The Niobrara

A River Running through Time

Paul A. Johnsgard

With chapters by
Jon Farrar & Duane Gudgel

University of Nebraska Press   Lincoln & London

Chapter 8 originally appeared in slightly different
form in *NEBRASKAland* magazine.

Chapter 8 © John Farrar.
Chapter 9 © Duane Gudgel.
© 2007 by the Board of Regents of
the University of Nebraska

Library of Congress
Cataloging-in-Publication Data
Johnsgard, Paul A.
The Niobrara : a river running through time /
Paul A. Johnsgard with chapters by Jon Farrar and Duane Gudgel.
p. cm.
Includes bibliographical references and index.
ISBN-13: 978-0-8032-5981-2 (pbk. : alk. paper)
ISBN-10: 0-8032-5981-6 (pbk. : alk. paper)
1. Natural history—Niobrara River (Wyo. and Neb.)
2. Niobrara River (Wyo. and Neb.)   I. Title.
QH104.5.N54J64   2007
508.782'7—dc22
2006030905

Dedicated to the memory of Fred Thomas (1/3/1931–1/29/1999),
Who completely understood the magic of the Niobrara

Contents

Illustrations

Maps

Tables

Preface and Acknowledgments

When I first visited the Niobrara River and its dramatically scenic valley in the early 1980s, after two decades of experience with the table-flat Platte River Valley and with similarly gentle Sandhills rivers, I immediately understood why so many people have fallen under its spell. I had already learned something of the region's special ecological and geological attributes by being involved in a grass-roots "Save the Niobrara" movement during the early 1970s.

At that time the U.S. Bureau of Reclamation had proposed to construct a large and predictably environmentally destructive dam in the most biologically interesting and scenically beautiful part of the Niobrara Valley, to irrigate land owned by a very few large property owners. The project was legally halted in the late 1970s after it was determined that the Bureau of Reclamation had failed to provide an adequate environmental impact analysis, and also after the U.S. Fish and Wildlife Service raised additional questions about the plan's potential violations of the Endangered Species Act.

The doomed Norden Dam project was followed by a 1985 U.S. Senate proposal to designate much of the central and lower Niobrara as a National Scenic River, thereby preserving its scenic, geological, paleontological, and biological attractions for posterity. This designation came to legal fruition in 1991, but divisive controversies and legal barriers still continue fifteen years later, especially as to defining the physical boundaries of the Scenic River corridor and developing a National Park management plan that is acceptable to all interested parties.

Also during the 1980s, Nebraska had entered into a proposal for an interstate compact to build a low-level radioactive waste site near the Niobrara River in Boyd County, although the site selected was in an ecologically sensitive and geologically unsuitable area. This proposal finally died after Nebraska unilaterally withdrew from the compact agreement, forfeiting over $150 million in legal penalties. Economic ramifications and political recriminations associated with the combined failures of the Norden Dam and low-level waste projects have continued to resonate through the Niobrara region down to the present.

It was against this contentious environmental backdrop and because of the Niobrara Valley's beauty, its biological richness, its fascinating geological and social history, and its unique contribution to the ecological diversity of Nebraska that I decided to write this book. In a way, I am simply completing a task that was begun by the late Fred Thomas, an outdoors columnist for the *Omaha World Herald*, an active conservationist, and a longtime friend. Many years ago he began to assemble materials for a book on the Niobrara Valley, so I then decided I should not follow up on my own vision of one day writing a Niobrara Valley book.

Sadly, Fred died unexpectedly in 1999, before he had managed to advance the project beyond collecting background reference materials and preparing some preliminary notes. I later contacted his family to see if any of his manuscript could be preserved. This was not possible, since the text materials either had been lost or were limited to notes in Fred's illegible shorthand. However, his daughter Amy offered to give me the reference materials Fred had accumulated. On a hot July day in 2003 I drove to Omaha, and she handed over two large cardboard boxes. They held several important in-house reports of the National Park Service and the U.S. Bureau of Reclamation that I had never seen, as well as various other documents and news articles that provided me with new historical and biological information on the middle and lower Niobrara Valley.

With these materials supplementing my own files, I decided I might as well go forward with my writing. In addition to covering the region's historical and biological treasures, I wanted to convey some sense of the region's current and future value as a recreational and scientific resource, and of the controversies that surround such uses. I thus asked Jon Farrar, senior editor of the Nebraska Game and Parks Commission magazine NEBRASKA*land*, for permission to reprint two articles he wrote in 2003 for that magazine, summarizing the Norden Dam controversies and the steps leading to the establishment of National Scenic River status for the Niobrara. These articles are reprinted here as a single chapter, with some shortening, editing, and updating as seemed necessary. I also asked Duane Gudgel, lifelong Nebraska resident and coowner of the Plains Trading Company in Valentine, if he would prepare something on the recreational values of the river from the viewpoint of a resident, canoeist, and local businessman. Both men very kindly and without hesitation agreed to help me.

Other people who have helped me along the way include Barbara Voeltz, librarian of the Nebraska Game and Parks Commission, as well as librarians of the University of Nebraska. Paul Hedren, superintendent of the National Park Service's Niobrara National Scenic River office, gave me advance information on their proposed management plans. Al Steuter, Jim Luchsinger, and John Ortmann provided biological information relative to the Nature Conservancy's Niobrara Valley Preserve, and the staff of the Fort Niobrara National Wildlife Refuge have been similarly helpful.

Several people read and sometimes edited various components of the manuscript for me, including Linda Brown (birds, general information), Robert F. Diffendal Jr. (geology), Duane Gudgel (human history), Paul Hedren (Scenic River management plan), and Scott Johnsgard (paleontology and geology). Personal observations or local information were provided by Kari Andresen, Lisa Beethe, Jackie Canterbury, John Dinan, James Ducey, Randy Harper, Mary Hunt, Robert Kaul, James Stubbendieck, and David Titterington. Two anonymous reviewers also critiqued the manuscript for the University of Nebraska Press. The University of Nebraska's School of Biological Sciences and School of Natural Resources have kindly continued to support my postretirement activities. Unless otherwise indicated, all unsigned drawings, diagrams, and maps are my own.

Last, I must also acknowledge the strong influence of the late Fred Thomas, without whose spadework I might never have begun the book, and give thanks to the late Lou Christiansen, who kept urging me to finish it. To all these people and their memories, I offer my heartfelt thanks.

Chapter One

The Ancient Niobrara Valley

The face of the earth is a graveyard, and so it has always been.
—PAUL SEARS

Like the rest of the world, the Niobrara River region is indeed a gigantic graveyard. A prodigious diversity of life forms has occupied its land surface ever since the region slowly emerged from the great Cretaceous sea that covered central North America until about 70 million years ago. These plants and animals left scattered mementos of their transient presence in the form of fossils and other permanent impressions upon the landscape.

Although today we can easily travel the Niobrara Valley and enjoy its vistas for their sheer beauty alone, we cannot really appreciate it without some sense of the vast amount of geologic time that is writ large on its surface and especially is made evident along roadcuts and the steep bluffs that line the river itself. Here decades, centuries, and millennia are compressed into paper-thin horizontal layers, and the transient significance of individual lives and collective human history shrinks into insignificance. Based on this sobering fact alone, it is important to know something of the true age of the Niobrara region and its geologic underpinnings (see maps 1 and 2).

The Cretaceous Period

Before emerging as land near the end of the Mesozoic era, much of interior North America was covered by a shallow Cretaceous ocean. Before

Map 1. Geologic bedrock map of the greater Niobrara region

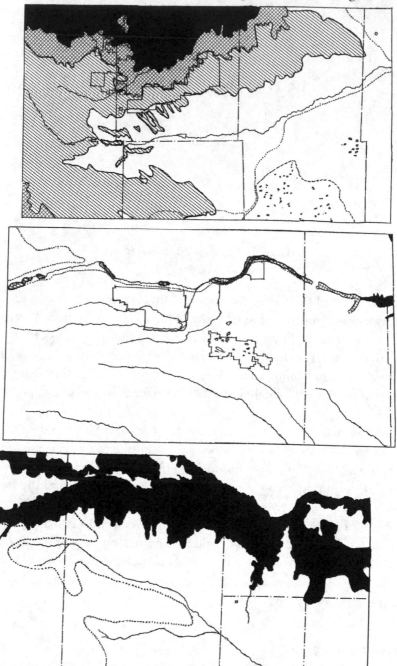

it disappeared under the combined influence of sediment accumulations and land uplifts, this Western Interior Seaway left a thick sedimentary deposit of whitish chalk over its vast bed. This chalk deposit, 82–88 million years old, is easily visible along the Niobrara and Missouri bluffs around Niobrara State Park, at the mouth of the Niobrara River. Microscopically, the chalk closely resembles the famous White Cliffs of Dover and is mostly composed of the same algal phytoplankton, called coccoliths, and calcareous foraminifera. Interred among these countless microscopic-sized skeletons are occasional larger fossils, the remnants of cephalopod ammonites and large clams. And living on such invertebrates as these were huge predatory reptiles and fish. One of these fish was the giant tarponlike *Xiphactinus*, ranging up to nearly twenty feet long. There were also diverse sharks with teeth of varied shapes, according to their food habits. Other major vertebrate predators of these late Cretaceous seas were large-jawed mosasaurs and long-necked plesiosaurs (Flowerday and Diffendal 1997).

One fossil mosasaur, *Mosasaurus missouriensis*, discovered in Niobrara State Park in 1986, is thirty-three feet long and is the largest known Nebraska fossil of that period. A few fossil fragments of sea turtles and of the flying reptiles called pterosaurs have also been found, but these are much better preserved in the vast and similar-aged Cretaceous chalk beds of Kansas.

As the Cretaceous seabed was slowly converted to low, moist shorelines and finally to dry uplands, it was certainly covered by relatively lush terrestrial vegetation, but apart from pollen evidence we have little direct knowledge of its specifics in the Nebraska region. An abrupt end of the

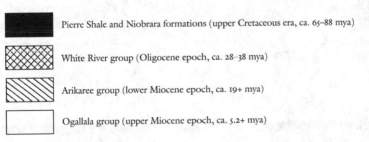

Pierre Shale and Niobrara formations (upper Cretaceous era, ca. 65–88 mya)

White River group (Oligocene epoch, ca. 28–38 mya)

Arikaree group (lower Miocene epoch, ca. 19+ mya)

Ogallala group (upper Miocene epoch, ca. 5.2+ mya)

MAP 1. *Source*: After a map by Burchett (1986), as updated by R. R. Burchett and R. K. Pabian in 1991. More recent and superficial deposits (Pliocene and Quaternary epochs, less than 5 mya) are not shown.

Map 2. Geologic map of the lower Niobrara Valley of Nebraska (west to the Niobrara Valley Preserve, or 100° west longitude)

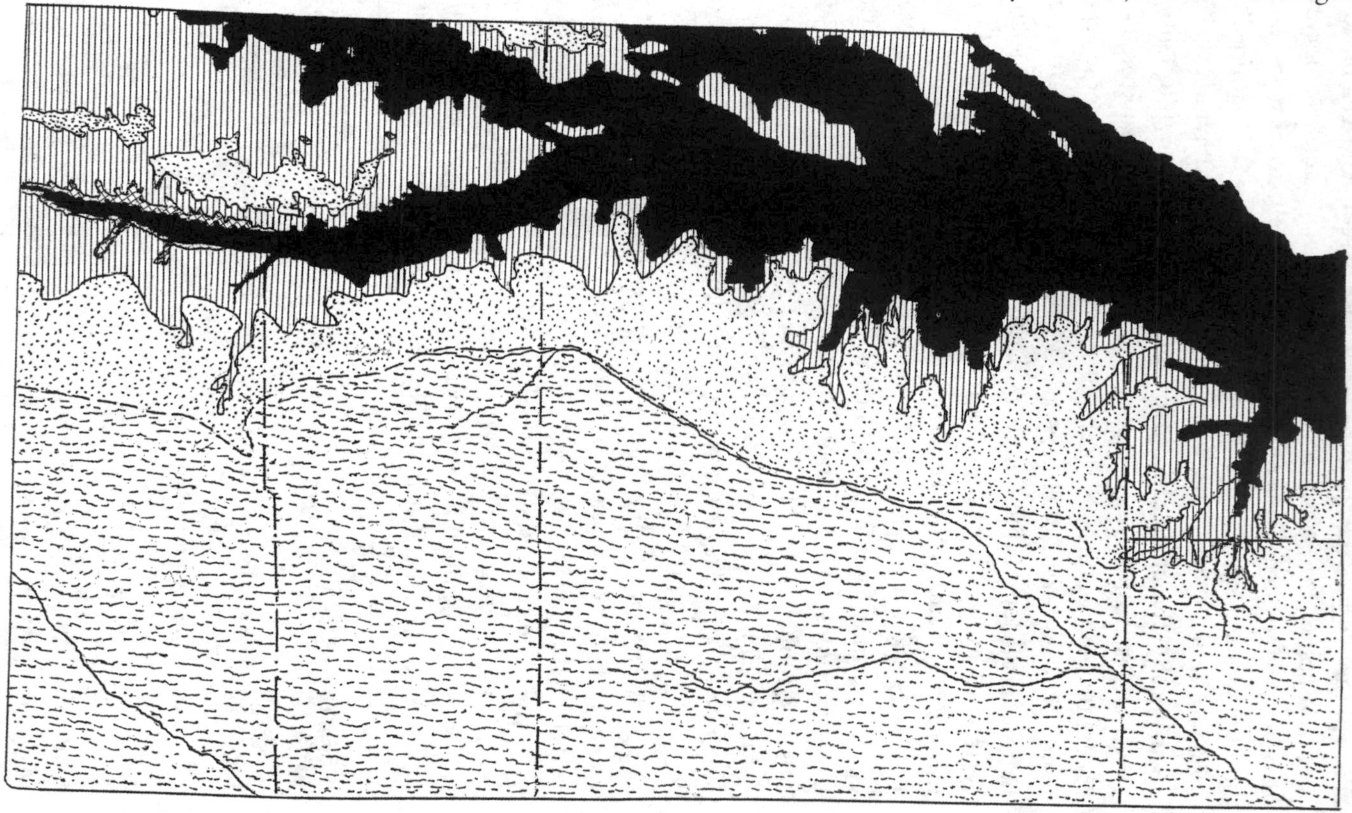

Cretaceous was marked by the massive die-off of most of the huge reptiles and many other marine and terrestrial species that dominated that period until a massive asteroid crashed into the sea near the present-day Yucatán peninsula. Suddenly the climate was drastically changed, and the earth began to undergo a rapid and prolonged cooling trend as its atmosphere became obscured by dust clouds. By the end of the Cretaceous crocodiles and other larger reptiles had become rare, but early mammals including primates were common in North America. Palm trees and other tropical plants still abounded in central North America in the early Paleocene of 65 million years ago (mya), but this situation would also gradually change.

The Eocene Epoch (35–54 mya)

A long-term cooling and drying trend was initiated in the central plains of North America during the Eocene, as mountain building in the Rocky Mountains and other western mountain ranges progressed. These mountains increasingly intercepted the moist westerly winds coming from the Pacific Ocean, producing arid "rain shadow" reductions in precipitation to the east and making the interior of North America both more arid and more seasonally variable, a climatic feature increasingly typical of the incipient Great Plains. Additionally, erosion along the eastern mountain slopes carried sediments into the interior plains via early river systems that were created and fed by mountain-caused (orographic) precipitation. Other clay- and silt-sized particulate materials were probably

 Cretaceous epoch (over 65 mya) exposures (Pierre Shale, except near the Niobrara's mouth and along the Missouri River, where replaced by Niobrara Chalk)

 Upper Eocene and Lower Oligocene epochs (Chadron formation of the White River group, less than 37 mya)

 Miocene (Ogallala group, 5–19 mya)

 Pliocene epoch (Long Pine formation, less than 5 mya)

 Holocene epoch (under 0.01 mya) deposits of eolian sand and alluvium

MAP 2. The location of a very confined exposure of the Rosebud formation (upper Oligocene and lower Miocene epochs, ca. 25 mya) is not indicated. *Source*: Modified from Diffendal and Voorhies (1994).

Table 1. Geologic timetable for life on planet Earth

Era	Period	Epoch	Years before the Present (mya)*	Major Events (with reference to Nebraska)
Cenozoic	Quaternary	Holocene	0–.011	Postglacial warming; Sandhills shaping
		Pleistocene	0.01–1.6	Several glaciations Sandhills forming; widespread loess, till, and alluvial deposits
		Pliocene	1.6–5.2	Grasslands spreading; cooler and drier climate
		Miocene	5.2–24	Ashfall Beds (ca. 10 mya); Agate Beds (ca. 20 mya)
		Oligocene	24–35	Mountain building in the west; spreading grasslands and grazing mammals on plains
	Tertiary	Eocene	35–54	Most modern mammal and bird families appearing
		Paleocene	54–65	Modern plants; North American interior emerging
Mesozoic	Cretaceous		65–135	Last of dinosaurs; North American interior submerged
	Jurassic		135–197	Peak of dinosaurs; early birds and mammals
	Triassic		197–225	Early dinosaurs appear
Paleozoic	Permian		225–280	Cooler and drier; many extinctions worldwide
	Carboniferous		280–345	Early reptiles appear
	Devonian		345–405	Seed plants appear
	Silurian		405–425	First land plants and early amphibians
	Ordovician		425–500	Early fishes appear
	Cambrian		500–570	Abundant marine life; many invertebrates

*mya = Millions of years ago

carried eastward by seasonal windstorms. Periodically, volcanism in the western mountains carried volcanic dust far eastward into the plains as well, sometimes smothering air-breathing animals but also adding to the mix of soil parent materials.

The central Rocky Mountains had their birth during the Laramide Revolution, a period of regional crustal uplifting that began in late Cre-

taceous times. By about 65 million years ago, the end of the Mesozoic era and start of the Cenozoic era or "Age of Mammals," the Tar-
ghee and Wind River uplifts in what is now western Wyoming had risen
and generated a massive amount of surface erosion, removing perhaps
15,000 feet of overlying Paleozoic and Mesozoic strata before expos-
ing their ancient quartzite core materials (Love and Reed 1971). These
eroded surface materials formed vast gravel deposits in the basins between the mountain ranges and eventually spilled out onto the eastern
plains. There early prairie rivers began to carry the smaller gravels and
sands eastward into what would become Nebraska and South Dakota's
portions of the Great Plains.

The Oligocene Epoch (24–35 mya)

Probably the major period of mountain building in western Wyoming
was nearly completed by 45 million years ago. But then volcanoes began
breaking though the earth's wrinkled crust, producing earthquakes and
lava flows and sending showers of volcanic rock and dust over vast areas. Starting about 35 million years ago, incalculable amounts of gravel,
sand, and clay sediments up to about 1,000 feet thick accumulated on the
plains to the east of the Rocky Mountains. These materials, extending
the length of the High Plains from present-day Saskatchewan to Texas,
were mostly laid down during the first 10 million years of the Oligocene
epoch, perhaps having originated from volcanic deposits in present-day
Colorado. Now called the White River group, the sediments are easily visible about thirty miles north of the Niobrara River in the exposed
strata of Toadstool Geologic Park northwest of Crawford, and also on
the nearby monolithic landmark appropriately called Sugarloaf Butte.

In western Cherry County, where the White River group may be up
to 1,000 feet thick, the top of these materials serves as the base of the
massive Ogallala aquifer. The Arikaree group, deposited above the White
River group materials in mid-Oligocene times, consists of alluvial and
aeolian sandstones and siltstones that continued to be laid down into
early Miocene times.

The base of Sugarloaf Butte near Toadstool Geologic Park is today
visibly tinted with the reddish sandstone strata of early Oligocene times,
which was deposited on a thin and even an earlier yellowish paleosol ("ancient soil") of Eocene times. These colorful layers cap the lower and still
earlier Pierre Shales of late Cretaceous times.

Table 2. Geologic timetable for the greater Niobrara region

Era	Period	Epoch	Years before the Present (mya)*	Geologic Group	Formations (F.) and Pleistocene Deposits
Cenozoic[a]	Quaternary	Holocene	0–.011	—	Recent deposits
		Pleistocene	0.01–1.6	—	
		Wisconsin phase	(0.01–0.075)		Wisconsin till
		Sangamon Interglacial			Loveland loess
		Illinoian phase	(0.125–0.265)		Illinoian till
		Yarmouth Interglacial			Kansas gumbotil
		Kansan phase	(0.3–0.435)		Kansan till
		Aftonian Interglacial			Nebraskan gumbotil
		Nebraskan phase	(0.5–1.6)		Nebraskan till
		Pre-Nebraskan			Pettijohn F.
					Duffy F.
		Pliocene	1.6–5	—	Long Pine F. (2–2.5 mya)
					Keim F. (2.5–3 mya)
		Miocene	5–24	Ogallala	Ash Hollow F. (6–10 mya)
			(5–19)		Valentine F. (11–14 mya)
					Runningwater F. (>14 mya)
			(19–28)	Arikaree	Harrison F. (19–23 mya)
					Monroe Creek F. (ca. 24 mya)
					Rosebud F. (24–25 mya)
		Oligocene	24–35		Gering F. (ca. 28 mya)
					Brule F. (28-32 mya)
			(28–38)	White River	Chadron F. (32– 36 mya)

(continued)

| Tertiary | Eocene | 35–54 | Chamberlain Pass F. (> 38 mya) (earlier Eocene strata absent) |
| | Paleocene | 54–65 | (Absent from region) |

Note: Adapted mainly from Swinehart and Diffendal (1998) and Diffendal and Voorhies (1993). Pleistocene periods and associated sediments after various sources. Some minor regional formations have been omitted. Associations of formations with specific geologic groups are identified combinations of italics and underlining.

[a]Cenozoic epoch limits based on Savage and Russell (1983).

* mya = millions of years ago (approximately).

Table 3. Paleontology of the greater Niobrara region

Era	Period	Epoch (mya)*	Formation (mya)	Typical Fossils and Environments
Cenozoic	Quaternary	Holocene (0–0.01)		Modern mammals; human occupation
		Pleistocene (0.01–1.6)		Alternating glacial and interglacial periods; many large mammals
		Pliocene (1.6–5.2)	Long Pine (ca.2) Keim (2.5–3)	Temperate grasses and woodlands; grazers, dogs, rodents
		Miocene (5.2–24)	Ash Hollow (6–11)	Savannas, warm and dry; many grazers, few browsers; tortoises
			Valentine (11–14)	Large streams and forests; warm climate; abundant and diverse fossils
			Turtle Butte (22–24)	Warm climate; channel and floodplain; fossils uncommon
		Oligocene (24–38)	Rosebud (24–28)	Seasonally arid; fossils rare
			Chadron (32–38)	Warm, humid fluvial; fossils unidentified
	Tertiary	(Paleocene and Eocene strata largely absent from region)		
Mesozoic		Cretaceous (65–135)	Pierre Shale (70–76)	Shallow marine; fish, reptiles, invertebrates
			Niobrara Chalk (82–88)	Shallow marine; fish, reptiles, invertebrates

Source: Adapted mainly from Diffendal and Voorhies (1993).
*mya = Millions of years ago (approximate).

Within Toadstool Park itself the Oligocene time span that is painted as horizontal bands on the steep slopes ranges from 36 to 24 million years ago, mostly in the form of softer light-buff claystones and darker and harder sandstones. An ancient river flowed through the area, along which lived now-vanished piglike entelodonts, camel-like oreodonts, and double-horned, rhinoceros-like titanotheres, as did ancestral forms of surviving mammal groups such as dogs, cats, horses, and deer. Fossilized tracks of rhinos, entelodonts, shorebirds, and waterfowl are still visible in the park, along what was once probably a muddy creek.

Between about 30 and 35 million years ago, the climate of Wyoming, Colorado, and probably also western Nebraska was shifting from warm-subtropical to warm-temperate, with increasingly familiar trees such as oaks, maples, beeches, alders, and ashes becoming evident. In the 34-million-year-old strata of Florissant Fossil Beds National Monument, east-central Colorado, at least 140 species of fossil plants have been found. The fossil trees include redwoods, cedars, pines, hackberries, walnuts, maples, hickories, and oaks. Shrubs included sumac and serviceberry, and there were also ferns, mosses, horsetails, and cattails growing in moist areas (National Park Service Web site: http://www.nps.gov/flfo/).

By these Oligocene times of about 30 million years ago, primitive horses, rabbits, rodents, camels, dogs, cats, and titanotheres were roaming the broad-leaved and coniferous woodlands, both in what is now Wyoming and also on the western plains of present-day South Dakota and Nebraska. By 25–30 million years ago the mountains of central Wyoming, such as the Beartooth Mountains and Wind River Range, were well formed. By about 20 million years ago the central Rocky Mountains were probably approaching their present-day heights, although in western Wyoming the now-spectacular Teton range had not yet begun to rise under the influence of continuing violent earthquakes (Love and Reed 1971).

The Miocene Epoch (5–24 mya)

Abundant evidence of the 20-million-year-old early Miocene landscape and its animal life has been preserved at Agate Spring Fossil Bed National Monument, in Nebraska's Sioux County. This internationally famous fossil site was discovered in 1885 by James H. Cook while he was courting Kate Graham at her father's cattle ranch along the upper Niobrara River near Harrison. After the two were married in 1886, Cook purchased the land and renamed it the Agate Spring Ranch. Cook then invited paleontologists from the University of Nebraska to his ranch to examine the fossil artifacts he had collected. The first director of the university's State Museum, Erwin Barbour, started his many visits in 1891 and soon realized the significance of Cook's discoveries. Later other famous paleontologists such as E. D. Cope from Yale University, O. C. Marsh from Philadelphia's Academy of Natural Sciences, and Olaf Peterson from the Carnegie Museum also excavated at the site. The site was also studied by H. F. Osborn and Albert Thompson of the Amer-

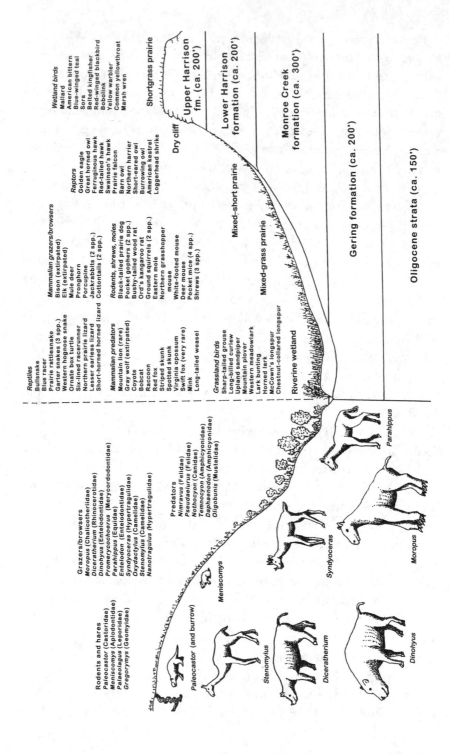

Reptiles
Bullsnake
Blue racer
Prairie rattlesnake
Garter snakes (3 spp.)
Western hognose snake
Ornate box turtle
Six-lined racerunner
Northern prairie lizard
Lesser earless lizard
Short-horned horned lizard

Mammalian predators
Mountain lion (rare)
Gray wolf (extirpated)
Coyote
Bobcat
Raccoon
Red fox
Striped skunk
Spotted skunk
Virginia opossum
Swift fox (very rare)
Mink
Long-tailed weasel

Grassland birds
Sharp-tailed grouse
Long-billed curlew
Upland sandpiper
Mountain plover
Western meadowlark
Lark bunting
Horned lark
McCown's longspur
Chestnut-collared longspur

Riverine wetland

Mammalian grazers/browsers
Bison (extirpated)
Elk (extirpated)
Mule deer
Pronghorn
Porcupine
Jackrabbits (2 spp.)
Cottontails (2 spp.)

Rodents, shrews, moles
Black-tailed prairie dog
Pocket gophers (2 spp.)
Bushy-tailed wood rat
Ord's kangaroo rat
Ground squirrels (2 spp.)
Eastern mole
Northern grasshopper mouse
White-footed mouse
Deer mouse
Pocket mice (4 spp.)
Shrews (3 spp.)

Raptors
Golden eagle
Great horned owl
Ferruginous hawk
Red-tailed hawk
Swainson's hawk
Prairie falcon
Barn owl
Northern harrier
Short-eared owl
Burrowing owl
American kestrel
Loggerhead shrike

Wetland birds
Mallard
American bittern
Blue-winged teal
Sora
Belted kingfisher
Red-winged blackbird
Bobolink
Yellow warbler
Common yellowthroat
Marsh wren

Rodents and hares
Paleocastor (Castoridae)
Meniscomys (Aplodontidae)
Palaeolagus (Leporidae)
Gregorymys (Geomyidae)

Grazers/browsers
Moropus (Chalicotheriidae)
Diceratherium (Rhinocerotidae)
Dinohyus (Entelodontidae)
Promerycochoerus (Merycoidodontidae)
Parahippus (Equidae)
Entelodon (Entelodontidae)
Syndyoceras (Hypertragulidae)
Oxydactylus (Camelidae)
Stenomylus (Camelidae)
Nanotragulus (Hypertragulidae)

Predators
Nimravus (Felidae)
Pseudaelurus (Felidae)
Nothocyon (Canidae)
Temnocyon (Amphicyonidae)
Daphaenodon (Amphicyonidae)
Oligobunis (Mustelidae)

Meniscomys
Paleocastor (and burrow)
Stenomylus
Syndyoceras
Diceratherium
Parahippus
Moropus
Dinohyus

Shortgrass prairie
Upper Harrison fm. (ca. 200')
Dry cliff
Mixed-short prairie
Lower Harrison formation (ca. 200')
Mixed-grass prairie
Monroe Creek formation (ca. 300')
Riverine wetland
Gering formation (ca. 200')
Oligocene strata (ca. 150')

ican Museum of Natural History. In 1965 it was officially recognized as Agate Fossil Beds National Monument (U.S. Department of Interior, National Park Service 1980).

Imagine the world of the upper Niobrara Valley some 21 million years ago. It is likely that it consisted of a vast grassland, with scattered trees and shrubs, especially along creeks and other wetlands. The major river then draining the region, perhaps a very early precursor of the Niobrara, was carrying great amounts of sand and silt east from what is now Wyoming, and during seasonal floods these sediments were spread out and deposited over the adjoining floodplain. These materials, now called the Harrison formation of the early Miocene, would bury the remains of animals that happened to drown in the river or die along its shores. Many of the hundreds of fossil camels and rhinoceroses discovered there were interred when two periods of catastrophic drought occurred, burying the camels under windblown sands and depositing the bodies of hundreds of small rhinos in a sandy river channel (fig. 1).

Among the largest of the mammals that trod these landscapes was *Moropus*, a horse-sized member of a now extinct family (chalcotheres) that was related to both horses and rhinos but had claws rather than hooves. Surviving from Eocene times, the chalcotheres were browsing mammals destined to become extinct by the mid-Miocene as ecological conditions on the interior plains changed. By then the ecological advantages of having tall and enamel-rich teeth suitable for grazing the increasingly abundant and nutritious but silica-rich and abrasive prairie grasses began to outweigh the advantages of having teeth adapted for browsing soft leaves of the ever diminishing forests.

Smaller but more dangerous than *Moropus* was *Dinohyus*, about six feet tall and a member of the entelodont group of piglike animals that were

---

FIGURE 1. Diagrammatic profile of the upper Niobrara Valley, showing (left side) fossil assemblages of major mammalian types existing about 21 million years ago (upper Harrison formation, Miocene epoch) at present-day Agate Fossil Beds National Monument, compared with a modern assemblage of typical plant community types and associated terrestrial vertebrates (right side). Reconstruction sketches of major fossil genera found at Agate are also shown at lower left (not to exact scale). Within groupings, species or genera are listed vertically downward in order of approximate descending size. Stratigraphy after Peterson (1906b). Fossil examples and sketches adapted from U.S. Department of Interior, National Park Service (1980); modern species listings based on available regional data.

both scavengers and plant eaters. With large tusks and massive heads, the animals were perhaps as fierce as modern-day wild pigs. About half the height of *Dinohyus* was *Entelodon*, and a third pig of the same region and time period was *Desmathus*, looking much like a modern peccary.

Another large mammal of the region was the rhinolike *Diceratherium*, which differed from modern rhinos by having a pair of horns near the end of its nose. There were also piglike oreodonts, including *Promerycochoerus* and a smaller relative, *Merycochoerus*, which survived until about 15 million years ago.

The early horses of this period included *Miohippus*, a genus approaching the end of its tenure on earth and already being replaced by *Parahippus*, a more modern horse with more efficient grass-grinding teeth. This three-toed horse would in turn become the ancestor of the many single-toed horses and zebras that have survived into modern times.

Other ungulates of this rich savanna habitat included a small deerlike mammal, *Nanotragulus*, with tall teeth well adapted for grazing. Another was *Syndyoceras*, a tiny prongbuck having two pairs of unbranched horns on its head. One pair was on the forehead, where similar horns occur in the modern (but only distantly related) pronghorn, and the other was near the end of the nose. Its Oligocene ancestor had six bumps on its skull that presumably supported short horns, and its Pliocene descendant *Synthetoceras* also had a pair of horns on its forehead, but the pair near the nose had fused into a single forked horn.

Of course there were a variety of large and small predators, such as nimravid cats (*Nimravus* and *Pseudaelurus*), leopardlike animals with very long canine teeth. There were probably also true saber-toothed cats present, although none has yet been found in the immediate region around Agate. Conspicuous members of the dog family (Canidae) included *Nothocyon* and *Daphaenodon*, but many other doglike or hyenalike predators probably also roamed the Miocene grasslands of Nebraska.

There were also various rodents, including a beaverlike creature, *Paleocastor*. Unlike the modern semiaquatic beaver, these rodents dug vertical and helically twisted tunnels up to eight feet deep in dry upland sites, with straight side-tunnel shafts slanted upward, so that any rainwater entering the tunnel would be unlikely to flood the animals' living quarters. These strangely shaped tunnels, after filling with sediments, eventually sometimes fossilized, forming "devil's corkscrews" that were once thought to be the fossilized roots of giant trees.

Another interesting rodent was *Meniscomys*, part of a very primitive group of rodents that has only a single surviving member, the relatively primitive mountain beaver (*Aplodontia*) of the Pacific Northwest's coniferous rainforests (U.S. Department of Interior, National Park Service 1980).

After this period of the early Miocene there was a phase of increased mountain building in the Rockies, bringing on alternating cycles of deep channel cutting in high plains rivers and new floodplain deposits. As the Rockies rose to approximately their modern height the climate of the western plains became increasingly drier, and the savannalike landscape of this region was gradually transformed into vast grasslands resembling those of the present day. As these grasslands spread, so did such grazing-adapted ungulates as the relatively modern horse *Merychippus* of the middle to late Miocene.

The Ogallala group was deposited during Miocene times some 5–19 million years ago, as sandy alluvial materials were carried eastward from Wyoming and settled into in a huge sedimentary basin. The Ogallala's sandstones, locally up to 800 feet thick in the middle Niobrara Valley, are the main source of Sandhills groundwater: the present-day Ogallala aquifer (Bleed and Flowerday 1989).

We might try to imagine the latter Miocene of about 15 million years ago. The climate of the Niobrara Valley was becoming drier yet, and there was still occasional volcanic activity in the mountains hundreds of miles to the west. Starting about 14 million years ago, vast deposits of sand, silt, and gravel were laid down in north-central and northeastern Nebraska, a process that lasted some 3 million years. This layer of soft, poorly cemented whitish sandstone about 11–14 million years old, the Valentine formation, may be up to 300 feet thick in places and is often exposed along the steep southern slopes of the lower Niobrara River (Voorhies 1994). It lies directly above the older (24–25 million years old) Rosebud formation, a harder pinkish gray to brown sandstone that often serves as bedrock for the middle Niobrara. The Valentine formation is typically capped by the Ash Hollow formation, a grayish layer of sandstone dating back some 6–10 million years that often is exposed as rocky cliff ledges.

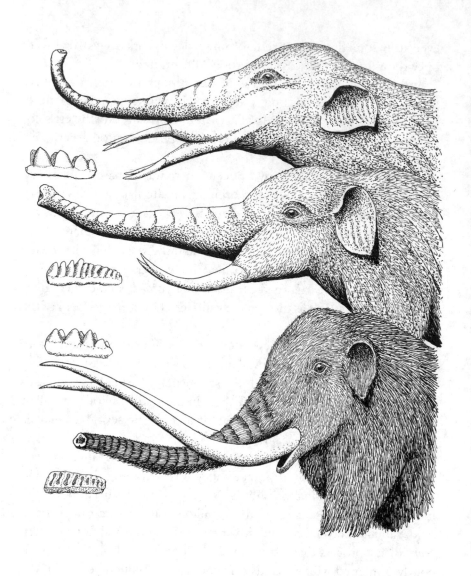

FIGURE 2. Representative Miocene mastodonts of the Niobrara region, including (top to bottom) *Gomphotherium*, *Stegomastodon*, and American mastodont (*Mammut*). Teeth of these respective genera are also shown, plus a tooth (bottom) of typical mammoth (*Mammuthus*). After various sources, including museum specimens.

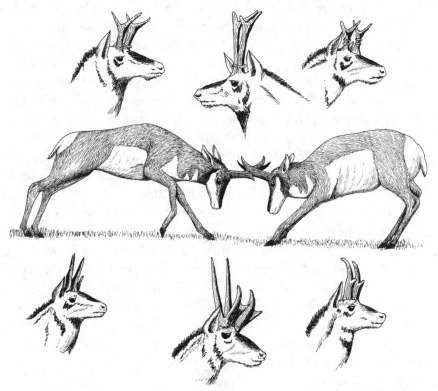

FIGURE 3. Three late Tertiary pronglets (top, left to right, *Meryceros*, *Paracosoryx*, and *Subparacosoryx*) and three Pleistocene-age prongbucks (bottom, left to right, *Capromeryx*, *Hayoceros*, and *Proantilocapra*) from the Niobrara region (after Frick 1937). In the center are two modern male pronghorns fighting (after a sketch in Kitchen and Bromley 1971).

At about 14 million years ago the first elephants (mastodonts) made their way across the Bering land bridge to North America and found their way to the Nebraska grasslands. There were numerous species, but all were of two general types, the very long-jawed "four-tusker" gomphotheres and the more typical mastodonts. Both of these families had sharp-edged molars that were probably best adapted for browsing in forests, the four-tuskers having strongly cusped teeth in transverse rows, and the mastodonts having rows of flattish cusps separated by open valleys. The four-tusker elephants evidently were especially common in the Niobrara Valley, judging from the abundance of their fossils there. Both families survived for millions of years, but the gomphotheres had mostly vanished by the late Pliocene (fig. 2).

In a Valentine-formation fossil site near the Norden Bridge, near Norden, Keya Paha County, at least eighty-nine species of fossil mammals have been found, including both four-tuskers and typical mastodonts. There an ancient river, both larger and deeper than the modern Niobrara, captured their bones and deposited them in its sediments, along with thousands of others. At another site, near Valentine (the Railway Bridge quarry), were found the fossil remains of ten horse species. Indeed, the number of fossil horses known from the Niobrara region alone approaches half the total number of fossil horses known for the entire world!

Additionally, there were fourteen species of cloven-hoofed ungulates (artiodactyls), as well as rhinos, a tapir, and a chalcothere, part of a group of horse-sized browsers with claws rather than hooves. Second only to the horses, the most abundant mammals found were small pronghorns (merycodonts) with forked horns on the males' foreheads similar to those of modern pronghorns. These must have been one of the most abundant ungulates of the Miocene grasslands, judging from the numbers of fossils known (fig. 3). All told, about 90 percent of the individual animals found at the Railway Bridge quarry were grazers, indicating that by then the area was probably mostly upland grassland-dominated savannas, but with well-watered floodplains supporting forests (Voorhies 1994; Voorhies and Corner 1993).

Approximately 10–12 million years ago a gigantic cloud of volcanic dust that had originated in the mountains of present-day Idaho settled over northern Nebraska nine hundred miles to the east, filling the air with choking particles of ash and enveloping entire herds of animals in an ash layer up to ten feet thick. Evidence of this lethal event may be seen at Ashfall Fossil Beds State Historical Park, in northwestern Antelope County. Here one can see the remains of an entire herd of about thirty small barrel-bodied rhinos (*Teleoceras*), lying in a huddle, where they slowly suffocated and died. The quarry also has revealed five species of horses, including both typically three-toed Miocene horses and *Pliohippus permix*, a more advanced, virtually one-toed species similar to modern horses except for its small size. There were also camels, turtles, and cranes, birds much more similar to still-living crowned cranes (*Balearica*) of Africa than to the currently surviving North American sandhill and whooping cranes (Voorhies 1990; Mosel 2004).

In a nearby quarry (Pratt Slide) in Brown County, these same mam-

Table 4. Regional summaries of Tertiary exposures
in the greater Niobrara region*

Geologic Epoch	Geologic Group*	Geographic Region		
		Pine Ridge	Upper Niobrara River	Lower Niobrara River
Pliocene			*Upper Snake Creek F.*	Pettijohn F. Long Pine F. Keim F.
Miocene	*Ogallala*		*Snake Creek F.* *Olcott F.* *Sheep Creek and* *Box Butte Fs.* *Runningwater F.* *Marsland F.* (Upper Harrison F.)	*Ash Hollow F.* *Valentine F.* Rosebud F.
Oligocene	Arikaree	Harrison F. Monroe Creek F. Ash Creek Beds	Harrison F. Monroe Creek F.	
Eocene	*White River*	*Brule F.* *Chadron F.* *Chamberlain* *Pass F.*		

Source: Adapted from Maher, Engelmann, and Shuster (2003).
*Formation (abbreviated F.) names associated with specific stratigraphic groups are identified by italics (*Ogallala group*), underlining (Arikaree group), or both (*White River group*).

mal species are present, as well as shovel-tusked elephants, tapirs, deer, and a large array of smaller animals, totaling about eighty species. Comparable species diversity is more characteristic of tropical habitats, such as African savannas, than of the modern Great Plains grasslands (Voorhies 1994).

As the Miocene epoch wound down, horses remained the more common grassland mammals, with four or five grazing species predominating, averaging larger than their ancestors. Likewise, species diversity among camels decreased as body size increased. Pronghorns, deer, and peccaries were other major large mammals of the late Miocene, in addition to shovel-tusked mastodonts (*Ambelodon*) with huge, flattened lower tusks that probably were used for scraping bark or scooping up aquatic vegetation (Voorhies 1994).

Pliocene Epoch (1.5–5 mya)

The relatively short Pliocene epoch in Nebraska was the calm before the storms and glaciers of the Pleistocene. Northern Nebraska was still a temperate grassland, with woods largely limited to riverine floodplains. Sands, gravels, and silts continued to be carried in from the west, covering earlier Miocene deposits. Grazing-adapted horses (*Equus*), giant camels (*Gigantocamelus*), gomphothere mastodonts, and bone-crushing dogs (*Borophagus*, "greedy eater") were abundant, and there were many burrowing rodents such as ancestral gophers and ground squirrels (Diffendal and Voorhies 1993).

In a Pliocene fossil quarry (Sand Draw) near Ainsworth, Morris Skinner discovered a herd of *Stegomastodon* elephants, as well as almost modern badgers (*Taxidea*) and burrowing gopher tortoises (*Gopherus*) similar to those still found in the southern United States. And in northern Antelope County, a site 2–5 million years old produced tapirs (Tapiridae), armadillos (Dasypodidae), and ringtails (Procyonidae), all representing mammal families that are still common in warmer parts of North and Central America (Skinner and Johnson 1984; Skinner and Hibbard 1972; Voorhies 1994).

Pleistocene Epoch (0.1–1.6 mya)

The Big Chill, in the form of several successive continental glaciations, began in North America about 1.6 million years ago. Since then, multiple glaciations have variously affected Nebraska. The total number is uncertain but is often assumed to be at least four, and probably several more. Each glaciation that reached Nebraska has tended to cover and obscure the earlier ones, making interpretation difficult. At the minimum we know that roughly the eastern fifth of the state has been covered by glacial till, the western limits of which approached the present-day mouth of the Niobrara River (see map 5, chapter 2).

By the Pleistocene a proto-Niobrara River probably existed, since there are tracks of east-west Tertiary-age river systems crossing northern Nebraska and incised into the underlying Pierre Shale. One river track closely parallels the modern Niobrara from Keya Paha to Boyd County. It eventually disappears to the west but perhaps is connected with similar paleovalleys in the Nebraska Panhandle. However, the deep valley that has been cut by the modern Niobrara River along its central reaches is now thought to be no more than about 10,000 years old (James Swine-hart, pers. comm.).

The glacial tills of northeastern Nebraska provide almost no clues to the Pleistocene fauna of the region, but to the west, where glacial out-wash deposits, ash beds, and other ice-age fossil sites exist, much has been learned of Nebraska in the Ice Age. Volcanoes in the Yellowstone region erupted at least twice in the Pleistocene, sending showers of ash eastward about 1.2 million years ago and again 600,000 years ago. Fossil sites associated with these ashfalls often contain the remains of mammoths, the last of the major elephant types to reach North America and the type best adapted to grinding grasses with their tall, flat-topped teeth made of alternating layers of enamel and softer materials. Fossil mammoths (*Mammuthus*) have been found in nearly every Nebraska county, including the entire length of the Niobrara Valley. A few relics of earlier elephant types also survived into the Pleistocene, such as the four-tusker *Stegomastodon* (Voorhies 1994), but the other gomphotheres had disappeared by the end of the Pliocene. The American mastodont survived until the end of the Pleistocene, about 10,000 years ago, perhaps competing with the tundra-adapted woolly mammoths by moving into the few remaining forested areas (Voorhies 1994).

Large and fearsome predators such as short-faced bears, saber-toothed cats, and dire wolves have been found in mid-Pleistocene deposits of Sheridan County, as have a variety of potential prey species such as horses and camels. These finds came from fossil quarries near Hays Springs and Rushville, the first discovered by "Old Jules" Sandoz, who sent the lower jaw of a giant beaver he had found to the University of Nebraska State Museum. Besides primitive mammoths, much the most common fossils found there were horses of the modern genus *Equus* (the basis for naming these the *Equus* beds) as well as nearly modern camels (*Camelops*). Other large ungulates found there included musk oxen, deer, and two species of pronghorns. Other nearly modern mammals included prairie dogs, ground sloths (*Megalonyx, Mylodon*), giant and modern-sized beavers (*Casteroides, Castor*), and muskrats (*Ondatra*) (Schultz 1934).

In a late Pleistocene site at Smith Falls, boreal and arctic-adapted species such as lemmings, pikas, snowshoe hares, wolverines, and mammoths have been located, attesting to the frigid conditions that must have once existed there. All these but the mammoths can still be found

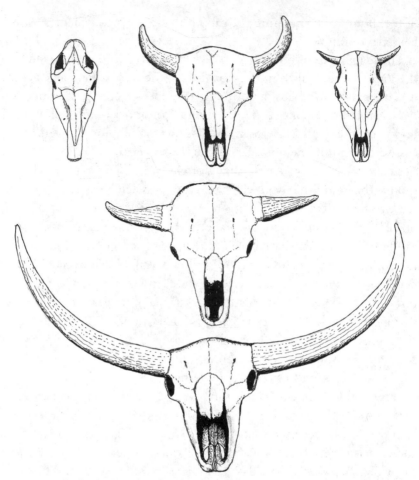

FIGURE 4. Skulls (bottom to top) of Pleistocene-age *Bison latifrons* and *Bison antiquus* and modern *Bison bison*. Also shown are domestic horse (top left) and domestic ox (top right), drawn to same approximate scale. After various sources, including Skinner and Kaisen (1947).

alive in northern Canada or in high mountain meadows. Spruces, firs, and other northern forest trees were probably widespread in the Niobrara Valley, and tundra-adapted herbaceous plants such as cotton grass were probably also common. Cotton grass still exists locally in the valley as a Pleistocene relict.

The first bison found their way to North America about 100,000 years ago, as did bighorn sheep and elk. One of the two known early bison species (*Bison latifrons*) had horns measuring up to eight feet across (fig. 4), while the other smaller and more common species (*B. antiquus*), with horns up to three feet across, was the direct ancestor of the modern species of bison. By about 10,000 to 12,000 years ago, when the first Native Americans were colonizing the Great Plains, the modern bison (*B. bison*) was the sole remaining North American member of the genus *Bison* (Voorhies 1994). By then the last glacier was retreating, the climate of the interior plains was becoming warmer and more arid, and temperate grasslands were replacing the tundra and boreal-forest communities that had dominated northern Nebraska during the previous glacial period. The modern pronghorn (fig. 2), likewise the sole surviving species representative of a great diversity of uniquely American antelopes that had once lived on the late Cenozoic plains of northern Nebraska, also became a major herbivore component of the developing grassland ecosystem.

Sands, gravels, and silts of the Pleistocene epoch gradually buried the Pliocene sediments and the still earlier Miocene deposits. Vast quantities of windblown sands were also transported in from the west and northwest, perhaps as recently as 10,000 to 15,000 years ago, shaping the present-day dunes of the Sandhills. At about that same time, during the final phases of the Pleistocene, waters from melting glaciers probably also began to carve the Niobrara Canyon into its present shape.

Between about 7,000 and 9,000 years ago the climate of the Great Plains became especially desertlike, producing major dune movements in the Sandhills, and subsequent cycles of high aridity and resulting dune movements occurred at about 6,000 to 7,000 years ago, about 3,000 years ago, and again about 600 to 900 years ago (Swinehart 2004). The nearly decade-long drought that modern residents of the Great Plains are gradually becoming accustomed to would barely make a blip on the long-term climatic trends of interior North America and is in fact very short in the greater scheme of things.

> With our short memory, we accept the present climate as normal. It is as though a man with a huge volume of a thousand pages before him—in reality, the pages of earth time—should read the final sentence on the last page and pronounce it history.
>
> —LOREN EISELEY, *The Unexpected Universe* (1969)

Chapter Two

Human Footprints in the Niobrara Valley

A people without history is like wind through the buffalograss.
— CRAZY HORSE (Tshunca Uitco)

The now quiescent surface lands of the Niobrara Valley mostly consist of materials brought in from great distances by wind and water during Tertiary times, at least 35 million years ago. Some Pleistocene deposits lay scattered in areas of glacial outwash and have accumulated just beyond the river's mouth, where glacial till deposits had their westernmost extensions during the Kansas and Nebraskan glaciations (map 3). Along the Niobrara's present route, many tributary streams feed into the river from both north and south, but especially from the south, where the high and stable water table of the Nebraska Sandhills provides a year-round source of freshwater seeps and springs (map 4). This pristine landscape was obviously once very rich in wildlife and also had great potential for eventual human occupation.

The exact time when Native Americans arrived in the Niobrara Val-

---

 Pleistocene-age loess deposits

 Areas of the saturated groundwater column in the Sandhills region that are at least 500 feet deep

MAP 3. *Source*: After Carlson (1993). Loess deposits after Condra, Reed, and Gordon (1950). Saturated groundwater column after Bleed (1998)

Map 3. Depths (in feet) of Tertiary waterborne (fluvial) sediments and
windblown (eolian) deposits in the greater Niobrara region

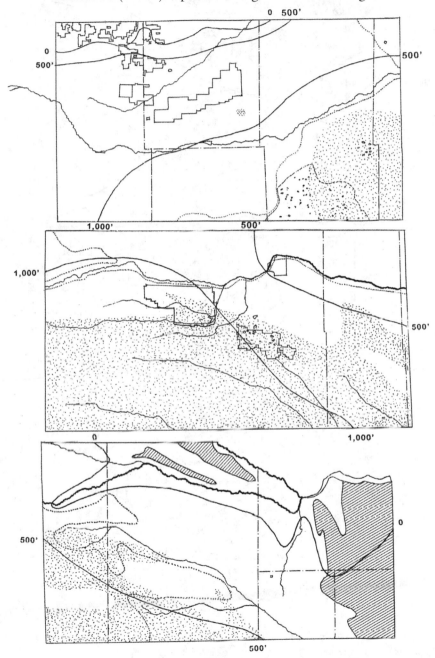

Map 4. Rivers and creeks in the greater Niobrara region

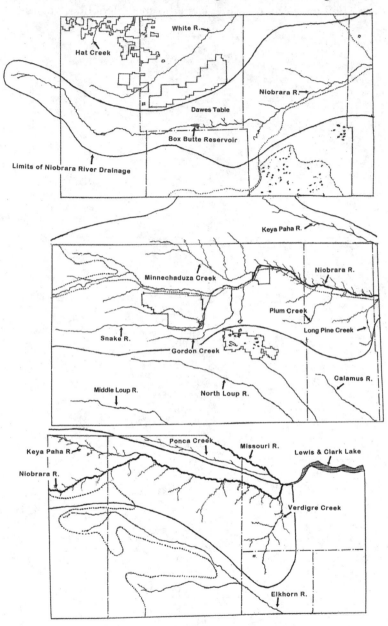

MAP 4. The dashed line indicating the geographic limits of the Niobrara drainage basin is only approximate and excludes Ponca Creek. After various sources.

ley is still shrouded in uncertainty. Very probably prairie river bottoms and adjacent floodplains, with abundant wildlife, were centers of early settlement. No intact Clovis or Folsom Paleo-Indian sites (named after their distinctively shaped arrow and spear points) have yet been reported from Nebraska. These ancient cultures of 13,500 to 10,500 years ago produced the beautifully shaped but deadly Clovis points used by early mammoth hunters and the similar but smaller and thinner Folsom points used by later hunters of bison. Paleo-Indian sites of this general period have been found in Colorado, Wyoming, Kansas, and South Dakota, and a few isolated points of these earliest weapon types have been found in Nebraska. However, somewhat more recent stone points found in western Nebraska lack fluting and represent late Paleo-Indian cultures of 10,500 to 8,000 years ago, thus establishing a tentative date for initial human settlement for the greater Niobrara region.

Our first good evidence of early humans on the plains of northern Nebraska comes from a site in Sioux County, north of Crawford and a few miles west of Toadstool Geologic Park. This archeological site, the Hudson-Meng Bison Bonebed Enclosure, is about 9,000 to 9,800 years old and contains the disjointed skeletal remains of more than six hundred now extinct bison (*Bison antiquus*) that either died naturally or perhaps were killed and processed there. Curiously, no skulls have been found at the site. Besides the skeletons, there are stone points of the type called Alberta—beautiful broad spearheads lacking the fluting of the earlier Clovis and Folsom types and with narrower rear portions for attachment to a lance (Agenbroad 1978; Bozell 1994).

After the Paleo-Indian period, an Archaic period began (ca. 6,000 BC–1 AD), during which Native Americans came to rely on a diversity of smaller game and plant materials. Most of the known Niobrara Valley sites of this period are from Boyd County (table 5). The Plains Woodland period (1 AD–1000 AD) followed, characterized by a combination of small-game hunting and subsistence gathering, but with the important addition of pottery manufacture, aiding food transport and storage. Many sites representing this period have been found in the Niobrara Valley, as far west as the Sandhills lakes of Cherry County, but the largest number are known from Keya Paha County (Falk, Pepperl, and Voorhies 1985).

The Plains Village period was marked by the construction of semiper-

Table 5. Distribution and temporal occcurrence of Native American
archeological sites in the Niobrara basin

Cultural Period	Time Span	Number of Known Sites and Counties
Paleo-Indian	10,000–6000 BC	6 (Box Butte to Boyd)
Plains Archaic	6000 BC–1 AD	13 (Box Butte to Knox)
Plains Woodland	1–1000 AD	29 (Cherry to Knox)
Undefined Plains Village	—	15 (Brown to Boyd)
Central Plains Tradition	900–1450 AD	7 (Keya Paha to Holt)
Coalescent Tradition	1450–1750 AD	24 (Sioux to Knox)
Historic/Proto-Historic[a]	After 1750 AD	12 (Sheridan to Knox)

Source: Adapted from Falk, Pepperl, and Voorhies (1985).
[a]Ponca, Omaha, and other unspecified components.

manent earth lodges and a more sedentary way of life, along with increased agriculture and gardening. The period may have begun as early
as 500 AD, but it extended through a prehistoric Central Plains tradition
(900–1450 AD) and later developed into a Coalescent tradition (1450–
1750 AD) of prehistoric and protohistoric phases. This later phase involved cultural and genetic contacts with groups from outside the central plains region. One cultural "focus" of this phase developed from
about 1450 to 1550 AD, at the eastern end of the Niobrara Valley (the
Boyd focus), with somewhat later villages (the Redbird focus) centered
in Boyd, Knox, and Holt counties between 1600 and 1700 AD (Falk,
Pepperl, and Voorhies 1985).

From about 1750 AD to the present, a variety of historical tribes of Native Americans have occupied the Niobrara Valley. Near its eastern end
the Poncas were probably the most common occupants, and they may
have made periodic hunting trips as far west as the Black Hills and Rocky
Mountains. To the west, the highly mobile Dakotas, especially the Brule
division of this bison-centered culture, seasonally followed the bison
herds south into the upper Niobrara Valley and beyond. These incursions
brought them into repeated conflict with the Poncas and, farther south,
the more formidable Pawnees (Falk, Pepperl, and Voorhies 1985).

The Poncas had settled the Niobrara Valley early, after having left the
Ohio Valley during the seventeenth century and, with the Omahas, settled first in what is now central South Dakota. Later the Poncas relo-
cated around the upper White River Valley of present-day western South
Dakota, and eventually they moved east to an area near the mouth of

the Niobrara, with the Omahas moving farther downstream along the Missouri. After fights about 1740 AD with the Comanches of the High Plains at their southwestern hunting boundaries, the Poncas finally settled their differences and even obtained horses from them. However, their battles with the Dakotas to the northwest would continue for another century (Hanson 1983). The Omaha and Ponca tribes may have split between 1650 and 1715, with the Omahas moving farther downstream along the Missouri (Howard 1965).

The Poncas typically placed their villages on river or creek terraces, most often at a river's fork. The soil at such places was often very fertile, and the river offered a source of fish, a nearby water supply, and perhaps some protection. An early (1780) estimate of the Ponca population before much Western influence was 800 (Lowie 1954). In the 1830s it was estimated at 1,750 by Prince Maximilian (Howard 1965).

The Poncas not only raised corn but also hunted big game, including bison, elk, deer, pronghorns, and even Rocky Mountain bighorns, which once ranged east to the central Niobrara Valley. They hunted the bison twice a year, in midsummer (June–July) and again in autumn (October–November). Bison herds were sometimes stampeded over small bluffs to disable them or chased out onto river ice, where they became much more vulnerable. The Poncas also hunted or trapped beavers, muskrats, geese, ducks, and grouse.

As with other Plains tribes, the roles of some birds in Ponca tribal symbolism and belief systems were great. Their symbolic birds included eagles, whose wings were used as fans in ceremonies, whose tail feathers were placed in roach headdresses, and whose bones were used for making whistles. Feathers of some bird species were accorded special significance; for example, owl feathers were used only by shamans. Bird skins or feathers were also often used in ceremonial bundles (Howard 1965; Ducey 2000).

By 1800 the Poncas had been devastated by smallpox, their numbers reduced by about 75 percent, so that only 200 survived when they were visited by Lewis and Clark at the mouth of the Niobrara River in 1804. In spite of having acquired horses, the Poncas also were no match for the much more numerous and aggressive Dakotas, and they had to abandon their western bison hunting grounds after suffering a series of massacres in the mid-1800s.

The Brule band of the western or Teton Dakotas (those speaking the Lakota dialect) moved into southwestern South Dakota and the Black Hills in the late 1700s, after evicting the resident Crows, Cheyennes, and Kiowa Apaches. Then the Oglala branch split off and settled into land between the Cheyenne and Bad rivers east of the Black Hills, and the Brules moved into lands on their south side, along the White River drainage. During the early 1800s the Dakotas expanded south and west into the Niobrara and Platte–North Platte valleys, eventually reaching northeastern Colorado. By ranging widely and avoiding most contacts with Europeans, the Dakotas largely escaped the epidemic diseases that ravaged the sedentary river-centered tribes such as the Mandans, Hidatsas, Poncas, and Omahas.

By the mid-1800s the Dakotas had more than 5,000 horse-mounted warriors and a total population of about 25,000 (Hanson 1983). The stage had by then been set for the Indian wars of the late 1800s, which would rapidly obliterate 8,000 years of Native American culture in the central plains, eliminate the bison, generate a fatally flawed celebrity in the person of General George A. Custer, and make a heroic martyr out of the near-mythic Oglala Lakota warrior Crazy Horse.

European Settlement of the Niobrara Valley

Journal notes of Capt. William Clark, Sept. 4, 1804:

> Passed the mouth of the River Que Courre on the L. S. [left side] and came to a short distance above, this river is 152 yards wide at the mouth and 3 feet deep Throwing out Sands like the Platt (only Corser) forming bars in it mouth, I went up this river three miles to a butifull Plain on the upper side where the Panias [Pawnees] once had a village this river widens above its mouth and is devided by Sand and Islands, the Current verry rapid, not navigable for even Canoos without great dificulty owing to its Sands. (Moulton 1983)

Captain Clark referred in his notes to the Niobrara River by the name that was then in use by French fur traders. However, the Poncas called the river *ni obhatha ke*, meaning "spreading water river," a meaning comparable to the Dakota's *mini tanka wakpa*. The Pawnees referred to it as *kitsu-kakis*, meaning "swift-running water," which was evidently the basis for the Rivere Que Courre version noted by Lewis and Clark.

Although Lewis and Clark were certainly not the first whites to see the Niobrara River, their expedition across the Missouri River drainage of the Louisiana Purchase opened the way for the region's colonization. Starting in the early 1800s, the western Plains tribes were subsequently inundated by U.S. government representatives offering the Native Americans trinkets and proposing a variety of treaties, all destined to soon be broken and forgotten.

One of the last of the Indian wars treaties was the Fort Laramie treaty of 1868. In return for the prospect of peace on the Great Plains, this treaty was to provide the western Dakotas with a massive reservation that encompassed essentially all of present-day western South Dakota, including the Lakotas' sacred Black Hills (a direct translation of the Lakota *paha sapa*). Food, clothing, and schools were to be provided, as well as knives, guns, and cattle. The areas of Wyoming and western Nebraska that the Dakota tribes had traditionally used for bison hunting were designated as unceded hunting preserves (Hanson 1983).

During the early 1870s the U.S. Army established a presence in the upper North Platte Valley (Fort Laramie) to try control the Cheyennes, the Arapahos, and the Lakota-dialect Miniconjou and Oglala Dakotas, all of whom were using their treaty-given rights to hunt on the unceded lands of that region. Assigned by the Fort Laramie treaty of 1868 to live in the Fort Randall area along the Missouri River of southern Dakota Territory, the Oglala chief Red Cloud initially refused to lead his 12,000 followers out of the North Platte Valley. Red Cloud had distinguished himself as a warrior against both the U.S. Army and the Crows and had served as a valuable spokesman for the Oglalas during the negotiations that led to the Fort Laramie treaty of 1868. It was not until 1873 that Red Cloud and his band of Oglalas finally agreed to settle in a new site on the White River, about fifteen miles north of the upper Niobrara River and near present-day Crawford. In 1874 a group of several hundred U.S. cavalry arrived to patrol and manage this new Red Cloud Agency, thereby establishing Camp Robinson, which in 1878 was renamed Fort Robinson (Nebraska Game and Parks Commission 1986).

The Red Cloud Agency became a major gathering place for Dakotas, Northern Arapahos, and Northern Cheyennes, who collected their regular government rations there. The discovery of gold in the Black Hills by George Custer's expedition in 1874 marked the end of a fragile peace, for within months the Black Hills had been invaded by 15,000 whites in search of gold. After unsuccessful efforts on the part of the U.S. government to buy the Black Hills back from the Dakotas, armed conflict broke out in 1876. By June of that year, Custer's fatal battle of the Little Bighorn had occurred, and all-out war was declared on Native Americans of the Great Plains. Red Cloud was arrested in the fall of 1876 after he and his followers were surrounded and captured while fleeing from the Red Cloud Agency.

By the following spring Crazy Horse had surrendered at Fort Robinson, only to be murdered there later. By the following winter the relatively few Dakotas still surviving in the Niobrara Valley and western South Dakota had been subdued and were confined to reservations north of the Niobrara Valley, including the Pine Ridge (the Oglalas) and the Rosebud (the Brules). By now the bison were also gone from the western plains, along with elk, grizzly bears, and wolves. The Wounded Knee Massacre of December 29, 1890, with the deaths of the Miniconjou chief Big Foot and most of his band of some 350 followers, largely women and children, represented a final bloody chapter of the Great Plains' 8,000-year Native American history.

The Homesteading Era

By the start of the twentieth century, settlement of the Niobrara Valley was well under way. The Homestead Act of 1862, supplemented by later federal legislation that encouraged farming and ranching in the arid parts of the Great Plains, was drawing people ever farther west.

By 1874 a trail linked Sioux City, Iowa, and the Black Hills, taking gold-seeking prospectors west and probably also encouraging settlement of the Niobrara Valley. Treaties of 1857 and 1876 had eliminated Indian rights to much of the Niobrara lands, allowing cattle ranches to develop in the central Niobrara Valley by the 1870s.

Fort Niobrara was established by the military in 1879 as a protection against Dakota raids from the north. The village of Valentine soon developed near Fort Niobrara. The first homestead claim at the current site of Valentine was filed in 1882 by David Mears, a surveyor for a railroad company, who evidently planned to subdivide his property. He was followed shortly by other claimants, mostly civilians at Fort Niobrara.

The Fremont, Elkhorn, and Missouri Valley Railroad had penetrated the central Niobrara Valley by 1883. With an initial population of 250, Valentine incorporated in January 1884, shortly after a railroad bridge had been completed across the Niobrara River (Duane Gudgel, pers. comm.; Van Metre 1977). Fort Niobrara was finally abandoned as a military post in 1906, and by 1913 most of its land area had been opened to settlement. However, in 1912 part of Fort Niobrara was designated as the Niobrara Big Game Reservation, later to be renamed the Fort Niobrara National Wildlife Refuge.

River-powered sawmills and flour mills were built as the land became more settled, with three mills appearing between 1881 and 1880, eighteen between 1881 and 1890, twelve between 1891 and 1900, and five after 1900. Additionally, five hydroelectric sites were built between 1900 and 1913. The largest of these, the Cornell Dam near Valentine, finished in 1916, provided hydro power for the city of Valentine for nearly seventy years (Clark 1997).

The passage of the Kincaid Act in 1904, allotting 640 acres per homesteader rather than 160, sent a new wave of settlers into thirty-seven counties of the Sandhills and Nebraska Panhandle during the early 1900s. The act encompassed all the counties lying within the Niobrara Valley except Antelope County. By 1910, 1,600 land patents representing 800,000 acres had been filed by these "Kincaiders." These homesteaders were required to live on the land for five years and make significant improvements on it before being granted permanent title, a process called "proving up." In the next seven years nearly 19,000 more land patents had been filed under the Kincaid Act, accounting for another 8 million acres of homesteaded land.

By 1910 Nebraska's human population (1,172,214) had reached nearly 75 percent of the state's present-day population (1,576,385 as of the 2000 census). Among the thirty-seven Kincaid counties, the population nearly doubled within two decades, from 136,616 people in 1900 to 251,830 in 1920, its approximate high point of the twentieth century.

By the 1920s many of these homesteads had already failed, and eventually nearly half were abandoned, even though favorable precipitation patterns persisted in the Great Plains until the late 1920s. Then a decade of severe drought hit the Plains states and began to eliminate homesteading farmers and ranchers alike. A continuing trend of rural depopulation throughout the twentieth century on the western plains has resulted in reductions in town sizes, elimination of many farms and ranches, consolidation and closing of schools, flight from the region by younger people, and other social hardships.

Between 1881 and 1916 some 196 land claims had been registered by 130 homesteaders within the 24,000–acre area that a half century later became a Bureau of Reclamation site for a prospective irrigation dam and reservoir planned south of Norden village. By 1900 only 30 of the names of the original 130 homesteaders in the Norden Dam study area appeared in national census records, suggesting a very high rate of homesteading failures and a correspondingly increased size of individual landholdings. County records for the Norden Dam study area indicate that between 1912 and 1919 thirty families held property in this same area. By the mid-1950s only seven families controlled the land, and by the mid-1980s a total of nine families lived on the entire 24,000–acre proposed Norden Dam project area, representing an average ownership of about 2,700 acres per family (Falk, Pepperl, and Voorhies 1985).

From an original estimated $230 million cost in 1980 the price tag for the Norden Dam project rose sharply to $454 million by 1985, with only $45 million to be paid by irrigators (Clark 1997). Plans for the Norden Dam and its associated irrigation development finally collapsed under evidence of unrealistic economic projections and the prospects of unacceptable environmental degradation of a unique river valley (see chapter 8).

The Niobrara River Today

The present-day Niobrara is notable among Nebraska's larger rivers for many reasons. Unlike the more famous Platte and Missouri rivers, 90 percent of the Niobrara is within the state's boundaries. Its overall stream length including the Wyoming headwaters component is 535 miles. Even excluding the roughly 50 miles of its headwater streams that flow out from the Hartville Uplift of eastern Wyoming near Man-

---

MAP 5. Elevation contours are listed in feet. Mean annual precipitation is in inches, thirty-year average. On this and following maps, major federal lands and larger state parks and historic sites are shown in outline (see appendix 3 for identifications of these sites). The edges of the Sandhills region are indicated by dotted lines, and a subregion of highly alkaline wetlands in the Sandhills is outlined by short dashes. *Source*: Precipitation data after Baltensberger (1985).

Map 5. Mean elevation contours and mean annual precipitation in the upper, central, and lower Niobrara Valley region

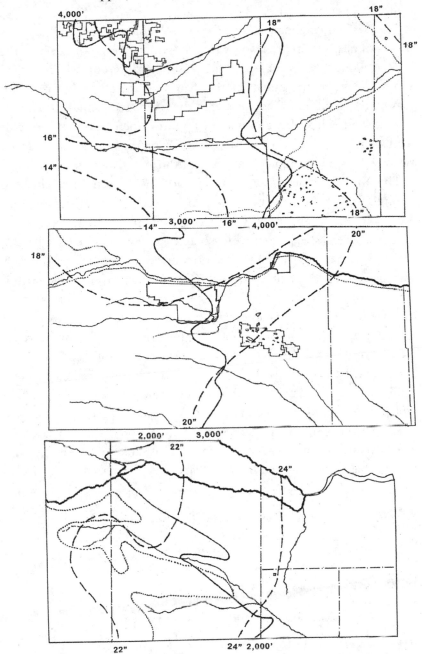

ville, it is Nebraska's longest river. With its 486 Nebraska stream miles, its in-state length exceeds that of its nearest competitor, the Big Blue, by about 20 stream miles.

The Niobrara gradually descends across Nebraska from an initial elevation of nearly 5,000 feet where it enters the western boundary of the state to about 1,100 feet at its mouth. This gradient represents a rather leisurely average descent rate of approximately eight feet per river mile, but it averages about nine feet per mile in the river's scenic middle reaches. Correspondingly, average annual precipitation increases from about fifteen inches annually near the Niobrara's Wyoming headwaters to about twenty-three inches annually at the mouth (map 5).

The Niobrara's deep canyon in its most scenic central reaches has strongly affected the microclimate and associated geographic distributions of numerous plants and animals and has provided a unique refugium for several species that were isolated here during the last phase of the Pleistocene, as glaciers retreated northward and the climate gradually warmed. And because of its steep cliffs and numerous spring-fed tributaries, it is the only Nebraska river to have waterfalls. Well over two hundred falls of varied heights occur within the seventy-nine-mile stretch that has been designated as the Niobrara National Scenic River, but nearly all are on private land, and the total has never been established.

Relative to the now largely impounded Missouri River, the free-flowing Niobrara carries a fairly heavy load of sand, silt, and clay, much of which is deposited as a broad delta near its confluence with the Missouri. In spite of its considerable length, the Niobrara drains a relatively small overall area of 12,800 square miles, thus ranking it smaller in surface drainage area than the Missouri, Platte, Republican, or Loup, among

---

 Niobrara Valley and its associated benches

 Sandhills

 Linear megadunes

— — Approximate western limits of Pleistocene-age glacial till deposits

MAP 6. *Source*: Mainly after Lugn (1935) and Carlson (1993)

Map 6. Contemporary surface topography of the greater Niobrara region

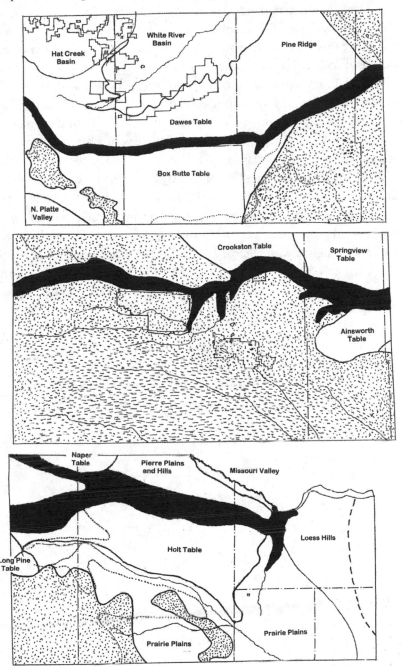

Nebraska rivers. In its magnitude of annual discharge the Niobrara likewise is only a minor state river, ranking behind the Missouri, Loup, and Platte, but because of its many spring-fed sources it maintains a more consistent seasonal flow rate and a cooler water temperature than either the Missouri River or the Platte.

The Niobrara is also unique as a prairie river in that over most of its middle and lower sections from Brown County east its channel flows directly over a bedrock of hard sandstone (the Rosebud formation) and shales (Pierre Shale), producing local areas of riffles and rapids. It was probably for these reasons that the early French fur traders called it L'Eau Qui Court, "The River That Rushes." In these same stretches the Niobrara River has carved a relatively steep and narrow canyon that in some places is 200–300 feet deep and up to two miles wide, most or all of it evidently excavated within the past 10,000 years. At its downstream confluence with the Missouri, the Niobrara almost reaches the westernmost edge of Pleistocene glacial till, and for nearly its entire length the river's southern shoreline follows the northernmost edge of the Nebraska Sandhills (map 6).

> I was born a Lakota and I have lived a Lakota and I shall die a Lakota. The white man came and took our lands. We told them that where the buffalo ranged, that was our country. Now where the buffalo ranged there are wires on posts that mark the land where the white man labors and sweats to get food from the earth.
>
> —RED CLOUD

Chapter Three

The Distributions and Habitats of Niobrara Plants

The most striking feature of the Niobrara Valley is the co-occurrence of 5 distinctly different major vegetation types all within 1–2 miles proximity of each other. There are few places in North America which have this kind of habitat and floristic diversity in such a small distance.

—A. T. HARRISON (1980)

When you set foot on a natural site for the first time, your perception of it is usually rooted in the present and is limited by your individual ability to evaluate the scene's environmental characteristics. Few people think about the fact that all the plants and animals now there have long and varied evolutionary histories, as does the land itself. My son, a geologist, and I, an ornithologist-biologist, tend to look respectively downward and upward as we walk about. I often completely overlook aspects of the land beneath our feet that are transparently obvious to him, and perhaps he at times fails to notice hawks circling high overhead or birds moving about in the canopies of tall trees. I usually try to think of what an animal might be responding to in its present-day environment, whereas I suspect Scott is constantly thinking of what might have happened here in times long past. We see the natural world in quite different ways, as would every other person who might happen to venture over the same ground.

I believe that nearly all animals except humans operate in the here and now, although within their genes they still carry with them, for better or sometimes for worse, the baggage of millions of years of evolutionary adaptations to past worlds. Those species that retained too many genes associated with past climates and past ecologies may exist only as fossil fragments under our feet or as rarely encountered individuals that have barely managed to persist in changing environments. A grove of ancient bur oaks growing beside a river canyon may just as much reflect ecological conditions occurring a century or two ago, when the plants first took root, as measure current environmental conditions. Furthermore, our human abilities to appreciate such facts in turn reflect our own individual backgrounds and educational experiences, often dating back to childhood.

At the time of the mid-1850s exploratory expedition by G. K. Warren and the U.S. Army Corps of Topographical Engineers, the western Niobrara Valley was predominantly grassland, with some pines in the middle reaches of the river and cottonwoods, elms, and ashes in the riverside canyons. Along the lower Niobrara there were grassy meadows, with riparian cottonwoods, oaks, walnuts, and ashes. Tributary streams supported pines, oaks, and ashes, and at its Missouri confluence the Niobrara was wider than the Missouri itself (Warren 1875).

Like the land where the plants of the Niobrara Valley now grow, the present-day constellation of plant communities is a compound reflection of previous climates, various historical and prehistoric events, and present-day adaptations to changing environments. Interspecies plant competition, warming climates, changing fire regimes, altered mixtures of grazing and browsing animals, chance or human-caused introductions of new plant and animal species, or other vagaries of nature may gradually tip the balance of survival for any single species or even influence an entire ecological community.

In sharp contrast to the Great Plains, many forest trees of the Pacific Northwest are extremely long-lived; there an individual tree might survive for many centuries and might not initially set seeds until it is many decades old. However, the plants of the Great Plains have long been subjected to vast seasonal variations in temperature and precipitation, and most of them have evolved relatively short life-history strategies to cope with such variable and unpredictable environmental events. It is thus relevant that the plant family with the largest number of species in the Niobrara Valley is the grasses, whose members avoid killing winter temperatures by setting seeds quickly each summer and dying back to ground level each autumn. Whereas shrubs and trees have much of their biomass exposed to the elements for most or all of the year, by storing their energy supplies in deep root systems and having their active growth areas (meristems) located basally rather than terminally, grasses are little affected by frosts, occasional droughts, prairie fires, or grazing. It therefore should not be surprising that at least 115 grass species (Poaceae) and 80 sedges (Cyperaceae) occur in the Niobrara Valley counties. A grand total of 376 species of grasses and sedges occur statewide in Nebraska, and the species of these two families constitute almost a quarter of the state's entire vascular plant flora (Kaul, Sutherland, and Rolfsmeier 2006).

Deciduous trees manage to avoid much of winter's worst freezing damage by seasonally dropping their leaves and forfeiting their photosynthetic capabilities, but they cannot avoid the occasional fires that sweep the region and sometimes incinerate them. There are only about thirty species of native broad-leaved trees in the Niobrara region, roughly half the state's total species. Some of these, such as the bur oak, have notably thick and fire-resistant bark. Others, such as quaking aspen, burn readily but are then stimulated to regrow through extensive suckering and may actually benefit from periodic fires. Most Niobrara Valley hardwood trees are rather closely associated with river-terrace bottomlands, where soil moisture and nutrient conditions are especially favorable and fires are less frequent than on the surrounding upland plains.

Conifers such as pines and junipers can continue their photosynthesis later into the autumn than can deciduous trees and can begin again earlier in the spring by keeping their photosynthetic structures year-round, but their tiny or needlelike leaves lack the large light-intercepting surface areas of broad-leaved plants. Furthermore, the turpene- and resin-rich leaves, although evolved to be highly distasteful to browsing animals, are extremely flammable. A fire that might infrequently sweep through a mixed grassland and coniferous forest will simply stimulate the grasses to put on a rapid new burst of growth as above-ground mineral nutrients are quickly recycled, but it can almost instantly transform a century's worth of woody growth into smoke and ashes.

There are only five native conifers in the entire state, including two pines and three cedars (= junipers). The Niobrara Valley can claim all

Map 7. Major natural plant communities in the greater Niobrara region

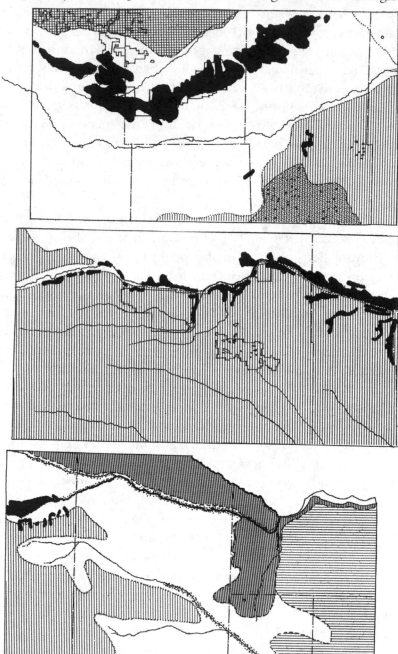

three cedars and one of the pines, the ponderosa (= yellow) pine. Although like other conifers the ponderosa is fire sensitive when small, it eventually acquires a thick, fire-resistant bark and sheds most of its lower needles, so that periodic prairie ground fires are unlikely to extend high enough to reach its vulnerable crown needles.

Ponderosa pines typically occur on sunny south-facing Niobrara canyon slopes and on cooler north-facing slopes, as well as in shady spring-branch canyons. They also often form a transitional open-forest zone between the springbranch canyon forests and the Sandhills prairies. Ponderosa pine reaches its eastern range limit in the Niobrara Valley in Holt County, about sixty miles west of the Missouri River confluence.

Cedars never attain the height of ponderosa pines in Nebraska, and at least in sunny environments they never lose their ground-hugging foliage. Their bark is both thin and highly resinous, making the trees virtual tinderboxes in spite of their evergreen foliage. As a result, cedars are highly vulnerable to ground fires and, unless otherwise protected from fire, tend to be confined to cool and shady ravines or to steep canyons, where they might escape most fire threats. Eastern red cedar extends the

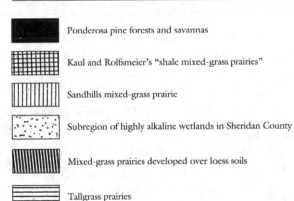

Ponderosa pine forests and savannas

Kaul and Rolfsmeier's "shale mixed-grass prairies"

Sandhills mixed-grass prairie

Subregion of highly alkaline wetlands in Sheridan County

Mixed-grass prairies developed over loess soils

Tallgrass prairies

MAP 7. Stippling along larger rivers indicates the distribution of eastern floodplain deciduous forests; upland deciduous forest distribution is not indicated. The remaining unpatterned areas represent mixed-grass communities that are variously transitional to shortgrass, Sandhills prairie, or tallgrass prairie. "Shale mixed-grass prairies" are here identified as the shortgrass and sagesteppe prairies subregion of the Northwestern Great Plains ecoregion. *Source*: Based largely on a map by Kaul and Rolfsmeier (1993), but with some modifications based on current ecoregion terminology.

length of the entire valley and is supplemented or replaced by western red cedar (Rocky Mountain juniper) from Sheridan County west into Wyoming and the Rocky Mountains (map 7).

Throughout the Great Plains, eastern red cedars have spread invasively into native grasslands since fires have become less frequent, and they are able to convert a tallgrass prairie in Kansas into a closed-canopy woodland within forty years (Briggs, Hoch, and Johnson 2002). Cedar seeds are primarily dispersed by birds, which eat them and later eliminate them at varied distances from the source tree. More than sixty species of North American birds eat cedar fruits, especially cedar waxwings, Townsend's solitaires, American robins, brown thrashers, gray catbirds, bluebirds, wild turkeys. and various thrushes and finches. Additionally, mammals such as deer, pronghorns, and coyotes may turn to junipers as easily available winter food (Farrar 1997).

Cedars produce vast quantities of seeds, but most seeds remain close to the parent unless eaten by animals. Additionally, seed viability is relatively low and seems to diminish both over time and with increasing distance from the parent. Increased cedar density on grasslands progressively reduces above-ground herbaceous productivity, decreases plant diversity, reduces plant understory cover, and causes an increase in cool-season relative to warm-season herbaceous cover plants (Gehring and Bragg 1992; Tunnell et al. 2004). The accumulation of dead cedar leaves on the soil produces a dense litter that impedes germination by other plants, and the decomposing litter also releases chemicals that further inhibit germination of other plants. All these ecological trends are undesirable in terms of overall ecosystem management.

Cedars can survive on dry and unstable substrates, and they do unusually well in overgrazed sites, owing to their inedible foliage. Their continued spread in the Great Plains during recent decades reflects the current relatively fire-free environment, and cedars have thereby degraded vast areas of high-quality grasslands. It has been estimated that between 1955 and 1994 the total acreage of red cedars in Nebraska increased from 12,500 to 91,700 acres, representing more than 10 percent of the state's overall woodland acreage (Farrar 1997). Periodic controlled burns on grasslands are the most effective way of containing this spread, but setting grassland fires always risks their getting out of hand and must be

Table 6. Typical native vegetation, upper Niobrara Valley and Pine Ridge*

Pine/Chokecherry Wooded Bottomlands	Mixed-Grass Prairie	Shortgrass Prairie
Prunus virginiana	Schizachyrium (Andropogon) scoparius	Bouteloua gracilis
Pinus ponderosa		Buchloë dactyloides
Fraxinus pennsylvanica	Poa pratensis	Aristida purpurea
Amelanchier alnifolia	Yucca glauca	Bouteloua curtipendula
Prunus americana	Mosses supp.	Festuca octoflora
Ulmus americana	Prunus virginiana	Plantago patagonica
Acer negundo	Stipa comata	Astragalus spp.
Cornus stolonifera	Bouteloua curtipendula	Opuntia polyacantha
Juniperus scopulorum	Andropogon gerardi-hallii	Gaura coccinea
	Symphoricarpos occidentalis	Oxytropis lambertii

Source: Data for wooded bottomlands and mixed-grass prairie from Nixon (1967), based on studies in Sheridan County. Species listed in sequence of decreasing densities. Data on short-grass prairie from Steinauer and Rolfsmeier (2003); this species sequence not organized by relative density.

done at times when they will do the least amount of damage to plants that land managers wish to preserve.

The Forest and Woodland Communities

Some riverine woody growth is typical along almost the entire length of the Niobrara Valley. However, from the river's High Plains Wyoming headwaters and eastward for a considerable distance into western Nebraska, only rather shrubby growth is typical. Sandbar willow and similar woody shrubs are usually present and are mostly confined to river shorelines (table 6).

As the ancestral upper Niobrara cut its way into the sedimentary strata of northwestern Nebraska, rocky and gravelly slopes were exposed. These slopes were at times too dry and too steep to allow grassland cover to colonize and form a closed herbaceous community (Harrison 1980). It was on these steeper inclines that ponderosa pine seedlings from the adjacent Pine Ridge uplands gained a precarious foothold, especially on south-facing slopes and on canyon rims along the north side of the river. Their seeds sometimes sprouted in shady rock crevices, where their root systems could gradually become deep enough and large enough not only to survive but to help stabilize the substrate.

Scattered stands of ponderosa pines that still occur around the boundaries of the Nebraska Sandhills suggest that during late Pleistocene times ponderosa pines had a much broader distribution in central Nebraska. With post-Pleistocene drying and warming these forests retreated, under the combined influences of drought, competition with nonwoody plants better adapted to shorter growing seasons, and increasingly frequent fires. Thus shaded, rocky canyons became refuges for the pines. Upland prairie fires often bypassed these valleys, eventually producing variably interrupted populations of pines that locally survive as far east as the steeper portions of the middle Niobrara Valley and its tributaries in Keya Paha, Rock, and Brown counties.

These ponderosa pine communities have established fairly dense forests in the canyon situations just described, but on the northern edges of the Sandhills they form a more open pine savanna mostly comprising fairly young trees that have probably benefited from increased fire controls in recent decades. In Cherry, Keya Paha, Rock, and Brown counties there were about 7,200 acres of dense pine forests during the 1940s, but about ten times that acreage was composed of scattered pine growth in mixed-prairie grasslands (Tolstead 1942).

Between the pines of the higher elevations and the hardwood forests of the lower elevations associated with floodplains, red cedars appear as a transitional community element (table 7). Thus they not only are a part of the pine savanna community but also occur as a transitional pine–red cedar community, situated ecologically between the ponderosa pine forest and hardwood forest.

In some upper parts of the Niobrara Valley, such as in Sheridan County (table 6), a mixed coniferous-hardwood community type occurs on bottomlands (the pine-chokecherry wooded bottomlands community). In sequence of decreasing plant densities, this transitional woodland community is characterized by chokecherry, ponderosa pine, green ash, Saskatoon serviceberry, wild plum, American elm, box elder, red osier dogwood, and red cedar (Nixon 1967).

Below these partially coniferous communities, pure hardwood lowland communities are present, primarily in the central and eastern parts of the Niobrara Valley. They develop best on the floodplain bottomlands, where the tree roots are able to reach a reliable source of water, and along the shady north-facing slopes, where a cooler microclimate keeps soils moist (table 7).

Compared with the coniferous communities, species diversity among

Table 7. Woody plant communities of the Niobrara Valley

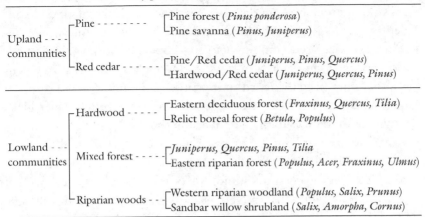

Upland communities	Pine	Pine forest (*Pinus ponderosa*) Pine savanna (*Pinus, Juniperus*)
	Red cedar	Pine/Red cedar (*Juniperus, Pinus, Quercus*) Hardwood/Red cedar (*Juniperus, Quercus, Pinus*)
Lowland communities	Hardwood	Eastern deciduous forest (*Fraxinus, Quercus, Tilia*) Relict boreal forest (*Betula, Populus*)
	Mixed forest	*Juniperus, Quercus, Pinus, Tilia* Eastern riparian forest (*Populus, Acer, Fraxinus, Ulmus*)
	Riparian woods	Western riparian woodland (*Populus, Salix, Prunus*) Sandbar willow shrubland (*Salix, Amorpha, Cornus*)

Source: Adapted mainly from Kantak (1995), plus Steinauer and Rolfsmeier (2003) for riparian community types.

Note: Representative genera are usually listed in decreasing frequency from selected sample sites.

woody plants in these lowland hardwood sites is considerable, with the dominant trees of this "eastern deciduous forest" outlier usually including green ash, bur oak, and basswood (= linden) and varying amounts of American elm, black walnut, box elder, and hop hornbeam (= ironwood) (Churchill, Freeman, and Kantak 1988; Kaul, Kantak, and Churchill 1988). The community was historically described as the "springbranch canyon formation," and more recently was called the "linden cedar ash association" by Raymond Pool, and it achieves its highest degree of development along the middle reaches of the Niobrara River. Farther downstream toward the Missouri River Valley confluence it merges with a "bur oak-elm-walnut association," a riparian forest type that is typical of the middle Missouri River floodplain. Basswoods range west to Cherry County in the Niobrara Valley, and black walnuts extend west to Dawes County. Bur oaks extend west into Cherry County in Nebraska and to Bennett County, South Dakota, with isolated populations occurring still farther west in the Black Hills and eastern Wyoming.

As a variant of the eastern deciduous forest community, a unique boreal relict community that includes a remnant paper birch population exists along a thirty-mile stretch of the middle Niobrara River, from Fort Niobrara National Wildlife Refuge east to Hazel Creek, along the south side of the canyon. Here freshwater springs seep out of nearly vertical slopes along the sharp boundary between the relatively soft and porous Valentine formation and the harder Rosebud sandstone formation. Paper birches once grew commonly in this cool and moist ecological situation, as well as in shady tributary "springbranch" canyons. In recent years they have been dying without reproducing, perhaps as a result of global warming. The nearest other current populations of paper birch are two hundred miles to the northwest in the Black Hills of South Dakota and about four hundred miles away in northern Minnesota.

In this special microclimate, other cool-adapted and shade-dependent plants also occur, sometimes hundreds of miles south of their normal Great Plains distributions. In Nebraska quaking aspens are mostly limited to the Pine Ridge and the vicinity of Smith Falls, Cherry County, where they have been reported to hybridize locally with bigtooth aspen, an eastern tree species not otherwise known from Nebraska. However, this interesting situation is still inadequately documented (Robert Kaul, pers. comm.). Similarly, wild lily-of-the-valley is known from a single population of about ten plants in a springbranch canyon of Brown County. It is a common plant from extreme eastern South Dakota eastward and has another disjunct population in the Black Hills (Robert Kaul, pers. comm.).

Two small ferns, prairie moonwort and least moonwort, are also known in Nebraska only from Brown County. The former is rare in red cedar–oak woods on the floodplain and in ponderosa pine forests on cool north-facing slopes, while the latter is even rarer in similar habitats, although it is common northward in the Great Plains (Robert Kaul, pers. comm.).

In some areas a mixed forest of pine, red cedar, oak, and linden can be found. A distinctive streamside community exists immediately beside the Niobrara River and its tributaries. This water-dependent community consists of classic riparian woody species such as peachleaf willow, sandbar willow, and eastern cottonwood. Besides occurring along streams, it also develops on larger stabilized sandbars. Farther from the river there is a transition to eastern deciduous forest, or there may also be adjoining tallgrass-dominated marshy wetlands, as where beavers have impounded tributary streams, and also close to the mouth of the Niobrara, where a broad deltalike marshy lowland gradually merges with Lewis and Clark Lake.

Table 8. Herbaceous plant communities of the central Niobrara Valley
and adjoining Sandhills

Upland communities	Sandhills communities	Prairie/thickets (*Festuca, Carex, Rhus, Rosa*)
		Dune prairie (*Carex, Festuca, Calamovilfa, Sporobolus*)
		Blowouts (*Redfieldia, Calamovilfa, Muhlenbergia*)
	Mixed prairies	Prairie slopes (*Ambrosia, Festuca, Lepidium*)
		Dry prairie (*Hedeoma, Conyza, Stipa*)
Lowland communities	Transitional grasslands	Transitional mixed prairie (*Festuca, Ambrosia, Bouteloua*)
		Transitional meadow (*Poa, Medicago, Panicum*)
	Tallgrass prairie	Tall prairie (*Poa, Sorghastrum, Equisetum*)
		Northern cordgrass wet prairie (*Spartina, Carex, Calamogrostis*)
	Wetland communities	Streamside meadow (*Eleocharis, Equisetum, Scirpus, Poa*)
		Marsh seep (*Carex, Eleocharis*)
		Spring seep (*Carex, Epilobium, Equisetum*)
		Sandhills fen (*Carex, Eleocharis, Onoclea*)
		Sandhills aquatic wetland (*Lemna, Potamogeton, Polygonum*)
		Sandhills freshwater marsh (*Phragmites, Typha, Scirpus*)
		Western alkaline marsh (*Chara, Ruppia*)
		Northern sedge wet meadow (*Carex, Juncus, Calamogrostis*)
		Sandbar/mudflat (*Cyperus, Echinochloa, Eragrostis*)

Note: Niobrara Valley communities are mainly after Kantak (1995). Representative genera are shown in decreasing frequencies within selected sites. The wetland community list is largely based on a classification of Steinauer and Rolfsmeier (2003) and is not comprehensive, nor are listed species always the most abundant. The listed communities also exclude some arid or alkaline types typical of the upper Niobrara Valley region.

The Grassland Communities

The herbaceous communities of the Niobrara Valley (table 8) are fairly similar throughout the valley's length, so an analysis by Gene Kantak (1995) for the central Niobrara Valley should provide a general pattern for the region.

On upland areas to the south of the Niobrara Valley, and locally also to the north in western Cherry County, several grass-dominated Sandhills communities are present (tables 6 and 7). On firmer soils and in relatively undisturbed sites, an upland mixed-grass prairie is present, with (in descending typical density) little bluestem, Kentucky bluegrass (introduced), small soapweed, wild plum, needle-and-thread, side-oats grama, big or Sandhills bluestem, and wolfberry. On drier sites, shorter grasses are typical, including blue grama, buffalo grass, three-awn, side-oats grama, and sixweeks fescue. A variety of forbs are typically also present, including several arid-adapted legumes such as various locoweeds as well as prickly pear cacti.

Like other Nebraska prairies, these upland grasslands are highly susceptible to eventual invasion and replacement by eastern red cedar if not periodically burned. Controlled burns in Nebraska usually take place in March and April, about a month after generally undesirable cool-season grasses such as annual bromes and Kentucky bluegrass have begun their growth but before the native warm-season grasses such as the bluestems, Indian grass, switchgrass, and grama grasses begin to grow. Periodic burning also helps control invasion by some relatively weedy annual forbs and fast-growing trees, such as Chinese elm (Farrar 2000). If these burns are done early enough in the season they are unlikely to affect successful nesting by most ground-nesting birds. In south-central Nebraska controlled burning of mixed-grass prairies is often done on a seven-year cycle, but local soils and growing conditions in the Niobrara Valley might require longer intervals.

On dry, sandy uplands ranging from level to gradually sloping, Sandhills prairie is typical, with sedges, fescues, little bluestem, Sandhills bluestem, hairy grama, and other grasses and forbs especially characteristic. Some shrubs such as poison ivy, prairie wild rose, and fringed sagebrush also occur. And in unstable "blowouts" where there is bare sand, blowout grass, prairie sandreed, sand muhly, and sand dropseed are common early colonizers.

Grassland fires on these prairies are potentially very harmful, since they can strip away the surface litter and expose the sandy substrate to erosion. Unlike the spring-burning regimes typical in southern Nebraska. managed fires on Sandhills grasslands are typically done during the plants' dormant season, when damage to valuable range plants such as little bluestem is least. It has been estimated that it may require up to five years for little bluestem to attain preburn levels. Species that tend to be favored during such planned or accidental burns are annual forbs and cool-season grasses.

On firmer upland soils, mixed prairies become more prevalent, with fewer sand-adapted species and more shortgrass prairie forms, such as grama grasses, fescues, and (in disturbed sites) annual weedy forbs such as ragweeds. On some steep northern dune slopes or depressions, or as a transitional community to pine savanna, a prairie thicket may occur, with smooth sumac and prairie wild rose growing luxuriantly. This community type, called the "sumac-dogwood shrubland" by Steinauer and Rolfsmeier (2003), is likely also to include wild plum, chokecherry, and perhaps buffaloberry, especially on firm soils. In lower and moister sites, a transitional meadow community potentially occurs but is now commonly overgrazed, with bluegrasses, panic grasses, and introduced sweet clovers. Still moister areas can support tallgrass meadows, most of which are now also hayed or cultivated but potentially support Indian grass and other native tallgrass prairie species.

The Wetland Communities

Wetland communities in the Niobrara Valley are widespread and fairly similar throughout (table 8). Northern cordgrass wet prairie is locally present in the central Niobrara region and is dominated by tall water-loving grasses such as prairie cordgrass and northern reedgrass, other grasses, sedges, rushes, spikerushes, and shrubs such as willows, false indigo, and red osier dogwood. The ground is often saturated, and standing water may be seasonally present (Steinauer and Rolfsmeier 2003).

Streamside meadow wetlands represent a transition between lowland prairies and wetland communities, since they are flooded for at least part of the year. Besides streamside sites, marsh seeps below groundwater levels might be included within this general category. The plants include such water-dependent types as horsetails, bulrushes, spikerushes, cattails, and many sedges. Shrubs that are present are likely to include false indigo, and the soils are organic, often having a thick layer of undecomposed peat or muck (Steinauer and Rolfsmeier 2003).

Spring seeps are similar to marsh seeps, with saturated groundwater levels, but they have sandy soils with some organic matter present and sometimes a zone of cold water rivulets flowing out from the groundwater seeps. In the seep zone the usual plants are bulrushes, bur reed, and cattail, various sedges and grasses, and sometimes willows and red osier dogwood. Liverworts, mosses, and horsetails are often present. In the spring-fed zone, partly emergent or submerged aquatic plants such as waterweeds and pondweeds are common, as are streamside forbs such as water parsnip and monkey flower (Steinauer and Rolfsmeier 2003).

True fens, boglike wetlands with undecomposed peatlike soils, occur in a few Sandhills sites, often near Sandhills stream headwaters in northwestern, southwestern, and central Cherry County. There the soils are deep peat or muck, constantly saturated with groundwater that is generally slightly acidic. The vegetation of fens is usually dominated by sedges and spikerushes but often also includes ferns and scattered shrubs, typically willows. Unlike marsh seeps, prairie fens can occur on slopes; the depth of the peat layer is quite variable, but it may be up to about five feet thick (Steinauer and Rolfsmeier 2003). Many species of plants typically found in more boreal climates have been reported from the Sandhills fens.

In the Sandhills proper, Sandhills aquatic wetlands and Sandhills freshwater marshes also occur. The aquatic wetlands are freshwater areas up to about five feet deep, dominated by submerged vegetation such as broad-leaved pondweeds, but with free-floating plants infrequent and emergent plants rare in deeper water. Water lilies may occur in shallow waters, along with the now rare wild rice. Sandhills freshwater marshes are also notable for their tall emergent species such as bulrushes and cattails, as well as having some submerged and floating-leaved pondweeds (Steinauer and Rolfsmeier 2003).

In southern parts of Sheridan County and its adjoining counties, there is a large "closed basin" region of interior drainage, with hundreds of moderately to strongly alkaline wetlands that lack sources of freshwater inflow or outflow and gradually accumulate high salt concentrations through evaporation. Many of these are too alkaline to support most aquatic vegetation, but some species of pondweeds, bulrushes, and other alkaline-tolerant flora sometimes occur (McCarraher 1977; Steinauer and Rolfsmeier 2003).

Other miscellaneous wetlands also occur locally in the Niobrara region, including northern sedge wet meadows, sandbars, and temporary mudflats. Perennial sandbars are common near the shorelines and shallow mouth of the Niobrara River and are usually dominated by shrubs, saplings, and grasses. The shrubs include sandbar and peachleaf willows, false indigo, and plains cottonwood saplings.

Shorelines and permanent sandbars may eventually consolidate and develop into river terraces, which over time may become populated with plains cottonwoods of substantial height as well as box elder, green ash, chokecherry, wild plum, willows, and buffaloberry (Steinauer and Rolfsmeier 2003).

River shoreline flats and nearby wet meadows of the Niobrara Valley have in recent years become infested with purple loosestrife, an introduced and escaped ornamental species that is highly aggressive and tends to replace native plants. Reed canarygrass is also a troublesome exotic invader in these wetlands.

Another recently invading exotic plant pest is saltcedar, a woody plant that in the American Southwest has clogged and sucked dry countless streams. As it increasingly invades western Nebraska it poses the potential for similar ecological damage in the Niobrara system. It has already affected the Republican, Platte, and Missouri rivers and is a serious threat to the Niobrara as well.

Chapter Four

The Distributions and Habitats of
Niobrara Animals

An incredible amount of biodiversity occurs in that stretch of [the Nio-
brara] river valley where east meets west and north meets south. These
ecologically diverse flora with their associated fauna meet, mix and hybridize in this thirty-mile stretch [of the central Niobrara Valley].
— CHARLES R. MAIER (1993)

Like natural communities everywhere, the animal populations of the Niobrara Valley are dynamic, each of its species fluctuating in numbers from
year to year and, over longer periods of time, ever changing in composition as a result of invasions, range retractions, and extinctions. Humans
usually notice only the larger and more conspicuous of a region's animals, and especially those that may be important to our hunting, fishing or recreational interests. The vast majority of all the countless other
animals live silent lives that are invisible to us. Some of the larger animals around us are nocturnal, others are subterranean or aquatic. Most
are too small to be detected without special effort and equipment, re-
gardless of where they live.

In our industrialized world, most people live in towns and cities and
have no concept of the variety of life that surrounds them. Earlier, less
formally educated generations had closer ties to the land and probably
had a much better knowledge of their surrounding natural worlds than
do most current college graduates. Only in rare circumstances—such as
when a graduate student selects a field-oriented thesis topic or a feder-

ally funded project is required to provide an environmental impact assessment—do biologists usually find the time to go beyond the relatively easy large-animal surveys and try to measure such things as invertebrate populations in local streams or search for microfauna hidden in prairie soils. At such times we begin to gain a slight insight into the tremendous diversity of life around us, and our own relatively insignificant position in the natural world is made clearer.

Niches and Species Diversity in the Niobrara Valley

The animal populations of the Niobrara Valley are tied directly to vegetation-defined communities. These animal populations are ultimately connected to one another and to the vegetation around them by energy-based food chains, but they also are compartmentalized into ecological niches that help reduce competition among species sharing the same basic energy resources. Generally speaking, species diversity among animals increases and ecological niches correspondingly multiply roughly parallel to increasing diversity of vegetation. Such diversity in turn mostly depends on available moisture, climate, and local variations in soil and surface topography. Therefore the western end of the Niobrara Valley, with its low annual precipitation, should be less able to support a high degree of plant and animal species diversity than the better-watered and more highly vegetated region near the river's mouth, which receives roughly 50 percent more annual precipitation and has a frost-free growing season that averages about a month longer (150 vs. 120 days).

However, this expected eastward trend of increasing biotic diversity with increasing moisture does not always materialize, at least among birds. Perhaps the topographic and vegetational diversity of the Pine Ridge region adjoining the upper Niobrara Valley may be the reason this semiarid region has a breeding-bird diversity closely comparable to that typical of the hardwood forested areas at the mouth of the river. For example, in 1998 I found that, using then available distributional information and a sample quadrant area (a latilong—one degree of latitude and longitude) of 1,351 square miles, the upper Niobrara Valley latilong quadrant supports an estimated 128 largely western-oriented breeding birds. Species diversity in more downstream latilongs of the Panhandle diminishes to a estimate of 105 probable breeding species in Sheridan County and western Cherry County (Johnsgard 1998). There the Niobrara River is relatively small, passes through an extensive area of Sand-hills, and has rather poorly developed valley topography.

In the Niobrara River's central reaches, steep pine-studded north-slope canyons occur, as do rich deciduous floodplain forests, moist south-side springbranch canyons, and grass-dominated uplands growing on sandy or loamy substrates. These diverse vegetational communities combine to support a great many vertebrate species of both western and eastern affinities. Breeding bird diversity increases eastward to an estimated maximum of about 125 species in the central Niobrara Valley and remains at this high level to the mouth of the Niobrara and beyond, where its avifauna is increasingly dominated by species of eastern zoogeographic orientation (Johnsgard 1998). The number of proven breeders in all these areas is in all cases somewhat less than my estimates, which relied on extrapolations from breeding distribution maps.

The Upper Niobrara Valley and Pine Ridge Fauna

The Niobrara Valley in western Sioux County is close to the uplands of the Pine Ridge, which in turn is a satellite of the Black Hills, at least in terms of its biotic associations. Breeding birds of the Black Hills that also nest in the ponderosa pine forests and rimrock cliffs of Nebraska's Pine Ridge include the mountain bluebird, western wood pewee, Townsend's solitaire, pygmy nuthatch, dark-eyed junco, red crossbill, white-throated swift, and violet-green swallow (fig. 5). The pinyon jay, Clark's nutcracker, northern saw-whet owl, plumbeous vireo, cordilleran flycatcher, and Lewis's woodpecker all breed in the Black Hills and either already nest in small numbers within the Pine Ridge or are likely to be documented there eventually.

Among mammals, the little brown myotis, long-legged myotis, fringe-tailed myotis, and Townsend's big-eared bat have Black Hills–oriented distributions that extend south into Nebraska's Pine Ridge, as does the pine-loving least chipmunk. However, the Black Hills populations of red squirrels, northern flying squirrels, and yellow-bellied marmots are not yet known to have reached northern Nebraska.

Shortgrass or mixed-grass plains surround the upper Niobrara in preserved sites such as Agate Fossil Beds National Monument, the Nature Conservancy's Cherry Ranch, and Sioux County Ranch of the Prairie-Plains Resource Institute. Farther north, the Oglala National Grassland

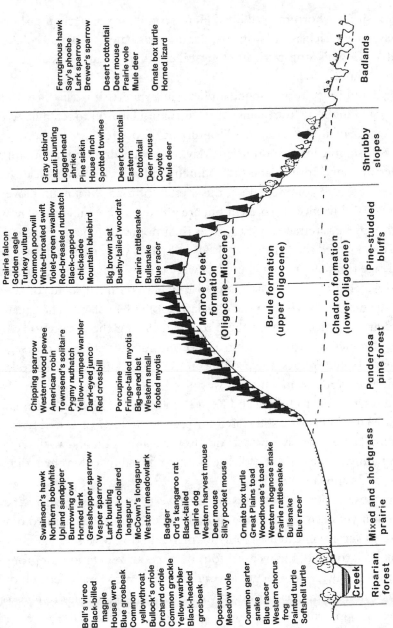

FIGURE 5. Cross-section view of typical western Panhandle habitats and some associated vertebrates (adapted from Johnsgard 1995). The stratigraphic sequence shown is that typical of the Pine Ridge region.

offers similar shortgrass habitats. Here several rare or declining short-grass species such as the swift fox, ferruginous hawk, chestnut-collared and McCown's longspurs, and long-billed curlew may still be regularly encountered.

Lark buntings are also abundant here; in an approximately thirty-mile stretch of highway from a mile or so south of Harrison to ten miles east of Agate Fossil Beds National Monument, I counted 123 lark buntings (mostly singing males) during late May 2003 while driving at about forty miles an hour! Horned larks (48 counted) and western meadowlarks (41 seen) were also common along this stretch of road. Mountain plovers were probably once also present but are unlikely to be found there now; their range has retracted westward as their population has diminished.

Sage-adapted species such as Brewer's sparrow, green-tailed towhee, and sage thrasher provide limited viewing possibilities for the dedicated bird-watcher in northwestern Nebraska where remnant stands of sage-brush still exist, such as in the Oglala National Grassland. The greater sage grouse once occurred there too, but during the past century its range retracted into Wyoming. However, another conspicuous sage-brush-adapted species, the pronghorn, is rather easily seen even today, having recolonized much of its western Nebraska range, and now extends east locally to Brown and Keya Paha counties. Golden eagles and prairie falcons likewise still search for prey along the rimrock outcrops, nesting conspicuously on their nearly vertical slopes, and rock wrens commonly probe eroded badlands, nesting invisibly within their abundant clefts and crannies.

In those relatively few areas of northwestern Nebraska where they have not yet been poisoned or shot out of existence, black-tailed prairie dogs survive in extensive burrow-marked "dog towns." They stimulate the growth of highly nutritious herbaceous vegetation for prong-horns and provide prey for golden eagles, prairie falcons, and ferruginous hawks, nesting cavities for burrowing owls, and temporary refuges or foraging opportunities for more than a hundred other vertebrate species (Johnsgard 2005).

Within Nebraska, prairie dogs are now most common in western counties having firm soils and native grassland vegetation, but they once extended to the glaciated tallgrass prairies of eastern Nebraska. They still occur locally in the Niobrara region, especially in Box Butte and Sioux counties, but are increasingly rare eastward.

In spite of the prairie dog's ecological value in contributing to species diversity and serving as a keystone grassland species, in the spring of 2004 the National Forest Service reauthorized poisoning prairie dogs on the publicly owned national grasslands of the Dakotas, Wyoming, and Nebraska. These include the Oglala National Grassland, where cattle ranchers can legally overgraze the prairies at bargain-basement prices. During August of the same year the U.S. Fish and Wildlife Service quietly removed the black-tailed prairie dog from its list of candidates for national protection as a threatened species, under intense political pressure from grazing interests and with urging from within the Bush administration.

Reptiles are common in the topographically diverse and generally arid upper Niobrara Valley. Western endemics include the many-lined skink, short-horned lizard, wandering garter snake, and western hognose snake. The many-lined skink and western hognose snake are likely to be found in sandy areas, whereas the horned lizard prefers more rocky habitats and the wandering garter snake is most often found near water.

The Central Niobrara Valley and Adjoining Uplands

The central Niobrara Valley, stretching roughly from Valentine east for about sixty miles to western Keya Paha and Boyd counties, encompasses some of the most beautiful valley scenery and most interesting biological communities in all of Nebraska. Within this corridor are Fort Niobrara National Wildlife Refuge, Smith Falls State Park, the Nature Conservancy's Niobrara Valley Preserve, and the upper portions of the Niobrara National Scenic River.

Besides including the highest waterfall in Nebraska (Smith Falls), this reach holds several hundred more small and mostly still unnamed waterfalls, a unique stand of relict paper birch trees, and an endemic race of the eastern wood rat. There are also nearly half a dozen pairs of closely related eastern and western birds that overlap and variably hybridize (see chapter 6). Additionally, there are many paleontological sites of national and international significance and the type localities of numerous species of fossil mammals (see chapter 10).

The northern and southern slopes of the Niobrara Valley in this river segment are more biologically different than the two sides of perhaps

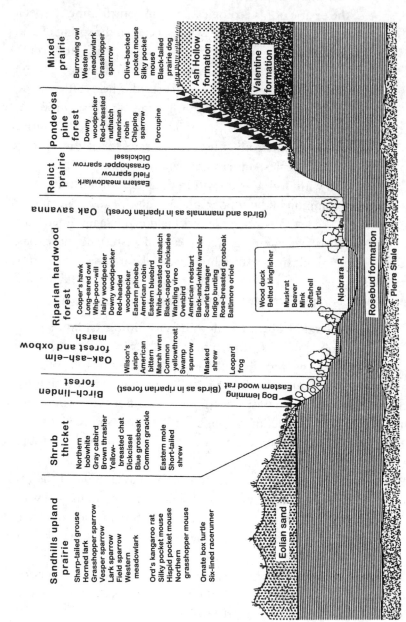

FIGURE 6. Cross-section view of typical central Niobrara Valley habitats and some associated vertebrates (after Johnsgard 1995).

any other river in the northern plains (fig. 6). The generally steep slope on the northern side of the river supports a usually thick stand of ponderosa pines, where western bird species such as the black-billed magpie and more northern ones such as the red-breasted nuthatch and red crossbill might be found. On the floodplain on both sides of the river a riparian forest of bur oak, green ash, and the now rare American elm is generally present, with a predominance of eastern or northeastern bird species, such as the whip-poor-will, eastern phoebe, eastern wood pewee, eastern bluebird, wood thrush, yellow-throated vireo, ovenbird, black-and-white warbler, and scarlet tanager.

Indigo buntings, rose-breasted grosbeaks, and northern orioles are also to be found, although sometimes these apparent sightings actually involve hybrids with their western counterparts, the lazuli bunting, black-headed grosbeak, and Bullock's oriole. On slightly drier terraces stands of bur oak form open, savannalike communities whose acorns provide important fall and winter food for fox squirrels, white-tailed and mule deer, wild turkeys, and sharp-tailed grouse. Bur oaks reach farther west (at least to Cherry County) into the Niobrara Valley than do any other of the half-dozen species of oaks native to Nebraska; their thick bark probably makes them particularly resistant to prairie fires.

On steeper, shaded slopes of the northern banks, stands of paper birch are conspicuous, supporting many of the same birds as found in the riparian forest and also some animals not found elsewhere, such as the southern bog lemming. Like the paper birch, the bog lemming is a Pleistocene relict now mostly found farther to the north and east.

Over forty species of mammals occur within the central Niobrara Valley (table 9). Upland prairies on either sandy or firm substrates probably support the largest number of species (at least twenty-six). Some of these are largely confined to Sandhills prairie, such as the Ord's kangaroo rat and the silky and hispid pocket mice. Plains pocket mice are also often very common on sandy substrates, especially in weedy, once-cultivated locations, and the spotted ground squirrel likewise favors sandy sites. Others, like the black-tailed prairie dog and thirteen-lined ground squirrel, prefer firmer substrates that are unlikely to cave in when they dig.

Second to prairie types, riparian hardwoods had the greatest number of mammalian residents (seventeen) in W. E. Beed's surveys done at Fort Niobrara National Wildlife Refuge (Beed 1936; table 9). They include

Table 9. Ecological associations of mammals in the central Niobrara Valley

Species*	Upland Prairie	Rock Outcrop	Pine Woods	Scrub Thicket	Riparian Forest	Dry Meadow	Wet Meadow	Swamp	Riparian Edge
Masked shrew					X		X	X	
Hayden's shrew	X								
Northern short-tailed shrew				X	X	X	X		
Eastern mole				X	X	X			
Eastern cottontail	X	X		X	X				
Black-tailed jackrabbit	X								
White-tailed jackrabbit	X	X	X	X					
Black-tailed prairie dog	X								
Thirteen-lined ground squirrel	X								
Spotted ground squirrel	X			X					
Fox squirrel				X	X	X			
Plains pocket gopher	X					X			
Olive-backed pocket mouse	X								
Plains pocket mouse	X								
Silky pocket mouse	X								
Hispid pocket mouse	X	X	X						
Ord's kangaroo rat	X	X							
Beaver									X
Plains harvest mouse	X								
White-footed mouse	X	X	X						
Deer mouse	X	X		X	X	X	X		
Grasshopper mouse	X	X							
Prairie vole				X	X				
Meadow vole				X	X	X			

continued

Muskrat	X							
Meadow jumping mouse				X	X			
Porcupine						X		X
Coyote			X	X	X	X		X
Raccoon		X	X	X			X	X
Long-tailed weasel			X	X	X	X		X
Least weasel			X	X	X			
Mink		X		X				
Striped skunk						X	X	X
Spotted skunk				X		X		X
Badger					X	X	X	X
Bobcat			X	X	X	X		X
Elk			X	X	X		X	X
Mule deer								X
White-tailed deer				X		X		
Pronghorn								X
Bison						X		X

*Species are listed according to currently accepted taxonomic sequence.

Source: Adapted from Breed (1936); data for the Fort Niobrara National Wildlife Refuge. The "upland prairie" was termed "shortgrass" by Beed. The "scrub thicket" community probably corresponds to the sumac-dogwood shrubland community of Steinauer and Rolfsmeier (2003).

Note: The white-tailed deer has been added, owing to its recent western range expansion. In contrast, the spotted skunk is now quite rare in the region.

such expected species as fox squirrel, raccoon, eastern cottontail, spotted skunk (now rare), eastern mole, and northern short-tailed shrew. White-tailed deer moved west into the hardwood forests of the central Niobrara region after Beed's surveys, as part of a general westward range expansion across Nebraska. However, the spotted skunk may now be declining as part of a general rangewide retreat. The relatively rare eastern wood rat is also a part of the eastern deciduous forest community; its local population is an endemic and geographically isolated race that seems to have adapted to both hardwood and coniferous forest life.

Like the ponderosa pine forest's low avian biodiversity in the central Niobrara Valley, its mammalian diversity is also generally low. Pine seeds are fairly small and are hard for most birds and mammals to extract, and sharp pine needles are bitter and provide little nourishment. Porcupines sleep in the forest crown and find food in the pine's cambium layer, below the bark. White-footed mice and deer mice are likely to survive here, as well as nearly everywhere, feeding mostly on diverse grass and forb seeds. Predators such as weasels and bobcats may find both prey and cover among the pines, and mule deer are more at home on the generally steep and rocky terrain associated with ponderosa pines than are white-tailed deer.

Scrub thickets support diverse mammals, including a considerable number of rodents and cottontails. These in turn attract predators such as coyotes, weasels, badgers, and bobcats.

Rock outcrops, favored by small rodents for hiding, are regularly visited by predators such as bobcats, weasels, and badgers. Dry meadows attract elk and mule deer (and locally also pronghorns) and are hunting grounds for coyotes searching for rodents. Minks and raccoons hunt in swampy areas, and riparian edges are used by beavers and muskrats (table 9).

Small-mammal trapping studies funded by the Bureau of Reclamation (1978) in the proposed Norden Dam area revealed that grassland habitats supported the greatest density of small mammals in June, totaling a mean of 15.4 per acre, and included six species, with Ord's kangaroo rats the most common. Evergreen forests were second in small-mammal density, having three species and an overall density of 6.5 animals per acre, with white-footed mice most common. Mixed forests had a mean density of 5.2 animals per acre, with four total species and white-footed mice most common. Lowland riparian forests supported a density of 3.4 animals per acre, with white-footed mice most common.

Hispid pocket mice were captured only in grasslands and mixed forests, and eastern wood rats were captured in measurable numbers only in coniferous forests. Prairie voles, northern grasshopper mice, Ord's kangaroo rats, and thirteen-lined ground squirrels were captured only in grasslands. Deer mice occurred in all the wooded habitats, but in lower densities than the widely ranging white-footed mice.

The major breeding birds of the central Niobrara Valley are summarized in table 10, and many of them also appear in figure 6. Not all the species Beed observed are shown in table 10—only those he considered characteristic of each major community type as well as some others he subjectively added. Considering all the habitats Beed analyzed, the riparian forest exhibited the greatest apparent vertebrate species diversity, followed by scrub thicket, riparian edge, upland prairie, and dry meadow. Considering only those species listed in table 10 as characteristic, the riparian forest also heads the list (with twenty-one species), followed by riparian edge (eight species) and upland prairie (seven species). A more quantitatively based survey of avian habitat associations is provided in chapter 6.

The twenty species of reptiles and amphibians listed for the central Niobrara Valley (table 11) include seven snakes, six amphibians, four turtles, and three lizards. All three lizards are open-country, sand-adapted species, especially the lesser earless and northern prairie lizards, whereas the six-lined racerunner prefers denser grassy vegetation. The Great Plains toad is also a widespread grassland species, whereas the Plains spadefoot toad is most common in rather sandy soils that are easy to burrow into. Toads are favored foods of hognose snakes; both eastern and western species are present in the Niobrara Valley. However, bull snakes and prairie rattlesnakes are more generalized and widespread open-country predators. The blue racer is also more likely to be seen in taller wet or dry meadows than in open, dry sand prairies. The Plains garter snake is more grassland adapted than is the red-sided garter snake, which like the northern watersnake prefers marshes. Although not observed during Beed's survey, the uncommon and beautiful milk snake also occurs in the central Niobrara Valley, where it is found in diverse habitats from grasslands to riparian forests.

Table 10. Ecological associations of typical breeding birds of the central Niobrara Valley

Species	Upland Prairie	Rock Outcrop	Pine Woods	Scrub Thicket	Riparian Forest	Dry Meadow	Wet Meadow	Swamp	Riparian Edge
Total reported species	18	6	11	28	37	14	8	7	14
Characteristic species									
Long-billed curlew	B								
Lark bunting	B								
Western meadowlark	J					J			
Eastern meadowlark							J		
Chestnut-collared longspur	B					J			
Rock wren		B							
Ferruginous hawk	B	J							
Red-tailed hawk	J	J	B		J				
Prairie falcon	J	J	B						
Say's phoebe		J							
Black-headed grosbeak			B		J				
Rose-breasted grosbeak					J				
Indigo bunting					J				
Lazuli bunting				J					
Bell's vireo					J				
Red-breasted nuthatch			J						
White-breasted nuthatch					J				
Loggerhead shrike				B					
Spotted towhee				B					
Eastern wood-pewee					J				
Red-headed woodpecker					B				
Hariy woodpecker					B				

continued

Species						
Downy woodpecker						B
Eastern kingbird						B
American crow	J					B
Black-capped chickadee						B
House wren						B
Black-and-white warbler						B
Yellow warbler						B
Common yellowthroat						B
Orchard oriole						B
Baltimore oriole						B
Common grackle		J				B
Upland sandpiper			B			
Black-crowned night heron				J		B
Mallard				J		B
Blue-winged teal				J		B
Wood duck					B	B
Spotted sandpiper						B
Least tern						J
Piping plover						J
Belted kingfisher						B

Source: Mainly after Beed (1936), based on surveys at Fort Niobrara National Wildlife Refuge. Habitat categories as described in table 9. Total reported species are those listed for the community type by Beed. Species are grouped according to favored habitats, from upland prairies to riparian edge.

Note: Characteristic species shown with the letter *B* are those that Beed regarded as unique to that single community type. The ruddy duck, northern shoveler, American coot, least tern, and black tern have been excluded as not typical of most Niobrara riparian habitats. Where the letter *J* appears it refers to additional species or additional typical habitats as judged by me and by Ducey (1989).

Wet meadows and swampy sites also support two cricket frogs, the tiger salamander, and all the native turtles except for the sand-adapted ornate box turtle. Although not reported by Beed and not included in table 11, the nationally rare and declining Blanding's turtle also enters the greater Niobrara region and reaches its southwestern range limits in the central Sandhills lakes and marshes, where it sometimes is fairly common.

Wetland habitats in the Niobrara Valley such as wet meadows and marshes are quite limited compared with nearby Sandhills wetlands (30,633 acres vs. 369,606 acres according to recent National Wetland Inventory data) yet not only are important to aquatic animals but also aid in filtering water, attenuating flood peak flows, and helping sustain river levels during dry periods.

The fishes of the Niobrara Valley have been sampled at various times by the Nebraska Game and Parks Commission. A statewide stream survey was performed in 1973, including the Niobrara River and its tributaries, when forty-one species of fish were collected within the entire Niobrara basin. The lower Niobrara's fish fauna were again sampled between 1976 and 1991, primarily between Spencer Dam (Holt County) and the river's mouth (Bliss and Schainost 1973; Hesse et al. 1979; Mestl 1993).

Between 1983 and 1988 about ninety localities in the Niobrara and Loup basins were surveyed with electrofishing equipment. The sites included two tributary streams in the central Niobrara Valley, Minnechaduza Creek in Cherry County, and Long Pine Creek in Brown County. Long Pine Creek is a cold-water stream with summer temperatures seldom exceeding 25°C and flow rates of 10–100 cubic feet per second (cfs). Minnechaduza Creek is a cool-water stream with average flow rates of under 10 cfs. Of four fish species and 159 specimens collected from Long Pine Creek, rainbow trout made up 42 percent, brook trout 36 percent, longnose dace 20 percent, and white sucker 2 percent. Of seven species and 142 specimens taken from Minnechaduza Creek, pumpkinseed made up 44 percent, rock bass 28 percent, golden shiner 10 percent, and black bullhead, green sunfish, largemouth bass, and northern pike the remaining 18 percent. Headwater reaches of this creek also support a few other species, such as the Plains topminnow and grass pickerel. These cool-water streams support the greatest diversity of fish species in

Table 11. Ecological associations of reptiles and amphibians in the central Niobrara Valley

Species	Upland Prairie	Rock Outcrop	Pine Woods	Scrub Thicket	Riparian Forest	Dry Meadow	Wet Meadow	Swamp	Riparian Edge
Eastern and western hog-nosed snakes	X		X						
Milk snake	X	X	X		X	X			
Prairie rattlesnake	X	X	X	X		X			
Bull snake	X		X	X		X	X		
Plains garter snake							X		
Red-sided garter snake							X	X	X
Blue racer				X		X	X		
Northern water snake							X	X	
Lesser earless lizard	X								
Northern prairie lizard	X	X	X						
Six-lined racerunner		X	X			X			
Great Plains toad	X	X	X		X				
Plains spadefoot toad	X								
Ornate box turtle	X								
Snapping turtle									X
Eastern painted turtle									X
Spiny softshell turtle									X
Northern leopard frog					X		X		X
Western chorus frog							X	X	X
Northern cricket frog							X	X	X
Tiger salamander							X	X	X

Note: Mostly after Beed's (1936) data from the Fort Niobrara National Wildlife Refuge, and from Freeman (1998). Habitat categories as described in table 9. Several species and a few additional habitat associations have been added.

Table 12. Aquatic macroinvertebrates reported from Long Pine Creek
and Bone Creek, Brown County

	Long Pine	Bone Creek
Coelenterata		
Hydrozoa		
Hydroidae: 1 genus (*Hydra*)		X
Platyhelminthes		
Turbellaria: 1 genus (*Cura*)	X	X
Nematoda	X	
Nematomorpha	X	
Annelida	X	X
Oligochaeta	X	X
Hirudinea	X	X
Anthropoda		
Arachnida		
Hydracarina	X	X
Crustacea		
Amphipoda: 2 genera	X	X
Insecta		
Collembola	X	
Ephemeroptera: 12 genera	X	X
Odonata		
Zygoptera: 3 genera	X	X
Anisoptera: 4 genera	X	X
Plecoptera: 8 genera	X	X
Hemiptera:		
Belastomatidae: 2 genera	X	X
Corixidae	X	
Naucoridae: 3 genera	X	X
Nepidae: 1 genus (*Nepa*)	X	
Notonectidae	X	
Pleidae: 1 genus (*Neoplea*)	X	
Vellidae	X	
Megaloptera: 1 genus (*Chauliodes*)	X	
Trichoptera: 16 genera	X	X
Lepidoptera: 1 genus (*Paragyractis*)	X	
Coleoptera		
Dytiscidae: 4 genera	X	
Dryopidae	X	
Elmidae	X	X
Haliplidae	X	X
Hydrophilidae	X	
Diptera		
Athericidae: 2 genera	X	X
Ceratopogonidae: 2 genera	X	X

continued

	Long Pine	Bone Creek
Chironomidae: 43 genera	X	X
Dixidae: 1 genus (*Dixa*)	X	X
Dolichopodidae	X	X
Empididae	X	X
Ephydridae	X	X
Muscidae	X	X
Psychodidae		X
Simulidae	X	X
Tabanidae	X	X
Tipulidae	X	X
Mollusca		
Gastropoda		
Physidae: 1 genus (Physa)	X	X
Planorbidae: 1 genus (Gyralus)	X	
Pelecypoda		
Sphaeridae	X	X

Source: Taxa reported by Maret (1988).

Nebraska and include some state-threatened species such as pearl and redbelly dace (Maret 1989; Mestl 1993).

Water-table-fed and gravel-bottom streams coming out of the Sandhills, such as Long Pine Creek and Bone Creek (before its pollution), have a very rich invertebrate life that contributes to their unusual capacity for supporting cold-water fish such as introduced brown and rainbow trout populations, as indicated in table 12.

Very few counterpart studies of terrestrial invertebrates of the Niobrara Valley have been performed, although surveys of butterflies, moths, dragonflies, and damselflies of the Niobrara Valley Preserve have been undertaken by the Nature Conservancy. Data for these groups have been incorporated into the checklists in appendixes E and F.

Subterranean invertebrate populations at Fort Niobrara National Wildlife Refuge were surveyed by Beed (1936), and an abbreviated summary of his listing for the upland prairie ("shortgrass" in his terminology) is provided in table 13. Remember that this survey was done nearly seventy years ago, and the soil conditions and biota may have changed considerably since that time.

Table 13. Terrestrial macroinvertebrates of the upland prairie,
Fort Niobrara National Wildlife Refuge

Class Insecta (insects)
  Order Orthoptera (grasshoppers, crickets, etc.): 19 genera and 22 species
  Order Homoptera (cicadas and relatives)
    Family Cicadellidae (leafhoppers): 6 genera and 7 species
  Order Hymenoptera (wasps, bees, ants): 22 genera and 29 aboveground species,
    plus 6 genera and 6 species of underground ants
  Order Diptera (flies): 5 genera and 5 species
  Order Coleoptera (beetles): 27 genera and 32 species, plus soil larvae of 6 genera
    and 9 species
  Order Hemiptera (true bugs): 4 genera and 4 species
  Order Neuroptera (lacewings and relatives): 3 genera and 8 species
Class Araneida (spiders and relatives): 14 genera and 14 species

Source: After Beed (1936).

The Lower Niobrara Valley and Missouri River Confluence

The lower reaches of the Niobrara River, from about the confluence of the Keya Paha and Niobrara rivers to the Niobrara's mouth, are marked by a rather broad valley, with the river flowing over a thick layer of the Pierre Shale and, near its mouth as the river turns northward, fairly steep, clifflike exposures of Niobrara Chalk.

Species diversity of vertebrates (fig. 7) is high here, based on currently available information. Ducey (1989) listed 107 known or suspected currently breeding birds for the vicinity of the Niobrara's mouth, as compared with 89 breeding species for the Fort Niobrara, Niobrara Valley Preserve region of the central Niobrara Valley. Some of these additional species include such forest- and thicket-adapted birds as the eastern screech owl, long-eared owl, willow and perhaps least flycatcher, brown creeper, and warbling vireo. There are also more mixed-grass prairie birds, such as the sharp-tailed grouse, long-billed curlew, short-eared owl, loggerhead shrike, lark bunting, vesper sparrow, and chestnut-collared longspur. Some swampland species also are present locally, such as the Wilson's snipe and swamp sparrow. And a few distinctly western-woodland species such as the black-headed grosbeak, Bullock's oriole, and lazuli bunting (or their respective hybrid combinations with the rose-breasted grosbeak, Baltimore oriole, and indigo bunting) extend this far east.

By the time the Niobrara River reaches its Missouri River confluence, it has descended about two thousand feet from its headwaters and has

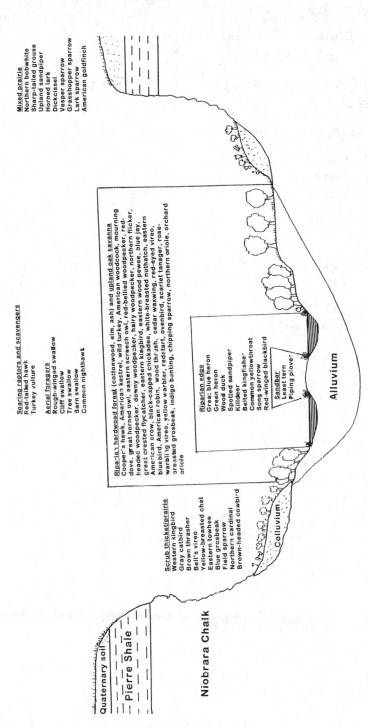

Soaring raptors and scavengers
Red-tailed hawk
Turkey vulture

Aerial foragers
Rough-winged swallow
Cliff swallow
Tree swallow
Barn swallow
Common nighthawk

Riparian hardwood forest (cottonwood, elm, ash) and **upland oak savanna**
Cooper's hawk, American kestrel, wild turkey, American woodcock, mourning dove, great horned owl, eastern screech owl, red-bellied woodpecker, red-headed woodpecker, downy woodpecker, hairy woodpecker, northern flicker, great crested flycatcher, eastern kingbird, eastern wood pewee, blue jay, American crow, black-capped chickadee, white-breasted nuthatch, eastern bluebird, American robin, wood thrush, cedar waxwing, red-eyed vireo, warbling vireo, yellow warbler, redstart, ovenbird, scarlet tanager, rose-breasted grosbeak, indigo bunting, chipping sparrow, northern oriole, orchard oriole

Riparian edge
Great blue heron
Green heron
Wood duck
Killdeer
Spotted sandpiper
Belted kingfisher
Common yellowthroat
Song sparrow
Red-winged blackbird

Sandbar
Least tern
Piping plover

Scrub thicket/prairie
Western kingbird
Gray catbird
Brown thrasher
Bell's vireo
Yellow-breasted chat
Eastern towhee
Blue grosbeak
Field sparrow
Northern cardinal
Brown-headed cowbird

Mixed prairie
Northern bobwhite
Sharp-tailed grouse
Upland sandpiper
Horned lark
Dickcissel
Vesper sparrow
Grasshopper sparrow
Lark sparrow
American goldfinch

Alluvium

Colluvium

Niobrara Chalk

Pierre Shale

Quaternary soil

FIGURE 7. Cross-section view of typical lower Niobrara Valley habitats (vicinity of Niobrara State Park) and some habitat-associated breeding birds (in part after data of Ducey 1989). The relative thicknesses of the Pierre Shale and Niobrara Chalk are not drawn to scale.

Table 14. Species richness of fish in the lower Niobrara River

Species (Percentage Composition)*	Explosive Charge		Seine Catch	
	1978	1991	1978	1991
Sand shiner (38.6)	37.8	1.2	14.9	25.3
Red shiner (34.0)	15.1	10.9	28.6	30.5
Flathead chub (12.2)	11.5	5.0	3.3	11.6
River carpsucker (5.6)	0.8	0.2	11.7	22.1
Channel catfish (3.9)	5.4	10.8	0.3	0.5
Bigmouth shiner (2.2)	—	—	11.0	Trace
Fathead minnow (0.8)	—	—	0.3	Trace
Emerald shiner (0.5)	1.0	1.8	13.7	Trace
Carp (introduced) (0.4)	< 0.1	< 0.1	0.1	Trace
Largemouth bass (0.3)	—	—	0.4	Trace
Bluegill (0.2)	0.3	0.2	0.6	1.1
Shorthead redhorse (0.1)	0.2	< 0.1	0.5	Trace
White sucker (0.1)	—	—	—	—
Yellow bullhead (0.1)	—	—	—	—
Black bullhead (0.1)	—	—	0.1	Trace
Brassy minnow (0.1)	—	—	—	—
River shiner (0.0)	—	—	14.3	7.7
Sauger (0.0)	< 0.1	0.2	0.1	Trace
Longnose dace (0.0)	—	—	—	—
Grass pickerel (0.0)	—	—	—	—
Stone catfish (0.0)	—	—	—	—
Yellow perch (0.0)	—	—	—	—
Silver chub	—	—	0.1	Trace
Green sunfish	0.9	0.1	0.1	1.0
Silvery minnow	1.0	< 0.1	—	—
Spotfin shiner	< 0.1	0.2	—	—
Plains minnow	—	—	0.1	Trace
Stoneroller	—	—	0.1	Trace
Total fish	20,744	< 2,000	2,882	< 2,000

Source: After Hesse et al. (1979) and Mestl (1993), sampled between Spencer Dam and mouth of Niobrara River. Figures for explosive charge data represent mean number of fish obtained per blast, not percentage species composition for samples.

*Species percentage composition based on estimates from electric shock and seine samples of 13,063 fish given for lower Niobrara River by Gutzmer et al. (2002). Estimate shown for river carpsucker includes highfin carpsucker. Figures given as "trace" represent relative sample percentages under 0.01; dashes indicate absence of species in sample.

become both warmer and more sluggish. Between the once-proposed Norden Dam area and the vicinity of the Missouri River confluence, the Niobrara's elevation diminishes from about nine to seven feet per mile, the river spreading out downstream to form a broadly braided, sand-bed channel as it approaches the confluence. The Niobrara River now carries about 2.9 million tons of sediment per year, of which about 2 million tons consist of sand and the rest is a mixture of silt and clay. A wide delta has formed at the confluence of the Niobrara and what is now actually the western end of Lewis and Clark Lake. These conditions have raised the groundwater table, depositing several feet of sediment and reducing the flood-carrying capacity of the river channel (Mussetter and Wolf 1993).

The Niobrara's rather turbid downstream waters no doubt carry less oxygen than is typical of the river's more upstream stretches and its cold-water tributaries. These conditions exclude most cold-water fishes and favor bottom-feeding species that are adapted to reduced visibility and low oxygen levels, such as catfish, carpsuckers, carp, and redhorse. Surveys of the lower Niobrara done from the vicinity of Spencer Dam to the confluence of the Niobrara and Missouri rivers (table 14) exhibit marked differences from the fishes of cool- or cold-water tributary streams that were mentioned earlier for Minnechaduza and Long Pine creeks. Between 1978 and 1991 there were also apparent declines in seine catches of several species found along the lower Niobrara, such as river shiner, emerald shiner, and bigmouth shiner. There were corresponding population increases in sand shiners, river carpsuckers, and flathead chubs. Explosive-charge samples suggest that population increases have also been typical of some warm-water species such as the channel catfish, but declines may have occurred in most other fish species (Gutzmer et al. 2002).

Chapter Five

Biogeography and Biodiversity in the Niobrara Valley

The Niobrara Valley of northern Nebraska contains numerous bryo-phyte, vascular plant, and animal species more typical of forests far to the east, north and west than to other forests in the grasslands that sur-round the valley. Some species are probably relics of cooler glacial and postglacial times, when much of what is now grassland was covered by boreal and cool-temperate forests. Others entered the Valley from the east in postglacial times, and some entered from the west as the climate became semi-arid.

—ROBERT KAUL, GENE KANTAK,
& STEVEN CHURCHILL (1988)

The Biogeography of Niobrara Valley Plants

The first time I walked up the beautiful wooded canyon of Long Pine Creek I thought I had suddenly been transported to South Dakota's Black Hills. A crystal-clear trout stream bubbled beside me, a black-headed grosbeak sang in hardwoods bordering the stream, and tall ponderosa pines towered above me. A friend who recently had moved from south-eastern Alaska to Nebraska evidently thought she was back home as she excitedly announced that she had just seen a black phoebe! It must have been an eastern phoebe, or perhaps its western relative the Say's phoebe, since black phoebes would be far out of range in Nebraska. But the inci-dent points out the confusing transitional character of the central Niobrara Valley, where you are not sure whether an eastern or western field guide is the appropriate reference book to carry.

It has long been recognized that, botanically speaking, the Niobrara Valley is a very special place. More than a century ago, Charles Bessey (1887) first described the Long Pine area of the central Niobrara Valley as a "meeting place of two floras." This area of Brown County lies almost exactly on the 100th meridian, the traditional east-west geographic divide in North America. Roscoe Pound and Frederic Clements (1900) described the pine forests, springbranch canyon forests, and hardwood floodplain vegetation of this portion of the Niobrara Valley as the only place across the present-day Great Plains grasslands where upland elements of the Rocky Mountain, boreal, and eastern deciduous forests meet. E. S. Nixon (1967) later analyzed the Pine Ridge vegetation of the upper Niobrara drainage in terms of its boreal, Rocky Mountain, southeastern, and southwestern plant representatives. Still later, the floristic geography of the entire Niobrara Valley was described in detail by A. T. Harrison (1980) and by Robert Kaul, Gene Kantak, and Steven Churchill (1988).

Table 15 presents a summary of the plants of biogeographic interest in the Niobrara Valley, selecting 105 species of "very special" geographic significance in the view of Harrison (1980) and species reaching the edges of their overall geographic distributions in the valley according to Kaul, Kantak, and Churchill (1988). Of the total number, about 70 percent are of eastern, northeastern, or southeastern geographic affinities, about 20 percent are of western or northwestern affinities, and 10 percent are of northern (boreal) affinities. It is clear that eastern forest or woody-edge species constitute a significant proportion (about 48 percent) of the flora of the Niobrara region, with eastern or southeastern mesic grassland types adding about 16 percent, drier western or northwestern grassland species contributing about 10 percent, and western woodland or woody edge species adding about another 9 percent. Meadow and marsh species contribute relatively little to the overall picture, accounting for about 18 percent collectively, with varied but mostly easterly affinities.

Although boreally oriented plants seem to make up a very small part of this overall picture, their occurrence in Cherry County fen wetlands accounts for almost half the total number of rare and disjunctively dis-

Table 15. Vascular plants of biogeographic significance in the Niobrara Valley

Eastern, Northeastern, and Southeastern Species
  Woody edge habitats:
    American bellflower, American potato bean, basswood, black walnut, bulblet bladder
    fern, bur oak, downy blue violet, downy yellow violet, enchanter's nightshade, erect
    dayflower, figwort, forktip three-awn, gerardia, grape fern, hazelnut, hog peanut,
    Iowa crab, jack-in-the-pulpit, lanceleaf buckthorn, large-flower tickclover, mulberry,
    ninebark, nodding fescue, pale touch-me-not, Peck's sedge, prickly ash, sharpwing
    monkey flower, silver maple, slippery elm, spikenard, spinulose wood fern, starry cam-
    pion, sweet cicely, tall anemone, virgin's bower, wahoo, white snakeroot, whitegrass,
    wild columbine, wild cranesbill, wild honeysuckle, wood nettle, woodbine, woodland
    bluegrass, woodreed
  Grassland habitats:
    Big tree plum (also in woody edge habitats), churchmouse three-awn, closed gen-
    tian (also in woody edge habitats), common elderberry (also in woody edge habi-
    tats), euthamia, fescue sedge (also in woody edge habitats), Grovonius's dodder (also
    in woody edge habitats), meadow willow, muhly (*Muhlenbergia glomerata*), prairie
    fringed orchid, rockpink, showy-wand goldenrod, slimspike three-awn, small skullcap
    (also in woody edge habitats), spikemoss, sweet flag, umbrella sedge, Virginia moun-
    tain mint, wild onion
  Meadow/marsh habitats:
    Allegheny monkey flower, arrowhead (*Sagittaria graminea* and *S. rigida*), false nettle,
    fimbristylis, hemicarpha, peppermint, rush (*Juncus scirpoides*), Virginia bugleweed

Western and Northwestern Species
  Woody edge habitats:
    Bristly gooseberry, pinedrops, snowberry, western clematis, wintergreen, yellow pine
  Grassland habitats:
    Blue lips (also in woody edge habitats), catchfly, draba milkvetch, fleabane (also in
    woody edge habitats), little breadfruit scurfpea, massive spike prairie clover, pale eve-
    ning primrose, Plains phlox, spikemoss, Sandberg's bluegrass, yellow whiteflower
  Meadow/marsh habitats:
    Harebell (also in woody edge habitats), obedient plant, sprangletop

Northern Species
  Woody edge habitats:
    Creeping blackberry, paper birch, wild sarsaparilla, wood fern
  Grassland habitats:
    Prairie chickweed
  Meadow/marsh habitats:
    Aster (*Aster pubentior*), buckbean, cottongrass, marsh Saint-John's-wort, sedge
    (*Carex diandra* and *C. saximontana*)

Source: Based on lists of species of "very major" biogeographic significance by Harrison (1990)
and of species reaching eastern or western range limits in the Niobrara Valley according to Kaul,
Kantak, and Churchill (1988). "Woody edge" includes woodland species. Lists are alphabeti-
cal by generic and, secondarily, specific names.

Table 16. Disjunct and rare plant species reported from
Sandhills fens in Cherry County

Bitter cress (*Cardamine pennsylvanica*)	Rush (*Juncus canadensis*)
Buckbean (*Menyanthes trifoliata*)*	Rush aster (*Aster junciformis*)*
Canada rush (*Juncus canadensis*)*	Sedge (*Carex diandra*)
Cottongrass (*Eriophorum polystachyion*)*	Sedge (*Carex prairea*)
Flatop aster (*Aster pubentior*)*	Slender cottongrass (*Eriophorum gracile*)*
Long-leaved stitchwort (*Stellaria longifolia*)*	Swamp lousewort (*Pedicularis lanceolata*)
Marsh marigold (*Caltha palustris*)*	Twayblade (*Liparis loeseli*)
Marsh Saint-John's-wort (*Triadenum fraseri*)*	Water horsetail (*Equisetum fluviatile*)
Mud sedge (*Carex limosa*)*	Water sedge (*Carex aquatilis*)
Muhly (*Muhlenbergia glomerata*)	Western lily (*Lilium philadelphicum*)
Northern bog violet (*Viola nephrophylla*)	Wild rice (*Zizania aquatica*)
Rush (*Juncus articulatus*)	

Source: After Steinauer (1993) and Steinauer, Rolfsmeier, and Hardy (1996), the latter listing
191 total plant species for Cherry County fens.
Note: Boreal relict disjunct species are indicated with asterisks. Listed alphabetically by common names.

tributed plants of the region (table 16). The cool groundwater environment surrounding these fens has apparently allowed at least some Pleistocene relict species populations to survive in these unique habitats, even though their current ranges are now otherwise mostly well to the north and west of the Great Plains. For example, the distinctive white-tufted heads of tall cottongrass (not a grass but part of the widespread sedge family) are familiar to all who have visited the arctic tundra during summer. This species extends south in the Great Plains along the glaciated moraines of the northern and eastern Dakotas, but in Nebraska it occurs only in the fens of Cherry County. Another isolated population of tall cottongrass occurs in the South Dakota Black Hills, and this cottongrass also extends southward from Alaska to New Mexico along the Rocky Mountain alpine communities.

The Biogeography of Niobrara Valley Birds

In addition to these plant geographic trends, very good information is available on the biogeography of breeding birds in the Niobrara Valley, thanks in large measure to the studies of James Ducey (1989), as well as statewide breeding bird surveys performed during the 1980s (Mollhoff 2001). Based on such studies, the breeding species of the region are indicated in appendix 1B.

Table 17. Bird Species of east-west biogeographic significance
in the Niobrara Valley

Eastern Species	Western Species
	Western grebe
	Clark's grebe
	Eared grebe
Greater prairie chicken	*Sharp-tailed grouse*
Northern bobwhite	
	Cinnamon teal
	Ferruginous hawk*
	Prairie falcon*
	Golden eagle
	Merlin
	Long-billed curlew*
	Willet
American woodcock	Wilson's phalarope
Barred owl (eastern population)	
Whip-poor-will	Common poorwill
Chimney swift	White-throated swift
Red-headed woodpecker	*Lewis's woodpecker*
Red-bellied woodpecker	Black-billed magpie
Blue jay	Pinyon jay
	Clark's nutcracker
Eastern wood pewee	*Western wood pewee*
Eastern phoebe	*Say's phoebe*
Great crested flycatcher	Cassin's kingbird

continued

Collectively, 185 bird species are currently known or believed to breed in the greater Niobrara region, which represents about 90 percent of Nebraska's entire breeding avifauna and about 87 percent of South Dakota's known breeding species (see appendix 1B). It is unlikely that any other segment of the state having a comparable area could document so much avian biodiversity. For example, a study area of about 1,900 square miles in the central Platte Valley, an area justly famous for its bird life, supports about 140 breeding species. Of the Niobrara region's total 185 breeding species, 43 percent (81) are widespread in North America. Additionally, 19 percent (35) are of western geographic orientation, 17 percent (31) are of eastern, and 2 percent (4) have southern, southeastern, or southwestern affinities. There are also 11 species (6 percent) that are here considered as having breeding ranges endemically centered in the Great Plains, 8 that have broader Great Plains–

Eastern Species	Western Species
Red-eyed vireo	Plumbeous vireo
Purple martin	Violet-green swallow
	Pygmy nuthatch
Blue-gray gnatcatcher	Rock wren
Wood thrush	Townsend's solitaire
Brown thrasher	Sage thrasher
Black-and-white warbler	Yellow-rumped warbler
American redstart	
Ovenbird	
Scarlet tanager	*Western tanager*
Eastern towhee	*Spotted towhee*
Rose-breasted grosbeak	*Black-headed grosbeak*
Indigo bunting	*Lazuli bunting*
Eastern meadowlark	*Western meadowlark*
Baltimore oriole	*Bullock's oriole*
Northern cardinal (eastern population)	Cassin's sparrow*
Orchard oriole	Brewer's blackbird

Note: Species reaching or nearly reaching their eastern or western Great Plains range limits in the greater Niobrara Valley region, based on various sources (see appendixes). Closely related (congeneric) species pairs are shown by italics; those pairs believed to hybridize in zones of secondary contact along the Niobrara Valley are connected by underlining.
*Species also having strong Great Plains affinities.

western or Great Plains–northern distributions, 9 that have northern or northwestern geographic affinities, and 6 breeding species that are introduced (table 17).

In contrast to the generally somewhat eastern-oriented plants, a majority (60 percent) of the sixty bird species reaching or nearly reaching the western or eastern edges of their geographic ranges in the Niobrara Valley are of western orientation. Since about two-thirds of the Niobrara Valley is geographically west of the 100th meridian, this relationship should not be too surprising. Many species reach or nearly reach the edges of their breeding ranges in the Niobrara Valley. Thus the eastern meadowlark (fig. 8) breeds west to about Cherry County, while the Western meadowlark extends east to beyond the Iowa border. Hybridization between the two is apparently rare. The Lewis's woodpecker (fig. 8) is limited to the pine forests of Sioux and Dawes counties, whereas

FIGURE 8. Adult plumages of western meadowlark (upper left), eastern meadowlark (upper right), Lewis's woodpecker (lower left), and red-headed woodpecker (lower left). Drawings by the author.

its congener the red-headed woodpecker ranges west into eastern Wyoming. Hybridization between the two has not been reported.

A few peripheral breeding species might be mentioned as being of generally southern geographic affinities, such as the distinctly infrequent northern mockingbird (one regional breeding record between 1980 and 1988 was reported by Wayne Mollhoff 2001) and the very rare scissor-tailed flycatcher (no regional records were reported by Mollhoff between 1980 and 1988). Several other rare or local breeders are of northern affinities, including the Wilson's snipe (mainly limited to northern Sandhills meadows), brown creeper (very few documented state records), and swamp sparrow (mainly limited to the lower Niobrara Valley). Possibly the Savannah sparrow (a probable but poorly documented nester in the Niobrara Valley), the tree swallow (which now breeds locally south to southern Nebraska in bluebird boxes), and the red-breasted nuthatch (which also breeds in the Rocky Mountains) should be added as species having boreal affinities.

There are also numerous birds whose breeding ranges center on the Great Plains and that commonly breed in the Niobrara Valley, including such shortgrass species as Swainson's hawk, lark bunting, and McCown's longspur. There are also several mixed-grass breeding species, such as vesper sparrow, lark sparrow, grasshopper sparrow, and chestnut-collared longspur. The Great Plains race of the sharp-tailed grouse (*Tympanuchus phasianellus jamesi*) might be mentioned here, although the species' overall North American range orientation is distinctly northern. And some other generalized grassland birds, like the ferruginous hawk, prairie falcon, long-billed curlew, and western meadowlark, might equally well be considered either as representing the Great Plains or as a part of the overall western North American avifauna.

Likewise, the greater prairie chicken, although historically best classified as an eastern tallgrass species, has a rapidly declining range that is now centered well to the west of its presettlement distribution in the upper Mississippi Valley prairies. Its current precarious status in the central and lower Niobrara Valley is a reflection of its generally threatened situation throughout the nation, since its tallgrass habitats have all but disappeared. In the Niobrara Valley it also overlaps with the more western- and northern-oriented sharp-tailed grouse. This region is one of the few left in the Great Plains where such contacts still regularly occur, inasmuch as where both species are present the greater prairie chicken tends to eventually be replaced.

Ecologically speaking, the region's 185 breeding birds occupy the following breeding habitats: wetlands 23 percent, forests 22 percent, open woods or woody edges 20 percent, grasslands 12 percent, general open-country habitats 7 percent, shrub-dominated habitats 5 percent, urban-human environments 4 percent, bank or cliff topography 4 percent, and riverine shorelines or sandbars 3 percent. It is worth noting that the relatively rare wetlands of the Niobrara region (especially the nearby Sandhills wetlands) represent its single most valuable breeding habitat for breeding birds, at least in terms of supporting the region's maximum species diversity. Wetlands are followed closely by the much more geographically widespread forest habitats and open woods or woody-edge habitats as important sources of species diversity in the region.

Of all these geographic affinities and interactions, the overlapping eastern and western species pairs of birds in the Niobrara Valley provide the most interesting examples of ecological and evolutionary processes. Along most of the Niobrara Valley genes are being exchanged between many bird species that over long periods of geologic time have become adapted to quite different vegetational and climatic conditions. New genetically based combinations of plumage patterns, songs, mate-selection behavior, and breeding adaptations are now being produced like randomly generated permutations, with natural selection becoming the final arbiter of which ones might survive and reproduce. This remarkable local situation will be examined in detail in chapter 6.

The Biogeography of Niobrara Valley Mammals, Reptiles, and Amphibians

Less specific information is available for the mammals, reptiles, and amphibians in the Niobrara Valley than for birds, but at least some trends are apparent (table 18). Of all the mammal species, the eastern and desert cottontail and the white-tailed and mule deer provide two clear examples of obvious east-west geographic replacement of mammal species pairs in the Niobrara Valley. Although there is considerable overlap in the ranges of the two deer, the mule deer is increasingly common to the west, especially in areas of rugged topography, and the white-tailed deer is progressively more common to the east, especially in hardwood forests. The desert cottontail likewise replaces the eastern cottontail in drier, rockier, and more open habitats. In a somewhat similar way the spotted ground squirrel gradually replaces the fairly closely related and shortgrass-adapted thirteen-lined ground squirrel in the still drier and sandier habitats of the western Niobrara Valley.

For the seventy-one mammal species documented for the greater Niobrara region collectively (see appendix 1A), the largest number (31 percent) are of widespread geographic distribution, and another 18 percent might be considered typical Great Plains species. The rest consist of western-oriented species (21 percent), eastern species (14 percent), northern or northwestern species (7 percent), and southern or southwestern species (6 percent). There are also two introduced species of Old World rodents. Thus, like the birds and in contrast to the situation with vascular plants, there is a preponderance of western over eastern species of mammals in the Niobrara Valley.

Table 18. Mammals, reptiles, and amphibians of east-west
biogeographic significance in the Niobrara Valley

Eastern Species	Western Species
Mammals	
Northern short-tailed shrew	Merriam's shrew
Least shrew	
Eastern mole	Little brown myotis
Northern myotis	*Western small-footed myotis*
Evening bat	Townsend's big-eared bat
Eastern cottontail	*Desert cottontail*
Southern bog lemming	Bushy-tailed wood rat
Woodchuck	Least chipmunk
Franklin's ground squirrel	Black-tailed prairie dog*
White-footed mouse	Northern pocket gopher
Meadow jumping mouse	Plains pocket mouse*
	Olive-backed pocket mouse*
	Silky pocket mouse
Gray fox	Swift fox (very rare)*
	Pronghorn (reestablished)
White-tailed deer	*Mule deer*
	Elk (reestablished)
	Bighorn sheep (reintroduced)
Reptiles	
Blanding's turtle	
Ornate box turtle	
Yellow mud turtle	
Eastern hognose snake	*Western hognose snake**
Ringneck snake	Wandering garter snake
Common (northern) watersnake	Prairie rattlesnake*
Fox snake	
Smooth green snake	
Six-lined racerunner	Short-horned lizard
Amphibians	
Northern cricket frog	
Plains leopard frog	
Great Plains toad*	

Note: Species reaching or nearly reaching their eastern or western range limits in the greater
Niobrara Valley region, based on various published sources (see species list in appendixes).
Closely related (congeneric) geographic replacement species pairs are shown by italics; other
pairings are not significant. Species with ranges centered on the Great Plains are indicated by
asterisks.

FIGURE 9. Male heads of eastern-oriented white-tailed deer (above) and western-oriented mule deer (below). Drawings by the author.

An example of an eastern mammal species' meeting a close western relative in the Niobrara Valley is the eastern white-tailed deer and the western mule deer (fig. 9). The Nebraska zone of 50:50 abundance ratios of the two was historically centered on Cherry County. However, in recent years white-tailed deer have moved westward along the Niobrara Valley, variably replacing the more open-habitat, smaller, and less adaptable mule deer. The two species sometimes hybridize in their broad zone of Great Plains overlap, which extends from Alberta to western Texas.

FIGURE 10. Elk (upper left), pronghorn (upper right) and bison (bottom) males, all grassland natives of the Niobrara Valley. Drawings by the author; bison based on sketch by Lott (1971).

The most famous all Great Plains mammals, the bison (fig. 10), has as its nearest living relative the European bison (*Bison bonasus*), from which it has been isolated since Pleistocene times. There is also a northern sub-species, the wood buffalo, limited to the aspen parklands of northwestern Canada. The American bison was historically distributed throughout all the grasslands of the Great Plains, extending east locally even to the Atlantic coast. It is now absent from the Niobrara Valley except for some captive herds, such as at Fort Robinson State Park and Fort Niobrara National Wildlife Refuge. There are also several privately owned herds in the Niobrara region.

During the colonial and westward expansion periods the bison gradually retreated west, but they could not outrun the long-range repeating rifles of the post–Civil War era. After being eliminated from western Nebraska in the early 1880s the species was reestablished in 1913, when a small herd was placed in Fort Niobrara Game Reserve, established by Theodore Roosevelt in 1906. This facility replaced an abandoned military outpost and was later renamed the Fort Niobrara National Wildlife Refuge.

Like the bison, the elk and the pronghorn (fig. 10) were also historically of western plains geographic orientation; the pronghorn was most closely associated with sagebrush and western shortgrass plains, and the now vanished prairie race of the elk was historically affiliated with the taller and moister prairies of the eastern prairies. The pronghorn currently ranges east occasionally to the lower Niobrara Valley (Boyd County, Nebraska, and Charles Mix County, South Dakota). Free-ranging elk occur east to Boyd County, and in South Dakota they locally occur east to Gregory County.

The black-tailed prairie dog, also a classic Great Plains mammal, may have historically ranged over 5.9 to 37 million acres in Nebraska, and billions probably existed over the Great Plains. Its population, like that of the other four species of prairie dogs, has declined nearly 99 percent in the past two centuries (Johnsgard 2005). As of 2003 its Nebraska range had been reduced to some 60,000 to 87,000 acres, based on recent estimates by Zachary Roehrs (2004). In the Niobrara region, only Sioux and Box Butte counties have maintained fairly high numbers and large sizes of prairie dog towns; counties farther east have exhibited declines both in their numbers and in the sizes of remaining towns. The prairie dog has now been essentially extirpated from those portions of its historical Nebraska range lying east of the 98th meridian (Roehrs 2004). In southern South Dakota it locally occurs east to Gregory and Charles Mix counties but is still abundant in Shannon, Burnett, and Todd counties.

The black-footed ferret and swift fox are perhaps the most characteristic of the Great Plains endemics whose ranges and populations have been strongly reduced or wholly eliminated by the demise of the prairie dog. Additionally, the ferruginous hawk, golden eagle, coyote, bad-

FIGURE 11. Niobrara herp species at their western range edges (left, top to bottom, plains leopard frog, Blanding's turtle, and Great Plains toad), or their eastern range edges (right, top to bottom, western hognose snake, wandering garter snake, and prairie rattlesnake). Drawings by the author.

ger, burrowing owl, and many other species rely on prairie dogs and their burrows for food or for nesting or foraging areas, and their abandoned burrows are often used for escape, shelter, hibernation, or other survival purposes.

Among reptiles, the eastern and western hognose snakes are the only closely related geographic species pairs represented in the Niobrara Valley, although several species reach the eastern or western edges of their ranges there (fig. 11). There seem to be no comparable examples among the amphibians of closely related western and eastern species pairs present in the Niobrara region. Among the thirty total species of reptiles and amphibians of the greater Niobrara region (see appendix 1C), most (58 percent) have ranges that are approximately centered within the Great Plains, 12 percent are western or southwestern in their geographic affinities, 9 percent are widespread, 9 percent are eastern to southeastern, 9 percent are northern to northeastern, and 3 percent are southern. As with the mammals, the strong influence of Great Plains endemics and western-associated species is apparent in the Niobrara Valley. Four western reptile species (wandering garter snake, western rattlesnake, short-horned lizard, and northern prairie lizard) reach their eastern range limits there. Likewise, three eastern or Plains-oriented amphibians (northern cricket frog, western chorus frog, and plains leopard frog) and three reptiles (Blanding's turtle, eastern hognose snake, and fox snake) reach their western limits in the Niobrara Valley. Several reptiles also reach their northern limits in the Niobrara region, such as the yellow mud turtle, ornate box turtle, many-lined skink, and lesser earless lizard.

Among native fishes, about a third have northern (cool-water) geographic associations, followed about equally by those with eastern geographic associations, Great Plains affiliations, or widespread distributions. Western and northwestern influences are minor among fish, perhaps because the headwaters of the Niobrara fail to reach the Rocky Mountains.

In contrast to the fish situation, among contemporary terrestrial vertebrates of the Niobrara Valley collectively there is a stronger colonization influence from western than eastern sources and also a fairly strong presence of typical Great Plains species, particularly among the relatively sedentary reptiles and amphibians. Likewise, geographically widespread species are most commonly represented among the more generally mobile groups, such as birds and mammals. The areas of North America that have apparently had the slightest zoogeographic influence in generating biodiversity within the vertebrates of the Niobrara Valley are the southern and southwestern regions.

The Biogeography of Niobrara Valley Insects
In spite of their vastly greater numbers of species, we know too little about most insect groups to try to identify and categorize all the species of the Niobrara region. Exceptions can be found among the Odonata (dragonflies and damselflies) and the diurnal Lepidoptera (butterflies and

Table 19. Geographic affinities of dragonflies and damselflies of the Niobrara Valley

Western Species	Eastern Species	Northern Species	Southern Species
Paddle-tailed darner*	Riverine clubtail*	Canada darner*	Stripe-winged baskettail*
Blue-eyed darner	Elusive clubtail*	Variable darner	Golden-winged skimmer (SE)
Brimstone clubtail	Common sanddragon*	Horned clubtail*	Eastern amberwing (SE)
Pale snaketail*	Prince baskettail*	Plains emerald*	Eastern pondhawk (SE)
Variegated meadowhawk*	Ruby meadowhawk	Saffron-winged meadowhawk	Double-striped bluet
Red-veined meadowhawk*	Calico pennant*	Hudsonian whiteface*	Great spreadwing (SW)
Striped meadowhawk*	Halloween pennant*	Western dark-winged damselfly	
Western (band-winged) meadowhawk	Fawn darner*	Tiaga bluet	
Piute dancer	Black-wirged damselfly	Marsh bluet**	
Emma's dancer	Sweetflag spreadwing	Sedge sprite	
Springwater dancer	Slender spreadwing		
Vivid dancer	Blue-frorted dancer		
Western forktail	Rainbow bluet		
River bluet	Stream Bluet		
	Skimming bluet		
	Hagen's bluet		
	Eastern forktail		

*Dragonflies at or near the edge of their ranges in the Niobrara Valley. Damselfly ranges are not yet well enough known to estimate range edges.
**The Plains Species plains forktail is also associated with these.

Table 20. Eastern, western, and Great Plains butterflies
of the Niobrara Valley

Western Species
  Rocky Mountain parnassian*, western black swallowtail, anise swallowtail*, indra swallowtail*, two-tailed swallowtail*, pine white*, spring white*, western white*, large marble*, Queen Alexandra's sulphur*, ruddy copper*, purplish copper*, western pine elfin*,
  western tailed-blue*, arrowhead blue*, silvery blue*, dotted blue, Melissa blue*, greenish blue*, Boisduval's blue*, shasta blue*, Acmon blue, Edwards's fritillary*, Coronis fritillary*, Zerene fritillary*, Callippe fritillary*, Mormon fritillary*, Arachne checkerspot*, field crescent*, pale crescent*, Anicia checkerspot*, satyr comma*, Zephyrus
  angelwing*, West Coast lady*, Weidemeyer's admiral*, common ringlet*, Mead's wood
  nymph*, small wood nymph*, Ridings' satyr*, Uhler's arctic*, Afranius duskywing*,
  Persius duskywing*, Garita skipperling*, Plains gray skipper*, Uncas skipper*, common
  branded skipper*, Pahaska skipper*

Eastern Species
  Eastern tiger swallowtail, little yellow*, Edwards's hairstreak*, banded hairstreak*, Baltimore*, Question mark*, eastern comma*, red-spotted purple*, northern pearly eye*,
  eyed brown*, little wood satyr*, Juvenal's duskywing*, mottled duskywing*, Little glassywing*, least skipper*, Leonard's skipper*, crossline skipper*, northern broken
  dash* Delaware skipper*, dusted skipper*, Hobomok skipper*, broad-winged skipper*,
  Dion skipper*, two-spotted skipper*

Great Plains Species
  Olympia marble, great gray copper, regal fritillary, Ottoe skipper

*Species at or near the edge of their ranges in the Niobrara River Valley.

skippers), both of which are large enough and colorful enough to attract
the attention of many amateur and professional field naturalists.

The dragonflies and damselflies, although less completely documented
for the Niobrara region than the butterflies, offer additional information of biogeographic interest (table 19). Geographic affiliations of these
species have been based on available range maps for dragonflies, such as
those of Dunkle (2000), and range descriptions by Kondratieff (2000) for
damselflies. The geographic affinities of these insects show nearly identical numbers of species with eastern and western affiliations, and progressively fewer species of northern or southern and Great Plains. Most
of the species reaching their apparent range limits in the Niobrara Valley (seventeen out of twenty-three) are of eastern or western geographic
orientation. A high proportion of the dragonfly and damselfly fauna (36
percent) are of widespread distribution, probably reflecting the relative
mobility of these strong-flying insects.

The butterflies and skippers of special zoogeographic interest are summarized in table 20, based on the species list (105 butterflies and 43 skippers) provided in appendix 1E and an evaluation of their geographic affinities, based on available range maps. A preponderance of western over eastern species is again evident. Species of widespread distribution, or those of northern or southern geographic affinities, are not listed in the table. However, as with birds, a high proportion (about 30 percent) of the highly mobile butterflies and skippers are of widespread distribution.

The Collective Biogeography and Biodiversity of Niobrara Valley Biota

A detailed analysis of the biogeographic aspects of the Niobrara River Valley has been provided by Kaul, Kantak, and Churchill (1988), especially in reference to its importance as a postglacial dispersion corridor and subsequent role as a refugium for cold-climate plants and animals. They found that seventeen butterflies and skippers, fourteen vascular plants, seven mosses, five birds, four reptiles, one fish, and one mammal represent western taxa (species, subspecies, or varieties) that reach their eastern range limits in the Niobrara Valley. By comparison, fifteen mosses, sixty-two vascular plants, sixteen birds, four reptiles, three fish, two butterflies, and one mammal having ranges generally oriented toward eastern North America reach their western limits there. Collectively, about 70 percent of all these edge-of-range taxa have eastern associations.

Using the data provided for the more geographically limited Niobrara Valley Preserve by Kantak and Churchill (1993), a similar floristic and faunistic analysis is possible for this central Niobrara Valley region in the heart of the east-west transition zone. Using their plant and aquatic insect data for the Niobrara Valley Preserve and information covering the entire greater Niobrara region relative to the other animal groups for which data are available, a general sense of the role of the Niobrara Valley as a biogeographic crossroads becomes apparent (table 21). Considering only the plants and animals that can be clearly assigned as having eastern, western, northern, southern, or Great Plains geographic associations, and excluding all intermediate and widespread taxa, a sample of 404 plant and animal taxa may be generated. Of these, 33 percent are eastern in geographic orientation, 32 percent are western, 15 percent are associated with the Great Plains, 14 percent are northern, and 6 percent

Table 21. Biogeographic affinities of plant and animal species in the Niobrara Valley

Taxon	Biogeographic Affinities						
	Plains	Eastern	Western	Northern	Southern	Widespread	Other
Mosses	—	15	10	7	1	?	
Vascular plants	1	12	5	9	—	?	—
Aquatic insects	—	8	1	—	1	?	1 southwestern 1 northwestern
Dragonflies and damselflies	1	17	15	10	2	28	3 southeastern 1 northwestern 1 southwestern
Butterflies	4	11	39	3	3	32	7 southwestern 3 southeastern
Skippers	1	13	7	—	—	13	6 southwestern 3 southeastern
Fish	8	13	1	18	10	7	1 Plains-northern 1 Plains-eastern 1 Plains-southern
Reptiles and amphibians	19	2	2	—	1	4	3 northeastern 2 southwestern
Birds	11	31	35	6	2	76	3 northwestern 1 southwestern 1 southeastern 7 Plains-western 1 Plains-northern
Mammals	14	11	15	5	4	22	1 southwestern 1 northwestern 2 introduced

Note: Plant and aquatic insect totals based on data from the Niobrara Valley Preserve (Kantak and Churchill 1993). Other insect and vertebrate data are for the entire Niobrara region (see text and appendixes for listings).

Table 22. Comparative species richness of plants and terrestrial
vertebrates along a Niobrara Valley gradient

	Geographic Location				
Taxa	Central Missouri River	Lower Niobrara	Central Niobrara	Upper Niobrara	Pine Ridge
Plants*					
Trees	25	24	23	—	—
Shrubs	34	31	33	—	—
Woody vines	10	8	7	—	—
Ferns	6	9	6	—	—
Mosses	30	32	55	—	—
Plant taxa	105	104	125	?	?
Breeding birds**	124–128	122–125	106–122	105–118	126
Mammals***	55	61	61	59	59
Reptiles***	10	22	18	13	12
Amphibians***	9	9	7	6	6
Vertebrate taxa	198–202	213–216	192–208	164–177	203

*Plant data from Kaul, Kantak, and Churchill (1988), based on collections. "Woody" vines in-
clude semiwoody species. Central Missouri River represents the forested Missouri Valley of
northeastern Nebraska, just below the Niobrara's mouth. Lower Niobrara and Central Niobrara approximately correspond to the lower and middle sections of the Niobrara Valley as
shown on regional text maps.
**Bird data from Johnsgard (1998), based on breeding range map interpretations. Pine Ridge
approximately corresponds with Sioux County; other areas are as indicated for plants.
***Mammal distributions (including extirpated/extinct species but excluding introductions)
based on range maps in Jones (1964); species-level taxonomies not updated. Herpetile data
from specimen records as mapped by Lynch (1985). Central Missouri = Cedar County to Dakota County; Lower Niobrara = Holt County to Knox County; Central Niobrara = Cherry
County; Upper Niobrara = Dawes and Sheridan counties; Pine Ridge = Sioux County.

are southern. At least by this criterion, the characterization of the Niobrara Valley as a true "biological crossroads" seems justified.

As a final examination of the role of the Niobrara Valley as a natural
corridor for the dispersion of plant and animal groups, a comparison of
relative species richness (biodiversity) estimates along different parts of
the Niobrara drainage system is of interest. Kaul, Kantak, and Churchill
(1988) provided such an analysis for the major life-form plant categories
from the mouth of the Missouri River to the central Niobrara region.
Table 22 includes their data, which extend from the Missouri River region of northeastern Nebraska (the vicinity of Cedar, Dixon, and Dakota counties) upstream along the Niobrara as far as the central Niobrara

Valley (Cherry County). Added to these data are figures for the Niobrara Valley's distributional affinities of breeding birds, mammals, reptiles, and amphibians, based on available documentation.

The general pattern shown in table 22 for plants is a slight downward trend in the biodiversity of woody plant taxa as you proceed westward upstream, but there is a considerable increase in moss biodiversity in the central Niobrara Valley, where shady and moist springbranch canyons probably favor survival. Bird biodiversity remains fairly high from the adjoining Missouri Valley west though the central Niobrara Valley, diminishes in the relatively unwooded portions of the upper Niobrara Valley, and increases again through the Pine Ridge region. Reptile biodiversity appears to reach a peak in the central and lower Niobrara Valley but tapers off in both directions. Finally, amphibian biodiversity gradually declines westward, probably in response to diminishing precipitation and humidity.

Chapter Six

Bird Populations and Interactions
in the Niobrara Valley

The Niobrara Valley is a modern faunal refugium from the arid and tree-less surrounding grasslands. The Valley provides important habitat for species hybridization and serves as a corridor to connect different populations of breeding birds. The key is retaining the habitat conditions necessary for the flora and fauna to thrive and maintain the ecological setting.
—JAMES DUCEY (1989)

Avian Transition and Hybrid Zones in the Great Plains

As documented in the previous chapter, it may be said that, botanically speaking, "East meets West" in few if any interior North American sites other than Nebraska's central Niobrara River Valley. Similar east-west transitions in breeding bird populations exist in Nebraska's Niobrara Valley, as well as in the state's well-documented Platte Valley.

The major hybridizing pairs of Great Plains birds are very closely related forest- or edge-adapted forms whose ancestors were probably geographically split and isolated to the east and west of the Great Plains during the last glaciation (Mengel 1970; Sibley and Short 1959, 1964; Sibley and West 1964). Most of these are deciduous forest- or woodland-adapted forms, since grasslands east of the Rocky Mountains were probably not so clearly split into eastern and western components by glacial advances.

Among grassland-adapted birds, only the eastern and western meadowlarks now form overlapping eastern and western counterpart distributions on the Great Plains, with hybridization occurring between them only rather rarely. Perhaps these two meadowlark populations were isolated earlier than were the woodland species pairs, or at least they have evidently been in secondary contact longer, since natural selection favoring avoidance of hybridization has developed more effectively in them.

In the Niobrara Valley the eastern meadowlark extends locally west to eastern Cherry County along the Niobrara River and to Sheridan County in the moist meadows of the saline wetlands in the western Sandhills. Probable local breeding overlap with the western meadowlark thus extends west to Sheridan County in Nebraska and to Shannon County in South Dakota. The eastern species is apt to choose isolated tallgrass prairie remnants or the tall grassy swales associated with Sandhills wet meadows. The western meadowlark breeds across the entire Niobrara Valley, usually selecting the shorter mixed-grass prairies on higher elevations for its territories. Often males of both species can be heard singing within earshot of one another. At times you can also hear songs that are somewhat intermediate between the rather slurred and less melodically complex songs of easterns and the sharply punctuated and many-noted songs of westerns. However, given the influence of learning on song development and associated vocal diversity among meadowlarks, such songs alone are not proof of hybridization.

Where both species occur locally, eastern meadowlarks do not respond differentially to the two song types, but those male eastern meadowlarks occurring in areas where there are no westerns do not respond to their songs. Evidently it is the female's responsibility to make the proper choice when forming pairs in areas where both species are present. When mistakes do occur and hybrids are produced, the offspring are sexually active but have reduced fertility (Lanyon 1994, 1995).

Since the Niobrara River does not offer a wooded corridor extending all the way to the Rocky Mountains comparable to that provided by the Platte River, the question remains of how such western riparian forest species as the black-headed grosbeak, Bullock's oriole, and lazuli bunting have managed to reach the central Niobrara Valley. All these species, as well as the conifer-adapted birds of the Pine Ridge such as the plumbeous vireo, cordilleran flycatcher, and western tanager, breed commonly in South Dakota's Black Hills, which was the likely point source of the Pine Ridge avifauna. The ancestral source of the Black Hills woodland birds was probably in turn the hardwood and coniferous forests of northeastern Wyoming.

Considering eight species pairs known to breed within the Niobrara Valley and for which hybridization has been documented or at least strongly suspected, an interesting range of interactions and hybridization rates occurs among them (table 23). At one extreme, the eastern (yellow-shafted) and western (red-shafted) races of the northern flicker interbreed so extensively across almost the entire Niobrara Valley that perhaps most if not all of birds examined carefully from the upper portions of the valley will show some signs of gene introgression. Typical yellow-shafted flicker phenotypes are likely to be consistently found only in the lower part of the valley, from about Holt County eastward (Moore and Koenig 1986). There is no evidence that hybrid matings between these two types result in reduced clutch sizes or smaller brood sizes, although it is possible that hybrid males might father statistically smaller brood sizes than result from other possible within-type or between-type mating combinations (Moor and Koenig 1986).

At the other extreme, the eastern and western wood peewees are nearly impossible to distinguish visually in the field, although they have distinctive song types, but it is doubtful that they hybridize across their apparently very limited zone of contact in the upper Niobrara Valley. There are recent probable or confirmed nesting records for the western wood pewee for Sioux, Dawes, and Sheridan counties and similar recent records for the eastern wood pewee from Sheridan County eastward through all the Niobrara Valley counties to the river's mouth (Mollhoff 2001). There is one earlier (1960s) nesting record of the eastern species for Dawes County as well (Ducey 1989), suggesting that Sheridan and perhaps Dawes counties are the most likely points of actual contact between the two species in the Niobrara Valley. The two species were reported to be heard singing "side-by-side" in Sheridan County in 1988 (*American Birds* 42:1309), and Ducey noted a bird singing a somewhat intermediate song in Cherry County during 1989 (Ducey 1989). The western species has been heard singing as far east as Norden and Niobrara, where easterns are known to nest. Pending more information, it seems probable that these two birds are effectively "allospecies," main-

Table 23. Hybridization and interactions among closely related bird taxa in the Niobrara Valley

Taxonomic Level	Representative Types		Zone of Sympatry in Niobrara Valley	Hybridization Rate in Niobrara Valley
	Eastern	Western		
Subspecies	Yellow-shafted flicker	Red-shafted flicker	ca. 300 miles	Extensive gene flow
Incipient species	Eastern towhee	Spotted towhee	ca. 200 miles	Frequent
	Baltimore oriole	Bullock's oriole	ca. 200 miles, declining?	Frequent, declining?
Full species	Indigo bunting	Lazuli bunting	ca. 250 miles, increasing?	Infrequent
	Rose-breasted grosbeak	Black-headed grosbeak	Fairly wide, ca. 150 miles	Infrequent
	Greater prairie chicken	Sharp-tailed grouse	Moderate, ca. 100 miles	Infrequent
	Eastern meadowlark	Western meadowlark	Fairly wide, ca. 200 miles	Rare
	Eastern bluebird	Mountain bluebird	Moderate, ca. 100 miles	Very rare
Allospecies	Eastern wood pewee	Western wood pewee	Very narrow, under 100 miles	Probably nil

taining only slightly overlapping and apparently nonhybridizing distributions in the Niobrara Valley. Rising and Schueler (1980) could find no convincing cases of hybridization between these species.

Something like the wood pewees, the mountain and eastern bluebirds have their most likely points of breeding overlap (sympatry) and interactions in the upper Niobrara Valley. Historical mountain bluebird records in the valley are for Sioux and Dawes counties, and historical eastern bluebird records extend west to Dawes and Sioux counties (Ducey 1988). More recent (1980s) mountain bluebird breeding records closely coincide with the Pine Ridge region in Sioux, Dawes, and Sheridan counties, and eastern bluebird records for the same period indicate a range overlap in the same three-county area (Mollhoff 2001). In adjacent South Dakota breeding by both species has been reported in Fall River County, and known or probable breeding by both was reported in Shannon and Bennett counties (Peterson 1995). In 1985 a mixed-species bluebird pair produced two broods in Dawes County (Sharpe, Silcock, and Jorgensen 2001). Otherwise there is no good evidence of hybridization in the Niobrara Valley, although hybrids have been documented in several other regions of the western states and southern Canada where the two species overlap in range. In overlap areas of Manitoba and Saskatchewan mixed pairing occurs among 0.1 to 0.6 percent of the total breeding pairs (Rounds and Munro 1982).

The black-headed (western) and rose-breasted (eastern) grosbeaks hybridize in several locations where they meet in the Great Plains, including the Republican, Platte, and Niobrara valleys of Nebraska (West 1962; Sharpe, Silcock, and Jorgensen 2001). It is believed that the black-headed grosbeak invaded central and eastern Nebraska during the early twentieth century, presumably aided by tree plantings and increased woody riparian growth along the Platte, Republican, and other western river systems. The black-headed grosbeak is adapted to breeding in a woodland-like habitat of shrubby box elders, green ashes, and small-stature cottonwoods, whereas the rose-breasted grosbeak is more likely to be found in open mature riparian forests with well-developed herb or shrub understories. Their adult male plumages are quite distinctive, but the primary advertising songs of both seem to be a rather unpatterned and prolonged series of whistled notes that, at least to human ears, seem very similar (fig. 12).

FIGURE 12. Comparison of male breeding plumages of rose-breasted (top left), black-headed (top right), and hybrid (center) grosbeaks; also indigo (bottom left) and lazuli (bottom right) buntings, plus typical male hybrid (center). Advertising song sonogram durations shown are for 4 seconds (grosbeaks) and 2.5 seconds (buntings); the intermediate bunting song type was from a male of indigo phenotype. Drawings by the author; bunting plumages and sonograms after Emlen, Rising, and Thompson (1975), hybrid grosbeak after Anderson and Daugherty (1974).

In Keith County, somewhat west of the primary Platte River hybrid zone, hybrid features were found in seven of forty-two grosbeaks netted (17 percent) (Brown et al. 1996). The relatively high hybridization rate in the Platte Valley may at least in part reflect this rather recent contact between the two species, since there has not been an extended time available for natural selection to reduce hybridization rates.

Less is known of the hybrid incidence in the Niobrara Valley. West (1962) reported a sight record for a hybrid near Spencer, Boyd County, and a hybrid has also been seen as far west as Box Butte Reservoir (Sharpe, Silcock, and Jorgensen 2001). The primary hybrid zone in the Niobrara and adjoining Missouri River valleys in the early 1960s appeared to extend from the vicinity of Bassett east beyond the mouth of the Niobrara to about the confluence of the Vermilion and Missouri rivers in southeastern South Dakota (West 1962). More recent (1980s) breeding records for the black-headed grosbeak extend from Sioux County to Keya Paha County, and the species nests commonly in the Niobrara Valley Preserve of Brown County. Recent rose-breasted grosbeak nesting records extend west to Holt and possibly Keya Paha counties (Mollhoff 2001), with reports also of breeding west to the Box Butte–Agate Fossil Beds region (Ducey 1989). This suggests that the current zone of interspecies contact is considerably farther west than visualized by West four decades ago, and it helps account for the seemingly extralimital hybrid sighting from Box Butte Reservoir.

In southern South Dakota the black-headed grosbeak is believed to mainly breed west of the Missouri River, with the hybrid zone extending locally west from Gregory County to Bennett County (Tallman, Swanson, and Palmer 2002). Of fifty-three male birds collected in the late 1960s at Springfield (Bon Homme County, about ten miles below the mouth of the Niobrara River), 42 percent were hybrid phenotypes, while the rest were classified as pure rose-breasted. The major hybrid zone occurred about twenty-five miles west of Springfield, in Charles Mix County. Field studies there indicated that, although mating appeared to occur almost at random among and between phenotypes, hybrid females had significantly smaller clutches than nonhybrids. The authors thus regarded the two forms as constituting semispecies.

The lazuli (western species) and indigo (eastern species) buntings have some ecological features in common with the grosbeaks. The lazuli is adapted to breeding in scrubby riparian woodlands, often with shrubs such as Juneberry or chokecherry and more arid-adapted shrubs or low trees such as mountain mahogany or juniper. However, the indigo bunting is a bird of deciduous forest edges, especially riparian forest edges, where a mixture of shrubs and taller trees is likely to be found. In their adult male breeding plumages the two species are easily distinguished, and their primary advertising songs, although geographically quite variable, can often be differentiated (fig. 12). The advertising songs of indigo and lazuli buntings are very similar, but those of the indigo tend to be slower, with longer internote intervals. Male hybrids are often visually identifiable in the field owing to their contrasting whitish abdomens, and they may sing songs that are not intermediate between the parental types but instead nearly identical to one or the other (Emlen, Rising, and Thompson 1975).

Lazuli and indigo buntings are both common in the lower Black Hills, where hybrids are fairly frequent (Peterson 1995; Emlen, Rising and Thompson 1975). They extend from there south into Nebraska's Pine Ridge, where Richard Rosche (1982) considered the hybrids more prevalent than pure indigo buntings. Breeding records for the lazuli buntings from the 1980s extend from Sioux County east possibly as far as the vicinity of Springview, and indigo bunting records extend throughout the entire Niobrara Valley west to Sioux County, Nebraska (Mollhoff 2001), to the Black Hills, and west into northeastern Wyoming, where there are a few records of lazuli × indigo hybrids (Luce et al. 1997). The range of the indigo bunting has spread westward in Nebraska at a very substantial rate, perhaps moving as much as 140 miles between 1955 and 1969 (Emlen, Rising, and Thompson 1975).

Early research on the hybridization of these buntings in the Great Plains (Sibley and Short 1959) provided considerable information on the Platte Valley, where hybridization is locally quite common. In eastern Nebraska, Lester Short (1961) found that nine of eighteen indigo buntings had backcross traits. In Keith County of western Nebraska, Brown et al. (1996) reported that six of twenty-seven birds (22 percent) netted at Cedar Point Biological Station were apparent hybrids, and later captures there by William Scharf determined that sixteen of seventy-nine birds (20 percent) had hybrid plumage characteristics.

The best information on bunting hybridization in the Niobrara Valley comes from the work of Emlen, Rising, and Thompson (1975). Their study of Great Plains bunting populations found that only 6-7 percent of the specimens they examined had hybrid traits. A "hybrid index" of male plumage types from specimens taken along the Niobrara River exhibits a gradual mean plumage shift from the Chadron area eastward (fig. 13). One of the highest apparent rates of hybridization these authors found was in the Bordeaux Creek area southeast of Chadron. They judged that mixed pairings and hybrids there may have been at a selec-

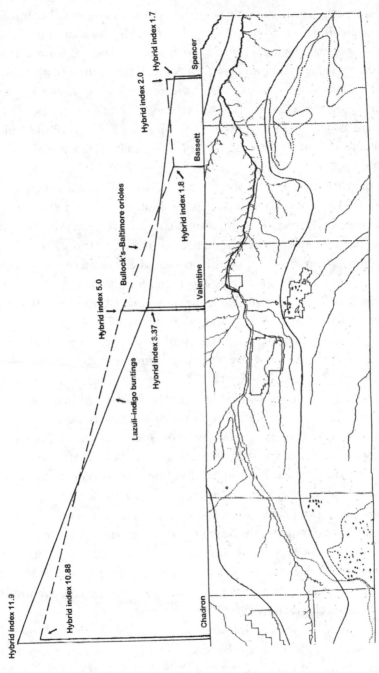

FIGURE 13. Mean male hybrid index trends of the Bullock's-Baltimore orioles and the lazuli-indigo buntings in the Niobrara Valley. Total index value 12 = western species plumage phenotype, to c = eastern species. Data from Sibley and Short (1959, 1964).

tive disadvantage, since not only were the hybrids uncommon but mixed pairs and hybrids seemed to occupy suboptimal habitats and bred relatively late compared with parental plumage types. They concluded that speciation in these two buntings has proceeded far enough that hybridization is so undesirable as to prevent the gene pools of the two species from merging in the future. In southernmost South Dakota the lazuli bunting is believed to breed east to the Missouri River, with the main hybrid zone occurring along that river (Rising 1983; Tallman, Swanson, and Palmer 2002).

Another of the well-documented cases of hybridization among species pairs in the Great Plains concerns the Bullock's (western) and Baltimore (eastern) orioles. This situation is confusing enough that in 1983 the American Ornithologists' Union merged these two forms, long considered separate species, into a single species (the "northern oriole") after hybrid studies by Charles Sibley and Lester Short (1964), only to "resplit" the two in 1995 after additional field research (Rising 1970, Corbin and Sibley 1977; Corbin, Sibley, and Ferguson 1979).

As in the lazuli bunting and black-headed grosbeak, the adult male plumages of these two orioles are highly distinctive, and their hybrid combinations are quite variable (fig. 14). Males of both species sing pulsed, loud, and highly variable song phrases that, at least for human ears, are difficult to distinguish. The Bullock's oriole is adapted to nesting in mature, openly spaced trees in western landscapes. In eastern Colorado they especially are likely to nest in narrowleaf cottonwoods and introduced Siberian elms, both common along riparian lowlands and farmsteads. The Baltimore oriole is more closely associated with eastern cottonwoods, American elms, ashes, and mature riparian forests.

Like the indigo bunting, the Baltimore oriole expanded its range west across the eastern Great Plains fairly rapidly during the late nineteenth and early twentieth centuries as trees planted around farmsteads and in shelterbelts matured and riparian woodlands protected from recurrent prairie fires developed into tall floodplain forests rich in cottonwoods. In Nebraska the Baltimore oriole was largely confined to the eastern half of the state about 1900, but by the 1980s its range had expanded west to Sheridan County in the Niobrara drainage, Scotts Bluff County in the North Plate drainage, and Dundy County in the Republican drainage

FIGURE 14. Comparison of male breeding plumages of Baltimore (top) and Bullock's (bottom) orioles and two hybrid male combinations (middle). Advertising song durations shown are for two seconds. Drawings by the author.

(Mollhoff 2001). However, some pioneering individuals apparently had already reached the Colorado border by the late 1890s, meeting the Bullock's oriole along the South Platte and Republican drainages (Kingery 1998). Between the 1950s and the 1970s the percentage of Baltimore orioles increased in the vicinity of Logan County, Colorado, while the percentage of hybrids and Bullock's orioles decreased (Corbin, Sibley, and Ferguson 1979).

Because between 1983 and 1995 the Baltimore and Bullock's orioles were regarded as a single species, no data are available to document any breeding range differences during that period (e.g., Ducey 1988). Wayne Mollhoff's (2001) summary of Nebraska breeding records for the 1980s shows breeding by the Bullock's oriole from Sioux County east to Sheridan County and the Baltimore oriole from Sheridan County eastward throughout the Niobrara Valley. Richard Rosche (1982) reported seeing "relatively frequent" hybrids in northwestern Nebraska (defined by him as extending from Sioux County to Sheridan County) as well as a few spring migrant Baltimore phenotypes, whereas Brogie and Mossman (1983) observed obvious hybrids as well as phenotypic Baltimore orioles in the Niobrara Valley Preserve area.

In an extensive field study, Charles Sibley and Lester Short (1964) analyzed oriole hybridization in the Great Plains, including Nebraska's Platte Valley and to a lesser degree the Niobrara Valley. Based on a male plumage index of 0 (phenotypically pure Baltimore oriole) to 12 (phenotypically pure Bullock's oriole), eight males collected near Chadron had a mean hybrid index of 10.88 (range 10 to 12). One male from Valentine had a hybrid index of 5, and four from near Bassett had a mean index of 1.8 (range 1-3) (fig. 13). Five from Spencer (Boyd County) had a mean index of 2.0 (range 0 to 4). Sibley and Short concluded that the center of the hybrid zone in the Niobrara Valley was then near Valentine and that most breeding Baltimore and Bullock's orioles in Nebraska were already affected by hybridization and gene introgression. I was told (pers. comm.) by Randy Harper, ranger naturalist at Gavins Point Dam, that as of 2004 Baltimore × Bullock's oriole hybrids were common as far east in South Dakota as the Yankton area. The apparent western edge of the hybrid zone in southern South Dakota is said to extend to Shannon County; however, many South Dakota orioles cannot be reliably assigned to species (Rising 1983; Tallman, Swanson, and Palmer 2002).

The last major passerine species pair known to hybridize extensively in the Niobrara Valley are the spotted and eastern towhees. Like the orioles, these two populations have been regarded at times (from the 1960s until the mid-1990s) as a single species ("rufous-sided towhee") owing to their strong tendency to hybridize. The adult plumage patterns (fig. 15) are quite similar, differing only in the degree of white spotting on the upperparts, especially the scapulars and wing coverts. The advertising songs of males are similar, that of the eastern usually being a three-part song ending in a long trill ("Drink your tea-eeeeeeee"). The spot-

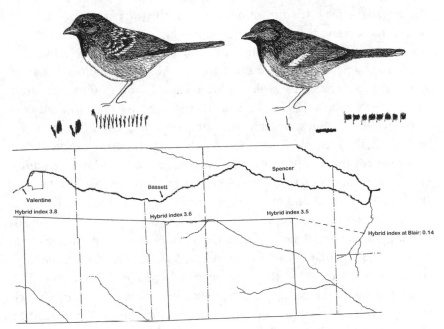

FIGURE 15. Male plumages of spotted (left) and eastern (right) towhees, and typical advertising song sonograms of each type. The mean hybrid index scores for four localities are based on extent of male back spotting (4 = typical spotted phenotype, 0 = typical eastern phenotype). Drawings by the author; data from Sibley and West (1959).

ted towhee's song in Nebraska often includes about four (but up to five) introductory notes rather than only one or two, followed by a trill that tends to be somewhat harsher and less musical than the eastern's. Songs of male hybrids can be quite variable.

Early studies on the hybridization of the towhees in Nebraska were performed by Charles Sibley and David West (1959). In the Niobrara Valley they obtained specimens from four localities: Chadron, Valentine, Bassett, and Spencer. They established a plumage hybrid index, ranging from 4 (phenotypically pure spotted towhee) to 0 (phenotypically pure eastern towhee). All the way east from Chadron to Spencer the plumage influence of the spotted towhee was very strong; ten adults averaged 3.5 in their plumage index (with six of ten specimens scoring as pure spotted). From Spencer east for more than one hundred miles along the Missouri Valley to the vicinity of Blair, Washington County, there was a sharper drop in plumage scoring, which declined at an almost ten times faster geographic rate (0.019/mile) than in the forty-mile segment between Bassett and Spencer (0.002/mile) (fig. 15). Sibley and West estimated that the middle of the hybrid zone during the 1950s was likely to be found somewhere east of the Niobrara-Missouri confluence. As of 2003, the birds breeding at Ponca State Park, Dixon County, appeared to be mostly hybrids (*Nebraska Bird Review* 71 [2005]: 124). In southernmost South Dakota, spotted towhee phenotypes apparently now breed east along the Missouri River counties almost to the Iowa border. Eastern towhees apparently now breed only along South Dakota's easternmost counties, but their actual western range limits are obscured by limited locality records and extensive hybridization (Rising 1983; Tallman, Swanson, and Palmer 2002).

Last, the range of the scarlet tanager of the eastern deciduous forests approaches that of the conifer-adapted western tanager in the central Niobrara Valley, and the birds possibly are in limited contact. The scarlet tanager breeds along the Niobrara River west to eastern Cherry County, where it is considered an uncommon breeder at Fort Niobrara National Wildlife Refuge. The western tanager is also ranked as uncommon during summer at Fort Niobrara National Wildlife Refuge, suggesting that some breeding overlap may occur along the Niobrara River in Cherry County. A few apparent hybrids have been reported from the Great Plains, but not yet from Nebraska or South Dakota.

One pair of nonpasserines that also is in contact and hybridizes in the eastern Sandhills immediately south of the central Niobrara Valley comprises the greater prairie chicken and the sharp-tailed grouse. In recent decades the eastern-oriented prairie chicken has been confined to the eastern edge of the Sandhills, where a mixture of small-grain agriculture in irrigated or subirrigated meadows is interspersed with native Sandhills grasses. In contrast, the Plains race of the sharp-tailed grouse is largely confined to the Sandhills themselves, with its eastern limits reaching the eastern Sandhills (Johnsgard and Wood 1968). In places such as Valentine and Fort Niobrara national wildlife refuges both species occur, the birds sometimes displaying on the same courting grounds and occasionally hybridizing (fig. 16). Such hybrids are relatively rare, and although the males engage to some degree in territorial behavior and are known to be fertile, they seem unable to compete effectively with males of either parental species and also fail to attract females.

FIGURE 16. Male courtship postures of greater prairie chicken (top), hybrid (middle), and sharp-tailed grouse (bottom). Drawings by the author.

Summer and Fall Bird Populations
of the Central Niobrara Valley

One of the few good results of the Norden Dam controversy was that a good deal of biological, paleontological, and anthropological research was performed around the site of the proposed dam near Norden, Keya Paha County. Among these studies were inventories of early summer (May and June) and fall bird populations by Stanley Longfellow (1977). Longfellow estimated bird species occurrences and densities per 100 to 106 acres in four major habitats, including mixed-grass prairie, coniferous (ponderosa pine) forest, open mixed hardwood forest interspersed with grasslands, and a dense mixture of riverine conifers and hardwoods (bur oak, cottonwood, hackberry, willow), along the Niobrara River (table 24). Of these, the open mixed forest had the highest species diversity during both late spring and fall. Not surprisingly, western meadowlarks were the most abundant species encountered in the grasslands. Mourning doves and American robins were the most abundant of the woodland and forest species. Fall population figures, especially in the mixed forest, were surprisingly high.

A two-year study in Sandhills prairie within the Niobrara Valley preserve studied the presence of summer birds where bison grazed under a controlled burning regime, compared with those where cattle grazed on unburned pastures (Griebel, Winter, and Steuter 1998). The controlled burning in this study was mainly done during the dormant growing season (80 percent), on an area being continuously grazed by bison. The total number of bird species seen in the bison enclosure were fourteen and fifteen during two summers, compared with ten and eleven in the cattle enclosure. The five most common species—mourning dove, grasshopper sparrow, horned lark, lark sparrow, and field sparrow—were present in descending frequency under the bison plus burning regime. The grasshopper sparrow was the most common species in the area grazed by cattle, the field sparrow was second, and the other three species were relatively rare. There were no significant differences in bird species richness or abundance, or in vegetation density or height, under the two differing management plans during the first year; but during the second year bird species richness was significantly higher in the bison en-

Table 24. Bird populations of Keya Paha and Brown counties, central Niobrara Valley

	Grassland*		Coniferous Forest		Open Hardwood–Grass		Riverine Forest	
	Summer	Fall	Summer	Fall	Summer	Fall	Summer	Fall
Birds/106 acre	319	1,328	239	623	593	2798	691	183
Total spp.	21	22.5	27	17	47	39	42	13

Most Abundant Species**

	Grassland*	Coniferous Forest	Open Hardwood–Grass	Riverine Forest
Summer	Western meadowlark	Lark sparrow	Mourning dove	Mourning dove
	Horned lark	Mourning cove	House wren	Baltimore oriole
	Lark sparrow	American robin	Black-capped chickadee	House wren
	Upland sandpiper	Blue jay	Great crested flycatcher	Western meadowlark
	Eastern kingbird	Black-capped chickadee	Blue jay	Eastern kingbird
				Brown thrasher
Fall	Western meadowlark	American robin	American robin	American goldfinch
	American goldfinch	American goldfinch	Mourning dove	Western meadowlark
	Mourning dove	Mourning dove	Common crow	Tree sparrow
	Horned lark	Northern flicker	American goldfinch	
			Black-capped chickadee	

*Grassland data represent mean of two transects; others are for single transects. Densities estimated as birds/approximately 106 per acre in spring, 100 per acre in fall. After Longfellow (1979).

**Listed in descending frequency of observed abundance.

closures. Both cattle and bison were found to prefer grazing on burned over nonburned grasslands.

In a study of the impact of river recreation on breeding riparian birds of the Fort Niobrara National Wildlife Refuge, Christopher Anderson and others (2004) found the most common neotropical migrant breeders to be the common yellowthroat, red-eyed vireo, ovenbird, and black-and-white warbler. The yellow-breasted chat, American redstart, and great crested flycatcher were also locally common.

Some Fish and Wildlife Service aerial river surveys conducted in the Norden area during October and November of 1976 and 1977 reported sandhill cranes as the most numerous species, followed by ducks, geese, herons, and white pelicans. Between 1943 and 1999 there were at least eighteen fall sightings of whooping cranes on the Niobrara River or its tributaries, as well as at least fourteen spring sightings (Austin and Richert 2001). In more recent years whooping cranes have been seen fairly regularly on the Niobrara River, perhaps as their numbers gradually increase. Presumably the wider downstream parts of the river best satisfy their roosting needs, although most sightings have occurred in the river's central stretches. In 2004 three pairs were seen on April 16 near the Carns Bridge (Rock and Keya Paha counties), and a family group was seen during October of that year near Valentine. At that time the wild Great Plains whooping crane flock numbered about two hundred birds, all of which presumably migrate through Nebraska each year.

Since the 1970s, wintering bald eagle populations along the river have increased. Bald eagles now regularly winter in the Niobrara Valley. During the fourteen years from 1990 through 2004 the average number of eagles seen during January aerial surveys extending from west of Valentine to the Niobrara- Missouri confluence was 52.3, with a maximum of 139 observed during the 2004 survey. A late spring Game and Parks survey in 2003 revealed 36 bald eagles from Springview downstream to the Niobrara-Missouri confluence, including at least two nests (John Dinan, pers. comm.). From 35 to 150 bald eagles winter along the lower Niobrara, and there may be as many as ten nesting sites along the lower 120 miles of river (LaGrange 2005). At least one active nest was present on the Niobrara near the Niobrara-Missouri confluence in 2004, and three juveniles were also seen in that area in early July (David Titterington, pers. comm.). These upward population trends reflect national bald eagle increases since the endangered species legislation of the late 1960s and 1970s. These acts not only have provided improved national and state protection for eagles but also have forced the elimination of reproduction-inhibiting pesticides such as DDT from animal as well as human food chains.

These conservation actions have also favored the osprey, a species absent as a breeder from Nebraska for more than a century. Young ospreys have recently been reared by South Dakota conservation workers, to be released along the Missouri Valley of southern South Dakota. Through this multiyear project, begun in 2003, ospreys should recolonize the lower Niobrara Valley over the foreseeable future. As a result of three decades of federal protection and pesticide controls, the osprey's population is now rebounding nationally, and the bald eagle has recently been removed from the national threatened species list. In spite of its many critics, the Endangered Species Act has in large measure fulfilled its promises.

Chapter Seven

Conservation Prospects and Portraits in the Niobrara Valley

Now the face of all the land is changed and sad. The living creatures are gone. I see the land desolate and I suffer unspeakable sadness.
— WHITE HORSE (Omaha tribe), 1912

The Niobrara Valley is in many ways nothing like what it was when Lewis and Clark passed by some two hundred years ago, when nearly uncountable bison and elk were in view. The gray wolf is now entirely gone from Nebraska, replaced by coyotes. The bison are now all confined, and the elk are barely starting to reoccupy the region. One of Lewis and Clark's Nebraska mammal discoveries, the black-tailed prairie dog, is gone from most areas east of Cherry County. Its major predator, the black-footed ferret, one of the rarest of North American mammals, has long been gone from the state.

Countering these dismal facts, grass-roots conservation organizations such as the Nature Conservancy's Niobrara Valley Preserve and the Audubon's Society's new Hutton Niobrara Ranch Wildlife Sanctuary have been important in supplementing the work of state and federal agencies such as the Nebraska Game and Parks Commission, the U.S. Fish and Wildlife Service, and the National Park Service in preserving large chunks of natural habitats in the Niobrara Valley. The Niobrara Council and the Friends of the Niobrara have helped guide many of these conservation efforts.

Other more recent entrants in the Niobrara Valley's conservation efforts include the Nebraska Lands Trust, concerned with conservation easements on the Niobrara Valley and elsewhere, and the Grassland Foundation (formerly the Conservation Alliance of the Great Plains), which concentrates on grassland preservation in northwestern Nebraska and the entire northern Great Plains region. The Nebraska Wildlife Federation, a state branch of the National Wildlife Federation, has also been promoting instream flow rights for the Niobrara River, an issue that will be of increasing importance considering the losses of flows that have occurred in recent decades on the Republican and Platte rivers owing to largely uncontrolled development of irrigation-based farming.

Because of the Niobrara Valley's high physiographic diversity and several distinctive habitats, many Nebraska plants and animals have survived almost uniquely in the Niobrara Valley, or at least are still more common there than elsewhere in the state. Some of them are now also rare elsewhere in their overall range. Others happen to be at or near the edges of their ranges in Nebraska, and in the Niobrara region they survive only precariously, within rather strict habitat, vegetational, and climatic boundaries. Of the twelve animals and four plants chosen for discussion here, all have been classified by state or federal authorities as being of special conservation concern.

Black-tailed Prairie Dog

The black-tailed prairie dog (fig. 17) is an authentic Niobrara Valley species, discovered by Lewis and Clark during their 1804 ascent of the Missouri River, just above its confluence with the Niobrara. Since then the prairie dog has become both a symbol of the native western plains and a favorite target for those who would prefer to see all these historic grasslands converted to cow pastures. After a century of being relentlessly poisoned, trapped, and shot, while the arid grasslands of North America were destroyed on a massive scale, the prairie dog is now gone from nearly 100 percent of its original range. Until the George W. Bush administration removed it from the list of candidate species warranting federal protection during the summer of 2004, it was afforded a modicum of concern by state and federal environmental agencies. That concern is now absent.

If ever a single "keystone" animal species was identified with the prairie ecosystems of North America, the black-tailed prairie dog would eas-

FIGURE 17. Male greater prairie chicken in courtship posture (above) and adult black-tailed prairie dog in alert posture (below). Drawings by the author.

ily qualify. Keystone species are those animals that tend to hold an ecosystem together and whose presence or absence has the greatest effect on the well-being of the other species. One can argue that historically predators such as the black-footed ferret, swift fox, coyote, ferruginous hawk, golden eagle, and prairie rattlesnake all largely or partly depended on the black-tailed prairie dog as prey. The ecological effects of prairie dogs on surrounding vegetation—keeping it short, stimulating new herbaceous growth, and bringing nutrients up from the subsurface— are variously exploited by the mountain plover, horned lark, lark bunting, several ground squirrels, and the northern grasshopper mouse. The abandoned burrows of prairie dogs are used for nesting or as retreats by burrowing owls, horned lizards, spadefoot toads, tiger salamanders, spiders, scorpions, and a variety of invertebrates. All told, well over a hundred species of vertebrates and invertebrates are ecologically associated in some way with the black-tailed prairie dog (Johnsgard 2005).

It has been suggested that uncontrolled overgrazing by ranchers principally accounted for the early historical spread of prairie dogs throughout the western rangelands by improving the "dog's" habitat requirements while simultaneously modifying the native grassland community in favor of fast-growing broad-leaved annuals. Prairie dogs and ranchers soon became bitter enemies, and the federal government, in the form of the U.S. Biological Survey, quickly joined the fray on the side of the ranchers. Large-scale poisoning and fumigation programs were instituted, and even after more than a century of unremitting effort the work of killing prairie dogs still goes on, using public funds. One of the worst examples is this program can be found in the Oglala National Grassland of northwestern Nebraska and the adjoining Buffalo Gap National Grassland of southwestern South Dakota. There the U.S. Forest Service, in spite of having internal regulations providing for the management of biodiversity and sensitive species, has long engaged in massive poisoning campaigns against prairie dogs. It was probably because of such government-sponsored poisoning in the past that Nebraska lost its black-footed ferret population, and the population remaining in South Dakota risks also being lost as a result of such federal contempt for the Endangered Species Act.

In the Niobrara Valley the prairie dog population is still mainly concentrated in the upper and more arid parts of the watershed. A study by the Nebraska Game and Parks Commission (Bischof, Fritz, and Hack 2004) estimated that the 2003 county acreages of active prairie dog colonies were Sioux, 7,758; Dawes, 2,949; Box Butte, 10,006; Sheridan, 1,158; and Cherry, 705. Survey data analyzed by Zachary Roehrs (2004) covered a broader period between 1978 and 2003 and came up with rather different mean acreage estimates: Sioux, 5,219; Dawes, 1,079; Box Butte, 4,377; Sheridan. 755; and Cherry, 2,721. In spite of these differences it seems clear that Sioux, Dawes, and Box Butte counties all have substantial numbers of active colonies, with federal lands such as the Oglala National Grassland (in Sioux and Dawes counties) probably supporting a significant proportion of the greater Niobrara region's totals.

Olive-backed Pocket Mouse

Of the four species of pocket mice that occur in the Niobrara Valley, the olive-backed seems to be the rarest. Like the others, this pocket mouse is named for its distinctive fur-lined cheek pouches, which allow it to stuff its cheeks full of small seeds and transfer them to underground caches without their getting wet from saliva, so they do not get moldy. The generic name *Perognathus*, meaning "pouch jaw," refers to this unusual trait, and *fasciatus* means "banded," referring to a buffy line that separates the dark olive back from the nearly white underparts. These are relatively small pocket mice; adults average only about ten grams, with a total length of up to about five inches, the tail constituting less than half the overall length.

All of the Niobrara's pocket mice seem highly attracted to sandy habitats, which can be easily excavated. Mixed-grass prairies, pastures, and shrub-dominated habitats reportedly are all used regionally, and the soils used range from pure sand to sandy loam. Sand is evidently important to pocket mice for taking sand baths and cleaning their cheek pouches. Although burrows in sandy soils can easily collapse, these mice typically dig their tunnels at the bases of grass or forb clumps where root systems probably provide support.

The mice feed on small seeds of grasses and forbs, which they gather from the ground surface at night. Typically they forage by rapidly sifting sand with their forelegs and sweeping any exposed seeds into their mouths. They get their water by touching wet vegetation with their front feet, then licking off the adhering water.

Their burrow entrances are plugged during daylight, making them hard for other animals to find. Pocket mice are rather solitary, spending their days in tunnels that may extend several feet, with side chambers for food storage, daytime resting, and defecation. During cold weather the animals become torpid, remaining in their grass-lined nests for long periods. Although little studied, it is believed that breeding occurs in late winter or early spring, and males in breeding condition have been found as late as July in Wyoming. The gestation period is believed to be about one month, and the usual litter size is five, with extremes of three to six. One or two litters may be produced during a single breeding season.

This is a little-studied species of the western high plains grasslands, reaching its eastern limits in the Niobrara Valley and adjacent Sandhills. It is considered sensitive by the Nebraska Natural Heritage Program and is evidently the rarest of Nebraska's four species of pocket mice, all of which are probably most common in the Sandhills.

Eastern Wood Rat

It is unfortunate that these attractive animals are called rats, since they have only a distant relationship to Old World rats and resemble giant mice, with large ears, enormous eyes, and a fur-covered tail. They are fairly large, somewhat over half a pound on average and up to about fifteen inches long, including a tail of six to eight inches. Except for white underparts the animals are uniformly medium brown to grayish brown, with a bicolored brown-and-white tail.

Eastern wood rats usually live in deciduous forests, especially riparian woods with nearby rocky cliffs, a habitat combination that is common in the Niobrara Valley. They are solitary and nocturnal but remain active throughout the year, living on a wide variety of plant materials. They are largely independent of water sources, since they can get the moisture they need from eating succulent plants such as cacti.

The den is a vital part of a wood rat's survival strategy and ecology. It constructs this structure within its small home range and defends it against intruders. The den's location is variable, such as in a brush pile, at the base of a tree or shrub, under a rocky overhang, or in a structure such as a barn or an abandoned building. It is constructed of materials gathered nearby, including twigs, bark, leaves, grass, and such diverse components as feathers, pebbles, bones, and pieces of glass, plastic, metal, and other found objects. The animals are prone to add colorful or bright objects to their dens; I have even had loose change stolen from my tent while I was asleep. This catholic choice of building materials has earned wood rats the popular name pack rats. Eventually they produce a dome-shape structure averaging about two feet across, with at least two openings. Although only one individual or a nursing female occupies a den at once, subsequent occupants often add to it, so that over time a den up to five feet high and three feet in diameter may evolve. Outside the den a waste pile of inedible food debris gradually accumulates. Inside there are tunnels and chambers that include separate nesting and food-storage sites.

These large and conspicuous structures may help protect the animals from invasion by some mammalian and avian predators, although weasels and snakes can readily enter. During early fall wood rats begin to accumulate fruits, seeds, and leaves to eat over the winter. By early spring mating begins, and in the Niobrara Valley breeding probably lasts only long enough for one litter to be raised.

After a five-week gestation the female bears a litter of up to six young. Since females have only four teats, it is likely that some young perish early. By fifteen days of age the youngsters' eyes open, and they are weaned in a month or less. Weaned young begin to disperse at about three months of age, and each must establish a den and provision it with an adequate supply of food if it is to survive the following winter. Those that live are able to breed by the following spring.

The population of eastern wood rats in the Niobrara Valley represents an endemic race (*Neotoma floridana baileyii*) that is well isolated geographically from one in southwestern Nebraska (*N. f. campestris*) and another in eastern Kansas (*N. f. attwateri*). The Niobrara population is evidently a glacial relict and is limited to a few counties in northern Nebraska and adjacent South Dakota. It is considered a sensitive subspecies by the Nebraska Natural Heritage Program.

Northern River Otter

River otters (fig. 18) once were distributed along nearly all the major streams of North America, from northern Alaska to Texas and Florida. Like beavers, river otters were historically trapped for their valuable pelts, and by the 1900s they had disappeared from much of the United States. The river otter was declared an endangered species in Nebraska in 1986. A restoration program began by releasing wild-trapped animals from a variety of geographic sites in several different Nebraska rivers. These sites included the Niobrara River as well as several others.

Although a member of the weasel family, the river otter seems to share few of the aggressive weasel traits and instead is remarkably playful. Otters live almost entirely on fish, captured mainly using visual cues, but they also have a keen sense of touch. They are apt to prey on the slowest-swimming and most abundant fish rather than the faster-swimming and more agile game fish such as trout. When underwater they use their forelegs for power and let their hind legs trail as rudders. They can run

FIGURE 18. Northern river otter (top), interior least tern (middle), and piping plover (bottom). Drawings by the author.

surprisingly fast on land, alternately flexing and extending their long, flexible backbones to provide power and lengthen their stride, much like a running cat.

Females care for their young for a long time, and in some national parks it is not rare to see a family group playing together, sliding down wet mud banks or running and then sliding on the ice during winter. Sometimes their seemingly carefree attitude can lead to dangerous encounters with predators. Yet they are very agile and can easily defend themselves against a single coyote. It is probably not unusual for an otter to live about fifteen years under natural conditions, or up to twenty-five years in captivity. In Nebraska the river otter was recently upgraded from endangered to threatened, and there have been several recent sightings in the Niobrara Valley.

Greater Prairie Chicken

The greater prairie chicken (fig. 17) is a grassland endemic species that has gradually lost its fight for survival over nearly all of its historical range of eastern North America. However, it continues to survive in various parts of Nebraska, especially in the eastern and northern Sandhills. Its Niobrara Valley range extends from western Cherry County east to Boyd and Holt counties and southward through much of the eastern Sandhills, where some grain crops supplement its native food plants in winter. On crisp spring dawns it is thus still possible to watch prairie chickens displaying in several Niobrara Valley locations, such as Valentine and Fort Niobrara national wildlife refuges and at Samuel R. McKelvie National Forest, all of which have observation blinds for public use.

Like all the other species of grassland-adapted grouse such as the sharp-tailed, prairie chickens display in competitive arenas, or leks, where adult males compete during long periods every spring, each trying to establish the most favorable territory. Roughly speaking, a lek resembles a round archery target, with the younger and less experienced males occupying the outer perimeter. These peripheral birds have no real ability to hold a female's attention long enough to mate with her, but they gradually gain experience during daily competitive male-to-male encounters.

The longer a male lives—and it may take three or four years for a male to work his way into the "bull's-eye"—the greater his chances of becoming socially dominant and attracting females. More aggressive males can gradually muscle their way toward the center, and by this location alone can evidently be recognized by females as vigorous enough to be desirable mating partners. Few if any copulations occur at the lek's edges, and apparently none occur beyond the lek boundaries.

Most evidence suggests that each female copulates only once, with this single mating providing enough sperm to fertilize her entire clutch of eggs, which she will tend wholly alone. Unlike most avian territories, the lek provides neither nest sites, foraging grounds, nor any other valuable resource; it is nothing more than a mating location that by its structure allows females to rapidly assess each male's desirability for mating.

Physical landscape features may help to make some sites more valuable than others for leks. Among prairie chickens, an elevated hill, providing panoramic visibility, and short grasses, which reduce the chances of a sneak attack by a ground-dwelling or low-flying predator, are both important landscape elements. Favored lek sites are used year after year as generation after generation of males replaces previous occupants.

Individual territories on the leks of greater prairie chickens are occasionally as little as twenty feet in diameter, and their margins are contested daily by aggressive calls and postural displays. However, the males spend most of their time uttering low-pitched "booming" calls while standing almost motionless in a highly stereotyped posture with tail cocked, pinnae erected, and wings drooping. The male produces these low-frequency calls by inflating his upper esophagus, which expands the sides of his neck into two bright orange esophageal enlargements called air sacs. Although the amplitude of sound generated is not great, the low frequencies resonated by these large air chambers carry a mile or more. Likewise, the males' colorful neck enlargements and white under tail coverts can be seen from far away, even in low light.

Should a female be attracted to the lek, the males' calls expand to include excited whooping notes, and the intensity and frequency of booming accelerate. Copulations require only a few seconds, and a single dominant male may mate with several females during a single morning.

After a successful mating, each female moves off some distance and finds a suitable nest site. Nests typically are in grasses, between about ten and thirty inches high, providing both vertical and horizontal cover. Eggs are laid almost daily until a clutch of ten to twelve is completed. The incubation period of twenty-three to twenty-five days begins only when the clutch is complete or nearly so.

The list of known egg predators is very long and includes snakes, mammals, and birds, but in the Niobrara Valley it probably especially includes bullsnakes. Nesting success is variable, but early-season efforts are more successful than later ones. Because of renesting, it is likely that most females will succeed in producing a brood each year, although there is also a high mortality rate among hatched chicks. The average longevity among fledged young is less than two years, so relatively few males survive the three or four years needed to attain the status of a lek's alpha male, or master cock (Johnsgard 2002).

In many places in the northern Sandhills the sharp-tailed grouse oc-

curs close to greater prairie chickens, and not only do the birds sometimes display at the same leks, but hybridization also sometimes occurs,
especially in the Nebraska Sandhills (Johnsgard and Wood 1968).

Interior Least Tern

Of the several species of terns that migrate through or nest in Nebraska,
the least tern (fig. 18) is by far the rarest and is also the smallest. Nebraska's birds are part of an inland geographic population (the interior race)
that once bred throughout the Mississippi, Ohio, and Missouri drainages;
two other races breed locally along the Atlantic and California coasts. The
interior population has been greatly affected by river dredging, channel-
izing, and changes in annual and seasonal flow rates. In 1985 the species'
interior population was federally listed as endangered.

The Nebraska nesting distribution of the least tern is now mostly
confined to the lower Niobrara Valley, the adjacent unchanneled Missouri River, and parts of the Loup River and especially the Platte (and
adjoining sandpits) from its mouth west to Keith County, plus the barren shorelines of Lake McConaughy. Nebraska's least tern population
is one of the largest components of the species' interior race and consists of about 1,200 to 1,400 birds, representing perhaps 25–30 percent
of the total.

The unvegetated sandbars and sandy islands that were once a typical part of the Missouri and Platte rivers of Nebraska have largely disappeared as annual river flow fluctuations have diminished. However,
nesting habitats for this sand-nesting tern have improved on the lower
Niobrara, from Keya Paha and Brown counties eastward. Here the channel has become wider and shallower. The river has also become rather
deltalike as it approaches the upper end of Lewis and Clark Lake, with
the development of many sandbars and low, sandy islands as the current gradually diminishes. Eight breeding surveys in the 1980s between
Norden Bridge and Niobrara documented 87 to 174 least terns, averaging 106 birds (Ducey 1989).

Birds nest on bare sand, often associating in a semicolonial manner,
probably because of limited nest sites. Both sexes help incubate the two-
or three-egg clutch, and both sexes collect food for the developing chicks.
Least terns catch their fish using vertical plunge dives similar to those of
kingfishers, and they feed exclusively on minnow-sized fish.

Least terns nest in a high-risk environment, often losing their nests to flooding, human disturbance, or predation by mammalian or avian predators. But they are persistent renesters, sometime making as many as three nesting attempts. Increasing protection of nesting areas of the least tern has begun to show positive effects, and it seems that the species is slowly recovering in Nebraska.

Piping Plover

In many ways the piping plover's story resembles the least tern's; both species need barren sandy areas near water for nesting, and they have suffered similar population decline as a result of habitat alterations that are mostly caused by humans. The interior breeding range of this federally threatened species encompasses the drainage of the upper Missouri River plus a few isolated outliers.

The piping plover's breeding range historically included all the larger rivers of Nebraska, such as the Niobrara, Platte, and Missouri. Its current range now mainly includes the lower Niobrara (from Brown County eastward), the adjoining unchannelized areas of the Missouri, and parts of the Loup and Platte and South Platte rivers, plus the sandy shorelines of Lake McConaughy. Seven breeding surveys done during the 1980s between Norden Bridge and Niobrara documented 12 to 109 plovers, averaging 53 (Ducey 1989). The Niobrara area originally designated as critical habitat for the piping plover begins at Norden Bridge and extends 120 miles downstream to the river's Missouri confluence. This region represents about a third of Nebraska's estimated total piping plover population. In 2002 an approximately forty-mile stretch of the river between Norden Bridge and the Highway 137 bridge north of Newport was reidentified as critical habitat for the piping plover.

The birds often nest very close to the water's edge, and the adults' back color closely matches dry sand. The eggs also perfectly match the color of sand and gravel, and the birds often place their nests where egg-sized gravel is nearby. The newly hatched chicks are just as cryptic (fig. 18) and tend to crouch motionless when danger threatens. Then they sprint away at the last possible moment, their tiny legs carrying them over the sand at a remarkable rate.

Blanding's Turtle

The Blanding's turtle is a little-studied species that reaches the western edge of its overall North American range in western Cherry County of

Nebraska. It is much more aquatic than the highly terrestrial and conspicuous ornate box turtle, and it is likely that most Nebraskans have never seen one, nor would they recognize it if they did. It is about the same size as the commonly encountered ornate box turtle, but instead of a radiating or starlike pattern of yellow lines on each large plate of the dorsal shell, there are a multitude of irregular tan to yellow dots. The underside is uniformly dark rather than crossed with many pale lines. The lower shell or plastron is not hinged, and from the side the outline of the mouth turns upward near its base, producing a permanent dolphinlike smile that is distinctive.

The Blanding's turtle spends nearly all its time in water, where courtship and mating occur, but females must lay their eggs on land. They usually do so at night, between mid-June and mid-July in Nebraska, often in grassy habitats near marshes. As with many other turtles, sex determination is temperature-dependent. If the eggs are incubated at 22.5 to 26.5°C, nearly all of the young will be males, but an incubation temperature of 30 to 31°C will result in nothing but females. Such a situation may limit the species' range to areas in which a mixture of sexes may be reasonably expected to hatch over several years.

Blanding's turtles continue to grow until they are about thirteen years old, and if they survive their vulnerable juvenile period they may possibly live well beyond twenty-five years. Raccoons, foxes, and skunks are known to be serious egg predators, and coyotes are also likely to be serious threats for eggs and young turtles. However, a substantial number also get run over by automobiles in late spring and early summer, during the mating and egg-laying period when the turtles are most mobile.

Until it was studied intensively at Valentine National Wildlife Refuge starting in 2002, nobody appreciated that this area of the Sandhills supports the largest known population of Blanding's turtles anywhere in the species' overall range. In studies done there by Jeff Lang, hundreds of the turtles were captured and marked. In the 2002 field season 757 turtles were captured, and 75 were fitted with radio transmitters for tracking their movements. One radio-tracked male moved about two miles from where it was tagged, then returned to the point of tagging within six weeks. Like ornate box turtles, males move great distances in search of mates, and females may also search widely for nesting sites.

Because of Lang's work, the world population of Blanding's turtles is

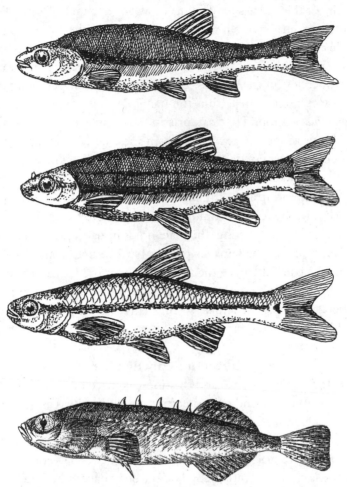

FIGURE 19. Males of finescale dace (top), redbelly dace (upper middle), blacknose shiner (lower middle), and brook stickleback (bottom). Drawings by the author.

now known to be much larger than previously believed, possibly as high as 100,000 on the Valentine refuge alone. Before his work the species' largest known population was in Minnesota, with an estimated 5,000 to 10,000 (Farrar 2003).

Finescale Dace

The finescale dace (fig. 19) is a state threatened species that is now largely limited to the Niobrara River of Sioux County and to cool tributary streams in Keya Paha, Rock, Brown, Sheridan, and Cherry counties.

Adults of this species may be up to about five inches long. They are dark olive green above, silvery white below, and have a dark stripe along the side of the body. Above the dark stripe is a narrow golden line, and below it is a bright red band in breeding males. Breeding males also develop tubercles on their scales, especially near their pectoral fins. The scales are extremely small, thus the name finescale dace.

This species is found in clear, pristine streams that are usually spring-fed and have a sandy or gravelly bottom and a fairly slow current. It may also occupy beaver ponds or similar standing-water habitats. The fish are carnivorous and eat a variety of small invertebrates.

During the spring and early summer breeding season males follow females closely, the females stimulating courtship by swimming in a zig-zag manner. While courting, the male holds his large, scooplike pectoral fins behind one of the female's pectoral fins to help control the swimming of the pair. The male then tries to direct the female against some solid object where he can curl his tail over hers, placing his anal fin and its tubercles against the female's vent. This evidently stimulates spawning. Although breeding males do not defend territories, they often fight with one another.

Northern Redbelly Dace

This little minnow (fig. 19) and the finescale dace have very similar Nebraska distributions, and both species are now classified as threatened in the state. Nebraska lies near the southern edge of both species' ranges, which extend north well into Canada and east to the Atlantic Ocean. Both species are glacial relicts, trapped in the cooler Nebraska streams when the last glaciers retreated. The redbelly dace is now found in the upper Niobrara River of Sioux County and in small, clear streams of Sheridan, Cherry, Brown, Rock, and Keya Paha counties.

This species is smaller than the finescale dace but also has very small scales. It too is olive green dorsally, with some dark flecking, and has a lateral black stripe, with a broad golden stripe above it and a bright red abdominal band below, at least in breeding males. There is a second narrow black line between the yellow lateral stripe and the dark olive back. Breeding males also develop tubercles on their pectoral fins and elsewhere.

This fish prefers small, quiet beaver ponds with slow flow rates, which often occur over silty bottoms and along well-vegetated shorelines. It is a summer spawner, and as in the finescale dace, males chase fertile females. Sometimes several males gather around single females, but it seems likely that only one is successful in fertilizing her. In streams where both species occur, hybridization between the two has sometimes been reported; the hybrids are mainly female and closely resemble redbelly females. Such hybrids may be fairly common in some areas.

Blacknose Shiner

The blacknose shiner (gig. 19) is usually no longer than two to three inches. A single black or dusky stripe extends from the snout through the eye and back along each lateral line to the base of the tail. Since 1939 this small cold-water species has been collected in only a few Nebraska streams, including Gordon Creek and Brush Creek in Cherry County, the Niobrara River in Dawes County, and Holt Creek in Keya Paha County. The species' status has recently been shifted from threatened to endangered in Nebraska.

The blacknose shiner is ecologically limited to cool, well-oxygenated waters. Its southern limits roughly correspond with the southern edges of the glaciers that once extended down to Kansas, Missouri, and the upper Mississippi–Ohio drainages. As the glaciers retreated, populations of cold-adapted fish were left in the cooler and clearer streams. Because of such factors as increased soil erosion and associated water turbidity and declining water flows, many of these populations disappeared during the early 1900s.

Like many endangered or threatened species, this one can be saved only by protecting its habitat, namely small clear-water streams with abundant aquatic vegetation and with substrates ranging from sand to mud. It also typically needs enough overhanging shoreline vegetation to shade the stream and help keep it cool.

Brook Stickleback

The brook stickleback (fig. 19) is found locally in the Niobrara River and several of its tributaries including the Snake River, Gordon Creek, and Bone Creek. It is a cold-water fish associated with shallow, clear creeks, well-vegetated streams, and stream headwaters. It is limited to those waters that are no warmer than about 65°F during the breeding season and that support prey populations of insects and crustaceans. It is a tiny fish, with adults only about two inches in length. It lacks scales and is named for the five sharp spines along its back, which probably help protect it from predators.

Brook sticklebacks spawn early in the spring, when adults leave the schools that are typical during the winter and males begin to establish territories. Breeding adult males are darker than nonbreeders, becoming jet black on their backs and their dorsal and anal fins. Their sides are variegated with yellow, which grades to a more coppery hue below. Males also have bright yellow eyes, with the iris crossed by a vertical black band. The black eye-stripe becomes more evident during aggressive and sexual situations. Females are much less colorful, changing from generally pale green in winter to more olive hues during the breeding season, with darker brown mottling or dotting on the upperparts.

Males establish territories and begin nest building during March or April in the Niobrara region. Within its small territory a male may build several nests of roots, twigs, algae, dead leaves, and other materials, attaching them to a vertical surface such as a rock or to the stems of emergent vegetation. These materials are attached using a sticky mucus produced by the male's kidneys, which is exuded and applied to the nest surface. Nests can be completed within a single day, although additions and repair may continue for a long time. The nest takes the general shape and size of a golf ball, with a lateral opening. Males defending larger territories may build as many as half a dozen nests; males defending smaller territories build fewer.

While the males are nest building, the females remain outside that area, and as they gradually become gravid with eggs, they become increasingly attractive to males. The male typically approaches such a female from above, with his spines erect and his caudal and pectoral fins vibrating. He then pushes and bumps the female downward and tries to lead her toward one of his nests by swimming with his body arched, his spines erect, and his mouth open. He then invites the female to enter the nest by placing his head in front of its opening or partially entering it himself. If the female enters the nest she will push her head through the nest's wall on the opposite side, so that only her head and tail are visible. At that point the male prods her underside with his snout, stimulating her to shed her eggs, typically up to a hundred.

After laying her eggs the female quickly leaves the nest. The male enters quickly, fertilizes the eggs without pausing, and leaves through the opening the female made. The female then leaves the male's territory, while he returns to guard the nest and repair the exit hole. Thereafter the male tends the nest closely, fanning it with his fins to provide oxygen to the eggs and retrieving any eggs that happen to fall out.

During the last week or so before hatching the male constructs a "nursery" by reorganizing the upper part of the nest so it forms a loose network of vegetation. As the young hatch, they drift upward and are usually caught in this mesh. Any that pass through are quickly caught by the male and returned to the nest. After a few days the young begin to actively escape from the nest, and thereafter they begin life on their own.

Hayden's (Blowout) Penstemon

This beautiful penstemon (fig. 20), the only plant known to be essentially endemic to Nebraska, was historically known from a few Sandhills localities, and at one time it was even believed to have become extinct. It was rediscovered in 1968, however, and is now known from more than dozen Sandhills sites, mostly in Cherry County. It was listed as nationally endangered in 1987.

This plant's range is narrow because of its specific adaptation to the bare sand environment of dune blowouts and their immediate edges, where loose sand prevents all but a few species from taking root. It is a short-lived perennial, surviving up to about eight years, but can spread vegetatively through underground rhizomes. It can also spread by roots forming at the plant nodes if the stem itself becomes buried in sand.

Although it produces great numbers of seeds, about 1,500 per plant per year, the seeds are often eaten, and those that survive are prevented from immediate germination by a thick seed coat that protects them from sand abrasion. To germinate, the seeds must remain damp for at least two weeks, and the developing root must then reach a source of moisture before the seedling's limited food reserves are used up. Because of these demanding conditions, seedlings rarely establish themselves even where the plants are abundant. However, since the seeds may remain viable for up to twenty years, the chances are good for ultimate germination if the seeds escape being eaten, being too deeply buried in sand, or blown into unsuitable habitats.

This penstemon species is one of Nebraska's most attractive, and the only one with fragrant flowers, which are usually blue to lavender. All

FIGURE 20. Hayden's penstemon (left) and Ute ladies' tresses (right). Drawings by the author.

penstemons have asymmetrical flowers, with two petal lobes above and three below, the latter making a convenient landing place for bees, wasps, and other potential pollinators. There are four functional stamens and one long, sterile one with a yellow hairy tip. This sterile stamen is the basis for the common name beardtongue that is sometimes applied to plants of this genus. Dark magenta guidelines on the inner surface of the corolla direct insects to the nectar, where they might also bring about pollination.

Hayden's penstemon is one of the first plants to invade fresh blowouts, but it disappears by the time the blowout is fully "healed." It is considered endangered by both state and federal agencies, and a program of greenhouse rearing and reintroduction into Sandhills habitats is under way, with the hope that eventually at least 15,000 plants can be established in the Sandhills. Currently there are known to be about 3,000 naturally occurring and 9,000 reintroduced plants in scattered Sandhills locations. Within the greater Niobrara region they occur natively in Box Butte, Cherry, and Sheridan counties. For the species to be reclassified from endangered to threatened status, 10,000 established plants must be present, and 15,000 will be needed for eventual delisting.

Ute and Hooded Ladies' Tresses

Nebraska has at least eighteen species of native orchids, but most are quite limited in distribution, and some are known from only one or two counties. The hooded ladies' tresses is known only from a single alkaline meadow in Sioux County. The Ute ladies' tresses (fig. 20) was initially known only from a few locations in Colorado, Utah, and Nevada but more recently has been found locally in the middle and upper Niobrara Valley. Like many orchids, this one may emerge only in very favorable years, then disappear again for many years. It also may germinate and remain underground for several years before appearing above ground for the first time.

The generic name of these two species, *Spiranthes*, refers to the way their blossoms are arranged in spirals along the stem of the plant. Each flower is built on a pattern of threes, including three petals and three sepals. The lowest petal is elongated into a decorative lip, two sepals extend sideways like wings, and the other two petals and the remaining sepal form a fused overhanging hood or tube that encloses the sexual parts of the flower. These parts are fused to form a central column, which in all orchids is highly specialized for ensuring fertilization.

The fertilizing insects for these species are not yet well known, but the fertilization biology of the Ute's ladies' tresses has been studied in Colorado and Utah. Small glands near the base of the column secrete a fluid that attracts insects, primarily bees and especially some long-tongued bumblebees. Of the two *Bombus* species observed at flowers there (*B. morrisoni* and *B. fervidus*), only the latter is common in the Niobrara Valley, although other bumblebee species are also present. Some long-tongued bees (*Anthophora*) were also observed carrying the plant's pollinaria, but their role as pollinators is uncertain. Only long-tongued insects are able to pollinate the plant; smaller bees cannot pick up the large pollinaria, or it may attach to an inappropriate location on their bodies.

The insect lands on the lip and extends its proboscis to reach the nectar, thereby touching the sticky mass of pollen as well and carrying it away when it leaves the flower. The bee ascends spirally up the flower stalk, leaving the lower and oldest flowers that are functionally female, and encountering the functionally male flowers toward the top of the stem. This differential rate of sexual development promotes cross-pollination as the insect visits one flower after another.

Paper Birch

The paper birch is a trans-Canadian species, occurring west to the Pacific and the Bering Sea and east to the Canadian Atlantic coast. It survives on a wide variety of soils but favors cool climates and well-drained, sandy loam. Toward the southern edges of its range it is increasingly limited to generally cooler and often higher sites, such as north-facing slopes of ridges or mountains. In addition to occurring south to the Black Hills of South Dakota, it extends south disjunctively into Nebraska, Missouri, and Illinois as glacial relict populations. In Nebraska the species is found only in Cherry and Brown counties. There it occurs on the south side of the Niobrara, and on the north-facing slopes of many shaded spring-branch canyons, such as those near Smith Falls.

Paper birch is probably best known for its papery white outermost trunk layer, called birchbark, which Native Americans have long used for the waterproof, flexible skin of birch canoes and lodges, for kindling, and for many other purposes. During winter grouse avidly eat paper birch buds, and during spring they eat its protein-rich catkins. Beaver and deer relish its leaves and twigs, which are important fall and winter foods for both.

Paper birch grows rapidly, producing seeds by the time the tree is about fifteen years old. Like aspens and poplars, it produces catkins each year, generating large numbers of tiny seeds that are wind dispersed. Also like these trees, the species benefits from periodic fires, since it can easily and quickly reproduce by "suckers" from its surviving roots. The trees usually do not grow very tall and have fairly short life spans. Then they fall and subsequently decay rather rapidly, usually leaving remnants of the apparently more decay resistant white bark as a visual reminder of their previous presence in the forest.

Perhaps owing to global climate changes, in the Smith Falls and Fort

Niobrara areas the paper birches have been inexplicably dying in recent years, leaving behind their gaunt white skeletons. It is possible that the entire population will soon disappear from the Niobrara Valley. The paper birch is classified as a sensitive species by the Nebraska Natural Heritage Program.

Chapter Eight

The Niobrara as a Scenic River

JON FARRAR

What happens over the next decade in the Niobrara Valley should prove
whether the land-use controls of environmentalism are any more condu-
cive to a free and prosperous society and a sound and healthy environment than was central planning and government ownership behind the
Iron and Bamboo Curtains.
— R. J. SMITH, Competitive Enterprise Institute,
Washington DC (1993)

Nearly two decades have passed since President George H. Bush signed
the Niobrara Scenic River Designation Act of 1991, protecting two segments of the middle Niobrara River under the Wild and Scenic Rivers Act
of 1968. The six miles separating those segments were later included, creating a continuous seventy-six-mile river corridor from Borman Bridge
east of Valentine downstream to Nebraska Highway 137 north of Newport. Born of controversy and plagued by lawsuits and conflicting de-
sires and visions, the present-day Niobrara National Scenic River is an
ongoing grand experiment, balancing citizens' rights and a nation's desire to protect in perpetuity a river unlike any other.

The Niobrara River flows almost entirely through private land. When
the Scenic River designation was first proposed, there was strong opposition, yet today some still resent the designation and many are uncertain what changes it will bring to the river. The Niobrara Scenic River
remains a work in progress.

A convincing argument could be made that the Niobrara Scenic River designation sprang from opposition to the Norden Dam project, which would have flooded nineteen miles of the river behind a 180-foot-high earthen dam on the river north of Johnstown. Thirty thousand acres of land would have been condemned for the project. As part of the Pick-Sloan Missouri Basin Program, the U.S. Bureau of Reclamation studied the feasibility of an irrigation reservoir on the middle Niobrara in the mid-1940s. The O'Neill Unit Irrigation project component of that plan, with the Norden Dam as a centerpiece, was authorized by Congress in 1954 and reauthorized in 1972 to provide irrigation for 77,000 acres of farmland in the O'Neill, Atkinson, and Springview areas. Just as the proposed Mid-State project on the central Platte River during the early 1970s rallied landowners and environmentalists in opposition, and as a by-product drew national attention to the spectacular spring migration of sandhill cranes, opposition to the Norden Dam brought national attention and a stream of canoeists to the Niobrara River.

The Niobrara between Gordon and Valentine was selected by the National Outdoor Recreation Resources Review Commission in 1962 as one of twelve American rivers for possible inclusion in a national system of wild and free-flowing rivers. But if the Niobrara National Scenic River story has a beginning, it was in 1972 when President Richard Nixon signed a bill approving construction of the O'Neill Unit Irrigation project.

Before 1970, floating the Niobrara below Valentine was mostly limited to Scout groups and local people, some of whom regularly bobbed down the river on inner tubes or in flat-bottom boats during the summer. Few canoeists came from outside the area, and there were no canoe outfitters. During the early 1970s, seat-of-the-pants outfitters began taking customers down the Niobrara east of Valentine, often camping overnight at Smith Falls for a steak dinner. Between 1985 and 1995, the number of people canoeing the river surged as outdoor recreation became increasingly popular. The Niobrara, with its reliable flows, scenic charms, and few water hazards, became the state's premier canoeing water. By the late 1980s, floating the river in tubes also grew more and more attractive.

Recognition of the Niobrara's scenic and recreational value played an important role in defeating the O'Neill Unit project and garnered support for a Scenic River designation. The other half of the equation was landowners' opposition to the Norden Dam. It was a strange marriage, urban canoeists and environmentalists gathered around riverside campfires with local ranchers and farmers plotting a course to keep the river wild and unencumbered. The controversy pitted environmentalists against corn farmers, canoeists against power boaters, and even neighbor against neighbor along the river.

In 1975 environmentalists and area ranchers organized to fight the O'Neill Unit project, founded the Save the Niobrara River Association, and filed a lawsuit to block construction of the Norden Dam. The next year, road and bridge work began to provide better access for construction of the dam. In 1977 U.S. District Judge Warren Urbom granted a temporary injunction halting the work, ruling that the Bureau of Reclamation's environmental impact statement was deficient. That same year, the Nebraska Legislature approved a resolution in support of the project, and the Nebraska Water Resources Association announced its support of a federal proposal to study a 120-mile stretch of the Niobrara River for inclusion in the National Wild and Scenic Rivers system. In 1979 Judge Urbom ruled that the Bureau of Reclamation's new environmental impact statement did not answer questions about the geologic stability of the proposed dam site and refused to lift the injunction. Then the U.S. Fish and Wildlife Service (USFWS) raised issues of threatened and endangered species.

In 1980 the Nature Conservancy, an international conservation organization, purchased 52,000 acres in the river valley in the area of the proposed reservoir. That same year, segments of the river included in the O'Neill Unit project area were designated as candidates to be a federal Wild and Scenic River. With opposition mounting in all quarters, the Bureau of Reclamation began to study less intrusive alternatives.

Although designation of seventy-six miles of the Niobrara as a Scenic River was more than ten years in the future, the writing was on the wall for the O'Neill Unit. The heyday of reservoir construction was over, grain prices were chronically depressed, congressional support for raising more grain with federal dollars was eroding, and preservation of wild lands was receiving wide public support. Opponents of the O'Neill Unit saw designation of the Niobrara River as Wild and Scenic as the last nail in the Norden Dam coffin.

Canoeists had discovered the Niobrara River in the 1970s, and by a decade later wall-to-wall crowds on summer weekends transformed the Niobrara into a party river. Canoe camps and private dwellings popped up like mushrooms after a spring rain. In response to these changes, a cry to preserve the Niobrara's scenic splendor grew loud and strident.

In the spring of 1985, a group of landowners along the Niobrara River signed letters asking the Nebraska congressional delegation to sponsor legislation designating a segment of the Niobrara River downstream from Valentine as a National Scenic River. U.S. Sen. J. J. Exon (D-NE) agreed to sponsor the bill and introduced it in the Senate in September 1985. At that time, no other river on the Great Plains had received a Scenic River distinction. In 1986 the Nebraska Natural Resources Commission opposed the designation, saying protection could be better provided by local or state agencies.

By the summer of 1986, mobile homes had appeared along the river south of Sparks, a harbinger of what the Niobrara might look like if development was not regulated. Some landowners saw a windfall in marketing the Niobrara's scenic charm or selling land to create a reservoir; others wanted to be left alone to raise cattle. As the debate heated, the question of who should protect the Niobrara became more of an issue than whether protection was needed.

In his bill Exon invoked the least intrusive land management and land acquisition alternatives allowed under the Wild and Scenic Rivers Act. Under that act there are three broad designations: a "Wild River" that is undeveloped, inaccessible, and free of dams or impoundments; a "Scenic River" that has some development such as access roads, farms, ranches, and other "compatible operations" but is free of dams and impoundments; and a "Recreational River" that is more intensively developed and commercialized.

The intent of Exon's bill was to keep the seventy-six-mile segment in private ownership as ranchland while protecting its undeveloped and scenic qualities. Although the bill did not restrict the agency selected to administer the act from acquiring land within the boundary from willing sellers, it restricted the amount of land acquired by condemnation to 5 percent of the area. The bill also mandated formation of a Niobrara Scenic River Advisory Commission composed of landowners, state and local government representatives, and others to advise the secretary of the interior "on matters pertaining to the development of a management plan." Existing land-use practices, such as grazing, farming, and renting private campgrounds, would continue.

The years between the introduction of the bill in 1985 and its passage in 1991 were contentious at all levels of government. A flurry of alternative legislation was proposed at state and federal levels, including a proposal to establish a national park on the Niobrara. Although there were conspicuous exceptions, support for and opposition to the Niobrara Scenic River bill split along urban and rural lines, and along party lines statewide and in the halls of Congress, with Democrats supporting the designation and Republicans opposing it. The *Omaha World-Herald*, the *Lincoln Journal*, and the *Lincoln Star* published editorials in support of the bill; most rural newspapers in north-central Nebraska strongly opposed it.

Exon's bill was reintroduced in 1989 and defeated in the House, introduced again in 1990 and defeated with four hours remaining in the congressional session in circumstances an *Omaha World-Herald* editorial labeled "tawdry." On May 24, 1991, President George H. Bush signed the Niobrara Scenic River Designation Act.

Supporters of the Scenic River designation sighed with relief—the battle had been won. Few envisioned the bumps, potholes, and broken glass in the road ahead. The National Park Service was selected to administer the nation's newest Scenic River. Most previously designated Scenic Rivers flowed principally through public land, and the agencies administering them were not burdened with the need to consult outside groups and landowners or build consensus with them. The Niobrara was a different matter—a Scenic River laid down over principally private land, and one that had to be fashioned by many hands.

Federal funding to formulate a management plan became available in late 1992. Warren Hill, the first superintendent of the Niobrara-Missouri National Scenic Riverways (since renamed the Niobrara National Scenic River and Missouri National Recreational River) had a huge job. Hill and his staff were charged with creating a national Scenic River on the Niobrara, administering national recreational rivers created by the same act of Congress on twenty miles of the lower Niobrara, thirty-nine miles of the Missouri River, and eight miles of Verdigre Creek; rewriting the management plan for the Missouri National Recreational River; and studying the feasibility of the Niobrara–Buffalo Prairie National Park on the Niobrara proposed by Rep. Douglas Bereuter (R-NE) in 1989. The Niobrara Scenic River Act established a planning partnership between local and state entities and the Park Service by way of a Niobrara Scenic River Advisory Commission composed of six landowners, two representatives of county governments or natural resources districts, and one member each representing the governor, a conservation organization, and a canoe outfitter.

The National Park Service completed its feasibility study of a Niobrara–Buffalo Prairie National Park in the spring of 1995. The report outlined four alternatives but did not identify one as preferred. The prospect of creating a national park on the Niobrara had diminished since 1989, when it was first proposed. Hill noted that the river resources were already protected by Scenic River designation, landowners opposed the idea, and in a period of strong ranch economy landowners were less inclined to sell land. And the political winds had shifted. The 1994 elections brought a wave of conservatism to Congress, and carving public lands out of privately owned land had become an unpopular concept.

In December 1996, after five years of planning and uncountable public meetings, the National Park Service issued its Niobrara National Scenic River General Management Plan and Final Environmental Impact Statement. At the core of the recommended plan was the creation of a local council to work as a partner with the Park Service in managing the Scenic River. The resulting Niobrara Council was created under the Nebraska Inter-local Cooperation Act in the spring of 1997 by the four counties in which the Scenic River designation was located: Brown, Cherry, Keya Paha, and Rock. The council ultimately grew to sixteen members to better represent all interests. Each of the four counties selects a commissioner to serve on the council, who in turn selects a landowner from the county. The remaining eight members include a representative from the USFWS, National Park Service, Nebraska Game and Parks Commission, one each from the two natural resources districts in the region, a private conservation organization, someone in the outdoor recreation business, and a representative of the timber industry.

Opposition to the Scenic River designation remained strong in north-central Nebraska and was reflected in proposed congressional legislation to revise the 1991 Scenic River Designation Act. Council members, though, recognized that the Scenic River designation was not going away.

There were stumbling blocks, such as differences of opinion over the composition of council membership and the fact that countywide zoning regulations complying with the Scenic River designation were slow in coming.

The keystone to success of the Niobrara Council would be whether county zoning had the clout to regulate development within the Niobrara corridor. However, by the summer of 1998, only two of the four counties in which the designated area existed had adopted zoning regulations. County zoning was a highly contentious issue, as contentious as the Scenic River designation.

In February 1997, even before the Niobrara Council and the National Park Service formally entered into a cooperative agreement, a Niobrara Valley landowner sued the National Park Service, challenging the way the Scenic River boundaries had been drawn. In March 1998 the National Parks and Conservation Association and the American Canoe Association filed a lawsuit against the National Park Service for "allowing the Niobrara National Scenic River to be managed by a local council consisting of local landowners, business owners, and politicians."

While management of the Niobrara Scenic River was being studied, litigated, cursed, and praised during the late 1990s, river recreation continued to swell. An estimated 50,000 canoeists and tubers floated the river in 1997.

Managers of the Fort Niobrara National Wildlife Refuge east of Valentine grew increasingly concerned that the mandate and mission of the refuge was compromised by increased river recreation. Although the refuge was included as part of the 1991 Niobrara National Scenic River legislation, management within refuge boundaries was left to the USFWS. About nine miles of river flow through the refuge, of which about five miles are open to canoeing. Nearly all of those five miles are within a federally designated wilderness area.

In 1999 the refuge placed a two-year moratorium on the number of outfitters launching from the Cornell Dam site on the refuge, capping it at eleven, the number using it in 1998. A recent Park Service study showed that over 90 percent of the people floating the Niobrara River use the services of outfitters. Royce Huber, Fort Niobrara National Wildlife

Refuge manager, said the cap was intended to better distribute canoeing and tubing through the week and to other segments of the river. The refuge levied a user fee on outfitters and individuals putting in at Cornell Dam to improve and maintain the site. In response to concern over rowdiness, inappropriate behavior, trash, and excessive use of alcohol, the refuge also stepped up law enforcement, hiring a full-time ranger to patrol the river and enforce federal regulations. That same year the refuge prohibited possession of alcohol.

To some, limiting the number of outfitters launching below Cornell Dam seemed arbitrary, depriving new outfitters of equal opportunity. One Niobrara River outfitter petitioned the USFWS to be allowed to launch at Cornell Dam, pointing out that the number of people floating the river has actually declined since 1999. But the number of people coming to the Niobrara was not the only issue. During the 1990s, it became obvious that the reason people floated the Niobrara River was changing.

The enactment and enforcement of the refuge's no alcohol regulation was a turning point in behavior on the river. Below the refuge, where the river courses through private land, possession and consumption of alcohol are not prohibited until Smith Falls State Park, where it is legal to have alcohol but not to drink it. The regulation cleaned up behavior through the refuge, but to some degree it just moved the problems downstream. After alcohol regulations were imposed on the Fort Niobrara refuge, some outfitters catering to clients who came to party started launching downstream from the refuge.

The Nebraska Legislature assigned the Niobrara Council the responsibility of rendering opinions to the State Liquor Commission before a license is granted within the river corridor, but the means by which the council can execute that authority were challenged in court. The National Park Service has broader authority. In fact, it could make it illegal to possess alcohol on the river tomorrow.

Although there were conspicuous problems on the Niobrara in the 1990s, nearby businesses boomed. It cannot be entirely attributed to river recreation, but Cherry County's lodging-tax revenue increased 102 percent between 1990 and 1998 compared with 59 percent statewide. In a decade, lodging in Valentine swelled from 150 rooms to 250. Taxable retail sales in Valentine grew from $29 million in 1989 to $48.5 million in 1997. Land and housing costs near Valentine skyrocketed, and new businesses catering to tourists appeared one after another. A national backpacking magazine named the Niobrara one of the nation's top ten canoeing rivers, and articles billing the river as the nation's "best kept secret" were increasingly frequent in national magazines and major newspapers outside Nebraska. According to the Valentine Chamber of Commerce, the number of canoeists and tubers on the Niobrara doubled in the 1990s.

During the same period, interest in buying a piece of heaven along the Niobrara increased dramatically.

Some people bought land with an eye toward development, others had fallen in love with the river and wanted a secluded hideaway. Property with a view brought premium prices. The average price of land adjacent to the Niobrara in Keya Paha County jumped from $200 an acre to $400 to $500 in just five years, and during that same period one-third of privately owned parcels of land along the river were sold.

Ranchers were concerned about the effect of inflated land values on property taxes and the cost of maintaining roads heavily used by vehicles from out of county or out of state. Even though the Park Service was operating without a management plan and the status of the Niobrara Council was uncertain for several years, both worked closely with counties to regulate development. Throughout the 1990s, Council members volunteered many hours, seldom receiving praise and frequently suffering abusive attacks at public meetings and in their private lives.

On June 15, 1999, a federal court judge in Washington DC, ruled that the National Park Service had unlawfully delegated its management responsibility to the Niobrara Council. The Park Service was ordered to prepare a new general management plan and environmental impact statement. On April 10, 2000, the Eighth Circuit Court of Appeals ordered the Park Service to redraw the Scenic River boundary in response to a second lawsuit.

There was good news on the river. The Middle Niobrara Natural Resources District established a public access site at Brewer Bridge southwest of Sparks in 1989. In 1992 the Nebraska Game and Parks Commission established Smith Falls State Park on the Niobrara south of Sparks, providing a third public access point and the first public campground along the most heavily floated segment of the river. In 1998 the Nebraska Legislature gave the Council $100,000 in funding. The Council had adopted a code of conduct on the river, local and Park Service law enforcement had been increased, and toilet facilities had been installed along the river. Rock County approved countywide zoning in June 1998, and Cherry County's zoning went into effect in October 2000.

But while counties were trying to hammer out zoning regulations, and while the Niobrara Council sought to define itself, cabins, concessions, and other developments were popping up along the river. Although the legislation declaring seventy-six miles of the Niobrara downstream from Valentine a National Scenic River had become law in 1991, the push-and-shove to develop or not develop, to protect private landowner rights or lock the river in time continued.

In 1996 the National Park Service proposed a Niobrara National Scenic River General Management Plan and Final Environmental Impact Statement to manage the Niobrara Scenic River as a partnership with the Niobrara Council. The Council was composed of a cross section of local and state representatives, a response to the concerns of Nebraska congressional representatives and many constituents who feared top-down management.

As a result of two lawsuits brought against the National Park Service in the late 1990s, the 1996 plan was voided by the courts. The Park Service was instructed to create a new plan meeting the intent of the Niobrara Scenic River Designation Act of 1991.

Some Council members believed the Council, not the Park Service, was the real target of the lawsuit and that Council representatives should have been allowed to testify in court in support of the partnership concept. Some even suggested that the Park Service did not fight the lawsuit vigorously enough, that at the national level there was a philosophy that managing the river would be easier without the Council.

The 1999 federal court decision was a huge setback in implementing the Niobrara National Scenic River and appeared to be the death knell for the Niobrara Council, but the Council did not go away. During its 2000 session, the Nebraska Legislature created a second Niobrara Council, providing it with legal status and authority the former Council had lacked. It charged the Council with reviewing, and either approving or rejecting, all existing, new, or proposed zoning regulations within the Scenic River boundary. In addition, the Council was permitted to make easement agreements with landowners to prevent unwanted development. The sixteen-member Council was composed of the same mix of interests and viewpoints as the old Council, including the representatives of the U.S. Fish and Wildlife Service and the National Park Service, both of whom participate as nonvoting members to avoid crossing legal conflict of interest rules.

In 2000, in response to a ruling on a second lawsuit challenging the 1996 Scenic River boundaries, the courts ordered the Park Service to redraw the Niobrara Scenic River boundary. During the early 1990s, Park Service staff at the O'Neill office both prepared the general management plan for the Niobrara Scenic River and studied the feasibility of establishing a national park on the Niobrara. Paul Hedren, superintendent of the Niobrara National Scenic River, explained that the lexicon used to describe resources worthy of protection is different in those two processes, and some Park Service terminology found its way into the Scenic River management plan. Because of that, the court ordered the Park Service to redraw and justify the boundaries of the Niobrara National Scenic River. A revised management plan was released by the National Park Service in 2005 but has not been implemented.

During the late 1990s and into the 2000s, much of the nuts-and-bolts work on the land within the Scenic River corridor—fire management, road and bridge concerns, controlling undesirable plants, stabilizing banks, removing junk cars along the river, installing portable toilets and signs—has been handled by the Park Service through the Niobrara Council, and often for the Council through one of the four counties in which the Niobrara National Scenic River exists.

The counties will continue to lead in managing development along the river corridor. Zoning by the county, backed by the zoning authority given to the Council by the state, provides the legal clout to keep the Niobrara Scenic River scenic. The National Park Service has limited authority to control development within the designated river corridor. It is restricted by law to acquiring title to no more than 5 percent of the land within the corridor by condemnation. The Niobrara Scenic River boundaries can encompass no more than 24,320 acres, so the Park Service could acquire no more than 1,216 acres by condemnation.

Management is a huge component of the Niobrara National Scenic River. The second component is the boundary. The new recommended boundaries, Hedren said, are not a rewrite of the 1996 proposal. During the past three years the Park Service started from scratch and studied the landscape to determine what could, should, and would be included.

The Wild and Scenic Rivers Act limits the size of the designated area to 320 acres of land per mile of river, so no more than 24,320 acres can be included along the seventy-six-mile segment. Congress identified seven resource types as worthy of protection, resources identified as "outstandingly remarkable values." Those outstandingly remarkable resources must be "unique, rare, or exemplary feature[s] in a regional or national context" and include scenic, recreational, geologic, fish and wildlife, historical, cultural, and "other similar values," which encompasses such features as hydrology, paleontology, and botany. The National Park Service identified resources along the seventy-six-mile river corridor that met five of the seven criteria. Historical and cultural sites within the corridor were not found to be unique. When the Park Service completed its boundary survey, it identified more than 150,000 acres in the corridor worthy of inclusion. Defining the lateral boundaries on each side of the river between Borman Bridge east of Valentine and Nebraska Highway 137 north of Newport and not exceeding 24,320 acres was the challenge Park Service staff faced.

The big questions remain: What will the Scenic River corridor look like when the new management plan is implemented? How conspicuous a presence will the National Park Service have within the corridor? The nearly twenty-year-old fear of creeping, incremental control by the Park Service is alive and well in north central Nebraska. Except for rangers patrolling the river for the past two years, and staff participation in uncountable public meetings, the Park Service has not been in the forefront of many of the issues for which it was assigned responsibility by Congress. Will all that change once a new management plan is adopted and increased funding becomes available?

Congress intentionally limited the National Park Service's authority to acquire land by condemnation in the Niobrara corridor. It did give it the authority to protect land by acquiring it by deed or through easements from willing sellers. Many landowners along the Niobrara objected to the Scenic River designation and to rural zoning because it took away their freedom to use or develop their land as they saw fit. The National Park Service and Niobrara Council see negotiated easements as the principal tool to maintain the landscape as it is while compensating landowners for lost economic opportunity.

Easements can be written in any form to which a seller and a buyer agree. In a perpetual easement, the landowner agrees to use the land in certain ways and not in others. The easement remains with the land title no matter who owns it in the future. For a price per acre now, the landowner sells the right to develop that land. In practice, that right was already limited by county zoning within the corridor and could be limited by the authority of the Niobrara Council if the counties fail to administer zoning laws in agreement with the Scenic River designation. Easements can be executed directly by the National Park Service. The Niobrara Council has the authority to execute easements independently within the Scenic River corridor and outside the corridor with county approval. Some observers note that time is running out to preserve the river corridor. County zoning does not prohibit development, it manages development. For both the Council and the Park Service, lack of funding has slowed protection of the Niobrara landscape through easements.

Other groups that are committed to preserving the character of the Niobrara Valley have already entered into easements. The Nature Conservancy, an international conservation organization, has purchased easements on about 6,500 acres of land, including about twelve miles of riverfront, within the Niobrara Scenic River corridor. The Nature Conservancy currently owns in fee title more than 50,000 acres in the corridor.

In 2001 the Nebraska Land Trust was formed as an all-volunteer organization, representing nearly a dozen federal, state, and private groups, to promote the development of conservation easements throughout the state. In 2004 the National Park Service signed a cooperative agreement with the Nebraska Land Trust to develop a local program of conservation easements, including a ranking system for evaluating lands, fund-raising tools, and a template for producing associated easement documents.

The type of easements the National Park Service seeks would allow a landowner to continue to use the land as pasture or cropland if crops are already being grown there. An old farmhouse or barn could be replaced with a new house or barn, but a landowner could not place a trailer on the riverbank or sell the back forty acres for a recreational home. It would still be a landowner's decision whether to allow hunting, trapping, or fishing. The essence of easements is that landowners can keep on doing what they have always done and get a substantial, one-time payment for not developing the land. Preexisting land uses and developments would continue, and public use would be regulated only when necessary. Unlike zoning, easements attempt to lock the landscape in time.

What will the seventy-six miles of Niobrara River downstream from Valentine look like in the next decade? If the plans, visions, and forces in play today continue, it will probably look much as it does today, and experiencing it will be more wholesome, convenient, and safer. Both the National Park Service and Fort Niobrara National Wildlife Refuge have the legal tools to regulate the number of people floating the Scenic River segment of the Niobrara River. The time might come when you can no longer pick the day you want to float the river; there might be regulations distributing the traffic away from weekends during the summer months.

Carl Simmons, a Niobrara River landowner and Niobrara Council member, said:

> If there had not been a scenic river designation, would we have been able to keep this place a secret for a little while longer? Probably. But eventually it would have been on the radar screens of enough people that it would have changed into that river wonderland playground and become something different. Good or bad, I don't know. But it would be something different. The scenic river designation was an opportunity and it is an opportunity, and we need to look for ways to make that opportunity work for us as landowners, as a community, as a county, and as a state in order to get what we all want. Very few people want to see a world-class fun park on the river. Generally, we are all going the same way, and we need to approach it with a spirit of cooperation and work together to get there. Are there going to be some issues that we can't agree on? Sure there are. Are there going to be some bumps in the road? You bet. Is there going to be another lawsuit? I suppose. But is that going to deter us? I hope not. I see it as a huge opportunity to get something good done, something lasting.

Chapter Nine

The Niobrara as a Recreational River

DUANE GUDGEL

Wilderness is a resource which can shrink but cannot grow.
—ALDO LEOPOLD, *A Sand County Almanac*

The reasons for coming to the Niobrara River have been as varied as the people who came and have changed with time. The Lakotas visited during the moons of ripening berries for fruit, game, and perhaps fish. The Poncas made permanent homes on the Niobrara, as did later settlers, who used the canyons to shelter themselves and their livestock from weather, authorities, or both. Wood, water, and edible flora and fauna were abundant during earlier centuries. Resource abundance allows time for leisure, and it is safe to conjecture that recreation on the Niobrara began when its plentiful natural resources were discovered.

Over much of the United States in this century, a landscape as desirable as the Niobrara Valley would not have remained so sparsely populated. No metropolitan area has developed near the river over its five-hundred-mile course. The largest nearby town is Valentine, a settlement of 2,800 people, and even its city limits are two or three miles from the banks of the Niobrara.

The Niobrara's lack of a concentrated human population has been beneficial for the river and attractive to its visitors. There are several possible reasons the population remained sparse. One may be that almost all towns in Nebraska were originally created along railroads. But the railroads, for various reasons including difficulty of construction, did not closely follow the Niobrara. Another reason may be that there was no compelling historical reason to establish a town along the river. Economically exploitable natural resources at the time of European settlement were largely limited to plains grasses and grazing opportunities. Few commercial centers were needed to supply the widely separated ranches that produced cattle and shipped them to market, and no concentrated industrial area or large labor force was required.

Box Butte Reservoir was built during the early 1940s to provide irrigation water, but economical farming also requires good arable land. The Sandhills region surrounding much of the Niobrara Valley provides little fertile farmland, and the irrigation reservoir on the upper Niobrara in Box Butte County remains the only one on the river. Perhaps for these reasons, and because of the generally inhospitable weather in the northern plains, the Niobrara River has escaped most development, making it a rarity among major western waterways.

In 1903 Nebraska State Museum director Erwin Barbour mentioned some "peculiarly attractive spots around Valentine," the only obstacle to visitors being "that the lakes and waterfalls are so inaccessible." That situation has changed, and today's generations may find it hard to imagine the pure joy to be felt in the cool forested canyons near streams or falls during earlier times. Before air-conditioning and public swimming pools became widespread, this river must have seemed a paradise to those living on the dry summer plains. Valentine once maintained a public swimming area on an impoundment of nearby Minnechaduza Creek, with lifeguards, changing house, and diving boards. Valentine City Park once also had several small cabins on public land along this tributary of the Niobrara. A current outfitter recalls camping and floating on the river on as many summer weekends as her family and friends could manage.

People have long hunted and fished along the Niobrara both for pleasure and from necessity. Searching for artifacts and fossils probably at first was incidental to general outdoor work, but it has become an important pastime for many and a profession for a few. Bird-watching was once not so much a leisure pursuit as an aspect of everyday life. The common thread of the Niobrara experience in the long period leading up to the recent "discovery" of the area's attractions was an increasingly widespread appreciation of the river and its remarkable biological diversity.

Today's opportunities for recreation on the Niobrara are limited only by imagination and by restrictions imposed by government and private landowners. The river's powerful attraction is attested by the thousands from around the nation who now visit this remote area each year. The valley's landscape has changed slowly, and for the most part without human interference. The Niobrara River still runs steady and unfettered for nearly all its route across the length of Nebraska. Despite more ambitious plans over the decades, there are still only three small reservoirs on the entire river, and a river voyager is interrupted by few obstacles other than natural ones.

The past century has nevertheless brought certain changes. Commercial recreation now encompasses a range of activities from guided "pay per animal" big-game hunts to trail rides with wranglers and canoe trips that are fully outfitted including meals. But humans also still come for the simpler aesthetic reasons that have drawn them for centuries. Cool canyons, fresh water, wildlife, and the opportunity to enjoy a beautiful river that is little changed from Lewis and Clark's time are made even more compelling by the visual contrast of the surrounding stark upland landscape.

While many people now talk about visiting the Niobrara, the masses of people who visit, canoe, and float this river each year actually are experiencing a very small sample of the nearly five-hundred-mile river.

The thirty-mile section downstream from Valentine is indeed beautiful, with graceful waterfalls and side canyons having a wide variety of wildlife, plant life, and unspoiled vistas. But many other miles of this river can boast of similar beauty and diversity.

There are many reasons for the current concentration of summer visitors in the central Niobrara Valley. The early development of recreational river use of the Fort Niobrara National Wildlife Refuge and the relatively untouched beauty of the Niobrara in that short stretch have much to do with the concentration of river use downstream from Valentine. Many landowners whose property borders the river below the refuge began to supplement their sometimes meager agricultural earnings with income from tourists, and a recreation-based industry was eventually born around a relatively short section of the river.

The roughly thirty miles of river east of Valentine boast a continuous flow of water that remains deep enough to float most popular watercraft during the summer. Farther east, as the river passes Norden Bridge north of Johnstown, it widens at times to become a mere shimmer of water over sand, and channels frequently change course in its broad sandy bed. This can produce an unpleasant experience that consists more of hiking and pulling watercraft over shallows than of floating or paddling serenely downstream.

West of Valentine the river traveler encounters different circumstances. Private property boundaries are often undefined, and ranchers frequently string fences across the river to restrict straying livestock. These fences have to be tight, and the water traveler needs some skill to navigate them.

The decreasing size of the river upstream also creates a challenge for navigation. A smaller river has greater seasonal variation in flow, and the Niobrara can develop some very shallow sections by mid- to late summer. Thus a canoeist normally can readily traverse less than 150 miles of the Niobrara during the summer.

The promise of income from river recreation remains elusive outside the immediate Valentine area, and landowners' tolerance of recreational users of the river significantly lessens west of Valentine. Access to the river also becomes more time-consuming to the west, because the Niobrara and modern highways diverge as they approach Wyoming. Communities with full services for travelers also become sparser westward. The first restaurant west of Valentine on Highway 20 is some sixty miles distant, and the first overnight accommodation is ninety miles away.

Nevertheless, each year more adventuresome paddlers explore western sections of the Niobrara. Article 15 of the Nebraska Constitution dedicates the water in each stream in the state to legal public use. This right is the basis for the premise of legally navigating any stream that will float a boat. A Nebraska statute further secures the right of the river traveler by allowing watercraft access to other bodies of water that are connected to a stream, such as a bayou or a cutoff.

Water travelers are given additional rights to transport their vessels around obstacles in Nebraska streams, and they are exempt from prosecution for trespassing. Wherever you can find public access at county roads or state highways, the river is free for entry and exit. However, only the water itself is legal for public use. It may be trespassing even to step on the bottom of the river, since landownership extends to the middle of all Nebraska rivers. There is an anecdotal report of a landowner's objecting to a visitor's walking on the bottom while pulling a canoe. This incident, while cautionary, should not be considered the norm in an area generally known for hospitality. Keeping legal limitations in mind, a modern-day river explorer can experience unbounded beauty and near-wilderness scenery on many additional miles of the Niobrara.

Travelers need to carefully estimate river distances and minimum times in order not be on the river after dark with nowhere to stop. Three access points are particularly useful west of Valentine: Anderson Bridge south of Kilgore, the Highway 97 bridge south of Nenzel, and a county bridge accessed by turning south from Highway 20 on a county road about fourteen miles west of Merriman. These bridges are not official launch sites, and it may be hard to find safe parking and both legal and safe access to the river. Outfitters in Valentine or Nenzel can help with arrangements for more demanding trips.

The crown jewel on the Niobrara, and arguably the most important scenic attraction, is the Fort Niobrara National Wildlife Refuge. The refuge covers more than 19,000 acres and was never settled or farmed because of its status as a military reservation dating from the 1880s. The transfer of the property to refuge status in 1911 ensured that it would remain largely pristine. In 1961 the administrators of the Fort Niobrara National Wildlife Refuge opened the portion of the Niobrara flowing though it to recreational watercraft. However, about four miles of the Niobrara River on the refuge's western border between Borman Bridge (southeast of Valentine) and Cornell Dam (northeast of town) remain closed to the public.

Organized recreation on the Niobrara is an industry that began when a Valentine Girl Scout troop purchased a few canoes in the 1970s, since privately owned campgrounds have been supplemented by modern, well-furnished cabins. "Here's your canoe and good luck" has been supplanted by coordinated shuttles of people, cars, canoes, and canvas-covered inner tubes. Set-up tents and prepared meals are now easy to arrange. Additionally, a nine-hole golf course in the Niobrara Valley and a Scottish-style course planned along the Snake River near the Niobrara will complete the transition from the original five-dollar-a-day canoe rental to membership fees in the thousands of dollars for golf and fishing clubs.

Partly because of the increase in services, and also its "discovery" by tourists, the river has seen a sharp increase in use over the past few decades. The discovery process has included several laudatory articles in national outdoor periodicals, including *National Geographic Explorer*, *Outside*, and *Backpacker*. The pinnacle of river use through the Fort Niobrara National Wildlife Refuge may have occurred in 1997, when more that 30,000 people floated from the Cornell Dam launch area five miles east of Valentine.

There is some evidence that increased enforcement of a prohibition on alcohol in Fort Niobrara National Wildlife Refuge may be moving recreational users to enter the river at sites below the refuge, where rules are not as stringent. Several outfitters report that clients who consider alcohol an integral part of the river experience are requesting launch sites downstream from the refuge. From 2001 through 2004, the National Park Service counted upward of 30,000 people a year using the river in the twenty-five miles downstream from Valentine, with a maximum of nearly 40,000 in 2003. Total river use may thus not be declining; instead, the location of use is changing.

In 2004 researchers for the National Park Service counted a daily average of more than 700 visitors passing Smith Falls State Park during just four hour-long counting periods on the busiest Saturdays of July and August. The number of people floating the river in various vessels, on occasion even metal stock tanks, is especially formidable on weekends.

Because of the scenic beauty, ease of river access, and overall convenience for users, the preponderance of river recreation centers on the Valentine area, with many river outfitters headquartered near that small city. At least twelve canoe and float-tube outfitters operated near Valentine in 2004, plus one near Nenzel. These seasonal businesses provide varied services, but their primary role is transporting people and watercraft. Many outfitters offer campgrounds or other overnight accommodations, and some provide meals. The fees during the summer of 2004 ranged from $25 to $30 per person each day for the basic service of furnishing transportation and watercraft. Buses, vans, and canoe-hauling trailers make daily trips to deposit river travelers at popular launch sites like Cornell Dam and Berry Bridge. The same vehicles then pick up the canoes and passengers at their destination. Trips are often of one day or less, but they can be stretched to a weekend of floating and camping.

There are no restrictions preventing any person with a nonpowered craft from using the Niobrara River, except for about four miles at the very beginning of the Niobrara Scenic River corridor through the Fort Niobrara National Wildlife Refuge.

There are several launch sites downstream from Valentine, three of them publicly owned. The launch site at Brewer Bridge, about fifteen miles downstream from Valentine by river, is free for public use. The Cornell Dam launch site, just east of Valentine, required a day-use fee of $2 in 2004. The launch sites at Smith Falls require a state park use permit. Landing or launching is allowed at many sites on private property. Berry Bridge and Rock Dam are two of the more heavily used sites. Travel times for canoeists from the Cornell Dam launch site will vary with the volume of water and the enthusiasm of the paddlers, but to give some idea, travel to Berry Bridge takes about two hours; reaching Smith Falls takes about three hours; and a trip to Rock Dam or Rocky Ford takes about seven hours.

By far the most water use on the Niobrara occurs on the weekends, with most launches on Saturday. The river experience will be improved for everyone as river use is spread more throughout the week. As many as fifty people per minute have been counted passing a point below the Cornell Dam launch site on Saturdays. Although this may represent an extreme, it may be advisable to use the river during the week. River outfitters or the National Park Service office personnel can help you choose the least busy days.

Using canvas-covered inner tubes rather than canoes to float the river may reflect a desire to recreate Huck Finn's experience. By 1995 such float tubes were nearly as popular as canoes, according to river counts done by the Fort Niobrara National Wildlife Refuge. Outfitters have scrambled to keep up with this trend, providing ever more tubes.

However, many people prefer to remember canoes on the Niobrara. Outfitters and chambers of commerce still use images of canoes in their promotions to convey an idyllic experience. And canoes remain a very practical method for transporting people and goods down the river. Unlike the float tube, which goes wherever the wind and water take it, the canoe is maneuverable with a few strokes of a paddle. Canoes and their transport are readily available, and the Niobrara is one of the more beginner-friendly rivers in the United States. Many tourists have become canoeists for the first time on this river.

The Niobrara River is now nearly mythical in the minds of many Nebraskans, and water recreation is just one of the things one can do in the river valley. The concentration of wildlife in conjunction with diverse outdoor activities provides a modern vision of the Old West.

The upper and clearer reaches of the Niobrara, as well as several smaller tributaries, have long supported trout. Trout fishing in tributaries of the Niobrara, particularly in the Snake River, Long Pine Creek, and Verdigre Creek, still entices fishermen from great distances. Except for a short distance at the outlet below Merritt Dam, there is no public access to the Snake River, and to fish there you must be friends with a landowner or a member of a fishing club. You can gain access to Long Pine Creek at Long Pine State Recreation Area or at Pine Glen Wildlife Management Area. Access to Verdigre Creek is at the Grove Lake Wildlife Management Area and nearby Grove Trout Rearing Station. Fishing for catfish in the deeper, quieter pools of the river is still popular.

The sparseness of the human population and abundance of remaining game animals and birds help make the Niobrara region a hunting mecca of sorts. Hunters often come to the valley to hunt deer, turkey, waterfowl, and upland game birds. The Nebraska Game and Parks Commission estimates that there are five times as many deer and turkeys close to the river as in the surrounding prairies. Some local residents also still hunt coyotes for sport.

Visiting hunters who travel to the Niobrara Valley must rely on using public access land or take on the time-consuming task of cultivating the trust of a local landowner. Some landowners now lease the hunting rights on their land to professional guides. The guides then assume responsibility for policing hunting behavior. The popularity of this arrangement may have less to do with money than with an indictment of the behavior of a few hunters. The end result is that hunters will increasingly pay for the privilege of hunting in an area of abundant game.

The first commercial fur-trading operation on the Niobrara was probably established near the mouth of the Snake River in about 1830. The traders likely shipped more buffalo robes than beaver pelts. Trapping fur-bearing animals has continued to be important, though it is declining. With the decreasing market price of furs, it is coming to be viewed as recreation.

Bird-watching is now the most popular outdoor activity in the United States, and it is actively pursued in the Niobrara Valley. The diverse biological habitats there create a special ornithological attraction, including some challenging identifications of hybrid birds whose parents' ranges overlap here on the Niobrara. During spring and fall migrations the air and wetlands along the river valley are filled with migrating waterfowl and shorebirds. Whooping cranes, though once considered only rare visitors, have been reported more often in recent years, and trumpeter swans and bald eagles are now regularly seen (see chapter 6).

There are not yet many designated hiking trails along the Niobrara. Most of the public lands listed in appendix 3 offer access to hikers, but in most places you must plan on bushwhacking or following unofficial trails. In the case of Fort Niobrara National Wildlife Refuge it is important to know if a particular area is open to visitors before hiking there.

Several designated hiking trails are available for sightseeing, bird-watching, or simply enjoying the scenery along the Niobrara. At Agate Fossil Beds National Monument visitors can experience the grasslands near the headwaters of the Niobrara over about 2.5 miles of trail. There are several hiking trails at Fort Robinson (totaling 67 miles) and Chadron (9.8 miles) state parks, and in the Pine Ridge unit of the Nebraska National Forest. The Pine Ridge Trail (32 miles) will eventually link Crawford and Chadron with the Cowboy Trail, which is still under construction. When completed, this rail-to-trail conversion will extend 321 miles from Chadron to Norfolk. It parallels the Niobrara and crosses the river on an old railway bridge about 2.5 miles south of Valentine.

At Fort Niobrara National Wildlife Refuge a .75-mile loop trail lets hikers experience a springbranch canyon that contains Fort Falls. Smith Falls State Park has a short hiking trail to the falls and a nature trail that traverses the canyon. The Nature Conservancy's Niobrara Valley Preserve maintains two hiking trails that total about 5 miles of the Niobrara Valley, one on the south side of the river and one on the north. Niobrara State Park boasts more than 14 miles of maintained trails, plus a 2.1-mile trail that starts at the park and crosses the Niobrara on a converted railroad bridge.

In many ways a tourism spotlight has been shined on the busiest parts of the Niobrara River, and additional recreational uses are under way. Leisure on the Niobrara, while not restricted to watercraft, is still largely defined by them. The National Park Service currently estimates that only about 30 percent of total summer visitors come to the Valentine area for reasons other than floating the river—about 10,000 visits each year.

These visitors have warranted little official attention so far. The federal government has offered significant funding to improve roads and access, but only in the area primarily affected by water users.

The Niobrara Council was created when seventy-six miles of the river was designated as nationally scenic. It was originally intended to partner with the National Park Service, and these two agencies along with the U.S. Fish and Wildlife Service are the primary government agencies seeking to retain some of the original wild nature of the stream and to minimize conflicts owing to increasing use. The Middle Niobrara Natural Resources District, like many local government agencies, is represented on the Niobrara Council and has provided funding and assistance for canoe-launching areas. County governments in the Niobrara Scenic River corridor have each implemented zoning regulations that require local government approval for development. Each county is also represented on the Niobrara Council. In the case of Cherry County, the zoning regulations affect about eighty additional miles of the Niobrara River to the west of Valentine.

The National Park Service and the Niobrara Council recently completed a code of mandatory and suggested behavior for river users. This code contains many commonsense items, including prohibitions against unlawful use of alcohol, indecent exposure, profanity, excessive noise, fireworks, firearms, any device that launches a projectile, and littering. The National Park Service and the U.S. Fish and Wildlife Service each now employ officers to encourage better behavior and educate visitors about the area. They may, of course, issue citations. Since 1994 the state has banned alcohol at Smith Falls State Park, and in 2001 the U.S. Fish and Wildlife Service banned it from the five-mile stretch of river passing through Fort Niobrara National Wildlife Refuge.

The Niobrara Council, the National Park Service, and other interested groups are currently seeking federal and private funding to purchase scenic easements along the Niobrara River. An easement can take many forms, but in this application they would purchase the future rights for development and in this way keep the land looking much as it does now. The goal is to protect the scenic and cultural qualities that have attracted so much attention. The Park Service and Niobrara Council are also pursuing additional launch sites for watercraft and more restrooms for river users. Each success is intended to prevent future crowding at existing facilities.

The U.S. Fish and Wildlife Service administers the Fort Niobrara Wildlife Refuge, and it implements its own rules on use of the river within its jurisdiction. The management plan includes several usage limitations. First among them is that river use can be increased somewhat beyond its current level without harming the wildlife or landscape on the refuge. The proposed limit for people using the river within the refuge boundaries is 20,300 per year. A minimum of 2,000 permits would be reserved for those who wish to use the river without hiring an outfitter.

In addition, an unlimited number of outfitters would be allowed to operate across the refuge, instead of following the current system that grants river rights based on the outfitter's past use. In the new system, anyone who wishes to operate a commercial outfitting business within the Fort Niobrara National Wildlife Refuge must bid on a minimum of 500 and a maximum of 2,500 permits each year. Approximately 18,000 permits would be sold in this way, each allowing one person to cross the refuge. Other provisions of the preferred plan would begin to limit Saturday launches after they reach 800 persons a day and would also encourage outfitters to launch watercraft between 10:00 a.m. and 4:00 p.m. The plan is final but will undergo scrutiny and some changes as management experience and additional studies indicate.

The Niobrara River is a national treasure. Relatively remote and in a lightly populated area, the Niobrara Valley has remained a microcosm of the western United States as it once was. If it is to remain so, the inexorable pressure of human use will have to be monitored. The immediate Niobrara Valley is almost entirely privately owned, making any input about the long-term public good more difficult. Almost all landowners want what is best for the land, but they also reasonably wish to protect their investment and property rights.

Historical circumstances have left the river largely untouched, but the history of many other once pristine areas suggests that development is inevitable. Houses sprouting on small canyon plots near Valentine are very likely the precursor of events for the entire river. Maintaining the Niobrara's solitude and wild beauty is a great challenge both for local residents and for America, and the best result will be a compromise. The river that has inspired and nurtured so many faces a multitude of tests if it is to remain the river that local residents have long enjoyed as more and more tourists seek to fulfill their recreational dreams.

Chapter Ten

The Now and Future Niobrara Valley

Unlike Native Americans, urban dwellers tend not to have a holistic approach to nature. They still do not feel intimately connected with the
natural world until immersed in it. This kind of connection to the environment can only be maintained through the preservation of the environment. That is why the Niobrara and efforts to preserve it are significant. The Niobrara is more than just a river. It is a means to reestablish
the connections between humans and nature.

—KURT M. CLARK (1997)

It is easy to love the Niobrara. The river has uncounted shady canyons
decorated by trickling brooks and hidden lacy waterfalls; exposed vertical bluffs whose layered bands of sand and clay have written the earth's
recent geological history as clearly and as logically as the chapters of a
book; and just enough rapid water to prevent a canoeist from falling
asleep at the paddle.

Especially evident when one is paddling the river are the constant
sounds of softly running water, ripples lapping at the canoe, and wind
rustling the leaves of cottonwood trees.

What are notably absent from such a trip are ringing telephones, traffic noises, radio talk shows, and all the other noise pollution we take for
granted as part of the price of modern living.

Canoeing the Niobrara brings often unforgettable vignettes of people who live along the river and scratch honest livings from the land—the sight of a ranch wife balancing twin daughters on her hips as she cooks dinner, her husband expertly handling a team of horses and equipment, and an array of mostly mongrel ranch dogs that seem delighted whenever they are minimally recognized as part of the overall scene.

The lives of rivers are much like human lives. During their youths they madly rush about, dashing wildly here and there, then they grow more predictable and reliable as they mature, grading into serenity and contemplative majesty in their old age, and finally they drift into obscurity and death by merging with some larger river or the sea.

Nebraskans should gratefully recognize the Niobrara not only for its a historical heritage as the home of our state's most authentic hero, Crazy Horse, but also for being a source of geological and biological instruction and endless pleasure. No other river in the state cuts through geologic time as clearly as the Niobrara, and no other pursuit cuts through the complexities and frustrations of modern life as cleanly as a canoe slicing through its cool waters like a knife through soft clay.

Like scanning the horizon ahead while canoeing a winding and unfamiliar river, peering into the future is an unpredictable venture at best. An optimist is likely to anticipate good weather, good currents, a favorable wind, and beautiful scenery rather than objectively assessing the situation and being prepared to accept whatever might be in store. A pessimist is more likely to anticipate dangerous rapids or thunderstorms and to imagine that other unpleasant surprises, if not government conspiracies, might be waiting around every bend. Often these differing expectations become self-fulfilling prophesies.

In trying to plot a pathway into the future by developing a workable management plan for the Niobrara National Scenic River, the National Park Service has been buffeted for more than a decade by contrasting attitudes, expectations, and hopes. What is the worth of the Niobrara Valley's unique ecological, biological, and geological-paleontological treasures relative to the region's traditional agricultural-ranching history and its potential for recreational and economic development? How can these diverse resources and attractions be preserved and also benefit the greatest number of human interests without being degraded or destroyed? Equally important, how they should *not* be used?

Paleontological and Geological Values of the Niobrara Valley
The scientific values of the Niobrara River valley are many. The valley
contains major deposits of Tertiary (Miocene, Pliocene) and Pleistocene
fossils, with over 160 cataloged fossil sites. As many as 146 vertebrate
species have been found at a single site, and one site (Norden Bridge
Quarry) has produced 89 fossil species of mammals. This is substantially
more than the total number of present-day mammals (72) known for the
entire Niobrara Valley and more mammal species than are known from
any other single fossil quarry in the world. The Norden Bridge site has
produced 146 vertebrata taxa, the nearby Engelhoff Quarry has generated 84 vertebrates, and Sand Draw sites near Ainsworth have accounted
for 85 vertebrates and 49 invertebrates (Voorhies and Corner 1993).

Eighty species of fossil vertebrates, including fifty-six mammals, thirteen reptiles, eight amphibians, two birds, and one fish, were initially
discovered within the Niobrara Scenic River corridor. As such, the valley represents a time capsule of the past 20 million years of planetary and
biological history. One fossil site in Brown County (Valentine Railways
Quarries) has generated more species of large fossil mammals than any
other North American Miocene site. Among a total of more than 83,000
fossil specimens from the site there are also the remains of twenty-six
reptiles, sixteen fish, fifteen amphibians, and an undetermined number
of birds (Voorhies and Corner 1993).

More than 160 mapped paleontological sites are known from within the
Niobrara River and its tributaries. Of the total sites, 15 have been identified as "world class," 46 are regarded as of national importance, and
106 are of regional significance. There are twenty-six localities within the
collective Scenic River corridor from which unique type specimens have
been described (those representing the first scientifically described examples of a particular fossil type). Among the mammals are ten new ar-
tiodactyl (cloven-hoofed) ungulates, ten carnivores, nine rodents, eight
gomphothere elephants, two horses, a shrew, a mole, and a bat. Twenty
of the fossil sites have been regarded as warranting inclusion in the National Register of Historic Places (Voorhies and Corner 1993). These sites
will have increased security from fossil destruction and potential commercial plundering under the protection of the National Park Service.

There are also probably more than 200 known waterfalls within the
geographical limits of the Scenic River designation, most on the steeper

south valley slopes. A recent unpublished survey of a twenty-mile stretch between Cornell Bridge and Rocky Ford by University of Nebraska professor Darryl Pederson revealed more than 180 waterfalls, almost twice as many as had previously been known for that river segment. Many of the Niobrara's waterfalls are small and inconspicuous, but with a vertical drop of about seventy feet, Smith Falls (in Smith Falls State Park) is the highest waterfall in Nebraska. There are also the sixty-foot Fort Falls at Fort Niobrara National Wildlife Refuge and the little-known but beautiful Stairstep Falls. At its deepest and widest, the Scenic River segment of the Niobrara Valley is as much as 300 feet deep and nearly two miles wide. Its canyon cuts through nearly 30 million years of time, and in some places a canoeist can pass directly over the Pierre Shale, the shale bed deposited by the great Cretaceous inland sea of 70 million years ago (fig. 21).

Botanical and Zoological Values of the Niobrara Valley

Biologically, the area's rich present-day plant and animal life is especially notable for its transitional attributes. The vascular plants of the Scenic River section include nearly one hundred species of state-listed sensitive, rare, or unusual plants, such as the blowout penstemon and the western prairie fringed orchid. Collectively about six hundred vascular plant species have been documented within the Scenic River corridor, and most of the area has not yet been thoroughly surveyed botanically. Although perhaps not rare nationally, some of these plants represent important local endemic populations, such as paper birch, quaking aspens, and numerous fen species that have been separated from other populations of these same species by thousands of years of postglacial time and may be now geographically separated from them by hundreds of miles. Unlike those of many other American rivers, the native plant communities of the Niobrara Valley are still largely intact.

Over two hundred species of birds have been reported for the designated Scenic River section of the Niobrara Valley, including breeding populations of the interior least tern (nationally endangered) and the piping plover (nationally threatened). The tern and plover are probably not going to be seriously affected by the prospective increased recreational uses of the river, since their nesting sites are not in the section that is primarily used for rafting and canoeing.

A recent field study by Christopher Anderson and others, undertaken

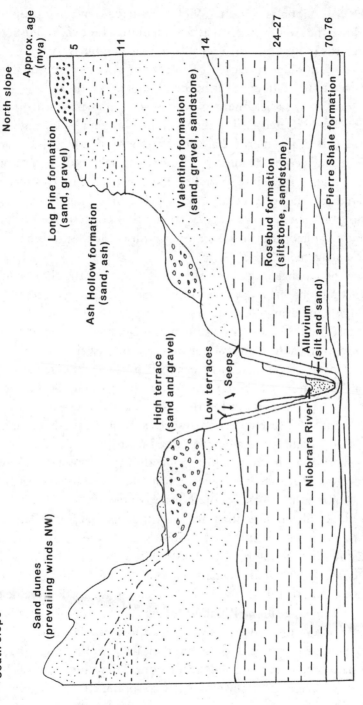

FIGURE 21. Cross-section view of the central Niobrara Valley, showing major geological features and their approximate timelines.

at the Fort Niobrara National Wildlife Refuge, found that people floating down the river frightened away water birds, herons, kingfishers, and
shorebirds more often than local breeding songbirds. And these same
water and shoreline species were more than twice as common in refuge
areas where recreational river traffic was not allowed.

As described earlier, there are also several interspecies hybrid zones
where closely related birds interact in the Niobrara Valley region, producing genetically intermediate populations of special evolutionary, behavioral, and ecological interest. Hundreds of species of migratory birds
use the region, including several rare to endangered species such as the
endangered whooping crane and the peregrine falcon. Since these migrating bird species of primary conservation concern are not present
during the major tourist season, their future is not a significant issue in
river management.

The still rare bald eagle is mostly only a winter visitor, though increasingly common, but several pairs now remain in the region to nest. Protecting them during the nesting season may become more important as
local tourism increases. The nationally endangered whooping crane has
been reported at least thirty-four times in the past sixty years. Twenty-
seven bird species classified as "sensitive" by the Nebraska Natural Heritage Program have been reported from the Niobrara Scenic River region (U.S. Department of Interior, National Park Service 2005).

There are over seventy mammal species in the greater Niobrara Valley
region, including the state-endangered northern river otter, plus several other species of conservation concern. One of these is the swift fox,
a shortgrass species that is now largely limited to Sioux County but also
occurs along the South Dakota border counties east to Todd County.
The black-tailed prairie dog is more widespread but is now largely limited to sanctuaries such as the Niobrara Valley Preserve, wildlife refuges
including Fort Niobrara National Wildlife Refuge, and other federally
owned lands such as the Oglala National Grassland and the Nebraska
National Forest. It is also still common along the northern edge of the
Niobrara drainage in the Rosebud Indian Reservation of South Dakota,
in spite of repeated federally sponsored efforts to poison it.

In Nebraska's national forest and national grassland areas the prairie
dog is exposed to unregulated "recreational" shooting as well as to periodic massive and politically motivated poisoning efforts, thereby reduc-

ing habitat for burrowing owls, swift foxes, and dozens of other species that are ecologically associated with prairie dogs. In the fall of 2005 the U.S. Forest Service expanded eradication efforts on the Oglala, Buffalo Gap, and Fort Pierre national grasslands to cover 3,000 to 7,000 acres of buffer zones adjacent to private lands, using zinc phosphide, a broad-spectrum metabolic poison.

The nationally endangered black-footed ferret, which has long been extirpated from Nebraska but which preys almost exclusively on the prairie dog, cannot be expected to be seen again in Nebraska until the prairie dog is finally given adequate state and federal protection. Furthermore, predators such as weasels and raptors such as golden eagles, prairie falcons, and ferruginous hawks risk dying from eating poisoned prairie dogs. Other apparently declining mammals in the Niobrara region include such typical grassland species as the long-tailed weasel and the white-tailed and black-tailed jackrabbits, all of which require substantial areas of grass for survival.

On the other hand, mountain lions increasingly enter the Niobrara Valley from the Black Hills, and elk regularly wander south into the central Niobrara Valley from adjacent South Dakota, where resident populations exist in Todd and Gregory counties. The white-tailed deer is slowly moving westward through the valley, affecting the resident mule deer. Several other woodland mammals are also expanding westward along the Niobrara Valley as the upper valley's forests mature, such as the Virginia opossum, northern myotis, eastern red bat, woodchuck, white-footed mouse, and gray fox (Benedict, Genoways, and Freeman 2000).

The Niobrara Valley supports an endemic but locally common race of the eastern wood rat that is a relict of postglacial climatic changes, with its nearest surviving relatives now living at least one hundred miles to the south, in south-central Nebraska. The Niobrara subspecies has some chromosomal differences from all other populations that suggest it may have been isolated for a substantial period. Six mammal species classified as "sensitive" by the Nebraska Natural Heritage Program have been reported from the Niobrara region (U.S. Department of Interior, National Park Service 2005).

There are at least twenty-nine species of reptiles and amphibians living within the Niobrara Scenic River corridor. Two of these (Blanding's turtle and yellow mud turtle) are of special conservation concern, especially the nationally declining Blanding's turtle, which is mostly associated with permanent Sandhills marshes. None of the other reptiles is likely to be seriously disturbed by increased recreational use, although some such as the prairie rattlesnake generally suffer from increased human contact, and ornate box turtles are far too frequently (and illegally) taken home by tourists as "pets." Two reptile species (yellow mud turtle and smooth green snake) that are classified as "sensitive" by the Nebraska Natural Heritage Program have been reported from the Niobrara region (U.S. Department of Interior, National Park Service, 2005).

The central stretch of the Niobrara River also still supports at least thirty-seven species of fish, although many are now rare or declining. Species of conservation concern within this region include several cold-water, minnow-sized fish (such as the pearl dace and black-nosed shiner) that occupy the Niobrara's tributary streams, but these are more likely to be affected by river pollution than by recreational river use. Ten fish species classified as "sensitive" by the Nebraska Natural Heritage Program have been reported from the Niobrara Scenic River corridor (U.S. Department of Interior, National Park Service 2005).

Butterflies of the immediate Scenic River corridor number at least fifty-six species, including the regal fritillary, a candidate for federal listing as threatened. Five other butterfly and skipper species classified as "sensitive" by the Nebraska Natural Heritage Program have been reported from the Niobrara region (U.S. Department of Interior, National Park Service 2005).

The federally endangered American burying beetle has been reported for the Niobrara region, and there are also nearly eighty species of dragonflies and damselflies known from the twelve-county greater Niobrara region (see appendix 1F). None of these other insect species is so far known to need special conservation action, nor is any likely to be obviously affected by increased recreational use of the river.

The other invertebrate groups of the Niobrara Valley are too diverse or too little studied to offer much information on their rarity and possible conservation concerns. Some invertebrate groups such as freshwater mussels clearly need taxonomic and ecological inventories in the Niobrara basin, since they are often among the first stream organisms to be deleteriously affected by pollution and thus are valuable indicators of declining water quality.

Among plants, the nationally endangered Hayden's (blowout) penstemon and the nationally threatened western prairie fringed orchid both have been reported from the Niobrara region, as well as ninety other species classified as "sensitive" by the Nebraska Natural Heritage Program (U.S. Department of Interior, National Park Service 2005). Probably the rarest of these is the hooded ladies' tresses, known in Nebraska only from a single alkaline meadow in Sioux County.

Although not yet listed as threatened, some heat-sensitive plants such as the paper birch are now limited to the shaded springbranch canyons and cool springs along a thirty-mile section of the Scenic River corridor between Fort Niobrara National Wildlife Refuge and Hazel Creek. They are most evident in and around Smith Falls, where the cool microclimate has permitted a precarious survival. The mature paper birches of these canyons are slowly dying without reproducing, so it may be that global warming is taking a toll on these cold-adapted relicts from the Pleistocene.

Scenic River Boundaries and Management Concerns

The legal width of the Scenic River boundaries determines how effectively the region's waterfalls, scenic views, biological resources, and paleontological sites can be protected. The interim boundary (Boundary Alternative 1), set by the original Wild and Scenic Rivers Act, would have extended only an average of 0.25 mile from the river's usual highwater mark and would encompass 24,320 acres of land. If adopted, this boundary alternative (favored by many landowners) would include habitat supporting at least ninety-five species of state-listed plants of conservation concern but would not take into account practical considerations such as roads and property lines or give maximum protection to the region's most important natural values. A variant alternative (Boundary Alternative 2), with a slightly smaller acreage total (20,205) and including as many significant natural resources as possible, would contain habitats supporting the same listed plant species, and would especially protect the scenic and paleontological resources. The width of the valley protected would extend nearly 3 miles from the river in two instances, and at minimum would measure 200 feet from the river's ordinary highwater mark. A third alternative (Boundary Alternative 3) is the option preferred by the National Park Service (U.S. Department of Interior,

National Park Service 2005). It would include 23,074 acres and would contain and protect as equitably as possible the scenic, recreational, geological, wildlife, and paleontological values of the region. At maximum it would extend 2.5 miles wide (at Fairfield Creek, an important paleontological site), and it would not measure less than 200 feet from the ordinary high-water mark except in the wilderness area of Fort Niobrara National Wildlife Refuge, where it would follow the river's high-water mark for 5.5 miles.

Several management options for the Scenic River corridor were also proposed by the National Park Service in 1996, and they were updated and revised in 2004. Alternative A would continue existing conditions, with no direct National Park Service action. Alternative B, the preferred alternative of the National Park Service (U.S. Department of Interior, National Park Service 2005), would draw on local Niobrara Council management advice from private, state, and other federal partners, but the land would remain largely privately owned. The Park Service would be the lead agency in core functions, such as law enforcement and resource management, and would be an adviser and helper in other relevant areas, such as resource protection on private lands. County planning commissions, the U.S. Fish and Wildlife Service, the Nature Conservancy, the Nebraska Game and Parks Commission, and local landowners would all be potentially significant local partners in the area's management. Alternative C would involve direct and independent management by the Park Service, much like the system now typically used in the national park system, on a landscape that in time would be federally owned within the limits of the Wild and Scenic Rivers Act. As of late 2006 the final management alternative had not been selected.

As noted in chapter 9, in 1997 the Niobrara Council was formed to help the National Park Service manage and protect the Valley's resources. Originally represented by an intercounty agreement among Brown, Cherry, Keya Paha, and Rock counties, in 2000 the Niobrara Council was recognized by the Nebraska state legislature and was mandated as the state-level authority for recommending river management practices and given responsibility for developing conservation easements and holding titles to land. The sixteen-member Council includes appointed representatives of local, state, and federal governments, local landowners, county commissioners, area industries, and environmentalists. It is headquartered in Valentine (www.niobraracouncil.com; tel. 402-376-2793). The Niobrara Scenic River Advisory Commission, with twelve appointed members from throughout Nebraska, also has contributed importantly in formulating management plans for the Scenic River corridor.

Of related interest and importance is the Friends of the Niobrara, a nonprofit corporation that evolved from the grassroots Save the Niobrara Association of the 1970s. The stated mission of the Friends of the Niobrara is to preserve the natural, historical, and scenic qualities of the Valley through education and projects that help to accomplish this preservation goal. The group is affiliated with the National Park Service, the Niobrara Council, the Nature Conservancy, and the Northern Prairies Land Trust. It is headquartered in Malcolm (9200 West Fletcher Avenue, Malcolm NE 68402).

The current economy of the Scenic River region is still based on farming and ranching, which contribute about a third of all regional jobs. During the late 1900s total employment decreased, as did government and agricultural employment. The human population of the greater Niobrara region has shown a pattern of gradual decline during the last decade of the twentieth century (table 25). This regional population decline of 5.6 percent within a single decade (and 9 percent within the four-county Scenic River region), at a time when the overall state population was essentially stable, is simply a continuation of a longer-term pattern of rural exodus that began during the first third of the twentieth century, with the regional population peaking about 1930. By the year 2000 the population of the twelve-county Niobrara region had declined to only 67 percent of the 1910 level, and it was continuing to drop at a rate approaching 1 percent a year.

The Niobrara Valley is now crisscrossed by numerous highways and populated by many villages and towns, of which the largest are Chadron (population ca. 5,600), O'Neill (ca. 3,900), Valentine (ca. 2,500), Ainsworth (ca. 1,900), and Crawford (ca. 1,100). The total human population in the twelve-county region of Nebraska that encompasses the Niobrara basin was about 80,000 as of the year 2000.

In parallel with human population losses during the 1900s, the number of farms and ranches in Brown County dropped by half, from 706 in 1935 to 345 in 2000, but the number of cattle in that county gradually increased from about 25,000 in 1920 to 105,000 in 2001. However, re-

Table 25. Areas and 1910–2000 human populations of
counties in the greater Niobrara Valley

	Area	Human Population			Ind./mile²	1990–2000
County	mile²	1910	1990	2000*	2000	Trend %
Sioux	2,067	5,598	1,549	1,475	0.71	−4.8
Dawes	1,396	8,240	9,021	9,060	6.48	−0.5
Box Butte	1,075	6,131	13,130	12,158	11.30	−7.4
Sheridan	566	7,328	6,750	6,198	10.90	−8.2
Cherry	5,961	10,414	6,307	6,148	1.03	−2.6
Brown	540	6,083	3,657	3,525	5.99	−3.7
Keya Paha	773	3,452	1,029	983	1.27	−4.5
Rock	1,008	3,617	2,019	1,843	1.82	−8.8
Holt	710	15,545	12,599	11,551	16.20	−8.4
Boyd	540	8,826	2,835	2,438	4.51	−14.1
Knox	1,108	18,358	9,584	9,374	8.46	−2.2
Antelope	857	14,003	7,965	7,425	8.66	−6.8
Total	16,601	107,595	76,445	72,178	4.34	−5.6

*Data from 2000 U.S. Census; counties are listed west to east.

gional irrigation, which became feasible with the construction of Merritt Dam and its associated reservoir, had reached 63,000 acres by 2000 and encouraged a regional shift from ranching to irrigation farming. With the advent of irrigation, fertilization, and modern farm technology, corn production in Brown, Rock, and Keya Paha counties increased from an average of 14 bushels an acre in 1910 to 142 bushels an acre by 2000 (Bauer 2004).

Some of the economic problems associated with these population losses and technological changes in the Niobrara Valley have been countered by increased tourism in the region. Between 1970, when 802 people launched canoes on the Niobrara River at Cornell Bridge near Valentine, and 1997, when 31,748 people did so, recreational use of the river expanded nearly fortyfold.

By 1993 the National Park Services estimated that annual recreational use in the Scenic River corridor area was then 30,000 visitor-days of direct river activities, plus 5,000 nonriver visitor-days. About 70 percent of these river activities occurred during July and August, with greatest use on Saturdays, when as many as 800 canoes were on the river. An estimated $918,800 in revenue was being generated annually from related direct tourism sales, which translates into $1,197,000 in indirect revenues. In 2002 over 72,000 visitors were recorded at Smith Falls State Park, including nearly 19,000 overnight campers.

By 2004 more than 54,000 people were annually participating in river-based activities in the upper Scenic River corridor, with an estimated 33,400 floating the river and another 21,000 tourists visiting the area. Tourism then still represented only about 6 percent of the total overall economy of the immediate four-county Scenic River region, but it was slowly growing. Future ways to accommodate tourists that are outlined in the draft management plan include adding access points for boaters at Berry Bridge and Rocky Ford, building six more public toilet sites, and possibly establishing a five- to six-mile hike-bike trail that would connect the river with the Cowboy Trail. The now obsolete Cornell Dam might also be removed to make water flow more naturally and promote fish movements (U.S. Department of Interior, National Park Service 2005).

The number of people floating the upper parts of the Scenic River corridor began to decrease in 1997, owing to some numerical restrictions on canoe launches within the boundaries of the Fort Niobrara National Wildlife Refuge and to better controls on alcohol use and rowdy behavior that were established in 2001. From 1993 through 1998 an average of 27,250 people floated the eight-mile river stretch within the refuge boundaries each year, compared with a mean of 17,350 floating that stretch annually between 1999 and 2003. An estimated 33,419 people used that same section in 2004. By 2005, when commercial outfitters were required to bid on a limited number of launching passes for traversing the Fort Niobrara river section, 20,300 passes were earmarked for outfitters and another 1,030 more were designated for independent users.

Alcohol and drug use on the river have declined sharply in recent years; arrests for drug use dropped from thirty-six in 2001 to ten in 2003. Most of the arrests by the National Park Service rangers during the summer of 2005 involved minors with alcohol. Thus canoeists wanting a near-wilderness experience may prefer to begin their trips at Cornell Bridge rather than starting from eight miles downstream at Berry Bridge, where alcohol use is not yet regulated.

In 2005 eleven canoe and raft outfitters had permits to operate within the Scenic River corridor. By then, usage limits had been established for the Cornell Bridge launch site. Lee Simmons, a local downstream resort owner who had initiated a lawsuit opposing the Fish and Wildlife Service's moratorium on granting new outfitter licenses, lost that lawsuit on appeal in 2004. That decision should allow the National Park Service to complete its plans for protecting the river's natural resources from excessive commercialization. However, a new lawsuit by William Mulligan, a retired Valentine businessman, has challenged the Fish and Wildlife Service's river management plan, including its restrictions on alcohol use.

Additionally, David Sokol, an Omaha businessman and owner of a 3,000-acre ranch in Cherry County, filed suit in 1997 in the Eighth U.S. District Court claiming that the Scenic River corridor should be limited to the bank-to-bank width of the river, claiming that the river's scenic values are not so "outstandingly remarkable" as to warrant national recognition. In contrast, a suit filed by the Minnesota-based Heartland chapter of the National Parks and Conservation Association claimed that the 1996 National Park Service plan did not "ensure long-term protection of the river and its immediate environment" (Clark 1997).

After long delays, in 2005 a revised General Management Plan and Environmental Impact Statement was released by the National Park Service (U.S. Department of Interior, National Park Service 2005). Among other proposals, it envisions improvements in river access, recreational facilities, and conservation easements collectively costing $11 million to $13 million. It also envisions a new research and education center, to be built in cooperation with the U.S. Fish and Wildlife Service, its location still to be determined. The cost of two new river access points and protecting about 17,000 by conservation easements under the preferred management proposal has been estimated at $5 million to $6 million, the money to be requested from Congress.

We may hope that decisions by well-intentioned people will set a course for the Niobrara River that will satisfy most, though probably not everyone. But the Niobrara River is, after all, a natural, living ecosystem, and not all living things need to conform to human wishes, nor will all humans agree on the river's attractions, their relative values, and how best to preserve them. Details of the Niobrara River management plan can be obtained from the Niobrara National Scenic River office, Box 319, 146 South Hall Street, Valentine NE 69201 (tel. 402-336-3970, or www.nps.gov/niob. The Nature Conservancy's establishment in 1980 of the

Niobrara Valley Preserve in the heart of the Niobrara National Scenic River corridor may have been the single most important step in preserving the Niobrara's critical habitats. It protects more than 60,000 acres from future development, abutting twenty-five miles of the Niobrara's south shoreline and several miles of the north shore. The preserve includes examples of riparian eastern deciduous, northern boreal, and western coniferous forests as well as extensive areas of Sandhills prairie and a combination of mixed-grass and tallgrass prairies. A herd of several hundred bison is present, and research is conducted on the effects of cattle and bison grazing and controlled fire management on plant and animal populations. Other studies involve remote sensing of rangeland vegetation, interactions between native thistles and insects, and woodland management in river canyons. There is a small visitor center that welcomes both general visitors and researchers. You can hike on two trails that pass through a variety of habitat types, and guided bison tours can be arranged for groups. Together with the Fort Niobrara National Wildlife Refuge and Smith Falls State Park, it provides visitors with easy access to some of the most attractive and biologically significant sites in the entire Niobrara Valley, as well as opportunities for learning about conservation progress and problems in the region.

In the past few years conservation opportunities and undertakings in Nebraska generally have greatly accelerated, thanks in large measure to the Nebraska Environmental Trust. This trust fund was established in 1992 when a state constitutional amendment brought the Nebraska Lottery into being. There was companion legislation establishing the Nebraska Environmental Trust, using some of the profits from the state-operated lottery. Initially 25 percent of these profits went to the Trust, but in 1997 the percentage was increased to 49.5 percent. By 2005 the Trust had already received and disbursed nearly $90 million. These funds have been competitively distributed statewide, with special emphasis on critical habit preservation, surface water quality, groundwater quality, and solid waste reduction. Individuals, organizations, and public entities are eligible to apply.

Some of the early grants that relate to the Niobrara watershed included awards to the Nebraska Game and Parks Commission totaling nearly $400,000 for Soldier Creek reclamation, Long Pine Creek habitat improvement, and shoreline stabilization of Lewis and Clark Lake. In

April 2005 the Nebraska Environmental Trust Fund awarded the Niobrara Council $250,000 for the purchase of conservation easements along the National Scenic River corridor. By 2005 the Trust had awarded over $1.3 million for conservation easements in the Valley and $2.75 million for land acquisition.

Almost every year political efforts have been made in the Nebraska state legislature to reduce the percentage of lottery funds allocated to protecting the natural environment, but so far they have been thwarted. Boldly inscribed on the north side of the Nebraska State Capitol is an epigram by Hartley Burr Alexander: "The Salvation of the State Is Watchfulness in the Citizen." Directly above, under the Capitol dome and its symbolic bronze Sower, is a giant mosaic of the Thunderbird. Its rain-making powers traditionally were thought to bring water, and thus also rivers, wetlands, and their multitude of animals and plants, to a grateful Native American nation below. We would do well to keep these symbols always in mind.

Afterword

A few summers ago I drifted in a canoe through nearly 15 million years of time along the Niobrara Valley. The time warp began with my witnessing fossil rhinos and bones of three-toed horses being excavated at a famous Miocene fossil site near Norden Bridge, and it ended with some frosty, clear, and astonishingly star-studded nights that brought an abrupt end to summer.

The trip was also a personal clock-setting experience for me. I had last canoed the Niobrara about twenty years before, during a dam-construction controversy over this portion of the river that finally brought the well-deserved death of the ecologically disastrous and financially foolish boondoggle but ironically also set the stage for discussion of how best to preserve the river for posterity. Now gone from the scene is Loren Wilson, an old friend whose many other "Save the Niobrara" ventures had indeed helped save the river from destruction, and in whose memory a memorial marker had since been erected along its north bank. As I looked at the memorial I realized that he had been born after me, so his life had been briefer than mine already is, but that his legacy of preserving the integrity of the river will last indefinitely. Two other old friends, Lou Christiansen and Fred Thomas, who for many decades were also strong supporters of the Niobrara River, are now also gone forever, but

Fred's work has been memorialized as the Fred Thomas Wildlife Management Area.

What is most worth remembering while enjoying the Niobrara are the efforts made and the price paid by people such as Loren Wilson, Lou Chistiansen, Fred Thomas, and the countless others who have also striven to protect the river from ecological destruction and, more recently, from commercial overdevelopment. What is most worth carrying away from a visit to the Niobrara are one's individual memories of the land, the sky, and the natural landscape, plus the hope that the river will run through the lives and dreams of the next generation just as it does through ours.

Nebraskans have already effectively lost their two other major rivers to agricultural "progress." These rivers, the Republican and the central Platte, now are virtual trickles if not entirely dry during midsummer owing to inadequate legal controls on upstream irrigation withdrawals, and irrigation-drained creeks such as Pumpkin Creek and Frenchman Creek are now usually no more than dusty memories. Some of the Niobrara's tributaries are in grave danger too, such as Bone Creek, which has been seriously polluted by a hog confinement operation near Ainsworth and has lost most of its valuable fish life. The biota of Keller Park State Recreation Area and Keller School Land Wildlife Management Area have thus been affected, as has the Bone Creek segment of Pine Glen Wildlife Management Area.

With persistent care and vigilance, the Niobrara River will continue to call softly to us for decades to come, will soothe us and our descendants with the whispered stories told by its running waters, and will provide both home and habitats for the plants and animals we are lucky enough to have as fellow travelers on our own brief journeys through this beautiful world.

> If the biota, in the course of eons, has built something we like but do not understand, then who but a fool would seemingly discard useless parts? To keep every cog and wheel is the first precaution of intelligent tinkering.
>
> —ALDO LEOPOLD, A Sand County Almanac

Appendix 1A

Mammals of the Niobrara Region

This species list is mainly based on data of Benedict, Genoways, and Free-man (2000) and Jones and Choate (1980). The geographic coverage of this list and the following ones includes the twelve counties listed in table 25, the three South Dakota border counties (Todd, Tripp, and Gregory) that in part occur within the Niobrara drainage (Higgins et al. 2000), and eastern Wyoming, specifically the Wyoming latilong that encompass-es the Niobrara's headwaters (Luce et al. 1997). The seventy-three species listed here represent 77 percent of the current Nebraska mammal list of ninety-five species. The list follows the traditional taxonomic sequence of families and genera; congeneric species are arranged alphabetically by their Latin specific names.

Asterisks (*) identify mammal species reputed to occur during envi-ronmental surveys within the now abandoned Norden Dam project area of Brown and Keya Paha counties (U.S. Bureau of Reclamation 1978). Those found during a 1982 survey of the Niobrara Valley Preserve (Kan tak and Churchill 1993) are identified by the pound symbol (#).

Indicated zoogeographic affinities are mostly after Freeman (1998); species with no clear zoogeographic affinities are termed "widespread." State and federally endangered and threatened species are noted, as are regionally "sensitive" species as defined by the U.S. Forest Service. A to-tal of six mammal species reported from the Niobrara Scenic River region are classified as "sensitive" by the Nebraska Natural Heritage Program (U.S. Department of Interior, National Park Service 2005). These species are shown in **boldface**.

Family Didelphidae—New World Opossums

Virginia opossum. *Didelphis virginiana.* Cities and woods; expanding west along Niobrara to Dawes and Box Butte counties in Nebraska, also in easternmost Wyoming and in South Dakota west to Todd County. At or near the northwestern edge of its Great Plains range. Southern affinities.* #

Family Soricidae—Shrews

Masked shrew. *Sorex cinereus.* Locally common. Mainly moist grasslands or somewhat brushy to wooded mesic habitats. Northern affinities.*

Hayden's shrew. *Sorex haydeni.* Local. Prairie grasslands. Great Plains affinities.#

Merriam's shrew. *Sorex merriami.* Very rare in Panhandle (Sioux, Dawes, and Sheridan counties) and in adjacent eastern Wyoming. Arid grasslands and sage. At eastern limits in Niobrara Valley. Western affinities.

Northern short-tailed shrew. *Blarina brevicauda.* Common eastward west to Cherry County in Nebraska and Tripp County in South Dakota; in diverse habitats, from grasslands to woods. At western range limits in Niobrara Valley. Eastern affinities.* #

Least shrew. *Cryptotis parva.* West regularly to Cherry County, local Panhandle records in Dawes and Sheridan counties. Open grassy or weedy habitats, especially tallgrass prairie. At or near western range limits in Niobrara Valley. Eastern affinities.*

Family Talpidae—Moles

Eastern mole. *Scalopus aquaticus.* Throughout region. Mostly subterranean, in loamy soils and taller grasses. At western range limits in upper Niobrara Valley of adjacent eastern Wyoming. Eastern affinities.* #

Family Vespertilionidae—Vespertilionid Bats

Western small-footed myotis. *Myotis ciliolabrum.* Throughout region (reported Sioux County to Keya Paha County). Rocky habitats; hibernator. At eastern range limits in lower Niobrara Valley. Western affinities. This taxonomically confusing species has at times been known as *M. keeni* and later as *M. subulatus leibii*; the epithet *M. keeni* is now used for a Pacific Northwest species, and *M. leibii* is now restricted in use to a very similar small-footed species of the eastern United States.*

Little brown myotis. *Myotis lucifugus.* Pine Ridge (Sioux, Dawes, and Sheridan counties in Nebraska) and adjacent eastern Wyoming; probably also lower Niobrara Valley (Todd County to Gregory County in South Dakota; single records exist for Nebraska's Cherry and Knox counties). Coniferous and deciduous forests; hibernator. Widespread.

Northern (long-eared) myotis. *Myotis septentrionalis.* West along Niobrara River from Knox County to Sheridan County. Wooded habitats; hibernator. At western range limits in Niobrara Valley. Eastern affinities. State-listed sensitive species.#

Fringe-tailed myotis. *Myotis thysanodes.* Pine Ridge counties (Sioux County to Sheridan County, also a Cherry County record). Coniferous habitats; hibernator. At eastern range limits in Niobrara Valley. Western affinities.

Long-legged myotis. *Myotis volans.* Pine Ridge (Sioux, Dawes, and Sheridan counties of Nebraska, Tripp County of South Dakota). Open forests and rock ledges; hibernator. At eastern range limits in Niobrara Valley. Western affinities.

Evening bat. *Nycticeius humeralis.* Reported only from Knox County. Deciduous woods; probably migratory. Eastern affinities.

Silver-haired bat. *Lasionycteris noctivagans.* Throughout region (scattered records). Forests and meadows; migratory. Widespread.*

Big brown bat. *Eptesicus fuscus.* Throughout region (Sioux County to Knox County). Diverse habitats including woods; hibernator. Widespread.* #

Eastern red bat. *Lasiurus borealis.* Throughout region (Sioux County to Knox County). Diverse habitats; migratory. Eastern affinities.* #

Hoary bat. *Lasiurus cinereus.* Throughout region (Sioux County to Knox County). Wooded areas; migratory. Widespread.* #

Townsend's (western) big-eared bat. *Plecotus townsendii.* Panhandle (Sheridan County) and adjacent eastern Wyoming. Coniferous forests; hibernator. At eastern limits in Niobrara Valley. Western affinities.

Family Leporidae—Hares and Rabbits

Desert cottontail. *Sylvilagus auduboni.* Common in west. Drier grasslands, especially mixed-grass and shortgrass prairies. At eastern range limits in Niobrara Valley (east to Todd County, South Dakota). Western affinities.*

Eastern cottontail. *Sylvilagus floridanus.* Throughout region. Woodlands and taller grasslands. At western range limits in Niobrara Valley. Eastern affinities.* #

Black-tailed jackrabbit. *Lepus californicus.* Uncommon to rare. Grasslands, especially mixed-grass prairies and disturbed habitats. Widespread.* #

White-tailed jackrabbit. *Lepus townsendii.* Local and increasingly rare. Grasslands, especially in mixed-grass or Sandhills prairies. Great Plains affinities.*

Family Sciuridae—Squirrels

Least chipmunk. *Eutamias minimus.* Sioux and Dawes counties of Nebraska and adjacent eastern Wyoming. Coniferous woods. At eastern range limits in Niobrara Valley. Western affinities.

Woodchuck. *Marmota monax.* Local; north rarely to Brown and Cherry counties. Open woodlands. At western range limits in Niobrara Valley, but still expanding westward. Eastern affinities.

Franklin's ground squirrel. *Spermophilus franklini.* West to Rock County. Tallgrass prairies. At western range limits in Niobrara Valley. Great Plains affinities.*

Spotted ground squirrel. *Spermophilus spilosoma.* Local in upper and central Niobrara Valley (Sioux County to Rock County, Nebraska, and adjacent eastern Wyoming, north to Todd County, South Dakota. Sandy soils with shrubby vegetation. At or near northern range limits in Niobrara Valley. Southwestern affinities.*

Thirteen-lined ground squirrel. *Spermophilus tridecemlineatus.* Throughout region. Grasslands, especially mixed-grass prairies. Great Plains affinities.*

Black-tailed prairie dog. *Cynomys ludovicianus.* Upper Niobrara Valley of Nebraska and adjacent eastern Wyoming, east to Boyd and Holt counties, Nebraska, and Gregory county, South Dakota. Drier grasslands. Surveys in 2003 estimated 17,361 acres of active colonies in the Niobrara region, with 58 percent in Box Butte County and most of the rest in Dawes (17 percent) and Sioux (16 percent) counties (Bischof, Fritz, and Hack 2004). Near eastern range limits in central Niobrara Valley. Great Plains affinities. Candidate for federal listing as threatened under the Endangered Species Act until August 2004, when delisted.*

Fox squirrel. *Sciurus niger*. Pine Ridge counties of Nebraska and adjacent eastern Wyoming; Todd County to Gregory County of South Dakota. Deciduous woods. Eastern affinities.*

Family Geomyidae—Pocket Gophers

Northern pocket gopher. *Thomomys talpoides*. Sioux and Dawes counties of Nebraska and adjacent eastern Wyoming; Todd County to Gregory County of South Dakota. Grasslands, especially mixed-grass or sandsage prairie. Probably declining. At eastern range limits in Niobrara Valley. Northwestern affinities.

Plains pocket gopher. *Geomys bursarius*. Throughout region. Grasslands, especially taller grasslands. Great Plains affinities.*

Family Heteromyidae—Heteromyid Rodents

Olive-backed pocket mouse. *Perognathus fasciatus*. Local from Pine Ridge counties of Nebraska and adjacent eastern Wyoming east to Cherry and probably Keya Paha counties in Nebraska, and to Gregory County in South Dakota. Shortgrass prairie, Sandhills. At eastern range limits in Niobrara Valley. Great Plains affinities. A state-listed sensitive species.*

Plains pocket mouse. *Perognathus flavescens*. Widespread, with no records from Pine Ridge, but reported from adjacent eastern Wyoming. Sandhills and sandsage or mixed-grass prairie. Near western range limits in Niobrara Valley. Great Plains affinities.*

Silky pocket mouse. *Perognathus flavus*. Rare in upper Niobrara Valley of Nebraska and adjacent eastern Wyoming, east to Cherry County in Nebraska, north to Todd County in South Dakota. Drier grasslands, especially mixed-grass prairie, Sandhills. At eastern range limits in Niobrara Valley. Western affinities.*

Hispid pocket mouse. *Perognathus hispidus*. Throughout region. Sandy grasslands. Great Plains affinities.*

Ord's kangaroo rat. *Dipodomys ordii*. Throughout region, common. Sandy grasslands. Western affinities.*

Family Castoridae—Beavers

Beaver. *Castor canadensis*. Throughout region. Creeks, rivers, riparian wetlands. Widespread.*

Family Cricetidae—Rats, Mice, Lemmings, and Voles

Western harvest mouse. *Reithrodontomys megalotis.* Throughout region. Taller grasslands. Western affinities.*

Plains harvest mouse. *Reithrodontomys montanus.* Throughout region. Mixed-grass grasslands. Rare. Western affinities.*

White-footed mouse. *Peromyscus leucopus.* Common, mainly east and central, but west to Sioux County, Nebraska, and adjacent eastern Wyoming. Diverse terrestrial habitats. Near western range limits in Niobrara Valley but expanding westward. Widespread.*

Deer mouse. *Peromyscus maniculatus.* Throughout region. Diverse open habitats. Widespread.*

Northern grasshopper mouse. *Onychomys leucogaster.* Widespread. Grasslands, especially sandy and mixed-grass prairies. Great Plains affinities.*

Bushy-tailed wood rat. *Neotoma cinerea.* Panhandle counties of Nebraska and adjacent eastern Wyoming. Rocky slopes and crevices. At eastern range limits in Niobrara Valley. Western affinities.

Eastern wood rat. *Neotoma floridana.* Endemic race (*N. f. baileyii*) in central Niobrara Valley (Cherry and probably Keya Paha counties, north to South Dakota's Todd, Tripp, and Gregory counties). Woodlands, buildings, rock outcrops. A relict and isolated population of a southern and eastern species. Eastern affinities. State-listed sensitive species.*

Southern bog lemming. *Synaptomys cooperi.* Local, Knox and Antelope counties west to eastern Cherry County; also Gregory County in South Dakota. Fens and dense grassy habitats. At northwestern range limits in Niobrara Valley. Eastern affinities.*

Prairie vole. *Microtus ochrogaster.* Throughout region. Taller grasslands. Great Plains affinities.*

Meadow vole. *Microtus pennsylvanicus.* Throughout region. Moist grasslands. Northern affinities.*

Muskrat. *Ondatra zibethicus.* Throughout region. Aquatic habitats. Widespread.*

Family Muridae—Old World Rats and Mice

House mouse. *Mus musculus.* Introduced; statewide near human habitations.*

Norway rat. *Rattus norvegicus.* Introduced; statewide near human habitations.*

Family Zapodidae—Jumping Mice

Meadow jumping mouse. *Zapus hudsonius.* East and central Niobrara Valley, locally reaching eastern Wyoming. Grassy or herbaceous habitats. Near western range limits in Niobrara Valley. Northern affinities.*

Family Erethizontidae—New World Porcupines

Porcupine. *Erethizon dorsatum.* Throughout region, more common in west. Diverse woodlands. Widespread.*

Family Canidae—Coyotes, Wolves, and Foxes

Coyote. *Canis latrans.* Throughout region. Open country, especially grasslands. Widespread.*

Swift fox. *Vulpes velox.* Rare and local in Sioux, Dawes, and Box Butte counties of Nebraska and adjacent eastern Wyoming. Native shortgrass prairies. Primarily limited to Sioux County, but reported east to Todd County in South Dakota. At eastern range limits in Niobrara Valley; no recent records exist for central Niobrara Valley. Great Plains affinities. State-listed as endangered; candidate for listing under the Endangered Species Act.

Red fox. *Vulpes vulpes.* Throughout region. Woodland edges, grasslands. Widespread.*

Gray fox. *Urocyon cineroargenteus.* Mainly from Boyd and Holt counties east, but increasing westward, with recent records to Sioux County, Nebraska, and adjacent eastern Wyoming. Deciduous woods. At western range limits in Niobrara Valley. Southern affinities.*

Family Felidae—Cats

Mountain lion. *Puma concolor.* Rare but increasing in Niobrara Valley; several recent regional records (Sioux, Box Butte, Dawes, Cherry, and Brown counties). Riparian woodlands and rocky topography. Western affinities.

Bobcat. *Felis rufus.* Increasingly common throughout region. Favors rocky topography. Widespread.*

Family Procyonidae—Raccoons and Allies

Raccoon. *Procyon lotor*. Throughout region. Riparian woodlands. Widespread.*

Family Mustelidae—Weasels, Badgers, Skunks, and Otters

Long-tailed weasel. *Mustela frenata*. Throughout region. Grasslands and woods. Widespread.*

Black-footed ferret. *Mustela nigripes*. Extirpated. Historical specimens are known from Sioux, Sheridan, and Box Butte counties, Nebraska, and from Todd County, South Dakota. Listed without documentation as "uncommon" in proposed Norden Dam project area (U.S. Bureau of Reclamation 1978). Open grasslands with prairie dogs. Great Plains affinities.

Wolverine. *Gulo luscus*. Extirpated; no specific regional locality records. Listed without documentation as "uncommon" in Norden Dam project area (U.S. Bureau of Reclamation 1978). No regional specimen records or other evidence of prior regional occurrence.

Least weasel. *Mustela nivalis*. Throughout region. Diverse habitats. Northern affinities.*

Mink. *Mustela vison*. Entire Niobrara Valley. Rivers and marshes. Widespread.*

Badger. *Taxidea taxus*. Throughout region. Grasslands, especially drier grasslands. Widespread.*

Spotted skunk. *Spilogale putorius*. Throughout region but rare and apparently declining. Forest edges. Southern affinities. A candidate for listing under the Endangered Species Act.*

Striped skunk. *Mephitis mephitis*. Throughout region. Diverse habitats. Widespread.*

Northern river otter. *Lutra canadensis*. Very rare; reintroduced along Niobrara and Elkhorn rivers. Rivers and streams with good fish populations. State endangered. Widespread.*

Family Cervidae—Deer, Elk, and Moose

Elk (wapiti). *Cervus elaphus*. The historical Plains race (*C. e. manitobensis*) was extirpated statewide by about 1900, but the Rocky Mountain race (*C. e. nelsoni*) has established itself in Pine Ridge (Sioux, Dawes, and Sheridan counties) and is local east to the central Niobrara Valley (Tripp County, South Dakota, and Boyd County, Nebraska). Grasslands and coniferous forests. Western affinities.

Mule deer. *Odocoileus hemionus*. West and central (most common from Cherry County west). Grasslands with hilly or irregular topography. Declining; at eastern range limits in Niobrara Valley. Western affinities.*

White-tailed deer. *Odocoileus virginianus*. Throughout region. Most common eastward but expanding westward and now constituting about 20 percent of combined population of mule deer and white-tailed deer as far west as Sioux County). Forests, riparian woodlands, and grasslands. Widespread.*

Family Bovidae—Cattle, Sheep, and Goats

Bison. *Bison bison*. Extirpated, but reintroduced locally as confined herds (Fort Robinson State Park, Fort Niobrara National Wildlife Refuge, Niobrara Valley Preserve, and private lands). Mixed-grass and shortgrass prairies. Widespread.

Bighorn sheep. *Ovis canadensis*. Extirpated (the Great Plains race *O. c. auduboni*) by 1900 from upper and middle Niobrara Valley. The Rocky Mountain race *O. c. canadensis* was successfully introduced in 1981 at Fort Robinson State Park, from where it has been slowly expanding northward. Rimrock, badlands, and similar rocky topography. Western affinities.

Family Antilocapridae—Pronghorns

Pronghorn. *Antilocapra americana*. Once nearly extirpated, but reestablished and most common in Panhandle. At eastern range limits in Nebraska's central Niobrara Valley (reaching Brown and Keya Paha counties); also locally east to the Missouri River in adjacent South Dakota. Open grasslands; Great Plains affinities.*

Appendix 1B

Birds of the Niobrara Region

This list of 323 species from the greater Niobrara region excludes several accidental, extirpated, and extinct species. Although the Niobrara region represents less than 20 percent of the state's total area, the 323 species represent 73 percent of the entire state's total list of about 440 bird species and nearly 90 percent of the approximately 365 species that are regularly reported from Nebraska. As here defined, the Niobrara region extends from the Nebraska-Wyoming border east to include the Pine Ridge counties and the entire Niobrara Valley of Nebraska to Knox County, north to include three adjoining counties of South Dakota that fall in part within the Niobrara drainage, and south as far as the southern limits of the Niobrara drainage, including Valentine National Wildlife Refuge in central Cherry County.

Regional bird surveys of five selected sections of the entire Niobrara Valley of Nebraska have been summarized by Ducey (1989). The birds of the upper Niobrara Valley and Pine Ridge region of northwestern Nebraska (Sioux, Dawes, Box Butte, and Sheridan counties) were documented by Rosche (1982). Brogie and Mossman (1983) and Mossman and Brogie (1983) surveyed spring and summer birds of the Niobrara Valley Preserve in the middle Niobrara Valley (Cherry, Brown, and Keya Paha counties).

The birds of three South Dakota counties (Tripp, Todd, and Gregory) that lie at least in part within the Niobrara drainage were documented by Tallman, Swanson, and Palmer (2002). Birds of the Wyoming latilong that includes the Niobrara's headwaters in Niobrara County were summarized by Luce et al. (1997). These two references are the basis for occasional comments about bird records from the edges of the Niobrara drainage occurring within the boundaries of southern South Dakota and eastern Wyoming. The following species list is based on the regional studies mentioned above, on local checklists for Fort Niobrara and Valentine National Wildlife Refuges, and on breeding data from the 1980s as mapped and summarized by Mollhoff (2001). Asterisks (*) identify 178 known historical or current breeders within the region. Parenthetical "east" and "west" designations indicate general geographic ranges within the Niobrara Valley. Zoogeographic affinity categories (Great Plains, northern, southern, eastern, western, and widespread) are indicated only for known breeding species and are based on my own judgment.

Abundance categories (common, uncommon, occasional, casual, and rare) are used as general descriptors for species with progressively fewer regional occurrences. "Vagrant" describes migrant species well out of their usual ranges, and "local" refers to species having geographically variable or relatively limited breeding distributions within the Niobrara region. Indicated habitat preferences are often generalized and may apply only to Nebraska. Month-defined occurrence statements for migrants are based on historical statewide averages of first and last sightings (Johnsgard 2005).

State and federally recognized "rare" and "threatened" species are noted, as are other species of state-level conservation concern, as judged by various authorities. Species shown with a pound symbol (#) are those recently identified by Partners in Flight (2004) as Prairie Biome species of continental conservation importance. A total of twenty-seven bird species reported from the Niobrara Scenic River region are classified as "sensitive" by the Nebraska Natural Heritage Program (U.S. Department of Interior, National Park Service 2005). These species are shown in **boldface**.

The list follows the traditional taxonomic sequence of families and genera; congeneric species are arranged alphabetically by their Latin specific names.

Family Anatidae—Swans, Geese, and Ducks

Greater white-fronted goose. *Anser albifrons.* Common spring (early March to mid-April) and fall (mid-October to mid-November) migrant. Marshy wetlands.

Snow goose. *Chen caerulescens.* Very common spring (early March to mid-April) and fall (early October to early December) migrant. Marshy wetlands.

Ross's goose. *Chen rossii*. Occasional migrant (early March to mid-April) and fall (early October to early December). Marshy wetlands.

Canada goose. *Branta canadensis*. Common semipermanent to permanent resident. Diverse wetlands. Widespread.*

Cackling goose. *Branta hutchinsii*. Common spring and fall migrant. Few available migration records, since these small arctic- to subarctic-breeding populations were only recently (2004) recognized as a distinct species. Previously they had been considered part of a multiple-subspecies complex (*B. hutchinsii*, *B. taverneri*, and other non-Nebraskan races) of the Canada goose. Marshy wetlands.

Trumpeter swan. *Cygnus buccinator*. Local semipermanent to permanent resident, breeding in larger Sandhills marshes, especially in Cherry and Sheridan counties and adjacent South Dakota (probably east to Todd County), wintering locally. Marshy wetlands, lakes. Great Plains and western affinities.*

Tundra swan. *Cygnus columbianus*. Casual migrant, March and November. Marshy wetlands, lakes.

Wood duck. *Aix sponsa*. Common summer resident, late March to late October. Wooded wetlands. Eastern affinities.*

Northern pintail. *Anas acuta*. Common summer resident, March to December, sometimes overwintering. Marshy wetlands. Widespread.*

American wigeon. *Anas americana*. Common summer resident, mid-March to late September. Marshy wetlands. Widespread.*

Northern shoveler. *Anas clypeata*. Common summer resident, March to November. Marshy wetlands. Widespread.*

Green-winged teal. *Anas crecca*. Common migrant and occasional summer resident, mid-March to early November. Marshy wetlands. Widespread.*

Cinnamon teal. *Anas cyanoptera*. Local summer resident, April to October (west). Western affinities; at eastern breeding limits in upper Niobrara Valley. Marshy, often alkaline, wetlands.*

Blue-winged teal. *Anas discors*. Common summer resident, early April to mid-October. Marshy wetlands. Widespread.*

Eurasian wigeon. *Anas penelope*. Rare spring and fall migrant. Marshy wetlands.

Mallard. *Anas platyrhynchos*. Common semipermanent resident, sometimes overwintering. Diverse wetlands. Widespread.*

American black duck. *Anas rubripes*. Rare migrant. Marshy wetlands.

Gadwall. *Anas strepera*. Common summer resident, late March to late November. Marshy wetlands. Widespread.*

Lesser scaup. *Aythya affinis*. Common migrant, sometimes summering, mid-March to mid-October. Deeper marshes and lakes.

Redhead. *Aythya americana*. Common local summer resident, mid-March to mid-November. Deeper marshes and lakes. Great Plains affinities.*

Ring-necked duck. *Aythya collaris*. Common migrant, sometimes summering, late March to mid-October. Deeper marshes and lakes.

Greater scaup. *Aythya marila*. Uncommon to rare wintering migrant, late October to April. Deeper marshes and lakes.

Canvasback. *Aythya valisineria*. Uncommon local summer resident, mid-March to mid-November. Deeper marshes and lakes. Great Plains affinities.*

White-winged scoter. *Melanitta fusca*. Rare fall migrant, October to December. Deeper marshes and lakes.

Black scoter. *Melanitta nigra*. Rare migrant, March to May and September to December. Deeper marshes and lakes.

Surf scoter. *Melanitta perspicillata*. Uncommon migrant, late April to late May and October to December. Deeper marshes and lakes.

Long-tailed duck. *Clangula hyemalis*. Rare migrant, February to April and October to December. Deeper marshes and lakes.

Bufflehead. *Bucephala albeola*. Common migrant, mid-March to late April and mid-October to late November. Marshes and lakes.

Common goldeneye. *Bucephala clangula*. Common migrant, early March to early April and mid-November to mid-December. Deeper marshes and lakes.

Barrow's goldeneye. *Bucephala islandica*. Rare migrant. Deeper marshes and lakes.

Hooded merganser. *Lophodytes cucullatus*. Uncommon migrant, casual summer resident, late March to late November. Clear rivers, marshes, and lakes.*

Common merganser. *Mergus merganser*. Common migrant, early March to late April and mid-November to mid-December, casual summer resident. Deeper marshes, clear rivers, and lakes.

Red-breasted merganser. *Mergus serrator*. Uncommon migrant, late March to late April and early to late November. Deeper marshes, clear rivers, and lakes.

Ruddy duck. *Oxyura jamaicensis*. Common local summer resident, early April to mid-November. Marshes and silt-bottomed lakes. Great Plains affinities.*

Family Phasianidae—Partridges, Grouse, and Turkeys

Gray partridge. *Perdix perdix*. Rare (introduced) resident. At or near southern breeding limits in Niobrara Valley (breedings reported from Cherry and Knox counties, southern range limits seemingly unstable). Grasslands, croplands, prairies.*

Ring-necked pheasant. *Phasianus colchicus*. Common (introduced) resident. Grasslands, croplands, prairies.*

Greater prairie chicken. *Tympanuchus cupido*. Uncommon resident. At western breeding limits in central Niobrara Valley (west to Cherry County, Nebraska, possibly also to Tripp County, South Dakota). Eastern affinities. Native grasslands, grainfields, prairies.* #

Sharp-tailed grouse. *Tympanuchus phasianellus jamesi*. Common resident. Great Plains affinities. Native grasslands, prairies.* #

Wild turkey. *Meleagris gallopavo*. Locally common (reintroduced) resident. Woodland edges. Eastern affinities.*

Family Odontophoridae—New World Quail

Northern bobwhite. *Colinus virginianus*. Rare to uncommon resident (east). Eastern affinities; at western breeding limits in central Niobrara Valley (Gregory County, South Dakota, and Cherry County, Nebraska. Grasslands, brush, woodland edges.*

Family Gaviidae—Loons

Common loon. *Gavia immer*. Common migrant, March to May and late October to early November. Rivers and lakes.

Pacific loon. *Gavia pacifica.* Rare migrant, April to May and October to November. Rivers and lakes.

Family Podicipedidae—Grebes

Pied-billed grebe. *Podilymbus podiceps.* Common summer resident, early April to early November. Marshy wetlands. Widespread.*

Horned grebe. *Podiceps auritus.* Uncommon migrant, mid-April to early May and early October to mid-November. Marshy wetlands.

Red-necked grebe. *Podiceps grisegena.* Extremely rare migrant, April and October to November. Larger wetlands.

Eared grebe. *Podiceps nigricollis.* Common local summer resident, mid-April to mid-October (west). Western affinities; at eastern breeding limits in Niobrara Valley (Valentine National Wildlife Refuge). Marshy wetlands. Widespread.*

Clark's grebe. *Aechmophorus clarkii.* Rare local summer resident, early May to early October. Western affinities; at eastern breeding limits in Niobrara Valley (Valentine National Wildlife Refuge). Larger marshy wetlands; lakes.*

Western grebe. *Aechmophorus occidentalis.* Common local summer resident, early May to early October. Western affinities; at eastern breeding limits in Niobrara Valley (Valentine National Wildlife Refuge). Larger marshy wetlands; lakes.*

Family Pelecanidae—Pelicans

American white pelican. *Pelecanus erythrorhynchos.* Common nonbreeding summer resident, late April to mid-October. Rivers and lakes.

Family Phalacrocoracidae—Cormorants

Double-crested cormorant. *Phalacrocorax auritus.* Common summer resident, mid-April to late September. Rivers, marshes, and lakes. Widespread.*

Family Ardeidae—Bitterns and Herons

American bittern. *Botaurus lentiginosus.* Common summer resident, early May to early October. Marshy wetlands. Widespread.*

Least bittern. *Ixobrychus exilis.* Rare summer resident, mid-May to mid-August. Marshy wetlands. Widespread.*

Great egret. *Ardea alba*. Occasional to rare nonbreeding summer resident, late April to early September. Diverse wetland edges.

Great blue heron. *Ardea herodias*. Common summer resident, early April to mid-October. Diverse wetland edges. Widespread.*

Little blue heron. *Egretta caerulea*. Occasional to rare nonbreeding summer resident, early May to mid-August. Wetland edges.

Snowy egret. *Egretta thula*. Irregular summer resident, rare breeder, early May to mid-August. Wetland edges. Widespread.*

Cattle egret. *Bubulcus ibis*. Rare summer resident, early May to late August. Pastures and wetlands. Self-introduced.*

Green heron. *Butorides virescens*. Common summer resident, late April to mid-September. Wooded wetland edges. Eastern affinities.*

Black-crowned night heron. *Nycticorax nycticorax*. Common summer resident, late April to early September. Marshy wetlands. Widespread.*

Yellow-crowned night heron. *Nyctanassa violacea*. Rare summer visitor or possible breeder, early May to early September. Wetland edges.

Family Threskiornithidae—Ibises and Spoonbills
White-faced ibis. *Plegadis chihi*. Rare and local (Valentine National Wildlife Refuge) summer resident, April to October. Marshy wetlands, meadows. Western affinities.*

Family Cathartidae—American Vultures
Turkey vulture. *Cathartes aura*. Common summer resident, mid-April to late September. Open country. Widespread.*

Family Accipitridae—Kites, Hawks, Eagles, and Allies
Osprey. *Pandion haliaetus*. Uncommon migrant, late April to early May and mid-September to mid-October. Recent releases of young birds in South Dakota below the Missouri confluence are likely to result in breeding populations in the Niobrara drainage. Clear rivers and lakes.

Bald eagle. *Haliaeetus leucocephalus*. Uncommon overwintering migrant, rare or local resident. Population increasing, with recent nestings in Gregory County, South Dakota, and along the middle and lower Niobrara River in Nebraska. Rivers, lakes, larger wetlands. Widespread.*

Northern harrier. *Circus cyaneus*. Uncommon summer resident mid-

March to early December. Prairies, meadows, and marshes. Great Plains affinities.*

Cooper's hawk. *Accipiter cooperii.* Uncommon wintering migrant, mid-September to late April, and local breeding resident. Mature forests. Widespread.*

Northern goshawk. *Accipiter gentilis.* Rare wintering migrant, September to late April. Mature forests.

Sharp-shinned hawk. *Accipiter striatus.* Rare resident, common wintering migrant. Forests, suburbs in winter. Widespread.*

Red-tailed hawk. *Buteo jamaicensis.* Common resident. Open plains and woodland edges. Widespread.*

Rough-legged hawk. *Buteo lagopus.* Common wintering migrant, early November to late March. Open plains.

Red-shouldered hawk. *Buteo lineatus.* Rare vagrant. Deciduous forests.

Ferruginous hawk. *Buteo regalis.* Uncommon to rare resident (west). Great Plains and western affinities. At eastern breeding limits in central Niobrara Valley (Cherry County). Open plains. Candidate for listing under the Endangered Species Act.*

Broad-winged hawk. *Buteo platypterus.* Rare migrant, late April to mid-May and mid-September to early October. Deciduous forests.

Swainson's hawk. *Buteo swainsoni.* Common summer resident, mid-April to late September. Open plains. Great Plains and western affinities.* #

Golden eagle. *Aquila chrysaetos.* Uncommon resident (west). Western affinities; at eastern breeding limits in upper Niobrara Valley (Sheridan County, Nebraska, probably east to Todd County, South Dakota). Open plains, rimrock.*

Family Falconidae—Falcons

Merlin. *Falco columbarius.* Uncommon wintering migrant, October to March, and rare summer resident (west). Northern affinities; at southern breeding limits in upper Niobrara Valley (Sioux County). Open plains, woodland edges.*

Prairie falcon. *Falco mexicanus.* Local resident (west). Great Plains and western affinities; at eastern breeding limits in upper Niobrara Valley (Sheridan County). Open plains, rimrock, bluffs.*

Peregrine falcon. *Falco peregrinus.* Occasional migrant, mid-September to late March. Previously listed as state- and federally threatened; recently delisted. Open plains, wetlands, cities.

Gyrfalcon. *Falco rusticolus.* Casual wintering migrant, November to March. Open plains, sandhills.

American kestrel. *Falco sparverius.* Common summer resident, often over-wintering. Open country, Woodland edges, suburbs. Widespread.*

Family Rallidae—Rails, Gallinules, and Coots
Virginia rail. *Rallus limicola.* Uncommon summer resident, early May to mid-September. Marshy wetlands. Widespread.*

Sora. *Porzana carolina.* Common summer resident, early May to late September. Marshy wetlands. Widespread.*

Common moorhen. *Gallinula chloropus.* Occasional summer resident, mid-May to late August. Marshy wetlands. Widespread.*

American coot. *Fulica americana.* Common summer resident, late March to early November. Marshy wetlands. Widespread.*

Family Gruidae—Cranes
Whooping crane. *Grus americana.* Rare migrant, late March to early May and mid-September to early November, and possible historical breeder. State and federally endangered. Wide rivers, meadows, large marshes.

Sandhill crane. *Grus canadensis.* Common migrant, early March to mid-April and early October to early November. A historical Sandhills breeder and an undocumented 2003 breeding observation in Sioux County (Mary Hunt, pers. comm.). Wide, braided rivers, marshes, grainfields.

Family Charadriidae—Plovers
American golden plover. *Pluvialis dominica.* Common migrant, May and late September to mid-October. Grasslands, open shorelines.

Black-bellied plover. *Pluvialis squatarola.* Common migrant, May and late August to early October. Grasslands, open shorelines.

Snowy plover. *Charadrius alexandrinus.* Rare migrant, April to May and August to September. Open sandy shorelines.

Piping plover. *Charadrius melodus.* Rare migrant and summer resident (east), mid-May to mid-September. Near southern Great Plains breeding limits in central Niobrara Valley (Cherry County to Knox County). State and federally listed as threatened. River sandbars, sandy shorelines. Widespread.*

Semipalmated plover. *Charadrius semipalmatus.* Common migrant, May and mid-August to mid-September. Open sandy shorelines.

Killdeer. *Charadrius vociferus.* Very common summer resident, mid-March to mid-October. Gravelly shorelines, roadsides. Widespread.*

Family Recurvirostridae—Stilts and Avocets

American avocet. *Recurvirostra americana.* Local summer resident, late April to early September. Open shorelines, alkaline wetlands. Western affinities, at eastern breeding limits in wetlands of central Niobrara Valley (Valentine National Wildlife Refuge).*

Family Scolopacidae—Sandpipers and Phalaropes

Lesser yellowlegs. *Tringa flavipes.* Common migrant, mid-April to mid-May and mid-August to early October. Muddy and grassy shorelines.

Greater yellowlegs. *Tringa melanoleuca.* Common migrant, mid-April to early May and mid-August to early October. Muddy and grassy shorelines.

Solitary sandpiper. *Tringa solitaria.* Common migrant, early to mid-May and early August to early September. Muddy and grassy shorelines.

Willet. *Catoptrophorus semipalmatus.* Local summer resident, late April to late August. Meadows, grassy shorelines. Great Plains and western affinities; at eastern breeding limits in central Niobrara Valley (Valentine National Wildlife Refuge).*

Spotted sandpiper. *Actitis macularius.* Common summer resident, early May to early September. Rocky shorelines.*

Upland sandpiper. *Bartramia longicauda.* Common summer resident, early May to late August. Meadows, prairies. Great Plains and northern affinities.*

Long-billed curlew. *Numenius americanus.* Common summer resident, mid-April to mid-August. Meadows, prairies, pastures. Great Plains and western affinities; at eastern breeding limits in Niobrara Valley (Valentine

National Wildlife Refuge, Nebraska; Todd County, South Dakota).*

Whimbrel. *Numenius phaeopus.* Rare spring migrant, April to mid-May. Marshes, shorelines.

Marbled godwit. *Limosa fedoa.* Uncommon migrant and very rare summer resident (late April to mid-September) in northern Sandhills (1990 and possible 2003 nestings in Sheridan County). Nesting along South Dakota's border counties is still undocumented. Meadows, marshes, prairies. Great Plains affinities.*

Hudsonian godwit. *Limosa haemastica.* Rare spring migrant, late April to mid-May. Shorelines, marshy wetlands.

Ruddy turnstone. *Arenaria interpres.* Rare spring migrant, April to May. Rocky shorelines.

Sanderling. *Calidris alba.* Occasional to rare migrant, early to mid-May and late August to early October. Sandy shorelines.

Dunlin. *Calidris alpina.* Rare migrant, May and September. Grassy and muddy shorelines.

Baird's sandpiper. *Calidris bairdii.* Very common migrant, mid-April to mid-May and mid-August to early October. Grassy and muddy shorelines.

Red knot. *Calidris canutus.* Rare migrant, May and September. Sandy shorelines, marshes.

White-rumped sandpiper. *Calidris fuscicollis.* Very common migrant, late April to mid-May and August, mainly in spring. Grassy and muddy shorelines.

Stilt sandpiper. *Calidris himantopus.* Common migrant, early to mid-May and mid-August to mid-September. Grassy and muddy shorelines.

Western sandpiper. *Calidris mauri.* Common migrant, early to mid-May and mid-August to early September. Grassy and muddy shorelines.

Pectoral sandpiper. *Calidris melanotos.* Common migrant, late April to mid-May and September to October. Grassy and muddy shorelines.

Least sandpiper. *Calidris minutilla.* Common migrant, May and early August to mid-September. Grassy and muddy shorelines.

Semipalmated sandpiper. *Calidris pusilla.* Common migrant, late April to mid-May and early August to mid-September. Grassy and muddy shorelines.

Buff-breasted sandpiper. *Tryngites subruficollis.* Rare migrant, May and September (east). Fields, pastures, meadows, shorelines.

Short-billed dowitcher. *Limnodromus griseus.* Casual migrant, May and August to September (east). Grassy and muddy shorelines.

Long-billed dowitcher. *Limnodromus scolopaceus.* Common migrant, early to mid-May and early August to mid-October. Grassy and muddy shorelines.

Wilson's snipe. *Gallinago delicata.* Local summer resident in wetlands, mid-April to mid-November. Marshy wetlands. Northern affinities.*

American woodcock. *Scolopax minor.* Local summer resident, mid-April to mid-October (east). Moist forest edges. Eastern affinities; at western breeding limits in lower Niobrara Valley (Boyd County, Nebraska, and Gregory County, South Dakota).*

Red-necked phalarope. *Phalaropus lobatus.* Uncommon migrant, May and mid-August to late September. Marshy and alkaline wetlands.

Wilson's phalarope. *Phalaropus tricolor.* Local summer resident, early May to early September. Marshy and alkaline wetlands. Northern affinities; near southeastern breeding limits in central Niobrara Valley (Valentine National Wildlife Refuge).*

Family Laridae—Gulls and Terns

Herring gull. *Larus argentatus.* Uncommon nonbreeding resident. Wetlands, fields, landfills.

California gull. *Larus californicus.* Rare vagrant (west). Wetlands, fields, landfills.

Ring-billed gull. *Larus delawarensis.* Common nonbreeding resident. Diverse wetlands, fields, landfills.

Lesser black-backed gull. *Larus fuscus.* Rare vagrant. Diverse wetlands.

Bonaparte's gull. *Larus philadelphia.* Rare migrant, April to May and September to October. Diverse wetlands.

Franklin's gull. *Larus pipixcan.* Common migrant, mid-April to mid-May) and early September to mid-October. Cultivated fields, pastures, marshes.

Least tern. *Sterna antillarum.* Local summer resident, late May to mid-August (Niobrara River, west to Fort Niobrara National Wildlife

Refuge). State and federally endangered species. River sandbars, sandy shorelines. Widespread.*

Caspian tern. *Sterna caspia*. Rare vagrant, early May to mid-September. Larger wetlands, clear rivers, lakes.

Forster's tern. *Sterna forsteri*. Local summer resident, late April to mid-September (Sandhills wetlands). Larger marshes, creeks. Widespread.*

Common tern. *Sterna hirundo*. Uncommon migrant, May and September (east). Lakes and clear rivers.

Black tern. *Chlidonias niger*. Local summer resident, mid-May to early September. At southeastern breeding limits in wetlands of Niobrara Valley (Valentine National Wildlife Refuge). Marshy wetlands. Widespread. Candidate for listing under the Endangered Species Act.*

Family Columbidae—Pigeons and Doves
Rock pigeon. *Columba livia*. Introduced. Common resident. Farms, cities.*

Mourning dove. *Zenaida macroura*. Common summer resident late March to early November. Diverse open habitats. Widespread.*

Family Cuculidae—Cuckoos and Anis
Yellow-billed cuckoo. *Coccyzus americanus*. Common summer resident, late May to mid-September. Woodland edges, forests. Eastern and southern affinities.*

Black-billed cuckoo. *Coccyzus erythropthalmus*. Occasional summer resident, late May to late August. Eastern affinities. Woodland edges, forests.*

Family Tytonidae—Barn Owls
Barn owl. *Tyto alba*. Rare resident. Open country. Widespread.*

Family Strigidae—Typical Owls
Eastern screech owl. *Megascops asio*. Common resident. Forests, parks, suburbs. Eastern affinities; at western breeding limits in upper Niobrara Valley (Sioux County, Nebraska, and adjacent eastern Wyoming).*

Snowy owl. *Bubo scandiaca*. Rare wintering migrant, November to April. Open plains, sandhills.

Great horned owl. *Bubo virginianus*. Common resident. Forests, woodland edges, open plains. Widespread.*

Burrowing owl. *Athene cunicularia.* Uncommon to rare summer resident, late April to mid-September (west). Prairie dog burrows, other mammalian burrows, or natural cavities. Candidate for listing under the Endangered Species Act. Western affinities; near eastern breeding limits in lower Niobrara Valley (Rock County).*

Great gray owl. *Strix nebulosa.* Accidental winter migrant. Coniferous forests.

Barred owl. *Strix varia.* Rare resident (east). Mature forests. Eastern affinities; at probable western breeding limits of Great Plains range in lower Niobrara Valley (possibly Knox County).*

Long-eared owl. *Asio otus.* Rare resident. Forests. Widespread.*

Short-eared owl. *Asio flammeus.* Uncommon resident. Grasslands, marshes. Widespread.* #

Northern saw-whet owl. *Aegolius acadicus.* Uncommon wintering migrant, November to February, possible rare summer resident in Pine Ridge (breeding record for Shannon County, South Dakota). Coniferous forests (breeding), juniper thickets (winter).

Family Caprimulgidae—Goatsuckers

Common nighthawk. *Chordeiles minor.* Common summer resident, late May to mid-September. Urban, open country. Widespread.*

Common poorwill. *Phalaenoptilus nuttallii.* Local summer resident, early May to early September (west). Rocky canyons, scrub. Western affinities; at eastern breeding limits in central Niobrara Valley (Keya Paha County, Nebraska, and Todd County, South Dakota).*

Whip-poor-will. *Caprimulgus vociferus.* Uncommon summer resident, early May to early September (east). Deciduous riverine forests. Eastern affinities; at western breeding limits in lower Niobrara Valley (possibly to Holt County).*

Family Apodidae—Swifts

Chimney swift. *Chaetura pelagica.* Uncommon summer resident, late April to early October (east). Urban. Eastern affinities; at western breeding limits in upper Niobrara Valley (Sioux County).*

White-throated swift. *Aeronautes saxatalis.* Local summer resident, mid-

May to late August (west). Steep cliffs, canyons. Western affinities; at eastern breeding limits in Pine Ridge (Sioux County).*

Family Trochilidae—Hummingbirds

Ruby-throated hummingbird. *Archilochus colubris.* Uncommon migrant and possible but unproven rare summer resident, mid-May to mid-September (east). Floodplain forest, woodland edges.*

Broad-tailed hummingbird. *Selasphorus platycercus.* Rare early fall migrant, August to September (west). Woodland edges.

Rufous hummingbird. *Selasphorus rufus.* Rare late summer migrant, August (west). Woodland edges.

Family Alcedinidae—Kingfishers

Belted kingfisher. *Ceryle alcyon.* Uncommon summer resident, mid-March to mid-November. Rivers, creeks. Widespread.*

Family Picidae—Woodpeckers

Red-bellied woodpecker. *Melanerpes carolinus.* Uncommon resident (east). Open woods. Eastern affinities; at western breeding limits in upper Niobrara Valley (Sioux County).*

Red-headed woodpecker. *Melanerpes erythrocephalus.* Common summer resident, May to mid-September. Open woods. Widespread.* #

Lewis's woodpecker. *Melanerpes lewis.* Local summer resident, May to September (west). Open woods (burned conifers, open hardwoods). Western affinities; at eastern breeding limits in Pine Ridge (Dawes County).*

Downy woodpecker. *Picoides pubescens.* Common resident. Forests, wooded suburbs. Widespread.*

Hairy woodpecker. *Picoides villosus.* Common resident. Forests, wooded suburbs. Widespread.*

Northern flicker. *Colaptes auratus.* Common resident. Yellow-shafted (eastern) and red-shafted (western) races overlap and hybridize extensively in central Niobrara Valley. Woodland edges, wooded suburbs. Widespread.*

Family Tyrannidae—Tyrant Flycatchers

Olive-sided flycatcher. *Contopus cooperi.* Uncommon migrant, mid-May to late May and early to late September. Woodland edges.

Western wood pewee. *Contopus sordidulus*. Local summer resident, late May to early September (west). Mature forests. Western affinities; at eastern breeding limits in upper Niobrara Valley (Sheridan County, Nebraska; probably also to Tripp County, South Dakota).*

Eastern wood pewee. *Contopus virens*. Local summer resident, mid-May to mid-September (east). Mature forests. Eastern affinities; at western breeding limits in upper Niobrara Valley (Sheridan County), probably locally hybridizing with the western wood pewee.*

Alder flycatcher. *Empidonax alnorum*. Rare migrant. Woodland edges.

Yellow-bellied flycatcher. *Empidonax flaviventris*. Occasional migrant, May and September. Brushy woodland edges.

Least flycatcher. *Empidonax minimus*. Common migrant, early to mid-May and September. Apparent occasional summer resident; breeding reported for central Niobrara Valley by Ducey (1989). A possible breeder in Todd County, South Dakota (Peterson 1995); no Nebraska breeding evidence reported by Mollhoff (2001). Forests, woodland edges. Widespread.*

Cordilleran flycatcher. *Empidonax occidentalis*. Very local summer resident, May to September (west). Pine forests in shady valleys. Western affinities.*

Willow flycatcher. *Empidonax traillii*. Common summer resident, mid-May to early September (east). Woodland edges, willow thickets. Widespread.* #

Acadian flycatcher. *Empidonax virescens*. Rare migrant, May and August (east). Deciduous woodland edges.

Eastern phoebe. *Sayornis phoebe*. Common summer resident, mid-April to late September (east). Woodland edges. Eastern affinities; at western breeding limits in upper Niobrara Valley (Sioux County).*

Say's phoebe. *Sayornis saya*. Local summer resident, mid-April to mid-September (west). Open country, near cliffs. Western affinities; at eastern breeding limits in upper Niobrara Valley (Sheridan County, rarely farther east).*

Great crested flycatcher. *Myiarchus crinitus*. Local summer resident, late April to early September (east). Deciduous forest edges. Eastern affinities; at western breeding limits in upper Niobrara Valley (Sioux County; accidental in Wyoming).*

Scissor-tailed flycatcher. *Tyrannus forficatus.* Occasional migrant and rare summer resident, early May to mid-September (east). Woodland-grassland edges. Southern affinities.*

Eastern kingbird. *Tyrannus tyrannus.* Common summer resident, early May to early September. Woodland edges. Widespread.*

Western kingbird. *Tyrannus verticalis.* Common summer resident, early May to early September. Woodland edges, woodlands. Widespread.*

Cassin's kingbird. *Tyrannus vociferans.* Local summer resident, early May to mid-September (west). Woodland edges. Western affinities; at eastern breeding limits in upper Niobrara Valley (Sheridan County).*

Family Laniidae—Shrikes

Northern shrike. *Lanius excubitor.* Uncommon wintering migrant, early November to mid-March. Open country.

Loggerhead shrike. *Lanius ludovicianus.* Common summer resident, mid-April to mid-September. Open country. Widespread. Candidate for listing under the Endangered Species Act.*

Family Vireonidae—Vireos

Bell's vireo. *Vireo bellii.* Common summer resident, mid-May to early September. Scrubby grasslands. Widespread.* #

Yellow-throated vireo. *Vireo flavifrons.* Occasional migrant, early May to early September (east). Forests.

Warbling vireo. *Vireo gilvus.* Common summer resident, early May to early September. Mature forests. Widespread.*

Red-eyed vireo. *Vireo olivaceus.* Local summer resident, mid-May to early September (east). Deciduous forests. Eastern affinities; at western breeding limits in upper Niobrara Valley (Sioux County, Nebraska, occasionally to eastern Wyoming).*

Philadelphia vireo. *Vireo philadelphicus.* Rare migrant, mid-May to late May and late August to late September (east). Deciduous forests.

Plumbeous vireo. *Vireo plumbeus.* Local summer resident, mid-May to mid-September (west). Forests. Western affinities; at eastern breeding limits in Pine Ridge (Dawes County).*

Blue-headed vireo. *Vireo solitarius.* Occasional migrant, early to mid-May and mid-September to early October (east). Forests.

Family Corvidae—Jays, Magpies, and Crows

Blue jay. *Cyanocitta cristata*. Common resident. Woodland edges. Eastern affinities.*

Pinyon jay. *Gymnorhinus cyanocephalus*. Rare and local resident in Pine Ridge (Sioux and Dawes counties). Woodland edges. Western affinities.*

Clark's nutcracker. *Nucifraga columbiana*. Rare resident in Pine Ridge (Sioux County). Woodland edges. Western affinities.*

Black-billed magpie. *Pica hudsonia*. Common resident (west). Woodland edges, open country. Western affinities; at eastern breeding limits in lower Niobrara Valley (Knox County, Nebraska; Gregory County South Dakota; sometimes farther east).*

American crow. *Corvus brachyrhynchos*. Common resident. Diverse habitats. Widespread.*

Family Alaudidae—Larks

Horned lark. *Eremophila alpestris*. Common resident. Open country. Widespread.*

Family Hirundinidae—Swallows

Purple martin. *Progne subis*. Rare summer resident, mid-April to late August (east). Near humans. Eastern affinities; at western breeding limits in central or lower Niobrara Valley (possibly to Brown County, Nebraska, and to Tripp County, South Dakota).*

Tree swallow. *Tachycineta bicolor*. Uncommon summer resident, late April to mid-September. Woodland edges. Northern affinities.*

Violet-green swallow. *Tachycineta thalassina*. Local summer resident, mid-May to late August (west). Near cliffs or forests. Western affinities; at eastern breeding limits in Pine Ridge (probably Sioux, Dawes, and Box Butte counties).*

Northern rough-winged swallow. *Stelgidopteryx serripennis*. Common summer resident, late April to early September. Near cliffs or steep banks. Widespread.*

Bank swallow. *Riparia riparia*. Common summer resident, early May to early September. Open country near steep banks. Widespread.*

Barn swallow. *Hirundo rustica*. Common summer resident, late April to late September. Open country near humans. Widespread.*

Cliff swallow. *Petrochelidon pyrrhonota*. Common summer resident, late

April to early September. Open country near cliffs or vertical surfaces. Widespread.*

Family Paridae—Titmice

Black-capped chickadee. *Poecile atricapillus.* Common resident. Forests, wooded suburbs. Widespread.*

Tufted titmouse. *Baeolophus bicolor.* Rare vagrant and possible summer resident (east). Forests.

Family Sittidae—Nuthatches

Red-breasted nuthatch. *Sitta canadensis.* Common migrant, early October to early April; local resident. At southeastern edge of breeding range in central Niobrara Valley (Cherry and Brown or Keya Paha counties). Coniferous forests. Western and northern affinities.*

White-breasted nuthatch. *Sitta carolinensis.* Common resident. Deciduous and pine forests. Widespread.*

Pygmy nuthatch. *Sitta pygmaea.* Local resident (west). Coniferous forests. Western affinities; at eastern breeding limits in Pine Ridge and upper Niobrara Valley (Sioux and Dawes counties).*

Family Certhiidae—Creepers

Brown creeper. *Certhia americana.* Uncommon resident. Forests. Northern affinities.*

Family Cinclidae—Dippers

American dipper. *Cinclus mexicanus.* Rare migrant (west). Near clear, rapid streams.

Family Troglodytidae—Wrens

Rock wren. *Salpinctes obsoletus.* Local summer resident, early May to late October (west). Rocky habitats. Western affinities; at eastern breeding limits in central Niobrara Valley (probably to Cherry County).*

Bewick's wren. *Thryomanes bewickii.* Rare vagrant. Scrub, woodland edges.

House wren. *Troglodytes aedon.* Common summer resident, late April to late September. Forests, woodland edges, suburbs. Widespread.*

Winter wren. *Troglodytes troglodytes.* Rare winter migrant, mid-October to mid-April. Forests.

Marsh wren. *Cistothorus palustris.* Local summer resident, early May to early October. Marshy wetlands. Widespread.*

Sedge wren. *Cistothorus platensis.* Local summer resident, early May to late September. Grassy wetlands. Widespread.*

Family Regulidae—Kinglets

Ruby-crowned kinglet. *Regulus calendula.* Common migrant, April to mid-May and September to October, sometimes overwintering. Conifer and hardwood forests, city parks.

Golden-crowned kinglet. *Regulus satrapa.* Common wintering migrant, mid-October to mid-April. Conifer forests.

Family Sylviidae—Gnatcatchers

Blue-gray gnatcatcher. *Polioptila caerulea.* Poorly documented regionally, with questionable reports from Sioux and Dawes counties (presumably the western race *P. c. amoenissima*) and a statement by Ducey (1989) that the species occurs in the lower Niobrara Valley and may breed there (presumably the eastern race, *P. c. caerulea*). Mature deciduous forests (east) and shrub-juniper woodlands (west).

Family Turdidae—Thrushes and Allies

Mountain bluebird. *Sialia currucoides.* Local summer resident, April to October (west). Coniferous woodland edges. Western affinities; at eastern breeding limits in upper Niobrara Valley (Sioux County to Sheridan County), locally hybridizing with eastern bluebird.*

Eastern bluebird. *Sialia sialis.* Local summer resident, late March to early November (east). Woodland edges. Eastern affinities; at western breeding limits in upper Niobrara Valley (Sioux County).*

Townsend's solitaire. *Myadestes townsendi.* Common winter migrant, September to March, rare breeding resident (west). Coniferous forests (summer), juniper scrub (winter). Western affinities; at eastern breeding limits in Pine Ridge (Sioux County to Sheridan County).*

Veery. *Catharus fuscescens.* Uncommon migrant, May and September. Forests.

Hermit thrush. *Catharus guttatus.* Uncommon migrant, May and September. Forests, brushy woodlands.

Gray-cheeked thrush. *Catharus minimus.* Common migrant, May and September. Forests.

Swainson's thrush. *Catharus ustulatus.* Common migrant, May and September. Forests.

Wood thrush. *Hylocichla mustelina.* Common migrant, local summer resident, mid-May to mid-September (east). Deciduous forests. Eastern affinities; at western breeding limits in upper Niobrara Valley (possibly west to Sioux County).*

American robin. *Turdus migratorius.* Common summer resident, late February to mid-December, sometimes overwintering. Forests, woodland edges, suburbs. Widespread.*

Family Mimidae—Mockingbirds and Thrashers

Gray catbird. *Dumetella carolinensis.* Rare to uncommon summer resident, mid-May to late September. Woodland edges. Widespread.*

Northern mockingbird. *Mimus polyglottos.* Rare summer resident, early May to mid-September. Woodland edges. Southern affinities.*

Sage thrasher. *Oreoscoptes montanus.* Local summer resident, mid-April to mid-September (west); undocumented nester in Sioux County. Sage scrub. Western affinities.*

Brown thrasher. *Toxostoma rufum.* Common summer resident, late April to late September. Woodland edges. Eastern affinities.*

Family Sturnidae—Starlings

European starling. *Sturnus vulgaris.* Common (introduced) resident. Diverse habitats, near humans.*

Family Motacillidae—Pipits

American pipit. *Anthus rubescens.* Common migrant, April and October. Open country, shorelines.

Sprague's pipit. *Anthus spragueii.* Rare migrant, April and September to October. Native grasslands, open country.#

Family Bombycillidae—Waxwings

Cedar waxwing. *Bombycilla cedrorum.* Uncommon summer resident, late February to early October, sometimes overwintering. Open forest, woodland edges, parks. Widespread.*

Bohemian waxwing. *Bombycilla garrulus.* Casual wintering migrant, late November to late February. Open forest, woodland edges.

Family Parulidae—Wood warblers

Orange-crowned warbler. *Vermivora celata.* Common migrant, late April to mid-May and mid-September to mid-October. Woodland edges, weedy sites.

Tennessee warbler. *Vermivora peregrina.* Common migrant, early to late May and early September to early October. Forests, flowering trees.

Blue-winged warbler. *Vermivora pinus.* Rare migrant, May and August to September (east). Woodland edges, brushy woodlands.#

Nashville warbler. *Vermivora ruficapilla.* Common migrant, early to mid-May and mid-September to early October. Low forests, brushy woodlands.

Northern parula. *Parula americana.* Rare migrant, May and September. Mature forests.

Black-throated blue warbler. *Dendroica caerulescens.* Casual migrant, May and September (east). Dense forests.

Bay-breasted warbler. *Dendroica castanea.* Uncommon migrant, May and September. Forests.

Cerulean warbler. *Dendroica cerulea.* Rare migrant, May and September. Deciduous forests.

Yellow-rumped warbler. *Dendroica coronata auduboni.* Common summer resident, late April to late October (west). Open forests, woodlands. Western affinities; at eastern breeding limits in Pine Ridge and upper Niobrara Valley (Dawes and probably Sioux counties).*

Blackburnian warbler. *Dendroica fusca.* Uncommon migrant, May and early September to early October. Mature forests.

Magnolia warbler. *Dendroica magnolia.* Common migrant, mid-May to late May and early September to early October (east). Forests.

Palm warbler. *Dendroica palmarum.* Uncommon migrant, May and September (east). Woodlands, weedy sites.

Chestnut-sided warbler. *Dendroica pennsylvanica.* Common migrant, mid- to late May and early to late September (east). Woodland edges.

Yellow warbler. *Dendroica petechia.* Common summer resident, early May to early September. Forests, Woodland edges. Widespread.*

Pine warbler. *Dendroica pinus.* Casual migrant, May and September (east). Coniferous forests.

Blackpoll warbler. *Dendroica striata.* Uncommon migrant, May and September. Forests.

Townsend's warbler. *Dendroica townsendi.* Rare migrant, May and September (west). Conifer forests.

Black-throated green warbler. *Dendroica virens.* Rare migrant, early to mid-May and mid-September to early October. Conifer forests.

Black-and-white warbler. *Mniotilta varia.* Local summer resident, early May to mid-September (east). Deciduous forests. Eastern affinities; at western breeding limits in Pine Ridge and upper Niobrara Valley (certainly to Cherry County; probably to Sioux and Dawes counties, Nebraska; also to Tripp County, South Dakota).*

American redstart. *Setophaga ruticilla.* Local summer resident, early May to early September (east). Deciduous forests. Eastern affinities; at western breeding limits in Pine Ridge and upper Niobrara Valley (Sioux County).*

Ovenbird. *Seiurus aurocapilla.* Local summer resident, mid-May to mid-September (east). Deciduous forests. Eastern affinities; at western breeding limits in Pine Ridge and upper Niobrara Valley (certainly west to Cherry County; probably to Sioux County).*

Northern waterthrush. *Seiurus noveboracensis.* Rare migrant, May and September (east). Forest wetlands.

Connecticut warbler. *Oporornis agilis.* Rare migrant, May and September (east). Forests.

Mourning warbler. *Oporornis philadelphia.* Uncommon migrant, mid-May to late May and early September to early October (east). Brushy forests.

MacGillivray's warbler. *Oporornis tolmiei.* Occasional migrant, May and September (west). Brushy forests.

Common yellowthroat. *Geothlypis trichas.* Common summer resident, early May to mid-September. Marshy wetlands. Widespread.*

Canada warbler. *Wilsonia canadensis.* Uncommon migrant May and September (east). Shady forests.

Hooded warbler. *Wilsonia citrina*. Rare migrant, May and August to September (east). Shady forests.

Wilson's warbler. *Wilsonia pusilla*. Common migrant, May and September. Dense, moist forests.

Yellow-breasted chat. *Icteria virens*. Common summer resident, mid-May to early September. Brushy grasslands, scrub woods. Widespread.*

Family Thraupidae—Tanagers

Western tanager. *Piranga ludoviciana*. Local summer resident, mid-May to late August (west). Coniferous forests. Western affinities; at eastern breeding limits in upper Niobrara Valley (Sheridan County), perhaps locally in contact with scarlet tanager.*

Scarlet tanager. *Piranga olivacea*. Local summer resident, mid-May to September (east). Mature deciduous forests. Eastern affinities; at western breeding limits in lower or central Niobrara Valley (certainly west to Knox County, possibly to Brown County).*

Family Emberizidae—Towhees, Sparrows, and Longspurs

Green-tailed towhee. *Pipilo chlorurus*. Rare migrant, May and September (west). Sage scrub.

Eastern towhee. *Pipilo erythrophthalmus*. Local summer resident, late April to mid-October (east). Woodland edges. Eastern affinities; at western breeding limits in lower Niobrara Valley (range limits obscured by hybridization with spotted towhee.*

Spotted towhee. *Pipilo maculatus*. Local summer resident, late April to mid-October (west). Woodland edges. Western affinities; at eastern breeding limits in lower Niobrara Valley, meeting (between about Cherry and Knox counties) and locally hybridizing with eastern towhee.*

Cassin's sparrow. *Aimophila cassinii*. Rare and erratic summer resident (west). Sandsage scrub. Southwestern affinities; at northern limits of occasional breeding at edge of upper Niobrara Basin (Box Butte County, Nebraska, and easternmost Wyoming).*

American tree sparrow. *Spizella arborea*. Common wintering migrant, late October to early April. Scrubby grasslands.#

Brewer's sparrow. *Spizella breweri*. Local summer resident (northwest).

Sage scrub. Western affinities; at eastern edge of breeding in upper Niobrara Valley (Sioux and probably Box Butte counties).*

Clay-colored sparrow. *Spizella pallida.* Common migrant, early to mid-May and mid-September to early October. Brushy grasslands.

Chipping sparrow. *Spizella passerina.* Common summer resident, late April to early October. Woodland edges. Widespread.*

Field sparrow. *Spizella pusilla.* Common summer resident, mid-April to early October. Scrubby grasslands. Widespread.*

Vesper sparrow. *Pooecetes gramineus.* Uncommon summer resident, mid-April to early October. Mixed-grass prairies. Widespread.*

Lark sparrow. *Chondestes grammacus.* Common summer resident, early May to early September. Grasslands. Great Plains affinities.*

Lark bunting. *Calamospiza melanocorys.* Common summer resident, early May to late August (west). Shortgrass and mixed-grass prairies. Great Plains affinities; at eastern breeding limits in Niobrara Valley (probably to Boyd County).* #

Savannah sparrow. *Passerculus sandwichensis.* Common migrant and probable rare summer resident, late April to mid-September. Breeding evidence includes a possible 1950s nesting at Fort Niobrara National Wildlife Refuge, and territorial birds seen in Sheridan County. Mixed-grass prairies.

Baird's sparrow. *Ammodramus bairdii.* Rare migrant, April to May and late September to mid-October (mainly in west). Grasslands.#

Le Conte's sparrow. *Ammodramus leconteii.* Rare migrant, late April to early May and late September to late October. Wet grasslands.

Nelson's sharp-tailed sparrow. *Ammodramus nelsoni.* Rare migrant, May and October. Wet grasslands.#

Grasshopper sparrow. *Ammodramus savannarum.* Common summer resident, early May to early September. Mixed and tallgrass prairies. Widespread.* #

Fox sparrow. *Passerella iliaca.* Uncommon migrant, late March to mid-April and mid-October to mid-November. Woodland edges.

Swamp sparrow. *Melospiza georgiana.* Local summer resident, late April to late October. Marshy wetlands. Northern affinities.*

Lincoln's sparrow. *Melospiza lincolnii.* Uncommon migrant, late April to mid-May and mid-September to mid-October. Woodland edges.

Song sparrow. *Melospiza melodia.* Common summer resident, early April to late December. Woodland edges, brushy wetlands. Widespread.*

White-throated sparrow. *Zonotrichia albicollis.* Common wintering migrant, early October to mid-May. Woodland edges.

White-crowned sparrow. *Zonotrichia leucophrys.* Common wintering migrant, early October to mid-May. Woodland edges.

Harris's sparrow. *Zonotrichia querula.* Common wintering migrant, early October to mid-May. Woodland edges.#

Dark-eyed junco. *Junco hyemalis.* Common wintering migrant, early October to late March; also local resident ("white-winged" race *J. h. aikeni*). Woodland edges, conifer forests. Western and northern affinities.*

Lapland longspur. *Calcarius lapponicus.* Common wintering migrant, mid-November to late February. Low grasslands, plowed fields.

McCown's longspur. *Calcarius mccownii.* Local summer resident, early April to early October (west). Grasslands, especially shortgrass prairies. Great Plains affinities; at eastern breeding limits in upper Niobrara Valley (Sioux County).* #

Chestnut-collared longspur. *Calcarius ornatus.* Local summer resident, mid-April to early October. Grasslands, especially mixed-grass prairies. Great Plains affinities; at southern breeding limits in central Niobrara Valley (Cherry County, Nebraska, and Tripp County, South Dakota).* #

Snow bunting. *Plectrophenax nivalis.* Occasional wintering migrant, mid-November to mid-February. Low grasslands, plowed fields.

Family Cardinalidae—Cardinals, Grosbeaks, and Allies
Northern cardinal. *Cardinalis cardinalis.* Forest edge, suburbs. Common resident. Eastern affinities.*

Rose-breasted grosbeak. *Pheucticus ludovicianus.* Common summer resident, early May to mid-September (east). Deciduous forests. Eastern affinities; at western breeding limits in upper Niobrara Valley (occasionally west to eastern Wyoming).*

Black-headed grosbeak. *Pheucticus melanocephalus.* Common summer resident, mid-May to late August (west). Forests. Western affinities; at eastern breeding limits in central Niobrara Valley (Keya Paha County,

Nebraska; probably to Gregory County, South Dakota), locally hybridizing with rose-breasted grosbeak.*

Lazuli bunting. *Passerina amoena.* Local summer resident, mid-May to late August (west). Scrubby grasslands. Western affinities; at eastern breeding limits in upper Niobrara Valley (possibly east to Keya Paha County).*

Blue grosbeak. *Passerina caerulea.* Common summer resident, mid-May to late August. Scrubby grasslands. Widespread.*

Indigo bunting. *Passerina cyanea.* Local summer resident, mid-May to late August (east). Woodland edges. Eastern affinities; at western breeding limits in upper Niobrara Valley (possibly to Sioux County, Nebraska; hybrids with lazuli buntings reported from eastern Wyoming), locally hybridizing with lazuli bunting.*

Dickcissel. *Spiza americana.* Common summer resident, mid-May to late August (mainly east). Tallgrass prairies. Great Plains affinities; near western breeding limits in upper Niobrara Valley (Dawes County, Nebraska, and adjacent eastern Wyoming; at least to Tripp County, South Dakota).* #

Family Icteridae—Meadowlarks, Blackbirds, Orioles, and Allies

Bobolink. *Dolichonyx oryzivorus.* Common summer resident, mid-May to mid-August. Meadows. Widespread.*

Red-winged blackbird. *Agelaius phoeniceus.* Common summer resident, early March to late November. Wetlands, ditches. Widespread.*

Eastern meadowlark. *Sturnella magna.* Local summer resident, early April to mid-October (east). Grasslands, especially tallgrass prairie. Eastern affinities; at western breeding limits in upper Niobrara Valley (Sheridan County, Nebraska, to Shannon County, South Dakota).*

Western meadowlark. *Sturnella neglecta.* Common summer resident, early March to late October. Grasslands, especially mixed-grass prairie. Western affinities.*

Yellow-headed blackbird. *Xanthocephalus xanthocephalus.* Common summer resident, mid-April to mid-September. Marshy wetlands. Widespread.*

Rusty blackbird. *Euphagus carolinus.* Uncommon migrant, late March to mid-April and early November to late December. Woodland edges.#

Brewer's blackbird. *Euphagus cyanocephalus.* Local; summer resident, mid-April to early November (west). Dry grasslands, scrub. Western affinities; at eastern breeding limits in Pine Ridge and upper Niobrara Valley (Sheridan County).*

Common grackle. *Quiscalus quiscula.* Common summer resident, late March to late October. Forest edge, suburbs. Widespread.*

Brown-headed cowbird. *Molothrus ater.* Common summer resident, mid-April to early October. Grasslands, woodland edges. Widespread.*

Bullock's oriole. *Icterus bullockii.* Common summer resident, early May to early September (west). Forests. Western affinities; at eastern breeding limits in upper Niobrara Valley (Sheridan County), locally hybridizing with Baltimore oriole.*

Baltimore oriole. *Icterus galbula.* Common summer resident, early May to early September (east). Deciduous forests. Eastern affinities; at western breeding limits in upper Niobrara Valley (Sheridan County) accidental in Wyoming.*

Orchard oriole. *Icterus spurius.* Common summer resident, mid-May to late August. Forests. Eastern affinities.*

Family Fringillidae—Finches

Gray-crowned rosy finch. *Leucosticte tephrocotis.* Casual wintering migrant, October to February. Open grasslands.

Cassin's finch. *Carpodacus cassinii.* Uncommon wintering migrant, October to mid-April. Sage scrub.

House finch. *Carpodacus mexicanus.* Local resident (mainly in west, but still expanding in range). Near humans. Western affinities.*

Red crossbill. *Loxia curvirostra.* Uncommon wintering migrant, mid-November to early April, local resident (west). Conifer forests. Western and northern affinities; at usually eastern breeding limits in Pine Ridge (Sioux and Dawes counties, local in Nebraska National Forest of Cherry County, occasionally farther east).*

Common redpoll. *Carduelis flammea.* Occasional wintering migrant, late November to mid-March. Woodland edges.

Pine siskin. *Carduelis pinus.* Uncommon wintering migrant, mid-October to mid-May; local resident (mostly in west). Woodland edges. Widespread.*

American goldfinch. *Carduelis tristis.* Common resident. Open country. Widespread.*

Evening grosbeak. *Coccothraustes vespertinus.* Local wintering migrant, early November to late April (west). Woodland edges.

Pine grosbeak. *Pinicola enucleator.* Rare wintering migrant, late November to mid-March (west). Conifer forests.

Purple finch. *Carpodacus purpureus.* Uncommon wintering migrant, late October to late April (west). Forests.

Family Passeridae—Old World Sparrows
House sparrow. *Passer domesticus.* Common widespread (introduced) resident. Near humans.*

Appendix 1c

Reptiles and Amphibians of the Niobrara Region

The thirty-three species listed here represent 53 percent of Nebraska's total known reptiles and amphibians, and their distributions are based primarily on Lynch (1985). The geographic coverage here includes the twelve Nebraska counties listed in table 25 as well as three South Dakota counties (Todd, Tripp, and Gregory) that lie in part within the Niobrara drainage (Ballinger, Meeker, and Thies 2000). Reptiles of the Niobrara's headwaters in eastern Wyoming were documented by Luce et al. (1997). Species reported as present in 1982 from the Niobrara Valley Preserve (Kantak and Churchill 1993) are identified by asterisks (*).

Zoogeographic affinities were subjectively based on various range map sources, including Behler and King (1979). Two reptiles reported from the Niobrara Scenic River region are classified as "sensitive" by the Nebraska Natural Heritage Program (U.S. Department of Interior, National Park Service 2005). These species are shown in **boldface**.

Be aware that all Nebraska herp species are now protected by state law and may not be collected without a permit.

Order Caudata—Salamanders

Tiger salamander. *Ambystoma tigrinum*. Throughout region; common in shallow ponds. Great Plains affinities.*

Order Anura—Frogs and Toads

Northern cricket frog. *Acris crepitans*. West to Cherry County, Nebraska; also in Tripp County, South Dakota. Common in streams and ponds. Great Plains affinities; at or near western range limits in central Niobrara Valley (Cherry County).*

Great Plains toad. *Bufo cognatus*. Throughout region, and west to northeastern Wyoming. Fairly common in dry grasslands. Great Plains affinities.*

Woodhouse's (Rocky Mountain) toad. *Bufo woodhousei*. Throughout region; common in grasslands and forest edges. Great Plains affinities.*

Western (striped) chorus frog. *Pseudacris triseriata*. Throughout region; common in ditches and marshes. Great Plains affinities.*

Plains leopard frog. *Rana blairi*. Boyd and Holt counties, Nebraska, and adjacent South Dakota; permanent wetlands. Great Plains affinities; at or near western range limits in central Niobrara Valley (Tripp County, South Dakota).

Bullfrog. *Rana catesbiana*. Throughout region; diverse aquatic habitats. Widespread.*

Northern leopard frog. *Rana pipiens*. Throughout region; sandy streams and marshes. Widespread.*

Plains spadefoot toad. *Spea bombifrons*. Throughout region, especially in sandy or loess soils. Great Plains affinities.*

Order Chelonia—Turtles

Snapping turtle. *Chelydra serpentina*. Throughout region, in permanent wetlands. Great Plains affinities.*

Painted turtle. *Chrysemys picta*. Throughout region, in all aquatic habitats. Great Plains affinities.*

Blanding's turtle. *Emydoidea blandingi*. Permanent Sandhills marshes from Cherry County east. Northern and eastern affinities; at or near western range limits in middle Niobrara Valley (western Cherry and Grant counties). A declining species over most of its range; a candidate for listing under the Endangered Species Act.*

Yellow mud turtle. *Kinosternum flavescens*. Local along central Niobrara River and in permanent Sandhills wetlands. Southwestern affinities; at northeastern range limits in Niobrara Valley. State-listed sensitive species; candidate for listing under the Endangered Species Act.

Ornate box turtle. *Terrapena ornata*. Cherry, Keya Paha, and Brown counties, Nebraska and Todd County, South Dakota; Sandhills and mixed-grass prairies. Great Plains affinities; at or near northwestern range limits in Niobrara Valley.*

Spiny softshell. *Trionyx spiniferus*. Local in eastern Nebraska streams and reservoirs. Not yet reported from the Niobrara River, but known from most other major state rivers and many smaller streams. Eastern affinities.

Order Lacertilia—Lizards

Six-lined racerunner. *Cnemidophorus sexlineatus*. From Cherry County east. Sandy habitats. Great Plains affinities; near western range limits in central or upper Niobrara Valley (Cherry County, but also known from Fall River County, South Dakota).*

Many-lined skink. *Eumeces multivirgatus*. Reported from Sioux County to Brown County, Nebraska, and Tripp County, South Dakota. Sandhills and sandsage prairie habitats. Southwestern affinities; near northern range limits in Niobrara Valley, reported north to Bennett and Tripp counties, South Dakota.*

Lesser (northern) earless lizard. *Holbrookia maculata*. Throughout region, in sandy habitats. Southwestern affinities; near northern range limits in Niobrara Valley; reported north to Bennett, Tripp, and Gregory counties, South Dakota.*

Short-horned lizard. *Phrynosoma douglasii*. From Sioux County east to Sheridan County, in dry, rocky habitats. Western affinities; at or near eastern range limits in upper Niobrara Valley (Sheridan County).

Northern prairie (fence) lizard. *Sceloperus undulatus*. From Sioux County east to Brown County, Nebraska, and north to Tripp County, South Dakota. Common in Sandhills; also present in rocky or wooded habitats. Great Plains affinities; at or near northeastern range limits in central Niobrara Valley (Brown County).*

Order Serpentes—Snakes

Blue (eastern, green) racer. *Coluber constrictor*. Throughout region; diverse grasslands. Widespread.*

Prairie (western) rattlesnake. *Crotalus viridis*. Throughout region; prefers rocky grasslands. Venomous. Great Plains affinities; near eastern range limits in lower Niobrara Valley (Knox County).*

Ringneck snake. *Diadophis punctatus*. From Brown County east; deciduous woods. Widespread.

(Western) fox snake. *Elaphe vulpina*. Lower Niobrara Valley from Holt

County east, especially in riparian habitats. Northeastern affinities; at or near southwestern range limits in lower Niobrara Valley (Keya Paha County).

Western hognose snake. *Heterodon nasicus.* Throughout region, especially in sandy habitats. Great Plains affinities; near eastern limits in lower Niobrara Valley (Boyd County).*

Eastern hognose snake. *Heterodon platyrhinos.* From Cherry County east. Prefers deciduous woodlands and wooded sandy streams. Eastern affinities; at or near western range limits in central Niobrara Valley.*

Milk snake. *Lampropeltis triangulum.* Probably throughout region (reported west to Sheridan County, Nebraska, and to eastern Wyoming). Varied habitats, especially open prairies, sandy areas, and rocky hillsides. Great Plains affinities; near western range limits in upper Niobrara Valley.*

Common (northern) watersnake. *Nerodia sipedon.* Probably throughout region (reported west to Sheridan County). Marshes, streams and rivers. Great Plains affinities; near western range limits in upper Niobrara Valley.*

Smooth green snake. *Opheodrys vernalis.* Rare, probably near extirpation. Reported from Boyd County only, in wet meadows. Northern and eastern affinities; the Great Plains subspecies *O. v. vernalis* is at or near western range limits in lower Niobrara Valley. State-listed sensitive species.

Bullsnake (gopher snake). *Pituophis catenifer.* Throughout region; common in varied habitats. Widespread.*

Wandering (northern terrestrial) garter snake. *Thamnophis elegans.* Sioux County, Nebraska, and adjacent eastern Wyoming. Diverse habitats; often near ponds or streams. Western affinities; at eastern range limits in upper Niobrara Valley (Sioux County).

Plains garter snake. *Thamnophis radix.* Throughout region. Common in diverse but usually dry habitats. Great Plains affinities.*

Common (red-sided) garter snake. *Thamnophis sirtalis parietalis.* Throughout region. Common along all watercourses. Great Plains affinities.*

Appendix 1D

Native Fishes of the Niobrara Region

This list of sixty-one fish species is based mainly on information provided by Johnson (1942), Jones (1963), and Morris, Morris, and Witt (1974). It excludes hypothetical and accidentally or purposely introduced species. It represents about three-fourths of Nebraska's approximate total of eighty native fish species and over four-fifths of the seventy-two native species that have been reported from the Missouri National Recreational River region (Berry and Young 2004), which extends west to include the last twenty miles of the Niobrara River. In addition to the Niobrara drainage itself, the list geographically encompasses the White River headwaters, the lakes of the northern Sandhills, and the upper sections of the Loup, Calamus, and Elkhorn rivers that occur within the twelve-county greater Niobrara region of Nebraska as defined earlier. It also includes the Wyoming headwaters area of the Niobrara River (Baker and Simon 1970).

Species that were collected in 1978, 1991, or both from the lower Niobrara River (Boyd-Holt counties region) by Mestl (1993) are indicated by a single asterisk (*). Species found from 1993 to 2001 from the same lower Niobrara by Gutzmer et al. (2002) are marked with double asterisks (**). Those reported by Hesse et al. (1979), also from the lower Niobrara, are indicated by a single pound symbol (#). Those reported from the Niobrara Valley Preserve (Kantak and Churchill 1993) are indicated by double pound symbols (##). Hrabik (1998) listed some other Sandhills species that might also extend locally into the Niobrara drainage. Several additional species are known from the adjacent Missouri River of northeastern Nebraska (Berry and Young 2004) and might also occur in the lower Niobrara drainage. Species they reported between

Fort Randall and the upper end of Lewis and Clark Lake and lowermost portions of the Niobrara River and that are already listed for the Niobrara River are marked with triple pound symbols (###).

Zoogeographic affinities are mostly based on subjective interpretations of range maps provided by Page and Burr (1991). "Streams" as used here describes smaller moving-water habitats positioned ecologically between creek headwaters and larger, often more sluggish rivers. A total of ten fish species reported from the Niobrara Scenic River region are classified as "sensitive" by the Nebraska Natural Heritage Program (National Park Service, 2005). These species are shown in **boldface**.

The list follows the traditional taxonomic sequence of families and genera; congeneric species are arranged alphabetically by their Latin specific names.

Family Lepisosteidae—Gars

Longnose gar. *Lepidosteus osseus.* Rare in mouth of Niobrara River. Slower streams, rivers, impoundments, and oxbow lakes. Eastern affinities.###

Shortnose gar. *Lepidosteus playtostomus.* Rare in mouth of Niobrara River. Larger streams and rivers, oxbow lakes. Southern (Mississippi Valley) affinities.###

Family Hiodontidae—Mooneyes

Goldeye. *Hiodon alosoides.* Lower Niobrara, Keya Paha, and White rivers. Streams, larger, often turbid, rivers, and lakes. Widespread.###

Family Clupeidae—Herrings

Gizzard shad. *Dorosoma cepedianum.* Lower Niobrara. Reservoirs and larger rivers. Widespread.###

Family Esocidae—Pikes

Northern pike. *Esox lucius.* Upper Niobrara and Elkhorn rivers; also widespread in Sandhills streams, reservoirs, and lakes. Northern affinities.###
Grass (redfin) pickerel. *Esox vermiculatus.* Upper Elkhorn, Snake, and Niobrara rivers. Well-vegetated streams, rivers, lakes. Eastern affinities.** ## ###

Family Cyprinidae—Minnows

Central stoneroller. *Campostoma anomalum.* Upper Niobrara, including Wyoming headwaters, Calamus, and White rivers, Sandhills lakes. Gravelly streams. Eastern affinities.* #

Northern redbelly dace. *Chrosomus eos.* Rare and local, mostly in spring-fed creeks in the Sandhills, the upper Niobrara River in Sioux County, and small streams in Sheridan, Cherry (Fairfield Creek), Brown (Bone Creek), Rock, and Keya Paha (Lost Creek, East Holt Creek, and Holt Creek) counties. Also reported from North Platte and Loup basins. State threatened, sometimes hybridizing with finescale dace. Cool, sluggish streams. Northern affinities; at southern edge of range.

Finescale dace. *Chrosomus neogaeus.* Rare and local, in the upper Niobrara River in Sioux County and the Wyoming headwaters and in small streams in Sheridan, Cherry, Brown, Rock, and Keya Paha counties, as reported for northern redbelly dace. State threatened. Cool streams. Northern affinities; at southern edge of range.##

Lake chub. *Couesius plumbeus.* Niobrara tributaries, Brown and Cherry counties. Cool streams. Northern affinities.

Brassy minnow. *Hybognathus hankinsoni.* Widespread in Niobrara, Loup, Calamus, and Elkhorn drainages, including the Niobrara's Wyoming headwaters. Cool, sluggish streams; northern affinities.** ## ###

Western silvery minnow. *Hybognathus argyritis.* Lower Niobrara River. Silt- or sand-bottom streams and rivers; Great Plains affinities.* ###

Plains minnow. *Hybognathus placitus.* Niobrara and White rivers. Sandy-bottom streams and rivers. Great Plains affinities. Candidate for federal listing under the Endangered Species Act.* #

Hornyhead chub. *Hybopsis biguttatus.* Elkhorn River. Clear gravel- or rubble-bottom streams; eastern affinities.

Flathead chub. *Hybopsis gracilis.* All major drainages. Locally common in clear sand- or gravel-bottom streams and rivers. Great Plains and northern affinities. Candidate for federal listing under the Endangered Species Act.* # ** ## ###

Silver chub. *Hybopsis storeriana.* Niobrara River. Slow streams and backwaters of rivers, natural lakes. Southern (Mississippi Valley) affinities.* # ###

Pearl dace. *Margariscus (Semotilus) margarita.* Rare; local in the upper Niobrara River in Sioux County, and small streams in Sheridan, Cherry, Brown, Rock, and Keya Paha counties (Lost Creek, Cottonwood Creek,

Holt Creek, and East Holt Creek). State threatened. Cool streams and headwaters. Northern affinities; at southern edge of range.

Golden shiner. *Notemigonus crysoleucus.* Widespread but local, upper and lower Niobrara River, White River, and Sandhills lakes and rivers. Lakes and slow-moving streams. Eastern affinities.## ###

Emerald shiner. *Notropis atherinoides.* Very common in Niobrara River. Larger streams and rivers. Northern affinities.* # ** ###

River shiner. *Notropis blennius.* Common in Sandhills drainages and Niobrara River. Larger streams and rivers. Mostly southern (Mississippi Valley) affinities.* # ** ###

Common shiner. *Notropis cornutus.* Upper Elkhorn River, Niobrara tributaries. Clear, rapid streams and headwaters. Eastern affinities. State-listed sensitive species.

Bigmouth shiner. *Notropis dorsalis.* Widespread in Niobrara and Sandhills drainages. Small, shallow, and slow streams. Great Plains affinities.* # ** ## ###

Blacknose shiner. *Notropis heterolepis.* Rare, now perhaps limited to the upper Niobrara River in Sheridan County, Brush Creek (Cherry County), and Holt Creek (Keya Paha River tributary, Keya Paha County). Since 1939 also found in the Niobrara River, Dawes County, and in one Holt County stream. State threatened. Small, clear prairie streams and headwaters. Northern affinities.

Red shiner. *Notropis lutrensis.* Widespread and very common in Niobrara and Sandhills drainages. Lakes, rivers, streams. Great Plains affinities.* # ** ##

Sand shiner. *Notropis stramineus.* Widespread and very common in Niobrara and Sandhills drainages, including the Wyoming headwaters. Sand-bottom streams. Eastern and Great Plains affinities.* # ** ###

Bluntnose minnow. *Pimephales notatus.* Elkhorn River, Ponca Creek. Backwaters of streams, rivers. Eastern affinities.###

Fathead minnow. *Pimephales promelas.* Upper White and Niobrara rivers, including the Wyoming headwaters, all Sandhills lakes and streams. Lakes, including alkaline lakes, and streams. Widespread.* # ** ## ###

Blacknose dace. *Rhinichthys atratulus.* Niobrara River and tributaries (Verdigre and Johnson creeks). Streams and headwaters. Eastern affinities.

Longnose dace. *Rhinichthys cataractae.* Niobrara River, including the Wyoming headwaters, upper Loup and upper White rivers, Sandhills streams. Streams. Widespread. State-listed sensitive species.##

Creek chub, *Semotilus atromaculatus.* Niobrara River including Wyoming headwaters, upper White River and tributaries, and most Sandhills streams. Small streams and headwaters. Eastern affinities.** ##

Family Catostomidae—Suckers

River carpsucker. *Carpoides carpio.* Fairly common in Niobrara River; also upper White, Loup, and Calamus rivers. Lakes, silt-bottom rivers and larger streams. Great Plains affinities.* # ** ## ###

Highfin carpsucker. *Carpoides velifer.* Lower Niobrara and Loup rivers. Streams and clear rivers. Southern (Mississippi Valley) affinities.** ###

White sucker. *Catostomus commersoni.* Throughout region, including the Niobrara's Wyoming headwaters, especially in cold-water lakes and rock-bottom streams. Northern affinities, near southern edge of range.** ## ###

Bigmouth buffalo. *Ictiobus cyrpinellus.* Eastern Nebraska streams. Lakes, gravel pits, rivers, and larger, often turbid, streams. Southern (Mississippi Valley) affinities.###

Black buffalo. *Ictiobus niger.* Local, near mouth of Niobrara, Elkhorn River, and some Cherry County lakes, where perhaps introduced. Lakes and larger rivers. Southern (Mississippi Valley) affinities.

Shorthead (northern) redhorse. *Moxostoma macrolepidotum.* Niobrara and other regional drainages. Lakes, rivers, and gravelly streams. Widespread.* # ** ###

Mountain sucker. *Pantosteus platyrhynchus.* Chadron and Hat creeks. Cold-water streams. Western affinities.

Family Ictaluridae—Freshwater Catfish

Black bullhead. *Ictalurus melas.* Widespread in Niobrara, upper White and Elkhorn drainages. Lakes and silt-bottom streams. Widespread.* # ** ##

Yellow bullhead, *Ictalurus natalis.* Upper Elkhorn River and Sandhills lakes (locally introduced); probably also lower Niobrara River. Lakes and silt-bottom streams. Eastern affinities.**

Channel catfish. *Ictalurus punctatus.* Common in Niobrara River and other regional drainages. Lakes, larger slow-moving rivers, and quiet streams. Widespread.* ** ###

Flathead catfish. *Pylodictus olivaria.* Missouri tributaries. Lakes, often more rapidly flowing rivers and gravelly streams. Southern (Mississippi Valley) affinities.

Stonecat. *Noturus flavus.* Local in Niobrara, upper White, and Elkhorn rivers, some Sandhills streams. Rivers and sand- or rock-bottom streams. Northern affinities.# ** ###

Family Cyprinodontidae—Killfish
Plains killifish. *Fundulus kansae.* Local in Niobrara River. Streams, including saline or alkaline streams. Great Plains affinities.# ##

Plains topminnow. *Fundulus sciadicus.* Niobrara drainage, including Wyoming headwaters, and many Sandhills streams. Clear, quiet, and vegetated streams, headwaters. Great Plains affinities. Candidate for federal listing under the Endangered Species Act.##

Family Gadidae—Codfish
Burbot. *Lota lota.* Middle and lower Niobrara River. Cool rivers and streams. Northern affinities; near southwestern edge of range.

Family Gasterosteidae—Sticklebacks
Brook stickleback. *Eucalis inconstans.* Local in Niobrara River, Niobrara tributaries (Snake River, Gordon Creek, Bone Creek), and Sandhills rivers. Shallow, clear creeks, ditches, well-vegetated streams and cool headwaters. Northern affinities; near southwestern edge of range. State-listed sensitive species.##

Family Serranidae (= Perichthyiidae)—Temperate Basses
White bass. *Roccus (Morone) chrysops.* Larger rivers; also in lakes and streams, where often introduced. Eastern affinities; near western edge of native range.# ###

Family Centrarchidae—Sunfishes
Rock bass. *Ambloplites rupestris.* Lower Niobrara River. Local in north-

ern Sandhills lakes, where introduced. Lakes and streams. Eastern affinities; near western edge of native range.###

Largemouth bass. *Micropterus salmoides*. Upper White, Niobrara, and Elkhorn drainages. Introduced into Sandhills lakes. Lakes and streams. Eastern affinities; near western edge of native range.* ** ##

Green sunfish. *Lepomis cyanellus*. Widespread in upper White, Niobrara, and Elkhorn drainages, including the Niobrara's Wyoming headwaters, Sandhills lakes. Lakes and streams. Great Plains and southern affinities.* ## ###

Pumpkinseed. *Lepomis gibbosis*. Local in Sandhills lakes (where introduced) and Niobrara tributaries. Lakes and streams. Eastern affinities; near western edge of native range.

Orangespotted sunfish. *Lepomis humilis*. Niobrara and Elkhorn drainages. Lakes and streams. Great Plains affinities.###

Bluegill. *Lepomis macrochirus*. Niobrara and Elkhorn drainages; introduced elsewhere. Lakes and streams. Eastern affinities; near western edge of native range.* # ** ##

White crappie. *Pomoxis annularis*. Middle and lower Niobrara River, White River, and Elkhorn drainages; locally introduced elsewhere. Lakes and streams. Southern (Mississippi Valley) affinities.# **

Black crappie. *Pomoxis nigromaculatus*. Middle and Lower Niobrara River, Elkhorn River, and Sandhills drainages, where at least in part introduced. Lakes and streams. Southern (Mississippi Valley) affinities.** ##

Family Percidae—Perches
Iowa darter. *Etheostoma exile*. Niobrara tributaries, including Niobrara's Wyoming headwaters, Elkhorn River, and Sandhills streams. Lakes, cool streams, and headwaters. Northern affinities; near southern edge of range.

Johnny darter. *Etheostoma nigrum*. Elkhorn River and tributaries. Sandy pools, streams, and rivers. Northern affinities.###

Yellow perch. *Perca flavescens*. Niobrara and Elkhorn tributaries; Sandhills lakes, where widely introduced. Lakes and streams. Northern affinities.** ###

Sauger. *Stizostedion canadensis*. Lower Niobrara River. Rivers and streams. Northern affinities.* # ** ###

Walleye. *Stizostedion vitreum*. Local in Niobrara and tributaries; Sand-hills lakes. Deeper lakes, rivers, and streams. Northern affinities.###

Family Sciaenidae—Freshwater Drums

Freshwater drum. *Aplodinotus grunniens*. Lower Niobrara River. Deeper lakes, impoundments, and larger rivers. Southern (Mississippi Valley) affinities.# ###

Appendix 1E

Butterflies and Skippers of the Niobrara Region

The geographic coverage of the following list includes all the Nebraska counties listed in table 25 plus three South Dakota counties lying partly within the Niobrara drainage. Nebraska county attributions are based on Dankert, Nagel, and Nightengale (1993) and an on-line list provided by the Northern Prairie Research station: http://www.npwrc.usgs.gov/resource/distr/liped/bflyusa/ne/toc.htm. The butterflies and skippers of the Niobrara Valley Preserve were also documented by Dankert and Nagel (1988); these species are marked with an asterisk (*). Species marked with a pound symbols (#) are described in detail and illustrated by Marrone (2002). Six butterfly species reported from the Niobrara Scenic River region are classified as "sensitive" by the Nebraska Natural Heritage Program (U.S. Department of Interior, National Park Service 2005). These species are shown in **boldface**.

The list contains 148 species, more than 70 percent of the 207 total species of butterflies reported for the entire state of Nebraska, and more than 90 percent of the total 177 species known for South Dakota (Marrone 2002). The English vernacular names, taxonomic sequence, and geographical associations are based on USGS range maps of butterflies of the United States (Opler, Stanford, and Pavulaan 2002).

The list follows the traditional taxonomic sequence of families and genera; congeneric species are arranged alphabetically by their Latin specific names.

Typical Butterflies

Swallowtails (Family Papilionidae)
Parnassians (Subfamily Parnassiinae)
Rocky Mountain parnassian. *Parnassius smintheus.* Sioux County. Western affinities; at eastern edge of range.#

Swallowtails (Subfamily Papilioninae)
Western black swallowtail. *Papilio bairdi.* Sioux County. Western affinities.

Giant swallowtail. *Papilio cresphontes.* Brown and Holt counties, Nebraska, and Gregory County, South Dakota. Southeastern affinities; at northwestern edge of range.#

Eastern tiger swallowtail. *Papilio glaucus.* Throughout region. Eastern affinities; near western edge of range.* #

Indra swallowtail. *Papilio indra.* Sioux County. Western affinities; at eastern edge of range.#

Two-tailed swallowtail. *Papilio multicaudata.* Sioux to Keya Paha counties. Western affinities; at eastern edge of range.* #

Palamedes swallowtail. *Papilio palamedes.* Brown County. Southeastern affinities; out of usual range.

Eastern black swallowtail. *Papilio polyxenes asterius.* Throughout region. Widespread.

Anise swallowtail. *Papilio zelicaon.* Sioux, Box Butte, and Dawes counties. Western affinities; at eastern edge of range.#

Whites and Sulphurs (Family Pieridae)
Whites (Subfamily Pierinae)
Pine white. *Neophasia menapia.* Sioux, Dawes, and Box Butte counties. Western affinities; at eastern edge of range.#

Western white. *Pontia occidentalis.* Sioux and Dawes counties, Nebraska, and Todd County, South Dakota. Western affinities; at eastern edge of range.#

Checkered white. *Pontia protodice.* Throughout region. Widespread.* #

Spring white. *Pontia sisymbrii.* Sioux, Dawes, and Sheridan counties. Western affinities; at eastern edge of range.#

Cabbage white. *Pieris rapae*. Throughout region. Widespread.* #

Large marble. *Euchloe ausonides*. Sioux and Dawes counties. Western affinities; at eastern edge of range.#

Olympia marble. *Euchloe olympia*. Throughout region. Great Plains affinities.* #

Sulphurs (Subfamily Coliadinae)

Clouded sulphur. *Colias philodice*. Throughout region. Widespread.* #

Queen Alexandra's sulphur. *Colias alexandra*. Sioux, Dawes, and Box Butte counties. Western affinities; at eastern edge of range.#

Orange sulphur. *Colias eurytheme*. Throughout region. Widespread.* #

Southern dogface. *Zerene cesonia*. Scattered throughout region. Southern affinities; near northern edge of range.* #

Cloudless sulphur. *Phoebis sennae*. Sheridan County. Southern affinities; near northern edge of range.#

Little yellow. *Eurema lisa*. Brown County. Eastern affinities; at western edge of range.* #

Mexican yellow. *Eurema mexicana*. Sioux, Dawes, and Brown counties. Southwestern affinities; near northern edge of range.#

Dainty (dwarf) sulphur. *Nathalis iole*. Throughout region. Southwestern affinities.* #

Gossamer-wing Butterflies (Family Lycaenidae)

Coppers (Subfamily Lycaeninae)

Purplish copper. *Lycaena helloides*. Throughout region. Western affinities; near eastern edge of range.#

Bronze copper. *Lycaena hyllus*. Throughout region. Northern affinities.* #

Ruddy copper. *Lycaena rubidus*. Sioux County to Cherry County. Western affinities; at eastern edge of range.#

Great gray copper. *Gaeides (Dione) xanthoides*. Scattered throughout region. Great Plains affinities.

Hairstreaks (Subfamily Theclinae)

Acadian hairstreak. *Satyrium acadica*. Throughout region. Northern affinities.#

Banded hairstreak. *Satyrium calanus.* Cherry, Brown, and Keya Paha counties, Nebraska, and Tripp County, South Dakota. Eastern affinities; near western edge of range.#

Edwards's hairstreak. *Satyrium edwardsii.* Cherry County. Eastern affinities; at western edge of range.#

Striped hairstreak. *Satyrium liparops.* Scattered records across region. Widespread.#

Coral hairstreak. *Satyrium (Harkenclenus) titus.* Scattered throughout region. Widespread.* #

Western pine elfin. *Callophrys eryphon.* Scattered records. Western affinities; at eastern edge of range.* #

Juniper hairstreak. *Mitoura siva.* Scattered records. Widespread.*

Gray hairstreak. *Strymon melinus.* Throughout region. Widespread.* #

Leda ministreak. *Ministrymon leda.* Sheridan County. Southeastern affinities; outside normal range.

Blues (Subfamily Polyommatinae)

Western pygmy blue. *Brephidium exile.* Dawes County. Southwestern affinities; at northeastern edge of range.

Marine blue. *Leptotes marina.* Sioux and Cherry counties. Southwestern affinities; at northeastern edge of range.#

Reakirt's blue. *Hemiargus isola.* Throughout region. Southwestern affinities; at northeastern edge of range.* #

Western tailed blue. *Everes amyntula.* Sioux County. Western affinities; at eastern edge of range.#

Eastern tailed blue. *Everes comyntas.* Throughout region. Widespread.* #

Spring azure. *Celastrina argiolus* ("*ladon*"). Throughout region. Widespread.* #

Silvery blue. *Glaucopsyche lygdamus.* Sioux, Dawes, and Sheridan counties. Western affinities; at eastern edge of range.#

Arrowhead blue. *Glaucopsyche piasus.* Sioux County. Western affinities; at eastern edge of range.#

Dotted blue. *Euphilotes enoptes.* Sioux County. Western affinities; outside normal range.

Melissa blue. *Lycaeides melissa*. Throughout region. Western affinities; at eastern edge of range.* #

Boisduval's blue. *Plebejus icarioides*. Sioux, Dawes, Box Butte, and Sheridan counties. Western affinities; at eastern edge of range.#

Greenish blue. *Plebejus saepiolus*. Sioux and Dawes counties. Western affinities; at eastern edge of range.#

Shasta blue. *Plebejus shasta*. Sioux, Box Butte, and Dawes counties. Western affinities; at eastern edge of range.#

Acmon blue. *Icaria acmon*. Scattered records. Western affinities; outside normal range.

Brush-footed Butterflies (Family Nymphalidae)
Snouts (Subfamily Libytheinae)

American snout. *Libytheana carinenta*. Sioux and Brown counties. Widespread.#

Heliconians and Fritillaries (Subfamily Heliconiinae)

Variegated fritillary. *Euptoieta claudia*. Throughout region. Widespread.* #

Aphrodite fritillary. *Speyeria aphrodite*. Cherry to Sioux counties. Northern affinities.

Atlantis fritillary. *Speyeria atlantis*. Sioux County. Widespread.#

Callippe fritillary. *Speyeria callippe*. Sioux County. Western affinities; at eastern edge of range.#

Coronis fritillary. *Speyeria coronis*. Sioux, Dawes, Box Butte, and Sheridan counties. Western affinities; at eastern edge of range.#

Great spangled fritillary. *Speyeria cybele*. Throughout region. Widespread.* #

Edwards's fritillary. *Speyeria edwardsii*. Sioux County to Keya Paha County, Nebraska; Todd and Tripp counties, South Dakota. Western affinities; at eastern edge of range.* #

Regal fritillary. *Speyeria idalia*. Throughout region. Great Plains affinities.* #

Mormon fritillary. *Speyeria mormonia*. Sioux and Dawes counties. Western affinities; at eastern edge of range.#

Zerene fritillary. *Speyeria zerene*. Sioux and Dawes counties. Western affinities; at eastern edge of range.#

Meadow fritillary. *Boloria bellona*. Sheridan and Boyd counties. Widespread.#

Silver-bordered fritillary. *Boloria selene*. Scattered records. Widespread.

Titania's fritillary. *Clossinia titiana*. Dawes County.

True Brush-foots (Subfamily Nymphalinae)

Arachne checkerspot. *Poladryas arachne*. Sioux and Dawes counties. Western affinities; at eastern edge of range.

Fulvia checkerspot. *Thessalia fulvia*. Brown and Keya Paha counties. Southwestern affinities; at northeastern edge of range.

Gorgone checkerspot. *Chlosyne gorgone*. Throughout region. Great Plains affinities.* #

Silvery checkerspot. *Chlosyne nycteis*. Throughout region. Widespread.* #

Tawny crescent. *Phyciodes batesii*. Sioux, Dawes, and Sheridan counties. Widespread.#

Pale crescent. *Phyciodes pallida*. Sioux and Dawes counties. Western affinities; at eastern edge of range.#

Phaon crescent. *Phyciodes phaon*. Sioux and Dawes counties. Southern affinities; at northern edge of range.

Painted crescent. *Phyciodes picta*. Dawes County. Southwestern affinities; at northeastern edge of range.

Field crescent. *Phyciodes pratensis*. Sioux County. Western affinities; at eastern edge of range.#

Pearl crescent. *Phyciodes tharos*. Throughout region. Widespread.* #

Anicia checkerspot. *Euphydryas (Occidryas) anicia*. Sioux, Dawes, and Sheridan counties. Western affinities; at eastern edge of range.

Baltimore. *Euphydryas phaeton*. Cherry County. Eastern affinities; at western edge of range.

Eastern comma. *Polygonia comma*. Throughout region. Eastern affinities; at western edge of range.* #

Question mark. *Polygonia interrogationis*. Throughout region. Eastern affinities; at western edge of range.* #

Gray comma. *Polygonia progne*. Scattered records. Widespread.#

Satyr comma. *Polygonia satyrus*. Sioux County. Western affinities; at eastern edge of range.#

Zephyrus angelwing. *Polygonia zephyrus*. Sioux, Dawes, and Cherry counties. Western affinities; at eastern edge of range.

Mourning cloak. *Nymphalis antiopa*. Throughout region. Widespread.* #

Milbert's tortoiseshell. *Nymphalis milberti*. Sioux, Dawes, Box Butte, Sheridan, and Cherry counties. Widespread.#

Compton tortoiseshell. *Nymphalis vaualbum*. Sioux, Dawes, and Keya Paha counties. Widespread.#

West Coast lady. *Vanessa annabella*. Dawes, Sheridan, and Cherry counties. Western affinities; at eastern edge of range.#

Red admiral. *Vanessa atalanta*. Throughout region. Widespread.* #

Painted lady. *Vanessa cardui*. Throughout region. Widespread.* #

American painted lady. *Vanessa virginiensis*. Throughout region. Widespread* #

Common buckeye. *Junonia coenia*. Throughout region. Widespread.* #

Admirals and Relatives (Subfamily Limenitidinae)
Viceroy. *Limenitis archippus*. Throughout region. Widespread.* #

Red-spotted purple. *Limenitis arthemis*. Cherry to Knox counties. Eastern affinities; at western edge of range. Hybrids with *L. weidemeyerii* reported from the Niobrara Valley Preserve.* #

Weidemeyer's admiral. *Limenitis weidemeyerii*. Scattered records. Western species, at eastern edge of range. Hybrids with *L. archippus* and *L. arthemis* reported from the Niobrara Valley Preserve.* #

Leafwings (Subfamily Charaxinae)
Goatweed leafwing. *Anaea andria*. Scattered records. Widespread.* #

Emperors (Subfamily Apaturinae)
Hackberry emperor. *Asterocampa celtis*. Throughout region. Widespread.* #

Satyrs (Subfamily Satyrinae)
Northern pearly eye. *Enodia anthedon*. Cherry, Brown, and Keya Paha counties, Nebraska; Tripp and Gregory counties, South Dakota. Eastern affinities; at western edge of range.* ##

Eyed brown. *Satyrodes eurydice*. Throughout region. Eastern affinities; near western edge of range.#

Little wood satyr. *Megisto cymela*. Throughout region. Eastern affinities; at western edge of range.* #

Common ringlet. *Coenonympha tullia*. Sioux to Keya Paha and Rock counties. Western affinities; at eastern edge of range.*

Mead's wood nymph. *Cercyonis meadii*. Sioux and Dawes counties. Western affinities; at eastern edge of range.#

Small wood nymph. *Cercyonis oetus*. Sioux and Dawes counties. Western affinities; at eastern edge of range.

Common wood nymph. *Cercyonis pegala*. Throughout region. Widespread.* #

Ridings's satyr. *Neominois ridingsii*. Sioux County. Western affinities; at eastern edge of range.#

Uhler's arctic. *Oeneis uhleri*. Sioux, Dawes, and Box Butte counties. Western affinities; at eastern edge of range.#

Monarchs (Subfamily Danainae)
Monarch. *Danaus plexippus*. Throughout region. Widespread.* #

Skippers (Family Hesperiidae)
Spread-wing skippers (Subfamily Pyrginae)
Silver-spotted skipper. *Epargyreus clarus*. Throughout region. Widespread.*

Southern cloudywing. *Thorybes bathyllus*. Cherry County. Southeastern affinities; at northwestern edge of range.

Northern cloudywing. *Thorybes pylades*. Scattered records. Widespread.*

Hayhurst's scallopwing. *Staphylus hayhurstii*. Boyd County. Widespread.#

Afranius duskywing. *Erynnis afranius*. Sioux, Dawes, Box Butte, and Sheridan counties. Western affinities; at eastern edge of range.#

Wild indigo duskywing. *Erynnis baptisiae*. Sioux, Cherry, and Keya Paha counties. Southeastern affinities; at northwestern edge of range.*

Horace's duskywing. *Erynnis horatius*. Sioux, Keya Paha, and Brown counties. Southeastern affinities; at northwestern edge of range.*

Juvenal's duskywing. *Erynnis juvenalis*. Cherry, Keya Paha, Brown, and

Rock counties, Nebraska; Todd and Tripp counties, South Dakota. Eastern affinities; at western edge of range.* #

Mottled duskywing. *Erynnis martialis*. Sioux, Dawes, Cherry, and Brown counties. Eastern affinities; at western edge of range.#

Persius duskywing. *Erynnis persius*. Sioux and Dawes counties. Western affinities; at eastern edge of range.#

Small checkered skipper. *Pyrgus scriptura*. Sioux County. Southwestern affinities; at northeastern edge of range.#

Common checkered skipper. *Pyrgus communis*. Throughout region. Widespread.* #

Common sootywing. *Pholisora catullus*. Throughout region. Widespread.* #

Grass Skippers (Subfamily Hesperiinae)

Least skipper. *Ancyloxypha numitor*. Throughout region. Eastern affinities; at western edge of range.* #

Garita skipperling. *Oarisma garita*. Sioux, Dawes, and Sheridan counties. Western affinities; at eastern edge of range.#

Plains gray skipper. *Yvretta rhesus*. Sioux, Dawes, and Sheridan counties. Western affinities; at eastern edge of range.

Uncas skipper. *Hesperia uncas*. Sioux to Cherry County. Western species; at eastern edge of range.*

Common branded skipper. *Hesperia comma*. Sioux to Keya Paha counties. Western affinities; at eastern edge of range.*

Leonard's skipper. *Hesperia leonardus*. Throughout region, west to Sioux County. Eastern affinities; at western edge of range.* #

Ottoe skipper. *Hesperia ottoe*. Boyd County to Dawes County. Great Plains affinities.* #

Pahaska skipper. *Hesperia pahaska*. Sioux, Dawes, and Sheridan counties. Western affinities; at eastern edge of range.#

Green skipper. *Hesperia viridis*. Sioux and Sheridan counties. Southwestern affinities; at northeastern edge of range.

Northern broken dash. *Wallengrenia egeremet*. Scattered records west to Dawes County. Eastern affinities; at western edge of range.* #

Yellowpatch (Peck's) skipper. *Polites coras.* Brown and Keya Paha counties. Widespread.*

Long dash. *Polites mystic.* Throughout region. Widespread.* #

Crossline skipper. *Polites origenes.* Sioux to Boyd County. Eastern affinities; at western edge of range.* #

Peck's skipper. *Polites peckius.* Throughout region. Widespread.#

Tawny-edged skipper. *Polites themistocles.* Throughout region. Widespread.* #

Little glassywing. *Pompeius verna.* Brown, Keya Paha, and Knox counties. Eastern affinities; at western edge of range.* #

Sachem. *Atalopedes campestris.* Throughout most of region. Widespread.#

Arogos skipper. *Atrytone arogos.* Scattered records, Knox County to Dawes County. Widespread.* #

Delaware skipper. *Anatrytone logan.* Scattered records west to Sioux County. Eastern affinities; at western edge of range.* #

Dusted skipper. *Atrytonpsis hiana.* Keya Paha and Brown counties. Eastern affinities; at western edge of range.* #

Hobomok skipper. *Poanes hobomok.* Scattered records west to Sioux County. Eastern affinities; at western edge of range.* #

Taxiles skipper. *Poanes taxiles.* Throughout most of region east to Keya Paha County. Southwestern affinities; at northeastern edge of range.* #

Broad-winged skipper. *Poanes viator.* Sheridan and Cherry counties. Eastern affinities; at western edge of range.#

Two-spotted skipper. *Euphyes bimacula.* Scattered records west to Sioux County. Eastern affinities; at western edge of range.#

Dion skipper. *Euphyes dion.* Knox County. Eastern affinities; at western edge of range.#

Dun skipper. *Euphyes (Vestris) rupicola.* Almost throughout region, Sioux County to Knox County. Widespread.* #

Oslar's roadside skipper. *Amblyscirtes oslari.* Sioux County to Keya Paha County. Southwestern affinities; at northeastern edge of range.* #

Simius roadside skipper. *Amblyscirtes simius.* Sioux County. Southwestern affinities; at northeastern edge of range.#

Common roadside skipper. *Amblyscirtes vialis*. Scattered records. Widespread.* #

Giant Skippers (Subfamily Megathyminae)

Strecker's giant skipper. *Megathymus streckeri* (*texanus*). Dawes to Keya Paha and Rock counties, Nebraska; Todd and Tripp counties, South Dakota. Southwestern affinities; at northeastern edge of range.* #

Appendix 1F

Dragonflies and Damselflies of the Niobrara Region

The following list is based on unpublished data of Roy G. Beckemeyer (pers. comm.), who has a very useful dragonfly Web site: http://www.windsofkansas.com/odonata/odonata.html. Another useful site is Dennis Paulson's: http://www.ups.edu/biology/museum/NAdragons.html. This list's geographic coverage encompasses the twelve Nebraska counties listed in table 25. Counties are named in west-to-east geographic sequence in range descriptions. North American range maps and illustrations of all the forty-four listed species of dragonflies are provided by Dunkle (2000) and by Kondratieff (2000) for the thirty-four listed species of damselflies. Zoogeographic affinities of dragonflies were estimated from available range maps and range descriptions; zoogeographic affinities and common names of damselflies were based on various sources. Species are listed alphabetically by their Latin names within genera, which are arranged in usual taxonomic sequence, as are families.

Dragonflies

Family Aeshnidae—Darners

Common green darner. *Anax junius*. Reported from Dawes County to Antelope County. Widespread.

Fawn darner. *Boyeria vinosa*. Reported from Cherry, Brown, and Keya Paha counties. Eastern affinities; at western edge of range in Niobrara Valley.

Canada darner. *Aeshna canadensis*. Reported from Sheridan County to Keya Paha County. Northern affinities; at southern edge of range in Niobrara Valley.

Lance-tipped darner. *Aeshna constricta*. Reported from Sioux County to Keya Paha County. Widespread.

Variable darner. *Aeshna interrupta lineata*. Reported from Dawes County to Cherry County. Northern affinities.

Blue-eyed darner. *Aeshna multicolor*. Reported from Sioux County to Keya Paha County. Western affinities.

Paddle-tailed darner. *Aeshna palmata*. Reported from Sioux, Dawes, and Cherry counties. Western affinities; at eastern edge of range in Niobrara Valley.

Shadow darner. *Aeshna umbrosa*. Reported from Sioux, Dawes, and Cherry counties. Widespread.

Family Gomphidae—Clubtails

Plains clubtail. *Gomphus (Gomphurus) externus*. Reported from Cherry and Brown counties. Widespread.

Pronghorn clubtail. *Gomphus (Gomphurus) graslinellus*. Reported from Sioux, Dawes, and Keya Paha counties. Widespread.

Riverine clubtail. *Stylurus amnicola*. Reported from Cherry, Brown, and Antelope counties. Eastern affinities; at western edge of range in Niobrara Valley.

Brimstone clubtail. *Stylurus intricatus*. Reported from Cherry and Brown counties. Western affinities.

Elusive clubtail. *Stylurus notatus*. Reported from Cherry County. Eastern affinities; at western edge of range in Niobrara Valley.

Horned clubtail. *Arigomphus cornutus*. Reported from Cherry County. Northern affinities; at southern edge of range in Niobrara Valley.

Common sanddragon. *Progomphus obscurus*. Reported from Cherry County. Eastern affinities; at western edge of range in Niobrara Valley.

Pale snaketail. *Ophiogomphus severus*. Reported from Sioux County to Brown County. Western affinities; at eastern edge of range in Niobrara Valley.

Family Corduliidae—Emeralds

Prince baskettail. *Epitheca (Epicordulia) princeps*. Reported from Cherry and Antelope counties. Eastern affinities; at western edge of range in Niobrara Valley.

Stripe-winged baskettail. *Epitheca (Tetragoneuria) costalis*. Reported from Sioux County to Holt County. Southern affinities; at northern edge of range in Niobrara Valley.

Plains emerald. *Somatochlora ensigera*. Reported from Cherry County. Northern affinities; at southern edge of range in Niobrara Valley.

Family Libellulidae—Skimmers

Golden-winged skimmer. *Libellula auripennis*. Reported from Cherry County. Southeastern affinities; outside normal range.

Widow skimmer. *Libellula luctuosa*. Reported from Sioux County to Antelope County. Widespread.

Twelve-spotted skimmer (tenspot). *Libellula pulchella*. Reported from Sioux County to Antelope County. Widespread.

Four-spot skimmer. *Libellula quadrimaculata*. Reported from Dawes, Cherry, and Brown counties. Widespread.

Common whitetail. *Plathemis (Libellula) lydia*. Reported from Sioux to Antelope counties. Widespread.

Variegated (robust pink) meadowhawk. *Sympetrum corruptum*. Reported from Sioux County to Antelope County. Western affinities.

Saffron-winged meadowhawk. *Sympetrum costiferum*. Reported from Sioux County to Antelope County. Northern affinities.

Cherry-faced meadowhawk. *Sympetrum internum*. Reported from Sioux County to Keya Paha County. Widespread.

Red-veined meadowhawk. *Sympetrum madidum*. Reported from Dawes County. Western affinities; at eastern edge of range in Niobrara Valley.

White-faced meadowhawk. *Sympetrum obtrusum*. Seven counties, Sioux to Holt. Widespread.

Western (band-winged) meadowhawk. *Sympetrum (semicinctum) occidentale*. Reported from Sioux County to Holt County. Western affinities.

Striped meadowhawk. *Sympetrum pallipes*. Reported from Sioux, Dawes, and Sheridan counties. Western affinities; at eastern edge of range in Niobrara Valley.

Ruby meadowhawk. *Sympetrum rubicundulum*. Reported from Sioux County to Holt County. Eastern affinities.

Autumn (yellow-legged) meadowhawk. *Sympetrum vicinum*. Reported from Sioux County to Antelope County. Widespread.

Eastern amberwing. *Perithemis tenera*. Reported from Dawes County to Antelope County. Southeastern affinities; at western edge of range in Niobrara Valley.

Blue dasher. *Pachydiplax longipennis*. Reported from Dawes County to Brown County. Widespread.

Eastern pondhawk. *Erythemis simplicicollis*. Reported from Dawes County to Antelope County. Southeastern affinities.

Wandering glider (globe skimmer). *Pantala flavescens*. Reported from Dawes and Cherry counties. Widespread.

Spot-winged glider. *Pantala hymenaea*. Reported from Cherry and Brown counties. Widespread.

Black saddlebags. *Tramea lacerata*. Reported from Dawes County to Brown County. Widespread.

Hudsonian whiteface. *Leucorrhinia hudsonica*. Reported from Brown County. Northern affinities; at southern edge of range in Niobrara Valley.

Dot-tailed whiteface. *Leucorrhinia intacta*. Reported from Dawes County to Holt County. Widespread.

Calico pennant. *Celithemis elisa*. Reported from Cherry County. Eastern affinities; at western edge of range in Niobrara Valley.

Halloween pennant. *Celithemis eponina*. Reported from Cherry and Brown counties. Eastern affinities; at western edge of range in Niobrara Valley.

Damselflies

Family Calopterygidae—Broad-winged Damselflies

Western dark-winged damselfly (river jewelwing). *Calopteryx aequabilis*. Reported from Sioux County to Brown County. Northern species. Widespread.

Black-winged damselfly (ebony jewelwing). *Calopteryx maculata*. Reported from Sioux County to Holt County. Eastern species.

Genus Heterina—Rubyspots

American rubyspot. *Heterina americana*. Reported from Sioux County to Holt County. Widespread.

Family Lestidae—Spreadwing Damselflies

Great spreadwing. *Archilestes grandis.* Reported from Sioux County. Southwestern affinities.

Spotted spreadwing, *Lestes congener.* Reported from Dawes County to Cherry County. Widespread.

Common spreadwing. *Lestes disjunctus.* Reported from Cherry and Brown counties. Widespread and common.

Sweetflag spreadwing. *Lestes forcipatus.* Reported from Dawes, Cherry, and Brown counties. Eastern affinities.

Slender spreadwing. *Lestes rectangularis.* Reported from Cherry, Brown, and Holt counties. Eastern affinities.

Lyre-tipped spreadwing. *Lestes unguiculatus.* Reported from Sioux County to Knox County. Widespread and common.

Family Coenagrionidae—Narrow-winged Damselflies

Paiute dancer. *Argia alberta.* Reported from Sioux, Brown, and Cherry counties. Western affinities.

Blue-fronted dancer. *Argia apicalis.* Reported from Cherry County to Antelope County. Eastern affinities.

Emma's dancer. *Argia emma.* Reported from Sioux County to Brown County. Western affinities.

Variable dancer. *Argia fumipennis.* Reported from Sioux County to Holt County. Widespread.

Powdered dancer. *Argia moesta.* Reported from Cherry County Widespread.

Springwater dancer. *Argia plana.* Reported from Cherry and Keya Paha counties. Western affinities.

Blue-ringed dancer. *Argia sedula.* Reported from Holt County. Widespread.

Vivid dancer. *Argia vivida.* Reported from Sioux County to Keya Paha County. Western affinities.

Tiaga bluet. *Coenagrion resolutum.* Reported from Cherry County. Northern affinities.

River bluet. *Enallagma anna.* Reported from Sioux County to Keya Paha County. Western affinities.

Rainbow bluet. *Enallagma antennatum*. Reported from Sioux County to Antelope County. Eastern affinities.

Double-striped bluet. *Enallagma basidens*. Reported from Sioux County. Southern affinities.

Double-striped bluet. *Enallagma carunculatum*. Reported from Sioux County to Holt County. Widespread and common.

Familiar bluet. *Enallagma civile*. Reported from Sioux County to Antelope County. Widespread and abundant.

Alkali bluet. *Enallagma clausum*. Reported from Dawes, Sheridan, and Cherry counties. Western affinities.

Northern bluet. *Enallagma cyathigerum*. Reported from Cherry and Antelope counties. Widespread.

Marsh bluet. *Enallagma ebrium*. Reported from Cherry and Antelope counties. Northern affinities.

Stream bluet. *Enallagma exsulans*. Reported from Cherry, Brown, and Holt counties. Eastern affinities.

Skimming bluet. *Enallagma germinatum*. Reported from Antelope County. Eastern affinities.

Hagen's bluet. *Enallagma hageni*. Reported from Sioux to Holt counties. Eastern affinities.

Arroyo bluet. *Enallagma praevarum*. Reported from Sioux and Dawes counties. Western affinities.

Plains forktail. *Ischnura damula*. Reported from Sioux County. Great Plains affinities.

Western forktail. *Ischnura perparva*. Reported from Sioux County to Brown County. Western affinities.

Eastern forktail. *Ischnura verticalis*. Reported from Sioux County to Knox County. Eastern affinities; abundant.

Sedge sprite. *Nehallenia irene*. Reported from Cherry and Brown counties. Northern affinities.

Appendix 1G

Vascular Plants of the Niobrara Region

The 650-plus plant species in the following list are ones reported by Barkley (1977) or others from the twelve-county Niobrara region as defined earlier. This is clearly an incomplete inventory; Churchill, Freeman, and Kantak (1988) listed 581 plant species from the ninety-square-mile Niobrara Valley Preserve alone. Species selected for inclusion here are mostly the more common or conspicuous ones that are illustrated in regional field guides, such as those of Larson and Johnson (1999), who documented 289 species of the north-central Great Plains grasslands, and Johnson and Larson (1999), who described 600 species of mostly forest and shrubland plants from South Dakota's Black Hills region. Although I list mostly native species, I also include some introduced species such as economically significant weeds or forage crops.

In the following summary, plant families are sequenced alphabetically by their Latin names, genera are sequenced alphabetically within families, and species are sequenced alphabetically within genera. Numbers directly following each family name in parentheses represent the minimum total species reported from Nebraska per family by Barkley (1977); newer state totals should soon become available (Kaul, Sutherland, and Rolfsmeier, 2006). These numbers are followed after a slash (3/1) by the total species per family reported from the Niobrara Valley Preserve by Churchill, Freeman, and Kantak (1988).

Species reported from the Niobrara Valley Preserve by Churchill, Freeman, and Kantak (1988) are identified by asterisks (*) in the following list; those documented by Larson and Johnson (1999) are marked with pound symbols (#). A total of ninety-two plant species reported from the Niobrara National Scenic River region have been classified as "sensitive" by the Nebraska Natural Heritage Program (National Park Service, 2005); such species are shown in **boldface**.

In the range descriptions that follow, the "entire" Niobrara region as defined here consists of plants reported from most and possibly all the twelve Nebraska counties listed in table 25. "Western Niobrara Valley" refers to county records extending roughly as far east as Cherry County; "eastern Niobrara Valley" refers to county records extending roughly as far west as Cherry County.

Native Trees, Shrubs, and Woody Vines

Aceraceae—Maple Family (3/1)
Box elder. *Acer negundo*. Entire Niobrara region. Mesic woods.* #

Agavaceae—Agave Family (1/1)
Great Plains yucca (small soapweed). *Yucca glauca*. Entire Niobrara region. Sandhills and mixed prairies.* #

Anacardiaceae—Cashew Family (6/3)
Aromatic sumac. *Rhus aromatica*. Entire Niobrara region. Wooded canyons and prairie slopes.* #

Smooth sumac. *Rhus glabra*. Entire Niobrara region. Disturbed habitats, prairies, and coniferous woods.* #

Poison ivy. *Toxicodendron* (*Rhus*) *radicans* and *T. rydbergii*. Entire Niobrara region. Prairies and wooded canyons.* #

Asteraceae—Aster Family (230/80)
Silver sagebrush. *Artemisia cana*. Northwestern Panhandle. Xeric prairies.#

Sand sagebrush. *Artemisia filifolia*. Western Niobrara Valley. Mixed prairie and gravelly ridges.*

Fringed sagebrush. *Artemisia ludoviciana*. Western Niobrara Valley. Sandy prairies.* #

Big sagebrush. *Artemisia tridentata*. Panhandle. Xeric upland prairies.#

Rabbitbrush. *Chrysothamnus naseosus*. Western Niobrara Valley. Xeric prairies.#

Berberidaceae—Barberry Family (1/0)

Oregon grape. *Berberis repens.* Western Panhandle. Coniferous woods.#

Betulaceae—Birch Family (4/3)

Mountain (water) birch. *Betula occidentalis.* Pine Ridge. Lowland woods.#

Paper birch. *Betula papyrifera.* Central Niobrara Valley. Shady streamsides and near springs.* #

American hazelnut. *Corylus americana.* Widespread. Riparian sites.* #

Hop hornbeam (ironwood). *Ostrya virginiana.* Entire Niobrara region. Near water.* #

Caesalpiniaccae—Senna Family (6/0)

Honey locust. *Gleditsia triacanthos.* Lower Niobrara Valley. Floodplains.

Kentucky coffee tree. *Gymnocladus dioca.* Central and eastern Niobrara Valley. Floodplains.

Caprifoliaceae—Honeysuckle Family (7/4)

Elderberry. *Sambucus canadensis.* Eastern Niobrara region. Mesic woods.

Snowberry. *Symphoricarpos alba.* Entire Niobrara region. Prairies and open woods.* #

Western snowberry. *Symphoricarpos occidentalis.* Entire Niobrara region. Prairies and open woods.* #

Celastraccae—Staff Tree Family (2/1)

Climbing bittersweet. *Celastrus scandens.* Entire Niobrara region. Xeric canyons, woods, thickets, and near water.* #

Wahoo. *Euonymus atropurpureus.* Eastern Niobrara Valley. Uplands.

Chenopodiaceae—Goosefoot Family (32/8)

Fourwing saltbush. *Atriplex canescens.* Panhandle. Alkali soils.

Winterfat. *Ceratoides lanata.* Panhandle. Alkali soils.#

Black greasewood. *Sarcobatus vermiculatus.* Panhandle. Alkali soils.

Cornaceae—Dogwood Family (4/1)

Rough-leaved dogwood. *Cornus drummondii.* Eastern Niobrara Valley. Uplands.

Red osier dogwood. *Cornus stolonifera.* Entire Niobrara region. Riparian and other wetlands.* #

Cupressaceae—Cypress Family (2/2)

Creeping juniper. *Juniperus horizontalis.* Rare in upper and central Niobrara Valley. Xeric uplands.#

Western red cedar (Rocky Mountain juniper). *Juniperus scopulorum.* Western Niobrara Valley. Relatively xeric habitats.#

Eastern red cedar (red juniper). *Juniperus virginiana.* Mainly eastern Niobrara Valley, apparently intergrading westward with *J. scopulorum.* Diverse xeric to mesic habitats.* #

Elaeaginaceae—Russian Olive Family (2/2)

Buffaloberry. *Shepherdia argentea.* Entire Niobrara region. Xeric uplands and bluffs.* #

Fabaceae—Bean Family (90/36)

Leadplant. *Amorpha canescens.* Entire Niobrara region. Native prairies.* #

False indigo. *Amorpha fruticosa.* Entire Niobrara region. Floodplains and near water.* #

Shrubby (bushy) cinquefoil. *Potentilla paradoxa.* Entire Niobrara region. Low, moist sites.

Fagaceae—Oak Family (8/1)

Bur oak. *Quercus macrocarpa.* Primarily in eastern half of Niobrara Valley. Floodplains and valley slopes.* #

Juglandaceae—Walnut Family (1/1)

Black walnut. *Juglans nigra.* Eastern half of Niobrara Valley. Floodplain woods.*

Oleaceae—Ash Family (3/2)

Green (and red) ash. *Fraxinus pennsylvanica* (including *F. subintegerrima*). Entire Niobrara region. Floodplain woods near rivers.* #

Pinaceae—Pine Family (2/1 + 1 introduced)

Western ponderosa (yellow) pine. *Pinus ponderosa.* Panhandle and western half of Niobrara Valley. Xeric north-side slopes and gravelly ridges south of Niobrara River.* #

Rhamnaceae—Buckthorn Family (4/2)

New Jersey tea. *Ceanothus americanus.* Eastern Niobrara Valley. Prairies.

Lance-leaved buckthorn. *Rhamnus lanceolata.* Eastern Niobrara Valley. Deciduous woods.*

Rosaceae—Rose Family (42/16)

Serviceberry. *Amelanchier alnifolia.* Entire Niobrara region. Pine forests.#

Juneberry. *Amelanchier canadensis.* Eastern Niobrara Valley. Floodplains.

True mountain mahogany. *Cercocarpus montanus.* Panhandle. Uplands.#

Hawthorn. *Crataegus succulenta.* Eastern half of Niobrara Valley Uplands.

Ninebark. *Physocarpus opulifolius.* Rare in central and western Niobrara Valley. Xeric uplands.#

Wild plum. *Prunus americana.* Entire Niobrara region. Open woods, wood edges, and thickets.* #

Sand cherry. *Prunus besseyi.* Entire Niobrara region. Sandhills.#

Chokecherry. *Prunus virginiana.* Entire Niobrara region. floodplain woods, woodland edges.* #

Prairie crab apple. *Pyrus iowensis.* Eastern Niobrara Valley. Uplands.

Prairie wild rose. *Rosa arkansana.* Entire Niobrara region. Woodland edges.* #

Western wild rose. *Rosa woodsi.* Western Niobrara Valley. Thickets and riverbanks.* #

Black raspberry. *Rubus occidentalis.* Eastern Niobrara Valley. Riparian woods and wooded tributaries in sandy soils.#

Catherinette's berry (creeping blackberry). *Rubus pubescens.* Rare in central Niobrara Valley. Moist woods.#

Rutaceae—Rue Family (1/1)

Prickly ash. *Zanthoxylum americanum.* Eastern Niobrara Valley. Thickets and woods.*

Salicaceae—Willow Family (18/6)

Narrow-leaved cottonwood. *Populus angustifolia.* Panhandle. Floodplains.#

Balsam poplar. *Populus balsamifera.* Pine Ridge. Floodplains.#

Eastern (plains) cottonwood. *Populus deltoides.* Entire Niobrara region. Floodplains.* #

Bigtooth aspen. *Populus grandidentata.* Reputed to occur as a hybrid population with quaking aspen near Smith Falls. This interpretation is now considered questionable (Robert Kaul, pers. comm.).

Quaking aspen. *Populus tremuloides.* Panhandle. Floodplains.#

Peachleaf willow. *Salix amygdaloides.* Entire Niobrara region. Riparian sites.* #

Bebb's (long-beaked) willow. *Salix bebbiana.* Panhandle. Moist sites.#

Sandbar (coyote) willow. *Salix exigua.* Entire Niobrara region. Riparian sites.* #

Shining willow. *Salix lucida.* Panhandle. Moist sites.#

Black willow. *Salix nigra.* Entire Niobrara region. Streamsides.

Diamond willow. *Salix rigida.* Entire Niobrara region. Riparian sites.#

Saxifraginaceae (Grossulariaceae)—Currant Family (7/4)

Black currant. *Ribes americanum.* Entire Niobrara region. Open woodlands.* #

Missouri gooseberry. *Ribes missouriense.* Entire Niobrara region. Moist woods.#

Buffalo currant. *Ribes odoratum.* Entire Niobrara region. Woodlands.#

Northern gooseberry. *Ribes oxycanthoides.* Entire Niobrara region. Springbranch canyons.* #

Tamaricaceae—Tamarisk Family (1/0)

Salt cedar. *Tamarix ramosissima*. Local in riparian habitats. Exotic invader in wetlands.

Tiliaceae—Basswood Family (1/1)

Basswood (linden). *Tilia americana*. Eastern Niobrara Valley. Spring-branch canyons.*

Ulmaceae—Elm Family (5/2)

Hackberry. *Celtis occidentalis*. Entire Niobrara region. Floodplains.* #

White (American) elm. *Ulmus americana*. Entire Niobrara region. Floodplains.* #

Siberian elm. *Ulmus pumila*. Introduced and widespread. Most common in towns and farmsteads, where planted.* #

Red (slippery) elm. *Ulmus rubra*. Eastern Niobrara Valley. Floodplains.

Cork (rock) elm. *Ulmus thomasi*. Eastern Niobrara Valley. Floodplains.

Vitaceae—Grape Family (7/2)

Woodbine. *Parthenocissus vitacea*. Entire Niobrara region. Woods and thickets.* #

Summer grape. *Vitis aestivalis*. Rare in central Niobrara Valley. Upland woods.

Riverbank grape. *Vitis riparia*. Entire Niobrara region. Floodplains and xeric canyons.* #

Forbs, Grasses, and Sedges

Alismataceae—Arrowhead Family (11/2)

Long-barb arrowhead. *Sagittaria longiloba*. Rare in central Niobrara Valley. Wetlands.

Sessile-fruited arrowhead. *Sagittaria rigida*. Rare in central Niobrara Valley. Wetlands.

Amaranthaceae—Pigweed Family (11/5)

Tumble pigweed. *Amaranthus albus*. Scattered records. Weedy sites.

Prostrate pigweed. *Amaranthus graecizans*. Scattered records. Disturbed sandy soils, weedy sites.*

Redroot pigweed. *Amaranthus retroflexus*. Entire Niobrara region. Disturbed soils, weedy sites.*

Common water hemp. *Amaranthus rudis*. Mostly eastern records. Weedy sites.

Field snakecotton. *Froelichia floridana*. Entire Niobrara region. Sand dunes, rocky open woods.*

Slender froelichia. *Froelichia gracilis*. Eastern Niobrara Valley. Sandy sites, rocky open woods.*

Anacardiaceae—Cashew Family (6/3)
Poison ivy. *Toxicodendron* (*Rhus*) spp. Entire Niobrara region; woodland edges, also grows as a woody shrub or vine in shaded woods.*#

Apiaceae—Parsley Family (= Umbelliferae) (30/11)
Spotted waterhemlock. *Cicuta maculata*. Entire Niobrara region. Near streams.* #

Poison hemlock. *Conium maculatum*. Scattered records. Disturbed soils, weedy sites; poisonous.* #

Queen Anne's lace. *Daucus carota*. Eastern Niobrara Valley. Weedy sites.#

Cow parsnip. *Heracleum sphondylium*. Scattered records. Shaded woods.#

Wild parsley (desert biscuitroot). *Lomatium foeniculaceum*. Eastern Niobrara Valley and Panhandle. Xeric prairies.#

Leafy musineon. *Musineon divaricatum*. Western half of Niobrara Valley. Rocky prairies, open woods.#

Narrow-leaved musineon. *Musineon tenuifolium*. Panhandle. Xeric prairies, open woods.#

Sweet cicely. *Osmorhiza claytonii*. Scattered records. Wooded hillsides.*

Apocynaceae—Dogbane Family (4/1)
Hemp (prairie) dogbane. *Apocynum cannabinum*. Entire Niobrara region. Prairies, open woods, weedy sites; poisonous.#

Araceae—Arum Family (3/0)
Jack-in-the-pulpit. *Arisaema triphyllum*. Eastern Niobrara Valley. Moist, humid woods; poisonous.

Aralaceae—Ginseng Family (1/0)

Wild sarsaparilla. *Aralia nudicaulis.* Scattered records. Springbranch canyon forests.*

Spikenard. *Aralia racemosa.* Reported from Cherry County. Wooded hillsides and ravines.

Asclepiadaceae—Milkweed Family (17/7)

Sand milkweed. *Asclepias arenaria.* Entire Niobrara region. Sandy upland prairies.*

Swamp milkweed. *Asclepias incarnata.* Entire Niobrara region. Wet prairies, moist banks.* #

Woolly milkweed. *Asclepias lanuginosa.* Scattered records. Sandy prairies.*

Plains milkweed. *Asclepias pumila.* Entire Niobrara region. Mixed prairies.* #

Showy milkweed. *Asclepias speciosa.* Western Niobrara Valley. Moist prairies, near water.#

Narrow-leaved milkweed. *Asclepias stenophylla.* Entire Niobrara region. Sandy or rocky prairies.#

Common milkweed. *Asclepias syriaca.* Entire Niobrara region. Streambanks, floodplains, disturbed sites.* #

Whorled milkweed. *Asclepias verticillata.* Entire Niobrara region. Sandy or rocky prairies.#

Green milkweed. *Asclepias viridiflora.* Entire Niobrara region. Sandy or rocky prairies.* #

Asteraceae—Sunflower Family (= Compositae). (230/80)

Common yarrow. *Achillea millefolium.* Entire Niobrara region. Grasslands, open woods, weedy sites.* #

Common ragweed. *Ambrosia artemisiifolia.* Widespread. Disturbed soils, weedy sites.* #

Western ragweed. *Ambrosia psilostachya.* Entire Niobrara region. Open prairie, disturbed sites.* #

Pussytoes. *Antennaria neglecta.* Entire Niobrara region. Prairies, open woodlands, pastures.* #

Rocky Mountain pussytoes. *Antennaria parviflora*. Entire Niobrara region. Prairies, open woods, roadsides.* #

Common burdock. *Arctium minus*. Scattered records. weedy sites.*

Biennial wormwood. *Artemisia biennis*. Scattered records. Damp, sandy soil, streambanks.

Western sagewort. *Artemisia campestris*. Entire Niobrara region. Upland grasslands.#

Silky wormwood (tarragon). *Artemisia dracunculus*. Scattered records. Xeric, open sites.#

Fringed sagewort. *Artemisia frigida*. Western Niobrara Valley. Shortgrass prairies.#

Cudweed sagewort. *Artemisia ludoviciana*. Entire Niobrara region. Xeric plains.* #

Rayless aster. *Aster brachyactis*. Rare in central Niobrara Valley. Moist, sandy lowlands.

White (heath) aster. *Aster ericoides*. Entire Niobrara region. Open, upland prairies.* #

White prairie aster. *Aster falcatus*. Entire Niobrara region. Xeric sites.#

Rush aster. *Aster junciformis*. Rare in central Niobrara Valley. Cool bogs and swamps.

New England aster. *Aster novae-angliae*. Eastern Niobrara Valley. Moist, sandy sites.* #

Aromatic aster. *Aster oblongifolius*. Entire Niobrara region. Rocky or sandy open sites.* #

Willowleaf aster. *Aster praealtus*. Central and eastern Niobrara Valley. Damp sites.*

Nodding beggarticks. *Bidens cernua*. Entire Niobrara region. Muddy, disturbed soils, weedy sites.*

Tickseed sunflower. *Bidens coronata*. Entire Niobrara region. Damp, sandy sites.* #

Devil's beggarticks. *Bidens frondosa*. Entire Niobrara region. Moist wooded sites.* #

Musk thistle. *Carduus nutans*. Entire Niobrara region. Pastures, prairies, weedy sites.#

Russian knapweed. *Centaurea repens*. Scattered records. Introduced weed.

Oxeye daisy. *Chrysanthemum leucanthemum*. Scattered records. Fields, disturbed soils, weedy sites.#

Golden aster. *Chrysopsis villosa*. Scattered records. Open, sandy uplands.

Chicory. *Cichorium intybus*. Entire Niobrara region. Introduced species. Weedy sites.

Tall thistle. *Cirsium altissimum*. Entire Niobrara region. Disturbed soils, weedy sites.*

Canada thistle. *Cirsium arvense*. Entire Niobrara region. Disturbed soils, weedy sites.#

Platte thistle. *Cirsium canescens*. Entire Niobrara region. Sandy upland prairies.* #

Flodman's thistle. *Cirsium flodmanii*. Entire Niobrara region. Moist, open pastures, weedy sites.* #

Wavyleaf thistle. *Cirsium undulatum*. Entire Niobrara region. Xeric prairies, weedy sites.#

Bull thistle. *Cirsium vulgare*. Entire Niobrara region. Introduced species. Disturbed soils, weedy sites.#

Horseweed. *Conyza canadensis*. Entire Niobrara region. Disturbed soils, weedy sites.#

Plains coreopsis. *Coreopsis tinctoria*. Entire Niobrara region. Sandy ground, disturbed sites.

Hawk's beard. *Crepis runcinata*. Western Niobrara Valley. Open, often damp, meadows.*

Fetid marigold. *Dyssodia papposa*. Entire Niobrara region Open fields, disturbed sites.* #

Purple coneflower. *Echinacea angustifolia*. Entire Niobrara region. Open, rocky prairies.* #

Western fleabane. *Erigeron bellidiastrum*. Entire Niobrara region. Open, damp, sandy sites.*

Spreading fleabane. *Erigeron divergens*. Rare in central Niobrara Valley. Open rocky or sandy sites.

Low fleabane. *Erigeron pumilus.* Western Niobrara Valley. Open, xeric prairies.#

Daisy (rough) fleabane. *Erigeron strigosus.* Entire Niobrara region. Moist, damp prairies.#

Spotted joe-pye weed. *Eupatorium maculatum.* Entire Niobrara region. Moist, wooded sites.* #

Boneset. *Eupatorium perfoliatum.* Entire Niobrara region. Damp, low ground.*

White snakeroot. *Eupatorium rugosum.* Eastern Niobrara Valley. Open woods, disturbed sites.

Curly-top gumweed. *Grindelia squarrosa.* Entire Niobrara region. Disturbed places, weedy sites.* #

Broom snakeweed. *Gutierrezia sarothrae.* Entire Niobrara region. Xeric, open plains.* #

Cutleaf ironplant. *Haplopappus spinulosus.* Entire Niobrara region. Open prairies.*

Common sneezeweed. *Helenium autumnale.* Entire Niobrara region. Moist, open sites.*

Common sunflower. *Helianthus annuus.* Entire Niobrara region. Open sites.* #

Sawtooth sunflower. *Helianthus grosseserratus.* Entire Niobrara region. Damp prairies, open bottomlands.

Maximilian sunflower. *Helianthus maxmiliani.* Entire Niobrara region. Xeric or damp prairies, sandy sites.* #

Nuttall's sunflower. *Helianthus nuttallii.* Scattered records. Mesic prairies and marshes.* #

Plains sunflower. *Helianthus petiolaris.* Entire Niobrara region. Open sandy sites.#

Stiff sunflower. *Helianthus rigidus.* Eastern Niobrara Valley. Xeric or damp prairies.* #

Jerusalem artichoke. *Helianthus tuberosus.* Entire Niobrara region. Open or shaded, moist sites.*

False sunflower (oxeye). *Heliopsis helianthoides.* Eastern Niobrara Valley. Xeric open woods, weedy sites.*

Stemless hymenoxys. *Hymenoxys acaulis.* Panhandle. Rocky breaks, calcareous soils.#

Poverty sumpweed. *Iva axillaris.* Western Niobrara Valley. xeric, often alkaline soils, prairies.

Marsh elder. *Iva xanthifolia.* Entire Niobrara region. Borders of streams and local drying sites.

False boneset. *Kuhnia eupatorioides.* Entire Niobrara region. Open prairies.* #

Blue lettuce. *Lactuca oblongifolia.* Entire Niobrara region. Low, moist meadows.* #

Prickly lettuce. *Lactuca serriola.* Entire Niobrara region. Disturbed soils, weedy sites.

Rough gayfeather. *Liatris aspera.* Eastern Niobrara Valley. Open woods on sandy sites.*

Blazing star (scaly gayfeather) *Liatris glabrata.* Entire Niobrara region. Especially Sandhills.

Dotted gayfeather. *Liatris punctata.* Entire Niobrara region. Xeric, sandy upland prairies.* #

Skeletonweed. *Lygodesmia juncea.* Entire Niobrara region. Open high prairies.* #

Viscid aster. *Machaeranthera linearis.* Western Niobrara Valley. Open, xeric, sandy sites.

Pineappleweed. *Matricaria matricarioides.* Scattered records. Disturbed soils, weedy sites.#

False dandelion. *Microseris cuspidata.* Entire Niobrara region. Open, xeric prairie.* #

Snakeroot. *Prenanthes racemosa.* Scattered records. Varied habitats.

Prairie coneflower. *Ratibida columnifera.* Entire Niobrara region. Prairies, woodland openings.* #

Gray-headed coneflower. *Ratibida pinnata.* Eastern Niobrara Valley. Prairies, open woods.

Black-eyed Susan. *Rudbeckia hirta.* Entire Niobrara region. Disturbed prairies, other disturbed sites.* #

Gray ragwort. *Senecio canus.* Western Niobrara Valley. Open plains.#

Lambstongue groundsel. *Senecio integerrinus.* Entire Niobrara region. Wooded canyons.* #

Prairie ragwort. *Senecio plattensis.* Entire Niobrara region. Open prairies.*

Riddle groundsel. *Senecio riddellii.* Western Niobrara Valley. Open sites, sandy sites.* #

Threetooth ragwort. *Senecio tridenticulatus.* Entire Niobrara region. Sandy plains.*

Cup plant. *Silphium perfoliatum.* Eastern Niobrara Valley. Moist, low ground.

Canada goldenrod. *Solidago canadensis.* Entire Niobrara region. Xeric or open sites.* #

Giant goldenrod. *Solidago gigantea.* Entire Niobrara region. Damp soils.* #

Prairie goldenrod. *Solidago missouriensis.* Entire Niobrara region. Open prairies, sparse woods.* #

Soft goldenrod. *Solidago mollis.* Entire Niobrara region. Xeric plains.* #

Rigid goldenrod. *Solidago rigida.* Entire Niobrara region. Sandy or rocky prairies, xeric sites.* #

Showy-wand goldenrod. *Solidago speciosa.* Eastern Niobrara Valley. Prairies, open, xeric woods.* #

Common dandelion. *Taraxacum officinale.* Entire Niobrara region. Introduced weed.*

Greenthread. *Thelesperma filifolium.* Entire Niobrara region. open, weedy sites.*

Large-flowered townsendia. *Townsendia grandiflora.* Panhandle. Xeric plains and hillsides.

Goat's beard (western salsify). *Tragopogon dubius.* Entire Niobrara region. Introduced weed. Disturbed sites.* #

Western ironweed. *Vernonia fasciculata.* Eastern Niobrara Valley. Damp prairies.*

Common cocklebur. *Xanthium strumarium.* Entire Niobrara region. disturbed soils, weedy sites.* #

Balsaminaceae—Touch-Me-Not Family (2/1)

Spotted touch-me-not. *Impatiens capensis*. Entire Niobrara region. Shady woods.*

Boraginaceae—Borage Family (23/8)

Butte candle. *Cryptantha celosoides*. Panhandle. Xeric hillsides.#

Miner's candle. *Cryptantha thyrsiflora*. Panhandle. Rocky outcrops, open pine forests.

Large-flowered stickseed. *Hackelia floribunda*. Panhandle. Moist creek-banks, open woods.#

Western sticktight. *Lappula redoweskii*. Entire Niobrara region. Open, often sandy, disturbed sites.* #

Hairy puccoon. *Lithospermum carolinense*. Entire Niobrara region. Sandy prairies, open woods.*

Narrow-leaved puccoon. *Lithospermum incisum*. Entire Niobrara region. Xeric prairies, open woods.* #

Lanceleaf bluebells. *Mertensia lanceolata*. Panhandle. Brushy prairies.#

False gromwell. *Onosmodium molle*. Entire Niobrara region. Prairies, meadows, open woods.* #

Brassicaceae—Mustard Family (64/19)

Hoary false alyssum. *Berteroa incana*. Entire Niobrara region. Disturbed soils, weedy sites.#

Indian mustard. *Brassica juncea*. Entire Niobrara region. introduced weed. Disturbed sites.

Hoary cress. *Cardaria draba*. Entire Niobrara region. Introduced weed.

Tansy mustard. *Descurainia pinnata*. Entire Niobrara region. Xeric prairie, open woods.*

Western wallflower. *Erysimum aspersum*. Entire Niobrara region. Prairies, Sandhills, open woods.* #

Bushy wallflower. *Erysimum repandum*. Scattered records. Disturbed soils, weedy sites.

Dame's rocket. *Hesperis matronalis*. Entire Niobrara region. Introduced weed. Roadsides, disturbed sites.* #

Greenflower pepperweed. *Lepidium densiflorum.* Entire Niobrara region. Disturbed soils, weedy sites.* #

Silvery bladderpod. *Lesquerella ludoviciana.* Entire Niobrara region. Sandy and gravelly soils.* #

Spreading yellowcress. *Rorippa sinuata.* Scattered records. Xeric and wet sites, ditches.

Tall hedge mustard. *Sisymbrium loeselii.* Entire Niobrara region. Introduced weed. Disturbed sites.* #

Prince's plume. *Stanleya pinnata.* Western Niobrara Valley. Xeric, selenium-containing soils.

Pennycress. *Thlaspi arvense.* Entire Niobrara region. Disturbed soils, weedy sites.* #

Callitrichaceae—Water Starwort Family (3/0)
Autumnal water starwort. *Callitriche hermaphroditica.* Rare in central Niobrara Valley. Aquatic.

Water starwort. *Callitriche verna.* Rare in central Niobrara Valley. Aquatic.

Cactaceae—Cactus Family (6/4)
Missouri pincushion. *Corypantha missouriensis.* Scattered records. Xeric soils.* #

Pincushion cactus. *Corypantha vivipara.* Entire Niobrara region. Xeric sandy or rocky prairie.* #

Little (brittle) prickly pear. *Opuntia fragilis.* Western Niobrara Valley. Sandy or rocky prairie.* #

Bigroot prickly pear. *Opuntia macrorhiza.* Entire Niobrara region. Sandy, gravelly, or rocky prairie.* #

Plains prickly pear. *Opuntia polyacantha.* Western Niobrara Valley. Xeric, sandy prairie.#

Caesalpiniaceae—Caesalpinia Family (6/0)
Partridge pea. *Cassia fasciculata.* Eastern Niobrara Valley. Rocky or sandy prairies.

Campanulaceae—Bellflower Family (12/6)
American bellflower. *Campanula americana.* Eastern Niobrara Valley. Open woods, wet sites.*

Harebell. *Campanula rotundifolia*. Entire Niobrara region. Xeric woods, meadows.* #

Blue lobelia. *Lobelia siphilitica*. Entire Niobrara region. Moist soil, woods and meadows.*

Palespike lobelia. *Lobelia spicata*. Entire Niobrara region. Prairies, meadows, open woods.*

Venus's looking glass. *Triodanis perfoliata*. Entire Niobrara region. Sandy to gravelly prairies, disturbed sites.*

Capparaceae—Caper Family (4/3)

Rocky Mountain beeplant. *Cleome serrulata*. Entire Niobrara region. Prairies, open woods.* #

Caryophyllaceae—Pink Family (30/5)

Sandwort. *Arenaria hookeri*. Panhandle. Sandy to rocky hillsides, ledges.

Grove sandwort. *Arenaria lateriflora*. Entire Niobrara region. Moist or xeric woods.* #

Prairie chickweed. *Cerastium arvense*. Western Niobrara Valley. Disturbed sites.#

Bouncing bet. *Saponaria officinalis*. Entire Niobrara region. Introduced weed. Disturbed sites.

Catchfly. *Silene noctiflora*. Entire Niobrara region. Introduced weed. Disturbed sites.#

Long-leaved stitchwort. *Stellaria longifolia*. Rare in central Niobrara Valley. Wet meadows and damp woods.* #

Chickweed. *Stellaria media*. Scattered records. Introduced weed. Disturbed sites.

Chenopodiaceae—Goosefoot Family (32/8)

Silverscale saltbush. *Atriplex argentea*. Western Niobrara Valley. Alkaline soils.

Shadscale. *Atriplex canescens*. Panhandle. Alkaline soils.

Nuttall's saltbush. *Atriplex nuttallii*. Rare in upper and central Niobrara Valley. Xeric soils.

Mapleleaf goosefoot. *Chenopodium gigantospermum* (*hybridum*). Entire Niobrara region. Disturbed sites.*

Winged pigweed. *Cycloloma atriplicifolium*. Entire Niobrara region. Sandy soils, weedy sites.

Kochia. *Kochia scoparia*. Entire Niobrara region. Introduced weed.*

Nuttall povertyweed. *Monolepis nuttalliana*. Entire Niobrara region. Disturbed soils, weedy sites.

Cistaceae—Rockrose Family (3/0)
Hoary frostweed. *Helianthemum bicknellii*. Rare in central Niobrara Valley. Xeric, sandy soils.

Upright pinweed. *Lechea stricta*. Rare in central Niobrara Valley. Xeric, sandy woods.

Clusiaceae—Saint-John's-Wort Family (= Hypericaceae) (4/1)
Common St.-John's-wort. *Hypericum perforatum*. Entire Niobrara region. Introduced. Open sites.#

Commelinaceae—Spiderwort Family (5/2)
Long-bracted spiderwort. *Tradescantia bracteata*. Entire Niobrara region. Prairies, disturbed sites.#

Prairie spiderwort. *Tradescantia occidentalis*. Entire Niobrara region. Prairies, disturbed sites.#

Convolvulaceae—Morning Glory Family (7/3)
Field bindweed. *Convolvulus arvensis*. Entire Niobrara region. Introduced weed.* #

Bush morning glory. *Ipomoea leptophylla*. Entire Niobrara region. Plains and prairies.*

Crassulaceae—Stonecrop Family (2/1)
Virginia stonecrop. *Penthorum sedoides*. Entire Niobrara region. Ditches, streambanks.

Stonecrop. *Sedum lanceolatum*. Panhandle. Open, rocky sites.#

Cucurbitaceae—Cucumber Family (4/1)
Wild cucumber. *Echinocystis lobata*. Entire Niobrara region. Moist and open woods.* #

Cuscutaceae—Dodder Family (10/1)

Field dodder. *Cuscuta pentagona.* Scattered records. Parasitic.

Cyperaceae—Sedge Family (117/40)

Fescue sedge. *Carex brevior.* Entire Niobrara region. Meadows and woods.* #

Brown bog sedge. *Carex buxbaumii.* Rare in central Niobrara Valley. Bogs and fens.

Lesser panicled sedge. *Carex diandra.* Rare in central Niobrara Valley. Fens and meadows.

Needleleaf sedge. *Carex eleocharis.* Entire Niobrara region. Prairies and meadows.* #

Threadleaf sedge. *Carex filifolia.* Western Niobrara Valley. Upland prairies.* #

Meadow sedge. *Carex granularis.* Rare in upper Niobrara Valley. Bogs and fens.

Sun sedge. *Carex heliophila.* Entire Niobrara region. Sandhills and mixed prairies.* #

Woolly sedge. *Carex lanuginosa.* Entire Niobrara region. Low prairies.* #

Nebraska sedge. *Carex nebraskensis.* Entire Niobrara region. Swamps, wet meadows.* #

Fox sedge. *Carex vulpinoides.* Entire Niobrara region. Marshes and ponds.* #

Schweinitz flatsedge. *Cyperus schweinitzii.* Entire Niobrara region. Sandy soils.

Tall (narrowleaf) cottongrass. *Eriophorum polystachion.* Cherry County. Fens and wet meadows.

Hall bulrush. *Scirpus hallii.* Rare in central Niobrara Valley. Wetlands.

Equisetaceae—Horsetail Family (5/4)

Field horsetail. *Equisetum arvense.* Entire Niobrara region. Disturbed sites.* #

Euphorbiaceae—Spurge Family (26/4)

Texas croton. *Croton texensis*. Western Niobrara Valley. Sandy soils, weedy sites.*

Toothed spurge. *Euphorbia dentata*. Entire Niobrara region. Prairies, disturbed sites.

Leafy spurge. *Euphorbia esula*. Widespread. Introduced noxious weed.#

Spotted spurge. *Euphorbia maculata*. Eastern Niobrara Valley. Prairies, disturbed sites.

Snow-on-the-mountain. *Euphorbia marginata*. Entire Niobrara region. Prairies, disturbed sites; poisonous.

Fabaceae—Bean Family (= Leguminaceae) (90/36)

Fragrant (dwarf) indigobush. *Amorpha nana*. Rare in central and lower Niobrara Valley. Xeric prairies and hillsides.

Standing milk vetch. *Astragalus adsurgens*. Entire Niobrara region. Xeric prairie, open woods.#

Field milk vetch. *Astragalus agrestis*. Rare in upper and central Niobrara Valley. Moist prairies and wooded hillsides.#

Barr's milk vetch. *Astragalus barrii*. Panhandle. Barren knolls.

Two-grooved milk vetch. *Astragalus bisulcatus*. Panhandle. Prairie, roadsides, hillsides; poisonous.

Canada milk vetch. *Astragalus canadensis*. Entire Niobrara region. Moist prairies, open woods.* #

Painted milk vetch. *Astragalus ceramicus*. Entire Niobrara region. Sandy prairies.*

Ground plum. *Astragalus crassicarpus*. Entire Niobrara region. Prairies, rocky soils.* #

Drummond milk vetch. *Astragalus drummondii*. Panhandle. Drier grasslands.

Plains milk vetch. *Astragalus gilviflorus*. Panhandle. Drier grasslands.

Lotus milk vetch. *Astragalus lotiflorus*. Entire Niobrara region. Upland mixed prairies.* #

Missouri milk vetch. *Astragalus missouriensis.* Entire Niobrara region. Prairies, bluffs, ravines.* #

Woolly locoweed. *Astragalus mollissimus.* Panhandle Xeric prairies; poisonous.

Alkali (creamy) milk vetch. *Astragalus racemosus.* Scattered records. Poisonous.

Draba milk vetch. *Astragalus spatulatus.* Panhandle. Rocky hills, prairies.#

Pulse (loose-flowered) milk vetch. *Astragalus tenellus.* Panhandle. Rocky plains.#

Golden prairie clover. *Dalea aurea.* Entire Niobrara region. Loamy prairies.*

Slender (nine-anther) dalea. *Dalea enneandra.* Entire Niobrara region. Mixed prairies.*

Canada tickclover. *Desmodium canadense.* Entire Niobrara region. Rocky or sandy prairies.*

Wild licorice. *Glycyrrhiza lepidota.* Entire Niobrara region. Prairie ravines, moist sites.*

Hoary vetchling. *Lathyrus polymorphus.* Entire Niobrara region. Xeric, sandy to rocky prairies, woods.*

Bird's-foot trefoil. *Lotus corniculatus.* Scattered records. Introduced crop and weed. Disturbed sites.

American deervetch. *Lotus purshianus.* Entire Niobrara region. Disturbed sites.*

Silvery lupine. *Lupinus argenteus.* Panhandle. Rocky prairies, open woods.#

Low lupine. *Lupinus pusillus.* Panhandle. Sandy prairies.

Alfalfa. *Medicago falcata.* Entire Niobrara region. Introduced forage crop.

Sweet clover. *Melilotis officinalis* and *M. albas.* Entire Niobrara region. Introduced weed and forage crop. Disturbed sites.*

Purple (Lambert) locoweed. *Oxytropis lambertii.* Entire Niobrara region. Drier grasslands.* #

White locoweed. *Oxytropis sericea*. Panhandle. Rocky prairie; poisonous.#

White prairie clover. *Petalostemon (Dalea) candida*. Entire Niobrara region. Disturbed soils, weedy sites.* #

Compact prairie clover. *Petalostemon (Dalea) compactus*. Rare in upper and central Niobrara Valley. Sandy prairies.

Purple prairie clover. *Petalostemon (Dalea) purpurea*. Entire Niobrara region. Rocky prairies, open woods.* #

Silky prairie clover. *Petalostemon (Dalea) villosa*. Entire Niobrara region. Sandy prairies, open woods.*

Silver-leaf scurfpea. *Psoralea argophylla*. Entire Niobrara region. Prairies, open woods.*

Tall breadroot scurfpea. *Psoralea cuspidata*. Entire Niobrara region. Prairies.

Palmleaf scurfpea. *Psoralea digitata*. Entire Niobrara region. Sandy prairie.

Broadleaf scurfpea (prairie turnip). *Psoralea esculenta*. Entire Niobrara region. Prairies, open woods.

Little breadroot scurfpea. *Psoralea hypogea*. Rare in upper Niobrara Valley. Rocky and sandy prairies.

Wild alfalfa. *Psoralea tenuiflora*. Western Niobrara Valley. Prairies, roadsides.* #

Prairie buckbean. *Thermopsis rhombifolia*. Western Niobrara Valley. Prairies, open woods.#

Clovers. *Trifolium* spp. Entire Niobrara region. Introduced and cultivated forage crop.* #

American vetch. *Vicia americana*. Entire Niobrara region. Mostly sandy soils.#

Fumariaceae—Fumitory Family (4/1)
Golden corydalis. *Corydalis aurea*. Panhandle. Prairies, open woodlands.* #

Gentianaceae—Gentian Family (4/1)
Prairie gentian. *Eustoma grandiflorum*. Western Niobrara Valley. Moist meadows and prairies.

Closed gentian. *Gentiana andrewsii*. Entire Niobrara region. Wet meadows, prairies, or woods.* #

Downy gentian. *Gentiana puberulenta*. Eastern Niobrara Valley. Xeric woods and prairies.

Hydrocharitaceae—Frog-Bit Family (3/0)
Water celery. *Vallisneria americana*. Rare in central Niobrara Valley. Marshes.

Hydrophyllaceae—Waterleaf Family (4/1)
Waterpod. *Ellisia nyctelea*. Entire Niobrara region. Sandy prairies, open woods.*

Scorpionweed. *Phacelia hastata*. Panhandle. Sandy to rocky soils, disturbed sites.

Iridaceae—Iris Family (7/1)
White-eyed grass. *Sisyrinchium campestre*. Eastern Niobrara Valley. Prairies, open woods.

Blue-eyed grass. *Sisyrinchium montanum*. Entire Niobrara region. Prairies, open woods.* #

Juncaginaceae—Arrowgrass Family (13/9)
Arrowgrass. *Triglochin maritimum*. Entire Niobrara region. Moist, alkaline sites.*

Marsh arrowgrass. *Triglochin palustre*. Rare in upper Niobrara Valley. Wetlands.

Laminaceae—Mint Family (= Labitae) (41/17)
American dragonhead. *Dracocephalum parviflorum*. Rare in central Niobrara Valley. Gravelly soils in open woods.* #

Rough false pennyroyal. *Hedeoma hispidum*. Entire Niobrara region. Disturbed sites, open ground.*

Motherwort. *Leonurus cardiaca*. Eastern Niobrara Valley. Disturbed soils, weedy sites.

American bugleweed. *Lycopus americanus*. Entire Niobrara region. Moist, exposed sites.* #

Field mint. *Mentha arvensis*. Entire Niobrara region. Moist sites.* #

Wild bergamot. *Monarda fistulosa*. Entire Niobrara region. Prairies, open woods.* #

Plains (spotted) beebalm. *Monarda (Alonarda) pectinata.* Western Niobrara Valley. Upland prairies.

Catnip. *Nepeta cataria.* Entire Niobrara region. Introduced weed. Disturbed sites.* #

Purple dragonhead. *Physostegia parviflora.* Rare in central Niobrara Valley. Meadows and streambanks.

Healall. *Prunella vulgaris.* Entire Niobrara region. Disturbed sites, streambanks.*

Virginia mountain mint. *Pycnanthemum virginianum.* Eastern Niobrara Valley. Moist woods, wetlands.*

Lanceleaf sage. *Salvia reflexa.* Entire Niobrara region. Disturbed sites.* #

Marsh scullcap. *Scutellaria galericulata.* Entire Niobrara region. Wet sites.* #

Leonard small scullcap. *Scutellaria parvula.* Eastern Niobrara region. Upland prairies, open woods.*

Marsh hedge nettle. *Stachys palustris.* Entire Niobrara region. Xeric to wet prairies.

American germander. *Teucrium canadense.* Entire Niobrara region. Streambanks, pastures.*

Liliaceae—Lily Family (29/5)
Wild onion. *Allium canadense.* Entire Niobrara region. Prairies, open woods.

Wild white onion. *Allium textile.* Western Niobrara Valley. Prairies, coniferous woods.#

Sego lily. *Calochortus gunnisonii.* Panhandle. Xeric prairies, open coniferous woods.#

Mariposa lily. *Calochortus nuttallii.* Pine Ridge. Open coniferous woods.#

Leopard lily. *Fritillaria atropropurea.* Rare in upper and central Niobrara Valley. Grassy slopes in pine woods.#

Yellow stargrass. *Hypoxis hirsuta.* Eastern Niobrara Valley. Prairies, open woods.*

Mountain lily. *Leucocrinum montanum.* Western Niobrara Valley. Shortgrass prairies, coniferous woods.#

Western red lily. *Lilium philadelphicum*. Entire Niobrara region. Open woods, prairies.#

Wild lily of the valley. *Maianthemum canadense*. Known from a population of about ten plants in a springbranch canyon in Brown County.#

Solomon's seal. *Polygonatum biflorum*. Entire Niobrara region. Moist deciduous woods.* #

False Solomon's seal. *Smilacina stellata*. Entire Niobrara region. Moist to rather dry woods.* #

Death camas. *Zigadenus venenosus*. Panhandle. Xeric prairies, open woods; poisonous.#

Linaceae—Flax Family (6/2)

Stiffstem flax. *Linum rigidum*. Entire Niobrara region. Sandy prairies and hillsides.* #

Grooved (prairie) flax. *Linum sulcatum*. Eastern Niobrara Valley. Prairies, open woods.

Loasaceae—Stickleaf Family (4/2)

Ten-petal stickleaf. *Mentzelia decapetala*. Western Niobrara Valley. Disturbed sites.* #

Lythraceae—Loosestrife Family (6/3)

Winged loosestrife. *Lythrum decotanum*. Entire Niobrara region. Wet soils.*

Purple loosestrife. *Lythrum salicaria*. Entire Niobrara region. Introduced weed. Moist sites.*

Malvaceae—Mallow Family (12/3)

Purple poppy mallow. *Callirhoe involucrata*. Scattered records. Xeric, sandy prairies.

Flower of an hour. *Hibiscus* (*Malviscus*) *trionum*. Eastern Niobrara Valley. Introduced weed. Disturbed sites.

Running mallow. *Malva rotundifolia*. Entire Niobrara region. Introduced weed. Disturbed sites.*

Red false (scarlet globe) mallow. *Sphaeralcea coccinea*. Entire Niobrara region. Xeric prairies, hillsides.* #

Mimosaceae—Mimosa Family (2/2)

Illinois bundleflower. *Desmanthus illinoensis.* Entire Niobrara region. Rocky or sandy prairies.*

Sensitive brier. *Schrankia nuttallii.* Scattered records. Rocky or sandy soils.*

Monotropaceae—Indian Pipe Family (1/0)

Giant pinedrops. *Pterospora andromedea.* Rare in upper Niobrara Valley. Pine woods.

Nyctaginaceae—Four-O'Clock Family (6/3)

Sweet sand verbena. *Abronia fragrans.* Panhandle. Sandy prairies, disturbed sites.

Hairy four-o'clock. *Mirabilis hirsuta.* Entire Niobrara region. Prairies, open woods.*

Wild four-o'clock. *Mirabilis nyctaginea.* Entire Niobrara region. Disturbed soils, weedy sites.* #

Nymphaeaceae—Water Lily Family (3/1)

Fragrant white water lily. *Nymphaea odorata.* Rare in central Niobrara Valley. Aquatic.*

White water lily. *Nymphaea tuberosa.* Rare in lower Niobrara Valley. Aquatic.

Onagraceae—Evening Primrose Family (29/14)

Lavender evening primrose. *Calylophus hartwegii*, var. *lavandulifolius.* Panhandle. Xeric prairies.

Plains yellow evening primrose. *Calylophus serrulatus.* Entire Niobrara region. Xeric prairies, open woods.* #

Fireweed. *Epilobium* spp. Entire Niobrara region. Disturbed sites, often appearing after fire.* #

Scarlet gaura. *Gaura coccinea.* Entire Niobrara region. Xeric prairies, open woods.*

Many-seed seedbox. *Ludwigia polycarpa.* Rare in central Niobrara Valley. Low woodlands and wetlands.*

Common evening primrose. *Oenothera biennis.* Entire Niobrara region. Streambanks, open woods.* #

Gumbo evening primrose. *Oenothera caespitosa*. Panhandle. Xeric prairies, open woods.#

Comb-leaf evening primrose. *Oenothera coronopifolia*. Panhandle. Sandy to rocky prairies, woods.#

White-stemmed evening primrose. *Oenothera nuttallii*. Entire Niobrara region. Xeric prairies, open woods.*

Four-point evening primrose. *Oenothera rhombipetala*. Entire Niobrara region. Sand dunes, sandy prairies.*

Ophiglossaceae—Adder's-Tongue Family (1/0)
Least moonwort. *Botrychium simplex*. Known only from Brown County. Moist woodlands.

Orchidaceae—Orchid Family (17/3)
Spotted coral root. *Corallorhiza maculata*. Panhandle. Xeric coniferous woods.

Small white lady's slipper. *Cypripedium candidum*. Rare in central Niobrara Valley. Moist prairies.

Northern green orchid. *Habenaria hyperborea*. Panhandle and western Niobrara Valley. Cool marshes.*

Frog orchid. *Habenaria viridis*. Rare in upper and central Niobrara Valley. Marshes and fens.#

Loesel's twayblade. *Liparis loeselii*. Rare in central Niobrara Valley. Open or shaded boggy sites.

Western prairie fringed orchid. *Platanthera praeclara*. Known only from east-central Cherry County. Prairies. State and federally threatened.

Nodding ladies' tresses. *Spiranthes cernua*. Eastern Niobrara Valley. Prairies, open woods.

Ute ladies' tresses. *Spiranthes diluvialis*. Rare, reported only from an alkaline meadow site in Sioux County. State and federally threatened species.

Hooded ladies' tresses. *Spiranthes romanzoffiana*. Rare in upper and central Niobrara Valley. Wet meadows, open woodlands.

Orobranchaceae—Broomrape Family (3/1)
Cancer root. *Orobranche fasciculata*. Entire Niobrara region. Xeric prairies, sandy soils.* #

Oxalidaceae—Wood Sorrel Family (3/2)

Gray-green wood sorrel. *Oxalis dillenii.* Entire Niobrara region. Open woods, disturbed soils, weedy sites.*

Yellow wood sorrel. *Oxalis stricta.* Entire Niobrara region. Open woods, disturbed soils, weedy sites.*

Violet wood sorrel. *Oxalis violacea.* Eastern Niobrara Valley. Open woods, disturbed soils, weedy sites.

Papaveraceae—Poppy Family (2/1)

Annual prickly poppy. *Argemone polyanthemos.* Entire Niobrara region. Sandy soils, disturbed sites.* #

Plantaginaceae—Plantain Family (9/2)

Buckhorn plantain. *Plantago lanceolata.* Scattered records. Introduced weed. Disturbed sites.

Woolly plantain (Indian wheat). *Plantago patagonica.* Entire Niobrara region. Disturbed soils, weedy sites.*

Blackseed plantain. *Plantago rugelii.* Entire Niobrara region; Disturbed soils, shady places, weedy sites.*

Poaceae—Grass Family (ca. 250/81)

Jointed goatgrass. *Aegilops cylindrica.* Scattered records. Introduced weed.

Slender wheatgrass. *Agropyron caninum* (*trachycaulum*). Entire Niobrara region. Dry woods.* #

Crested wheatgrass. *Agropyron cristatum.* Entire Niobrara region. Introduced. Xeric prairies.* #

Thickspike wheatgrass. *Agropyron dasystachium.* Panhandle.

Intermediate wheatgrass. *Agropyron intermedium.* Scattered records. Introduced.#

Quackgrass. *Agropyron repens.* Entire Niobrara region. Introduced. Weedy sites.#

Western wheatgrass. *Agropyron smithii.* Entire Niobrara region. Xeric prairies.#

Bluebunch wheatgrass. *Agropyron spicatum.* Panhandle. Xeric prairies.#

Redtop bent. *Agrostis stolonifera*. Entire Niobrara region. Introduced weed. Mesic sites.*

Water foxtail. *Alopecurus geniculatus*. Rare in central Niobrara Valley. Moist places.

Big bluestem. *Andropogon gerardii*. Entire Niobrara region. Mesic tall-grass prairies.* #

Sandhills bluestem. *Andropogon hallii*. Entire Niobrara region. Sand-hills prairies.*

Prairie three-awn. *Aristida oligantha*. Eastern Niobrara Valley. Sandy or disturbed ground.

Purple (red) three-awn. *Aristida purpurea* (including *A. longiseta*). Entire Niobrara region. Mixed prairies, weedy sites.#

Wild oats. *Avena fatua*. Entire Niobrara region. Introduced weed.

American sloughgrass. *Beckmannia syzigachne*. Entire Niobrara region. Wetlands.

Side-oats grama. *Bouteloua curtipendula*. Entire Niobrara region. Mixed-grass prairies.* #

Blue grama. *Bouteloua gracilis*. Entire Niobrara region. Mixed-grass prairies.* #

Hairy grama. *Bouteloua hirsuta*. Entire Niobrara region. Shortgrass prairies.* #

Smooth brome. *Bromus inermis*. Entire Niobrara region. Introduced weed.* #

Japanese brome. *Bromus japonica*. Entire Niobrara region. Introduced weed.* #

Downy brome. *Bromus tectorum*. Entire Niobrara region. Introduced weed.* #

Buffalo grass. *Buchloe dactyloides*. Entire Niobrara region. Shortgrass prairies.* #

Bluejoint. *Calamagrostis canadensis*. Entire Niobrara region. Sandbars and marshes.* #

Northern reedgrass. *Calamogrostis inexpansa*. Entire Niobrara region. Sandy prairies.

Prairie sandreed. *Calamovilfa longifolia.* Entire Niobrara region. Sand-hills and mixed prairies.* #

Longspine sandbur. *Cenchrus longispinus.* Entire Niobrara region. Weedy sites in sandy soils.* #

Orchard grass. *Dactylis glomerata.* Entire Niobrara region. Introduced weed.* #

Smooth crabgrass. *Digitaria ischaemum.* Eastern Niobrara Valley. Introduced weed.

Large crabgrass. *Digitaria sanguinalis.* Entire Niobrara region. Introduced weed.*

Saltgrass. *Distichlis spicata.* Entire Niobrara region. Saline soils, weedy sites.

Barnyard grass. *Echinochloa crusgalli.* Entire Niobrara region. Introduced weed.

Canada wild rice. *Elymus canadensis.* Entire Niobrara region. Streams and roadsides.* #

Stinkgrass. *Eragrostis cilianensis.* Entire Niobrara region. Weedy annual.*

Purple lovegrass. *Eragrostis spectabilis.* Eastern Niobrara Valley. Weedy sites.*

Sand lovegrass. *Eragrostis trichodes.* Entire Niobrara region. Sandhills prairies.*

Sixweeks fescue. *Festuca (Vulpia) octoflora.* Entire Niobrara region. Weedy annual.* #

Small floating manna grass. *Glyceria borealis.* Rare in central Niobrara Valley. Wetlands.

Fowl manna grass. *Glyceria striata.* Entire Niobrara region. Moist soils.* #

Foxtail barley. *Hordeum jubatum.* Entire Niobrara region. Weedy.* #

Little barley. *Hordeum pusillum.* Entire Niobrara region. Weedy sites.*

Prairie junegrass. *Koeleria pyramidata.* Entire Niobrara region. Sand-hills and mixed prairies.* #

Bearded sprangletop. *Leptochloa fascicularis.* Entire Niobrara region. Weedy sites.

Plains muhly. *Muhlenbergia cuspidata*. Entire Niobrara region. Xeric soils.*

Sand muhly. *Muhlenbergia pungens*. Sandhills. Dune blowouts.

Marsh muhly. *Muhlenbergia racemosa*. Entire Niobrara region. Weedy sites.* #

Mat muhly. *Muhlenbergia richardsonis*. Rare in central Niobrara Valley. Moist to xeric prairies.

False buffalo grass. *Munroa squarrosa*. Western Niobrara Valley. Xeric plains.*

Indian ricegrass. *Oryzopsis hymenoides*. Western Niobrara Valley. Sandy soils.

Witchgrass. *Panicum capillare*. Entire Niobrara region. Weedy sites.*

Proso millet. *Panicum miliaceum*. Scattered records. Introduced weed.

Small (scribner) panicgrass. *Panicum oligosanthes*. Entire Niobrara region; mostly east.

Switchgrass. *Panicum virgatum*. Entire Niobrara region. Tallgrass prairies.* #

Reed canarygrass. *Phalaris arundinacea*. Entire Niobrara region. Moist soils.#

Timothy. *Phleum pratense*. Entire Niobrara region. Introduced. Disturbed sites.* #

Common reed. *Phragmites australis*. Entire Niobrara region. Wet soils.*

Canada bluegrass. *Poa compressa*. Entire Niobrara region. Introduced.* #

Kentucky bluegrass. *Poa pratensis*. Entire Niobrara region. Introduced weed.* #

Blowout grass. *Redfieldia flexuosa*. Sandhills. Dune blowouts.*

Tumblegrass. *Schedonnardus paniculatus*. Entire Niobrara region. Weedy sites.*

Little bluestem. *Schizachyrium* (*Andropogon*) *scoparium*. Entire Niobrara region. Mixed prairies.* #

Spangletop (whitetop). *Scolochloa festucacea*. Scattered records. Wetlands.

Giant foxtail. *Setaria faberi.* Scattered records. Introduced weed.

Yellow foxtail. *Setaria glauca.* Entire Niobrara region. Introduced weed.*

Bristly foxtail. *Setaria verticillata.* Entire Niobrara region. Introduced weed.

Green foxtail. *Setaria viridis.* Entire Niobrara region. Introduced weed.*

Indian grass. *Sorghastrum nutans.* Entire Niobrara region. Mesic prairies and near water.* #

Johnsongrass. *Sorghum halepense.* Scattered records. Weedy sites.

Alkali cordgrass. *Spartina gracilis.* Western Niobrara Valley. Alkali soils.

Prairie cordgrass. *Spartina pectinata.* Entire Niobrara region. Mesic soils and wetlands.* #

Alkali sacaton. *Sporobolus airoides.* Western Niobrara Valley. Alkali soils.

Tall dropseed. *Sporobolus asper.* Entire Niobrara region. Sandy soils.#

Sand dropseed. *Sporobolus cryptandrus.* Entire Niobrara region. Sandy soils.* #

Prairie dropseed, *Sporobolus heterolepis.* Entire Niobrara region. Native prairies.#

Poverty dropseed. *Sporobolus vaginiflorus.* Eastern Niobrara Valley. Weedy sites.

Needle-and-thread. *Stipa comata.* Entire Niobrara region. Native prairies.* #

Porcupine grass. *Stipa spartea.* Entire Niobrara region. Native prairies.* #

Green needlegrass. *Stipa viridula.* Entire Niobrara region. Upland prairies, roadsides.* #

Wild rice. *Zizania aquatica.* Sandhills. Fens and freshwater marshes.

Polemoniaceae—Phlox Family (= Polemonium) (12/3)

Slenderleaf collomia. *Collimia linearis.* Scattered records. Native prairies.* #

Gilia. *Ipomopsis longifolia*. Western and central Niobrara Valley. Xeric, sandy soils.*

Slender phlox. *Microsteris gracilis*. Rare in upper and central Niobrara Valley. Xeric or gravelly soils.

Plains phlox. *Phlox andicola*. Western and central Niobrara Valley. Xeric, sandy prairies.* #

Hood's phlox. *Phlox hoodii*. Panhandle. Rocky soils.#

Polygalaceae—Milkwort Family (4/2)
White milkwort. *Polygala alba*. Entire Niobrara region. Rocky prairie hillsides.* #

Polygonaceae—Buckwheat Family (36/6)
Umbrella plant. *Eriogonum annuum*. Entire Niobrara region. Xeric open grasslands.* #

Yellow wild buckwheat. *Eriogonum flavum*. Panhandle. Xeric plains and ridges.#

Littleleaf eriogonum. *Eriogonum pauciflorum*. Panhandle. Rocky slopes, xeric prairies.#

Common knotweed. *Polygonum arenastrum*. Entire Niobrara region. Introduced weed. Disturbed sites.

Pink smartweed. *Polygonum bicorne*. Eastern Niobrara Valley. Wet sites.

Pale smartweed. *Polygonum lapathifolium*. Entire Niobrara region. Damp soils.*

Pennsylvania smartweed. *Polygonum pennsylvanicum*. Entire Niobrara region. Disturbed soils, weedy sites.

Bushy knotweed. *Polygonum ramosissimum*. Entire Niobrara region. Damp, brackish soils.

Climbing false buckwheat. *Polygonum scandens*. Entire Niobrara region. Introduced weed. Disturbed sites.*

Wild begonia (veiny dock). *Rumex venosus*. Entire Niobrara region. Sandy dunes and riverbanks.*

Polypodiaceae—Fern Family (13/5)

Subarctic lady fern. *Athyrium filix-femina.* Rare in central Niobrara Valley. Moist thickets, bogs.#

Common bladder fern. *Cystopteris fragilis.* Throughout the Niobrara Valley. Rocky hillsides.* #

Spinulose wood fern. *Xericopterus spinulosa.* Rare in springbranch canyons. Low, rich woodlands.* #

Portulacaceae—Purslane Family (3/2)

Large-flower fameflower. *Talinum calycinum.* Rare in central Niobrara Valley. Sand and rocky soils.*

Primulaceae—Primrose Family (10/4)

Fringed loosestrife. *Lysimachia ciliata.* Entire Niobrara region. Moist woods and wetter sites.* #

Lance-leaf loosestrife. *Lysimachia hybrida.* Rare in central Niobrara Valley. Wetlands.

Tufted loosestrife. *Lysimachia thyrsiflora.* Entire Niobrara region. Moist to wet sites.* #

Pyrolaceae—Wintergreen Family (2/0)

Elliptical-leaf wintergreen. *Pyrola elliptica.* Rare in central Niobrara Valley. Rich woods.

Ranunculaceae—Buttercup Family (37/13)

Meadow anemone. *Anemone canadensis.* Eastern Niobrara Valley. Wet prairies, wet woods.#

Candle anemone. *Anemone cylindrica.* Entire Niobrara region. Open prairies and pastures.* #

Pasqueflower. *Anemone patens.* Entire Niobrara region. Open prairies, often rocky soil.* #

Wild columbine. *Aquilegia canadensis.* Entire Niobrara region. Moist woods.* #

Western clematis. *Clematis ligusticifolia.* Western Niobrara Valley. Creeks and roadsides.* #

Virgin's bower. *Clematis virginiana.* Eastern Niobrara Valley. Partially woody, climbing vine.*

Blue larkspur. *Delphinium nuttallianum.* Panhandle. Varied habitats.#

Prairie larkspur. *Delphinium virescens.* Entire Niobrara region. Prairies and pastures.*

Early wood (smallflower) buttercup. *Ranunculus abortivus.* Entire Niobrara region. Moist woods.*

Threadleaf buttercup. *Ranunculus flabellaris.* Scattered records. Moist and wet sites.

Macoun's buttercup. *Ranunculus macounii.* Western Niobrara Valley. Streambanks, wet meadows.#

Purple meadow rue. *Thalictrum dasycarpum.* Entire Niobrara region. Moist habitats.*

Rosaceae—Rose Family (42/16)

Sulphur cinquefoil. *Potentilla recta.* Eastern Niobrara Valley; disturbed sites, prairies.#

Rubiaceae—Madder Family (10/3)

Catchweed bedstraw. *Galium aparine.* Entire Niobrara region. Woods, prairies, disturbed ground.* #

Northern bedstraw. *Galium boreale.* Panhandle. Rocky prairies, woods, roadsides.#

Santalaceae—Sandalwood Family (2/1)

Bastard toadflax. *Comandra umbellata.* Entire Niobrara region. Xeric, sandy to rocky soils, open woods.* #

Scrophulariaceae—Figwort Family (46/16)

Rough purple gerardia. *Agalinis aspersa.* Entire Niobrara region. Xeric prairie, open woods.*

Slender gerardia. *Agalinis tenuifolia.* Entire Niobrara region. Moist woods and prairies.*

Hedge hyssop. *Gratiola neglecta.* Rare in central Niobrara Valley. Moist sites.

Butter-and-eggs. *Linaria vulgaris.* Entire Niobrara region. Disturbed soils, weedy sites.#

Sharpwing monkey flower. *Mimulus alatus.* Rare in central Niobrara Valley. Moist banks.

Allegheny monkey flower. *Mimulus ringens*. Eastern Niobrara Valley. Wet streamsides, sometimes emergent.*

White beardtongue. *Penstemon albidus*. Entire Niobrara region. Sandy to gravelly soils, open prairie.* #

Narrow beardtongue. *Penstemon angustifolius*. Entire Niobrara region. Sandhills and sandy prairie.* #

Crested beardtongue. *Penstemon eriantherus*. Western Niobrara Valley. Sandy to gravelly soil, xeric prairies.

Sawsepal penstemon. *Penstemon glaber*. Panhandle. Sandy to gravelly soil, prairies.#

Slender penstemon. *Penstemon gracilis*. Entire Niobrara region. Sandy to gravelly soil, xeric prairies.* #

Shell-leaf penstemon. *Penstemon grandiflorus*. Entire Niobrara region. Prairies with sandy to loamy soils.* #

Hayden's (blowout) penstemon. *Penstemon haydenii*. Sandhills. Bare dunes. Nationally endangered; native Niobrara regional populations are known from southern Box Butte County, southwestern Sheridan County, and north-central and east-central Cherry County. Reestablishment efforts are under way in various locations.

Common mullein. *Verbascum thapsus*. Entire Niobrara region. Introduced weed. Disturbed sites.* #

Brooklime speedwell. *Veronica americana*. Entire Niobrara region. Emergent in aquatic sites.* #

Water speedwell. *Veronica anagallis-aquatica*. Entire Niobrara region. Emergent in aquatic sites.* #

Solanaceae—Nightshade Family (20/6)

Jimsonweed. *Datura stramonium*. Eastern Niobrara Valley. Disturbed sites; poisonous.

Clammy ground-cherry. *Physalis heterophylla*. Entire Niobrara region. Prairies, open woods.* #

Virginia ground-cherry. *Physalis virginiana*. Entire Niobrara region. Open woods, disturbed sites.#

Buffalo bur. *Solanum rostratum*. Entire Niobrara region; disturbed sites.*

Sparganiaceae—Bur Reed Family (2/1)
Greenfruit bur reed. *Sparganium chlorocarpum.* Rare in upper and central Niobrara Valley. Wetlands.

Urticaceae—Nettle Family (5/5)
Pennsylvania pellitory. *Parietaria pennsylvanica.* Entire Niobrara region. Shaded woods.*

Stinging nettle. *Urtica dioica.* Entire Niobrara region. Moist woods, streambanks.* #

Verbenaceae—Vervain Family (9/5)
Dakota vervain. *Verbena bipinnatifida.* Entire Niobrara region. Xeric plains and prairies.#

Prostrate vervain. *Verbena bracteata.* Entire Niobrara region. Disturbed sites, prairies.* #

Blue vervain. *Verbena hastata.* Entire Niobrara region. Moist meadows, woods, seepage sites.* #

Hoary (woolly) vervain. *Verbena stricta.* Entire Niobrara region. Pastures, prairies, disturbed sites.* #

Violaceae—Violet Family (10/3)
Canada violet. *Viola canadensis.* Entire Niobrara region. Shaded woods.* #

Northern bog violet. *Viola nephrophylla.* Rare in central Niobrara Valley. Bogs and fens.#

Nuttall's violet. *Viola nuttallii.* Entire Niobrara region. Xeric prairies, bluffs.#

Prairie violet. *Viola pedatifida.* Eastern Niobrara Valley. Prairies, open woodlands.#

Blue prairie violet. *Viola pratincola.* Entire Niobrara region. Open woods, prairie hillsides.* #

Downy yellow violet. *Viola pubescens.* Entire Niobrara region. Woods, thickets.#

Downy blue violet. *Viola sororia.* Eastern Niobrara Valley. Woods, streamsides.

Zygophyllaceae—Caltrop Family (1/1)

Puncture vine. *Tribulus terrestris.* Entire Niobrara region. Disturbed soils, weedy sites.*

Appendix 2

English Names of Plants Text-Referenced by Latin Names

Acer, genus of maples and box elders
Acer negundo, box elder
Acer saccharinum, silver maple
Acorus calamus, sweet flag
Agalinis purpurea, gerardia
Allium perdulce, wild onion
Ambrosia, genus of ragweeds
Amelanchier alnifolia, Saskatoon serviceberry
Amorpha, genus of indigo and leadplant
Amphicarpaea bracteata, hog peanut
Andropogon gerardi/A. hallii, big/Sandhills bluestem
Anemone virginiana, tall anemone
Apios americana, American potato bean
Aquilegia canadensis, wild columbine
Aralia nudicaulis, wild sarsaparilla
Aralia racemosa, spikenard
Arisaema triphyllum, jack-in-the-pulpit
Aristida basiramia, forktip three-awn
Aristida dichotoma, churchmouse three-awn
Aristida longespica geniculata, slimspike three-awn
Aristida purpurea, purple three-awn
Aster pubentior, aster
Astragalus, genus of milk vetches
Astragalus spatulatus, draba milk vetch
Betula papyrifera, paper birch
Boehmeria cylindrica, false nettle

Botrychium campestre, grape fern
Bouteloua, genus of grama grass
Bouteloua curtipendula, side-oats grama
Bouteloua gracilis, blue grama
Buchloë dactyloides, buffalo grass
Calamovilfa, genus of sandreed grass
Campanula americana, American bellflower
Campanula rotundifolia, harebell
Carex, genus of sedges
Carex diandra, lesser panicled sedge
Carex peckii, Peck's sedge
Carex saximontana, sedge
Carex tribuloides, sedge
Cerastium arvense, prairie chickweed
Chara, genus of stonewort
Cinna arundinacea, woodreed
Circaea lutetiana canadensis, enchanter's nightshade
Clematis ligusticifolia, western clematis
Clematis virginiana, virgin's bower
Collinsia parviflora, blue lips
Commelina erecta, dayflower
Conyza, genus within the Asteraceae (sunflowers)
Conyza canadensis, horseweed
Cornus, genus of dogwoods
Cornus stolonifera, red osier dogwood
Corylus americana, hazelnut
Cuscuta grovonii, Gronovius's dodder
Cyperus, genus of flatsedges
Cyperus engelmannii, umbrella sedge
Cystopteris bulbifera, bulblet bladder fern
Dalea cylindriceps, massive spike prairie clover
Desmodium glutinosum, large-flowered tickclover
Draba nemorosa, yellow whitlowwort
Dryopteris carthusiana (= *spinulosa*), spinulose wood fern
Echinochloa, genus of barnyard grasses
Eleocharis, genus of spikerushes
Epilobium, genus of willow herbs

Eragrostis, genus of lovegrasses
Erigeron divergens, fleabane
Eriophorum, genus of cottongrasses
Euonymus atropurpurea, wahoo
Eupatorium rugosum, white snakeroot
Euthamia graminifolia, euthamia
Festuca, genus of fescue grasses
Festuca obtusa, nodding fescue
Festuca octoflora, sixweeks fescue
Fimbristylis puberula, fimbristylis
Fraxinus, genus of ashes
Fraxinus pennsylvanica, red ash
Gaura coccinea, scarlet guara
Gentiana andrewsii, closed gentian
Geranium maculatum, wild cranesbill
Habenaria leucophaea, prairie fringed orchid
Hedeoma, genus of mock pennyroyals
Hedeoma hispida, rough false pennyroyal
Hemicarpha micrantha, hemicarpha
Impatiens pallida, pale touch-me-not
Juglans nigra, black walnut
Juncus scirpoides, rush
Juniperus scopulorum, Rocky Mountain juniper
Laportea canadensis, wood nettle
Leersia virginica, whitegrass
Lemna, genus of duckweeds
Lepidium, genus of pepperweeds
Lonicera dioca glaucescens, wild honeysuckle
Lycopus virginicus, Virginia bugleweed
Medicago, genus of medic legumes
Mentha piperata, mint
Menyanthes trifoliata, buckbean
Mimulus alatus, sharpwing monkey flower
Mimulus ringens, Allegheny monkey flower
Morus rubra, red mulberry
Muhlenbergia, genus of muhly grasses
Muhlenbergia glomerata, muhly

Oenothera latifolia, pale evening primrose
Onoclea, genus of ferns
Onoclea sensibilis, sensitive fern
Opuntia polyacantha, plains prickly pear
Osmorhiza claytonii, sweet cicely
Oxytropis lambertii, purple locoweed
Panicum, genus of panic grasses
Parthenocissus quinquefolia, Virginia creeper
Phlox andicola, plains phlox
Phragmites, genus of common reed grasses
Physocarpus opulifolius intermedia, ninebark
Physostegia parviflora, obedient plant
Pinus ponderosa, yellow (ponderosa) pine
Plantago patagonica, Patagonian plantain
Poa, genus of bluegrasses
Poa juncifolia, bluegrass
Poa pratensis, Kentucky bluegrass
Poa sylvestris, woodland bluegrass
Polygonum, genus of smartweeds
Potamogeton, genus of pondweeds
Prunus, genus in Rosaceae family, including plums and chokecherries
Prunus americana, wild plum
Prunus mexicana, big-tree plum
Prunus virginiana, eastern chokecherry
Psoralea hypugaea, little breadroot scurfpea
Pterospora andromedea, pinedrops
Pycnanthemum virginianum, Virginia mountain mint
Pyrola virens, wintergreen
Pyrus iowensis, Prairie crab apple
Quercus, genus of oaks
Quercus macrocarpa, bur oak
Redfieldia, genus of blowout grass
Rhamnus lanceolata, lance-leaved buckthorn
Rhus, genus within Anacardiaceae family, including poison ivy
Ribes setosum, bristly gooseberry
Rosa, genus of roses
Rubus pubescens, creeping blackberry

Ruppia occidentalis, ditchgrass
Sagittaria graminea, arrowhead
Sagittaria rigida, sessile-fruited arrowhead
Salix, genus of willows
Salix petiolaris, meadow willow
Sambucus canadensis, common elderberry
Schizachyrium scoparius, little bluestem
Scirpus, genus of bulrushes
Scolochloa festucacea, spangletop
Scrophularia marilandica, figwort
Scutellaria parvula leonardi, small skullcap
Selaginella densa, spikemoss
Selaginella rupestris, rock spikemoss
Silene menziesii, campion
Silene stellata, starry campion
Solidago speciosa, showy-wand goldenrod
Sorghastrum, genus of Indian grasses
Stipa, genus of needlegrasses
Stipa comata, needle-and-thread
Symphoricarpos albus, snowberry
Symphoricarpos occidentalis, wolfberry
Talinum calycinum, Large-flower fameflower
Tilia americana, basswood (linden)
Triadenum fraseri, marsh Saint-John's-wort
Typha, genus of cattails
Ulmus, genus of elms
Ulmus americana, American elm
Ulmus rubra, red (slippery) elm
Viola pubescens, downy yellow violet
Viola sororia, downy blue violet
Yucca glauca, small soapweed (Great Plains yucca)
Zanthoxylum americanum, prickly ash

Appendix 3

Sites of Biological Interest in the Greater Niobrara Region

This appendix lists federal, state, and some other biologically significant sites, primarily those having public access. Federal sites include national wildlife refuges, national forests, national grasslands, and national monuments. State-owned sites include state parks, state wildlife management areas (WMAS), and state recreation areas (SRAS). Other listed sites include municipal parks, private nature preserves such as Nature Conservancy holdings, and miscellaneous sites of biological interest.

Sites on the associated map are identified by letter codes for the counties where each occurs (S = Sioux, D = Dawes, etc.). Some of these sites, especially those in the Sandhills, are on unmarked county roads, and you may need a good state atlas to find them. Such atlases include the *Nebraska Atlas and Gazetteer* (Freeport ME: DeLorme, 1996) and the *Nebraska Sportsman's Atlas* (Lytton IA: Sportsman's Atlas, 1994). The latter atlas is especially good for locating sites of outdoor interest such as WMAS and SRAS and provides better road information, but the former atlas illustrates natural features (elevations, river drainages, and forested areas) more effectively and also provides latitude-longitude axis points.

Although the sites listed nearly all have public access, state parks and state recreation areas require annual Nebraska park permits or daily admission fees. State wildlife management areas offer free access, as do both of the national wildlife refuges included here. Detailed information on all Nebraska SRAS, WMAS, and state parks can be found at the Nebraska Game and Park Commission's Web site: www.ngpc.state.ne.us. Aerial photographic maps of state lands can be found at: http://www.ngpc.state.ne.us/realty/gpland/landatlas.asp.

Sites of special biological interest in the upper, central, and lower Niobrara Valley

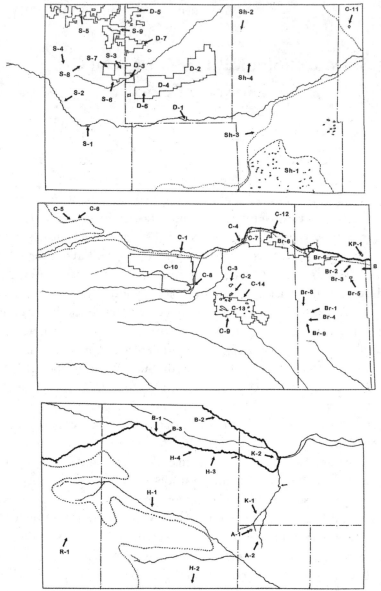

Sites in each county are identified numerically under the following county abbreviations: Antelope (A), Boyd (B), Brown (Br), Cherry (C), Dawes (D), Knox (K), Keya Paha (KP), Rock (R), Sioux (S), and Sheridan (Sh). Locations of known fens in Cherry County are shown by inked circles (after Steinauer, Rolfsmeier, and Hardys 1996).

Sioux County

Sioux County is in the heart of the Pine Ridge country, a multicounty region of ridge-and-canyon topography that is largely a north-facing, east-west escarpment mostly covered by ponderosa (yellow) pine and streamside deciduous forests, totaling some 68,000 acres. There once were more than a million acres of grasslands in Sioux County, mainly shortgrass plains. Most of those that survive are included in the Oglala National Grassland, which supports a typical high plains avifauna. Sioux County has several bird species that rarely occur elsewhere in Nebraska, such as the pinyon jay, Lewis's woodpecker, Clark's nutcracker, cordilleran flycatcher, and plumbeous vireo. There are also several unique Pine Ridge mammals, such as Merriam's shrew, long-legged and fringe-tailed myotis, Townsend's big-eared bat, and least chipmunk. There are tourist accommodations at Harrison. The birds of Sioux, Dawes, and Sheridan counties were documented by Richard Rosche (1982).

Agate Fossil Beds National Monument

Area about 3,000 acres. Managed by National Park Service. Located twenty-two miles south of Harrison, off U.S. Highway 29. Consists of shortgrass plains and world-famous Miocene fossils from about 20 million years ago. No formally published bird checklist is yet available, but a total of 156 species have been reported at the site, including many western forms such as ferruginous hawk, mountain plover, burrowing owl, Cassin's kingbird, pinyon jay, western tanager, black-headed grosbeak, lazuli bunting, and both McCown's and chestnut-collared longspurs. Information is available via the Web (www.nps.gov/agfo), or contact the park headquarters at 301 River Road, Harrison NE 69346. There is a one-mile trail through shortgrass prairie up to the Fossil Hills, making the trail a two-mile return-trip walk, or you can take the Fossil Hills loop trail to Carnegie Hill, then down to the Bone Cabin and across the terrace back to the Fossil Hills trail. There is also a one-mile Daemonelix Trail, passing helical fossil burrows of the beaverlike *Paleocaster*. The Niobrara River here is only a narrow creek, with wet meadows supporting willow thickets and associated wetland birds. There is a modern air-conditioned interpretive center, with many fossils from the site. Be aware that rattlesnakes are common along pathways during warmer months. Admission fee or national park permit required. For information check URL: www.nps.gov/agfo/. U.S. Map location S-1.

Cherry Ranch

Area 7,620 acres. A working ranch owned by the Nature Conservancy, about ten miles south of Harrison and along the Niobrara River. Located a short distance southeast of the Guadalcanal Ranch (see below). Not open to the public without special permission; contact the Nature Conservancy's Chadron field office or its Omaha state headquarters (1019 Leavenworth, Suite 100, Omaha NE 58102) for information.

Fort Robinson State Park

Area 22,000 acres, including portions in Dawes County. Managed by Nebraska Game and Parks Commission. Consists of mixed ponderosa (yellow) pine forests and shortgrass prairies near the White River. It is a restored military outpost dating from the Indian Wars of the late 1800s and has ties to such historic figures as George Custer, Crazy Horse, and Red Cloud. Although the park still provides extensive coniferous habitat, a forest fire in 1989 damaged much of the forested sections. There are sixty-seven miles of hiking, biking, and horse trails. Raptors include nesting golden eagles, prairie falcons, red-tailed and ferruginous hawks, and great horned owls. Confined bison and wild pronghorns and elk are present, as is a small herd of bighorn sheep. A steep cliff used by nesting white-throated swifts is six miles west of headquarters. No complete bird list is yet available. Peterson Wildlife Management Area and Soldier Creek Wilderness are both nearby. Lodging and food are available. Address: Box 392, Crawford NE 68339, or URL: http://www.stateparks. com/fort_robinson.html. Map location s-3.

Gilbert-Baker WMA

Area 2,537 acres. Managed by Nebraska Game and Parks Commission. Located about four miles north of Harrison via oil-surfaced county road. This is an area of ridges covered with ponderosa (yellow) pines, with scattered areas of grassland at the forest fringes. Monroe Creek traverses the area and is a popular trout stream. Elk can sometimes be found here, and you might also see bighorn sheep. Pinyon jays have nested here (the only documented location in the state), as well as white-throated swifts, and possibly even Swainson's thrushes and Lewis's woodpeckers. Monroe Canyon supports several distinctly western species, such as Townsend's solitaire, cordilleran flycatcher, plumbeous vireo, and violet-green swallow. Nearby Sowbelly Canyon (see below) supports many of these same highly localized species, such as cordilleran flycatcher, plumbeous vireo, violet-green swallow, and white-throated swift. Other western species to be found here include the least chipmunk, mountain birch, and mountain maple. Map location s-4.

Guadalcanal Ranch

Area 5,000 acres. A working ranch owned by Prairie-Plains Resource Institute of Aurora. Located about five miles southwest of Harrison and along the Niobrara River. For information contact the Aurora office at 1307 I Street, Aurora NE 68818. Not open to the public without advance permission. Not shown on map.

Harrison-Henry Road

A gravel road going south along the Wyoming border (turn south off Highway 20 eight miles west of Harrison) crosses the Niobrara River and passes into ridge-and-valley topography that supports McCown's and chestnut-collared longspurs, Say's phoebes, and rock wrens as well as Brewer's sparrows, ferruginous hawks, and long-billed curlews. At about eight miles south of the highway turning a gravel road goes east and leads back to State Highway 29. For the more adventurous, an unimproved road (perhaps impassable in winter or bad weather) continues south to Henry through high plains grasslands and photogenic badlands topography. Not shown on map.

Hudson-Meng Bison Bonebed Enclosure

Managed by the U.S. Forest Service. Located in the Oglala National Grassland near Toadstool Geologic Park (see below). Drive 4 miles north of Crawford on Highway 2, go west on Toadstool Road for 7.4 miles to Sand Creek Road, then follow Sand Creek Road 6.3 miles. Over 600 ancient bison (*B. antiquis*) skeletons have been discovered at this actively studied and now-enclosed archeological site that is about 9,000 to 9,800 years old. Once believed to be the location of a paleo-Indian kill, the site has recently been interpreted as resulting from massive natural mortality. Admission fee; handicap-accessible. Open mid-May to mid-September. Information at URLs: http://www.fs.fed.us/r2/nebraska/units/prrd/hm/hudsonmeng or www.hudsonmeng.org. Not shown on map.

Nebraska National Forest, Pine Ridge District

Area 50,853 acres. Managed by U.S. Forest Service. See description under Dawes County. Map location D-4.

Oglala National Grassland

Area 93,344 acres. Managed by U.S. Forest Service. Located in several separate units in northernmost Sioux County and adjacent Dawes County, about fifteen miles north of Harrison (via county road) or Crawford (State Highways 2 and 71). The area offers state rarities such as Brewer's sparrows and sage thrashers as well as long-billed curlews, Swainson's and ferruginous hawks, and chestnut-collared longspurs. Horned larks, western meadowlarks, and lark buntings are common breeders in this region. Grassland hawks (red-tailed, Swainson's, and ferruginous) are common here, and golden eagles are also frequent. The highest point in the Niobrara region, Roundtop Butte (4,501 feet), is near Toadstool Geologic Park (see below). For information check URL: http://www.fs.fed.us/r2/nebraska/units/prrd/oglala.html or contact the Forest Service office at HC 75, Box 13A9, Chadron NE 69337. Map location S-5.

Peterson WMA

Area 2,460 acres. This area, near the southeast corner of Soldier Creek Wilderness (south of U.S. Highway 20), consists of habitats alternating between mature ponderosa (yellow) pine forests and grasslands in typical ridge-and-canyon topography. Two streams pass through the area. No campground. Map location S-6.

Soldier Creek Wilderness

Area 7,794 acres. This is a large roadless area that has an extensive hiking trail network (Boots and Saddle Trail, six miles; Trooper Trail, nine miles). Both are loop trails over ridges and canyons with trailheads at the picnic area of Soldier Creek Road. You must carry in your water, and there are no facilities. Much of the area was burned in a 1989 fire, so Lewis's woodpeckers might occur here. To reach it, follow Soldier Creek Road at the northwest end of the Fort Robinson State Park headquarters complex. For information contact the Forest Service office mentioned above or check URL: http://www.fs.fed.us/r2/nebraska/units/prrd/soldier.html. Map location S-7.

Sowbelly Canyon

A beautiful forested canyon northeast of Harrison. Drive three miles east of Harrison on U.S. Highway 20, north on Pants Butte Road for five miles, then southwest on Sowbelly Road. Or drive one mile north of Harrison on State Highway 29, then turn east on a gravel road and proceed for several miles until you reach Sowbelly Road. This road soon enters a narrow canyon and extends northeast along a creek-bottom area at the bottom of the canyon (Coffee Park, a public-access park), where you can do birding on foot. The adjoining lands are privately owned, but a bed-and-breakfast (Sowbelly B and B Hideaway, 407 Sowbelly Road) is near the bottom of the canyon (five and a half miles northeast of Harrison) and caters to naturalists. Many distinctly western species occur in the canyon, including the very local cordilleran flycatcher, white-throated swift, violet-green swallow, and plumbeous vireo. Other western species reported here include common poorwill, Cassin's kingbird, Say's phoebe, rock wren, western tanager, Bullock's oriole, prairie falcon, pygmy nuthatch, and the endemic white-winged race of the dark-eyed junco. During 2006 this canyon was engulfed by fire, burning much of the forest and destroying the bed-and-breakfast. One should inquire at Harrison for current road and environmental conditions before visiting the site.

Toadstool Geologic Park

Area about 300 acres. Located within the Oglala National Grassland and Managed by the U.S. Forest Service. This area of typical badlands (White River Group, lower to mid-Oligocene) supports breeding-season rock wrens and Say's phoebes, with golden eagles and prairie falcons as seasonal visitors. A one-mile loop trail through part of the park begins at the picnic area, taking you past fossilized tracks of rhinos and piglike entelodonts as well as tracks of wading and swimming birds. Water is essential here, and you should carry a canteen during hot weather. There are outdoor toilets and a small campground. Information is available at URL: http://www.fs.fed.us/r2/nebraska/units/prrd/toadstooltemp. html. Free admission. Map location S-9.

Dawes County

Dawes County is one of Nebraska's most scenic regions, with nearly 100,000 acres of wooded habitats, and historically with almost 600,000 acres of grasslands within its boundaries. There are tourist accommodations at Chadron and Crawford.

Bordeaux WMA

Area 1,841 acres. Managed by Nebraska Game and Parks Commission. Located three miles southeast of Chadron via Highway 20, on Bordeaux

Road. A three-mile stretch of Big Bordeaux Creek passes through a valley of ponderosa (yellow) pines and deciduous wooded habitats, providing an important wintering area for elk. Bighorn sheep have also been seen here. Not shown on map.

Box Butte SRA

Area 612 land acres plus a 1,600-acre reservoir (the largest reservoir on the Niobrara River). Managed by Nebraska Game and Parks Commission. Except for tall cottonwoods lining the reservoir, this area is largely treeless, with the Niobrara River here being barely more than a creek. This is an outstanding birding area in the Panhandle; over two hundred species have been tallied here. Rock wren, Say's phoebe, and ferruginous hawk are among the more interesting western species, and probable eastern-oriented breeders include eastern bluebird, eastern wood pewee, and wood thrush. Small woodland passerines such as warblers and vireos are abundant during migration. Park entry permit required. Map location D-1. See URL: http://www.ngpc.state.ne.us/parks/guides/parksearch/showpark.asp?Area_No=31.

Chadron State Park

Area 801 acres. Managed by Nebraska Game and Parks Commission. This is one of the best places in the region to see Lewis's woodpeckers, and it also supports pygmy nuthatches, western tanagers, and common poorwills. On the way to the Black Hills lookout, watch for Lewis's woodpeckers perched on the tops of snags. At the lookout you might search for pinyon jays (rare), yellow-rumped warblers, western tanagers, and mountain bluebirds as well as western raptors. The Spotted Tail hiking trail extends eight miles from the park boundary through the Nebraska National Forest, and the Black Hills Overlook trail extends four miles from the park campground. State park entry permit required. Check URL: http://www.ngpc.state.ne.us/parks/guides/parksearch/showpark.asp?Area_No=42 for information. Map location D-2.

Fort Robinson State Park

See Sioux County account. Map location D-3.

Nebraska National Forest

Pine Ridge District (50,803 acres), and Pine Ridge National Recreation Area (6,600 acres). Managed by U.S. Forest Service. Mostly consists of ponderosa (yellow) pine forest and intervening grasslands. The topography of this area is generally rugged, and the roads may not be in good condition, so it is well to check with the ranger office on U.S. Highway 385 before venturing far from the main road. Cattle grazing is permitted here, so pay attention to gates. There is a fairly difficult four-mile hiking trail starting at the Iron Horse Road meadow, and a less difficult three-mile trail with its trailhead at East Ash Road. A fairly difficult eight-mile trail leading to Chadron State Park begins at a gravel road off U.S. Highway 85. The National Recreation Area does not allow motorized vehicles. For more information check URL: http://www.fs.fed.us/r2/nebraska/units/prrd/prnatrecareatemp.html or contact the Forest Supervisor at 270 Pine Street, Chadron NE 69337. Map location D-4.

Oglala National Grasslands
See Sioux County account. Map location D-5.

Ponderosa WMA
Area 3,659 acres. Managed by Nebraska Game and Parks Commission. Located about seven miles southeast of Crawford (drive two and a half miles south on U.S. 20, then four miles east). This area is largely covered by ponderosa (yellow) pine forest, with grasslands on level areas and some deciduous trees lining Squaw Creek. A hiking trail (Rim of the World Trail) starting at parking area 5 provides excellent panoramas and may offer views of such raptors as prairie falcons, golden eagles, and ferruginous hawks. Lewis's woodpeckers have been found nesting in a burned-over area, and Clark's nutcrackers have also been seen here. National Forest land adjoins the area to the south and southwest. About ten miles south of Crawford along State Highway 2 are ridgetop pine woodlands where Cassin's kingbirds are often present, especially during fall migration in September. Map location D-6.

Whitney Lake WMA
Area 900 acres. Managed by Nebraska Game and Parks Commission. Located two miles northwest of Whitney. This is a privately owned irrigation reservoir in the White River basin (a region where surface water is rare) that is stocked with game fish. The lake is little studied ornithologically but should seasonally attract fish-eating birds and waterfowl. Map location D-7.

Box Butte County

Box Butte County is only slightly forested (about 5,000 wooded acres) and historically had over 300,000 acres of grasslands. There are tourist accommodations at Alliance. There are no sites of special biological interest in the mapped portion of this county, but just beyond its southern edge is Kilpatrick Lake, about twenty miles west of Alliance. (Drive west on 10th Street for eleven miles, then south one mile, and west again for five more miles.) A trail begins at a sign saying that the route to Snake Creek Ranch goes to the left and leads to the dam. This small reservoir is a major stopover point for snow geese and a few Ross's geese in spring. The meadows to the south of the dam around Snake Creek support willets, long-billed curlews, Wilson's snipes, eastern meadowlarks (near the western edges of their Nebraska range), and the very local Savannah sparrow. Scan the drier shrubby areas of sandsage for Cassin's sparrows, which are also local and usually rare in Nebraska. These sparrows selectively inhabit sandsage grassland and are not present every year.

Sheridan County

Sheridan County has about 50,000 acres of wooded habitats, and historically it had nearly 1.2 million acres of grasslands. It also has over 20,000 acres of surface wetlands, mostly alkaline Sandhills marshes. There are tourist accommodations at Gordon, Merna, and Rushville.

Alkali Lake Region

The area enclosed within a dashed line in western Sheridan County (see the southwestern corner of map) contains more than 150 lakes of at least five acres, most of them moderately to highly alkaline. They often are attractive to migratory shorebirds such as phalaropes and avocets, since many support large populations of alkali-tolerant crustaceans (e.g., brine shrimp) and insects (especially brine flies). Map location Sh-1.

Metcalf WMA

Area 3,076 acres. Managed by Nebraska Game and Parks Commission. Located about ten miles north of Hay Springs, this site has typical Pine Ridge upland pine-covered habitats but also some open grasslands. It is crossed by Little Beaver Creek, with ponderosa (yellow) pines on the uplands and deciduous wooded habitats along the creek. The bird fauna is little known, but white-throated swifts, pinyon jays, and Clark's nutcrackers have all been seen here. This site may be the easternmost Nebraska location for these western species. There are no camping facilities. Map location Sh-2.

Smith Lake WMA

Area 640 acres. Managed by Nebraska Game and Parks Commission. Located twenty-seven miles south of Rushville on State Highway 250. Includes a 200-acre lake and about 20 acres of marsh. At least 145 species have been seen here, including 49 nesting species, plus 18 probable breeders and 36 possible breeders. Marbled godwits nested here in 1990, their only proven nesting location in Nebraska. Other typical Great Plains species include the lark sparrow, lark bunting, vesper sparrow, western grebe, and Forster's tern. Eastern and northern breeding species include wood duck, eastern screech owl, tree swallow, white-breasted nuthatch, warbling vireo, swamp sparrow, orchard oriole, Baltimore oriole, and bobolink. Some western species such as Swainson's hawk, long-billed curlew, western wood pewee, mountain bluebird, black-headed grosbeak, Brewer's blackbird, and Bullock's oriole are also likely or known western breeders. Other raptor species of widespread distribution include long-eared owl, northern harrier, Cooper's hawk, red-tailed hawk, and American kestrel. Map location Sh-3.

Walgren Lake WMA

Area 130 acres. Managed by Nebraska Game and Parks Commission. Drive three miles east of Hay Springs on U.S. Highway 20, then three miles south. A great variety of migrant species are attracted to this lake, including some rarities. Just a mile south of Walgren Lake is a prairie dog town, which usually supports nesting burrowing owls and occasional chestnut-collared longspurs. Longspurs are most common along the first road going east along the north edge of the prairie dog colony. There is a primitive campground at Walgren Lake. Map location Sh-4.

Cherry County

Cherry County, the largest county in the state, consists mostly of Sandhills habitats, with 3.7 million acres of grasslands historically (still mostly intact Sandhills prairies), about 17,000 acres of wooded habitats, and 41,000 acres of surface wetlands. There are tourist accommodations at Cody, Merriman, and Valentine. Known fen locations are indicated on the map by inked circles (after Steinauer 1993).

Anderson Bridge WMA

Includes 137 acres of river valley bottomland forest and a mile of river frontage (south side of river). Managed by Nebraska Game and Parks Commission. Drive five and a half miles south of Kilgore, two miles east, and then five miles south. The gravel road going west for about seven miles from this bridge, along the north side of the Niobrara River, passes through many meadows where species such as indigo buntings, blue grosbeaks, and lark sparrows are common and shrubby wetlands where yellow-breasted chats and common yellowthroats are abundant. This is one of the best stretches along the entire middle section of the Niobrara for roadside birding near the river. The road eventually turns north and provides a return route north to Highway 20 at Nenzel, or a route south across the river to the Samuel R. McKelvie National Forest. Map location C-1.

Arthur Bowring Sandhills Ranch State Historical Park

Area 7,200 acres. Managed by Nebraska Game and Parks Commission. Located one mile north of Merriman. There often are trumpeter swans on a marsh just north of this park, which is still a working cattle ranch. Park entry permit required. Map location C-5. See URL: http://www.byways.org/browse/byways/16471/places/38093/.

Ballard's Marsh WMA

Area 1,561 acres. Managed by Nebraska Game and Parks Commission. Includes a large marsh and adjoining Sandhills grasslands. Campground. Map location C-2.

Big Alkali WMA

Area about 900 acres. Managed by Nebraska Game and Parks Commission. Consists of 47 grassland acres and an 842-acre Sandhills lake. Campground. Map location C-3.

Borman Bridge WMA

Area 159 acres. Managed by Nebraska Game and Parks Commission. Located a mile and a half southeast of Valentine, off U.S. Highway 20. Consists of bottomland along the Niobrara River in transitional east-west forest. This point represents the upstream end of the Niobrara National Scenic River, which extends east from here for seventy-six miles to the Highway 137 bridge (north of Newport), where it is replaced downstream to the Missouri confluence by the Missouri National Recreation River. There are only a few public restrooms along this entire stretch of river: at Fort Niobrara NWR, Brewer Bridge, Smith Falls State Park, and Rocky Ford. Except for public-access points at about ten bridges, virtually this entire seventy-six-mile stretch of river is private property, and you need the landowners' permission for other access. For information see URL: http://www.nps.gov/niob/. Map location C-4.

Brewer Bridge Public-Access Area

Area two acres. Middle Niobrara Natural Resources District. Located along the north shore of the Niobrara, four and a half miles south of Sparks. Picnic tables, restrooms, and canoe launch site. Not shown on map.

Cottonwood Lake SRA

Area 180 acres, including a 60-acre Sandhills lake. Managed by Nebraska Game and Parks Commission. Located one mile southeast of Merriman. Canada geese and other waterfowl breed here. Five miles east of Merriman, off the north side of U.S. Highway 20, is a Sandhills marsh where trumpeter swans have nested. Park entry permit required. Campground. Map location C-6.

Cottonwood/Steverson Lakes WMA

This new WMA consists of 2,919 acres, encompassing three Sandhills lakes (Cottonwood, Steverson, and Home Valley). About thirty miles south of Cottonwood Lake SRA on Highway 61. The western end of Steverson Lake has a fen and associated cold-climate plants that are relicts of the Pleistocene. Other fens also occur in this headwaters area of the North Loup River. Not shown on the map. See URL: http://www.ngpc.state. ne.us/parks/guides/parksearch/showpark.asp?Area_No=53.

Fort Niobrara National Wildlife Refuge

Area 19,122 acres. Managed by U.S. Fish and Wildlife Service. This refuge, established in the early 1900s to propagate bison and other then rare big game, lies in the western portion of the primary east-west ecological transition zone between coniferous and deciduous forest types and thus has a fine mixture of eastern and western fauna and flora. The refuge has 14,400 acres of native prairie, 4,345 acres of wooded habitats, and 375 acres of wetlands. About two-thirds of the refuge consists of Sandhills prairie, and the rest is mostly mixed riparian hardwoods. Western-eastern species pairs of woodland birds that occur and may hybridize include such forms as western and eastern wood pewees, black-headed and rose-breasted grosbeaks, eastern and spotted towhees, and Bullock's and Baltimore orioles. A total of 225 species (77 breeders) have been reported here. There is a good population of sharp-tailed grouse, some greater prairie chickens, and wild turkeys. There are also breeding burrowing owls, yellow-breasted chats, American redstarts, grasshopper and Savannah sparrows, and both meadowlarks. There is an interpretive center at refuge headquarters (tel. 402-376-3789). The refuge address is HC 14, Box 27, Valentine NE, 6920l, or see URL: http://fort-niobrara.fws.gov. The west end of the Niobrara National Recreational River is at Borman Bridge near the refuge's west boundary (see Brown County, below). Map location C-7.

Merritt Reservoir WMA

Area 2,906-acre reservoir and 350 acres of upland Sandhills. Managed by Nebraska Game and Parks Commission. Located twenty-six miles southwest of Valentine, this large reservoir abuts the Samuel R. McKelvie National Forest. The reservoir attracts large numbers of migrant waterfowl, white pelicans, western grebes, and other aquatic birds, but no bird list is yet available. Map location C-8.

Niobrara Valley Preserve

See Brown County.

Rat and Beaver Lake WMA

Area 240 acres. Managed by Nebraska Game and Parks Commission. Drive twenty-nine miles south of Valentine on U.S. 20, then six miles west on a sand road. Consists of Sandhills grassland and two marshy lakes. Map location C-9.

Samuel R. McKelvie National Forest

Area 115,703 acres. Managed by U.S. Forest Service. This section of planted coniferous forest in an otherwise Sandhills grassland environment is similar to that of the Bessey District to the south and is quite different from the naturally forested Nebraska National Forest to the west. The adjoining Merritt Reservoir (see above) attracts many waterfowl. There is a sharp-tailed grouse blind available in spring that accommodates four people, first-come. For information check URL: http://www.fs.fed.us/r2/nebraska/units/mckelvie/mckelvienf.html. Map location C-10.

Schlegel Creek WMA

Area 600 acres. Managed by Nebraska Game and Parks Commission. Drive thirteen miles south of Valentine on U.S. Highway 83, then four miles west on an unmarked sand road. Consists of Sandhills grassland, including two miles of Schlegel Creek. Not shown on map.

Shell Lake WMA

Area 640 acres. Managed by Nebraska Game and Parks Commission. Located fourteen miles northeast of Gordon, via a county road. Consists of Sandhills grassland, including a 162-acre lake. Map location C-11.

Smith Falls State Park

Area 244 acres. Managed by Nebraska Game and Parks Commission. Drive twelve miles northeast of Valentine on Highway 12, then four miles south. You can cross the river by a footbridge for a close view of the seventy-foot falls, which is in a side canyon. No bird list is available, but the riparian forest is much like that of the Niobrara Valley Preserve (see Brown County), and its bird life is probably very similar. Park entry permit required (tel. 402-376-1306). Map location C-12. See URL: http://www.ngpc.state.ne.us/parks/guides/parksearch/showpark.asp?Area_No=308.

Valentine National Wildlife Refuge

Area 71,516 acres. Managed by U.S. Fish and Wildlife Service. Located about thirty miles south of Valentine, via U.S. Highway 83 and State Highway S-1B. This is Nebraska's largest national wildlife refuge, with 270 bird species (105 breeders) reported. Most of the refuge consists of Sandhills prairie, with dunes forty to two hundred feet high, and intervening interdune depressions that often contain shallow, marshy lakes. Some of the lakes are open for canoeing or boating, offering great birding opportunities. Driving on the sandy and hilly roads requires special care; a supply of water and a tow rope are recommended. There are several prairie chicken and sharp-tailed grouse leks in the refuge (viewing blinds are available; you may make reservations), and the numerous marshes and shallow lakes offer breeding habitat for eared, western, and pied-billed grebes and a few Clark's grebes. There are also a dozen breeding species of waterfowl and shorebirds such as soras, Wilson's snipes, Wilson's phalaropes, and American avocets. The higher grasslands provide habitat for long-billed curlews, upland sandpipers, and Swainson's hawks. The refuge manager's address is the same as that of the Fort Niobrara refuge; for information check URL: http://valentine.fws.gov. Map location C-13.

Willow Lake WMA
Area 440 acres, including 240 acres of marsh, and surrounded by Valentine NWR. Managed by Nebraska Game and Parks Commission. Drive twenty miles south of Valentine on U.S. Highway 83, then go two miles west on a Sandhills road. (Note: There is also a Willow Lake WMA in Brown County.) Map location C-14.

Keya Paha County
Keya Paha County is often pronounced locally as *kip'-aha*, but the Lakota-based name is properly pronounced *ke'ya pa-ha'* and means "turtle hills," probably in reference to the hills' rounded shapes. It has over 37,000 acres of wooded habitats, historically had over 400,000 acres of grasslands, and has about 1,300 acres of surface water. There are tourist accommodations in Springview.

Cub Creek Recreation Area
Area 300 acres. Maintained by the city of Springview and owned by the Middle Niobrara Natural Resources District. Eight miles west of Springview and about four miles north of the Niobrara River, consisting of woods, prairie, and a small reservoir. Camping is permitted.

Fred Thomas Overlook
Managed by Nebraska Game and Parks Commission. Located ten miles north of Bassett on State Highway 7. A scenic overlook named in the memory of Fred Thomas (1931-99), a longtime *Omaha World Herald* outdoors columnist and environmentalist who was dedicated to the preservation of the Niobrara Valley.

Niobrara Valley Preserve
See Brown County.

Thomas Creek WMA
Area 1,154 acres. Managed by Nebraska Game and Parks Commission. Located two miles south of Springview, three miles east, and then two

more miles south on county roads. Consists of steep topography around Thomas Creek, with grasslands on the hills, ponderosa (yellow) pines (near their eastern range limit) on the canyon walls, and deciduous wooded creek-bottoms. Map location KP-1.

Brown County

Brown County has over 21,000 acres of wooded habitats, historically had nearly 700,000 acres of grasslands, and has about 8,000 acres of surface water. Tourist accommodations are available at Ainsworth.

American Game Marsh WMA

Area 160 acres. Managed by Nebraska Game and Parks Commission. Located thirteen miles northeast of Elsmere along the county road to Johnstown. Consists of a large Sandhills marsh and surrounding grasslands. No facilities. Map location Br-1.

Bobcat WMA

Area 893 acres. Managed by Nebraska Game and Parks Commission. Located three miles west of Springview (on U.S. Highway 12), eight miles south (on Meadville Road), and one mile west. Nearly 90 percent of this area consists of steep pine- and cedar-covered canyons bordering Plum Creek. The rest is Sandhills grassland and shrubland on the west side. Map location Br-2.

Keller Park SRA (196 acres) and Keller School Land WMA (640 acres)

Managed by Nebraska Game and Parks Commission. Keller Park SRA is three miles west of Long Pine (via U.S. Highway 20) and six and a half miles north (via U.S. Highway 183), off the west side of this highway along Bone Creek. From Ainsworth drive four miles east on U.S. Highway 20, then north six and a half miles. Keller School Land WMA is directly south of Keller Park SRA, These areas consist of native prairies and wooded canyons beside Bone Creek. Five small fishing ponds in the SRA are stocked with trout and other game fish. The ponds attract eagles, ducks, and other waterbirds, the prairies support grassland sparrows, and the mixed wooded habitats have a variety of both western coniferous and eastern deciduous forest birds, including wild turkeys, scarlet tanagers, and American redstarts. Greater prairie chickens and sharp-tailed grouse both occur, as well as wild turkeys and northern bobwhites. Mule deer and white-tailed deer are also present in this east-west transition zone. Park entry permit required for the SRA. Map location Br-3.

Long Lake WMA

Area 80 acres. Managed by Nebraska Game and Parks Commission. Located twelve miles northeast of Elsmere on the west side of the county road to Johnstown. Consists of a lake and Sandhills grasslands. Map location Br-4. See URL: http://www.ngpc.state.ne.us/parks/guides/park-search/showpark.asp?Area_No=250.

Long Pine WMA and Long Pine SRA

Area 160 acres. Managed by Nebraska Game and Parks Commission. Located just south of Highway 20, near the town of Long Pine. Consists mostly of ponderosa (yellow) pine and red cedar wooded habitats; the rest is native Sandhills grasslands, bisected by Long Pine Creek. The terrain is steep, and camping facilities in the SRA are primitive. Map location Br-5.

Niobrara National Scenic River and Missouri National Recreation River

The Niobrara National Scenic River is a federally protected stretch of the Niobrara River that extends seventy-six miles downstream from Borman Bridge east of Valentine to the common boundary of Holt and Knox counties. The Missouri National Recreation River begins there and continues an additional twenty miles downstream to the mouth of the Niobrara River; it also extends eight miles up Verdigre Creek from the Niobrara-Missouri confluence to the town of Verdigre. For information check URL: http://www.nps.gov/niob/. The National Park Service's local address is Box 591, O'Neill NE 68763.

Niobrara Valley Preserve

Area approximately 60,000 protected acres (56,000 fee-title and 4,000 leased acres), including about twenty-five miles on the south side of the Niobrara River, in the heart of the transition zone between western coniferous and eastern deciduous forest types. Owned and managed by the Nature Conservancy, with the preserve headquarters about sixteen miles north of Johnstown, via a county road. A published list of 125 of the site's spring and summer birds exists (Brogie and Mossman 1983), and 213 have been seen in total. A collective list of more than 230 Niobrara Valley bird species reported from Mariaville (Highway 137) west to Fort Niobrara NWR has also been published (Ducey 1989). Among the breeding birds of special interest are several species pairs that hybridize here, such as Baltimore and Bullock's orioles, lazuli and indigo buntings, rose-breasted and black-headed grosbeaks, and spotted and eastern towhees. The yellow- and red-shafted races of northern flicker extensively hybridize here. Western-oriented bird species include the burrowing owl, black-billed magpie, common poorwill, sharp-tailed grouse, and (in winter) Townsend's solitaire. Eastern birds include the greater prairie chicken, American woodcock, whip-poor-will, red-bellied woodpecker, great crested flycatcher, eastern phoebe, eastern bluebird, black-and-white warbler, American redstart, ovenbird, and scarlet tanager. The blue-gray gnatcatcher has also been reported; if it breeds here it would be at the extreme western edge of the range of the eastern race (*P. c. caerulea*). Typical Great Plains species include the federally threatened piping plover, the endangered interior race of the least tern, and several arid-adapted grassland sparrows, such as the vesper sparrow, lark sparrow, and lark bunting. At least 47 species of mammals have also been documented here, including the rare Hayden's shrew, and there is a managed herd of over 500 bison. Along with about 2,000 cattle, these are the subjects of ecological studies on the effects of cattle and bison grazing and of managed fire on the grasslands. The preserve has also developed local lists of fishes (25 species), amphibians (8 species), and reptiles (17 species). There are lists of lichens (86 species), mosses, and moths and of the preserve's 70 known species of butterflies (Dankert and Nagel 1988). Churchill, Freeman, and Kantak (1988) documented 581 plant species in the preserve, or almost a third of the total known Nebraska species. Attempts have been made to reestablish the rare and endangered Hayden's (blowout) penstemon on barren dune slopes. The highly local paper birch occurs on the preserve, and cattle, bison, and fire are being managed to promote biological diversity. Kantak and Chuchill (1993) have summarized the special biogeographic significance of the preserve. Two hiking trails begin near the preserve headquarters, passing through several forest and prairie types. Each trail has a short loop and a long loop; the northern trail is somewhat longer (three miles) and steeper. Visitors are welcome. Parts of the preserve lie within the Niobrara National Scenic River corridor. The preserve's address is

Route 1, Box 348, Johnstown NE 69214 (tel. 402-722-4440). For information see URL: http://nature.org/wherewework/northamerica/states/nebraska/preserves/art9162.html. Map location Br-6.

Pine Glen WMA

Area 960 acres. Managed by Nebraska Game and Parks Commission. Located three miles west of Long Pine and six and a half miles north (via U.S. Highway 183). There a gravel road leaves the east side of the highway and leads to the WMA in about three miles. It consists of steep canyons covered with ponderosa (yellow) pine, red cedar, bur oak, and mixed native grasslands. A once excellent but now polluted trout stream (Bone Creek) passes through the area, as does the still unpolluted Long Pine Creek. No facilities. Map location Br-7.

Plum Creek WMA

Area 1,320 acres. Managed by Nebraska Game and Parks Commission. Located one and a half miles west via U.S. Highway 20 and one and a half miles south of Johnstown via a county road. Consists of two miles of Plum Creek, which passes through a wooded canyon of red cedars and bur oaks, with native Sandhills prairie on the eastern half. Not shown on the map.

South Pine WMA

Area 420 acres. Managed by Nebraska Game and Parks Commission. Located about eleven miles south of Long Pine WMA (see above). Consists of varied Sandhills habitats, including 80 acres of open water and 152 acres of marsh. Not shown on the map.

South Twin Lake WMA

Area 160 acres. Managed by Nebraska Game and Parks Commission. Located fifteen miles northeast of Elsmere off the west side of the county road leading to Johnstown. Consists of a 60-acre lake and Sandhills grasslands. This lake, American Game Marsh, Long Lake, and Willow Lake WMA are all close together, are ecologically similar, and should offer naturalists some excellent views of Sandhills habitats and wetland wildlife. Map location Br-8.

Willow Lake WMA

Area 511 acres. Managed by Nebraska Game and Parks Commission. Located seven miles northeast of Elsmere along the county road to Johnstown. Consists of a Sandhills lake (about 450 acres) and surrounding grasslands within an area of several large Sandhills marshes and lakes. Map location Br-9.

Rock County

Rock County, despite its name, mostly comprises Sandhills habitats. It historically had over 600,000 acres of grasslands, about 11,000 acres of wooded habitats, and about 11,000 acres of surface water. Tourist accommodations are available at Bassett.

Hutton Niobrara Ranch Wildlife Sanctuary

A 4,500-acre ranch along the south side of the Niobrara River, about twelve miles north of Bassett. Recently bequeathed to the Kansas Audubon Society and still under development. Not open to the public as of 2006. For information contact aok@audubonofkansas.org.

John W. and Louise Seier National Wildlife Refuge

Area 2,200 acres. Managed by U.S. Fish and Wildlife Service. This new national wildlife refuge, twenty-six miles south of Bassett and several miles west of Rose, is still under development and as of 2006 was not yet open to the public. It consists of Sandhills grasslands and marshy wetlands. For information see URL: http://seier.fws.gov.

Twin Lakes WMA

Area 143 acres. Managed by Nebraska Game and Parks Commission. Located eighteen miles south and two miles east of Bassett. It includes 113 acres of surface water (two lakes) and 30 acres of grassland. Map location R-1.

Boyd County

Boyd County is a Niobrara Valley county with about 2,500 acres of surface water and 1,600 acres of wooded habitats, and historically it had 200,000 acres of grasslands. Tourist accommodations are available at Lynch, Naper, and Spencer.

Hull Lake WMA

Area 36 acres. Managed by Nebraska Game and Parks Commission. Located three miles south and one mile west of Butte. Consists of hilly uplands with oaks, conifers, and grasslands around a three-acre lake. Map location B-1.

Old Baldy ("the Tower")

Located seven miles north of Lynch via gravel road; on private land. This distinctive, nearly barren butte is the place (described as the "Cupola") where Lewis and Clark discovered one of their major mammal species, the black-tailed prairie dog. Prairie dogs still exist in small numbers within Boyd County (their eastern limits in the Niobrara Valley), but they no longer are found at this historic site. Although on private land, there is a small public parking lot where you can obtain a good view of the butte, the Missouri River, and its associated valley. Map location B-2. For information, see URL: http://www.lewisandclarktrail.cjb.net.

Parshall Bridge WMA

Area 230 acres. Managed by Nebraska Game and Parks Commission. Located five miles south of Butte. Consists of riparian wooded habitats along the Niobrara River. Map location B-3.

Spencer Dam WMA

See Holt County account below.

Holt County

Holt County is a mostly Sandhills county with over 12,000 acres of surface water and almost 69,000 acres of wooded habitats, and historically it had 1.2 million acres of grasslands. There are tourist accommodations at Atkinson, O'Neill, and Stuart. The headquarters of the Niobrara National Recreational River are in O'Neill (Box 591, O'Neill NE, 68763; tel. 402-336-3970). For information check URL: http://www.nps.gov/niob/.

Atkinson Lake SRA

Area 54 acres. Managed by Nebraska Game and Parks Commission. Located at the northwest edge of Atkinson. Includes a fourteen-acre reservoir of the Elkhorn River. State park entry permit required. Map location H-1.

Goose Lake WMA

Area 349 acres. Managed by Nebraska Game and Parks Commission. Located twenty-three miles south and four miles east of O'Neill. Includes a Sandhills lake as well as grassy and wooded uplands. Map location H-2.

Redbird WMA

Area 433 acres. Managed by Nebraska Game and Parks Commission. Located one mile south of the U.S. Highway 281 bridge over the Niobrara. Mostly bur oak and red cedar, the area is bisected by Louse Creek, with adjacent steep wooded slopes and rolling grasslands. Map location H-3.

Spencer Dam WMA

Managed by Nebraska Game and Parks Commission. Located nine miles south of Spencer, or twenty-three miles north of O'Neill, via U.S. Highway 83, on the Holt-Boyd county line. Consists of nine acres of Niobrara River public access, including a hydro-power dam (the only mainstream dam in the Scenic River stretch) and a 1,200-acre reservoir. Map location H-4.

Knox County (Western Portion)

Knox County is bounded by the Niobrara and Missouri rivers and thus has over 41,000 acres of surface water as well as 38,000 acres of wooded habitats, and historically it had almost 320,000 acres of grasslands. There are tourist accommodations at Bloomfield, Creighton, Crofton, Niobrara, and Wausa.

Bazille Creek WMA

Area 4,500 acres. Managed by Nebraska Game and Parks Commission. Located between the city of Niobrara and the west end of Lewis and Clark Lake. Bordered for nine miles by the Missouri River and Lewis and Clark Lake, the site includes mixed woods, grasslands, and marshy areas. This area is extensively marshy, since it includes the area where the Missouri River is impounded to form the upper end of Lewis and Clark Lake. Immediately north of the city of Niobrara; not shown on map.

Greenville WMA

Area 200 acres. Managed by Nebraska Game and Parks Commission. Located ten miles west and three miles south of Verdigre. Mostly wooded, and bisected by Middle Verdigre Creek. Map location K-1.

Niobrara State Park

Area 1,632 acres. Managed by Nebraska Game and Parks Commission. This state park is at the confluence of the Niobrara River and the Missouri River. It is partly upland grassland but also has riparian wooded habitats, wet meadows, and extensive wetlands. There are more than fourteen miles of hiking trails, and a two-mile hike-bike trail extends along the park's northern boundary. Bald eagles have nested nearby, ospreys are regularly present, and golden eagles are occasional visitors. Eastern woodland birds include whip-poor-wills (near the northwestern edge of their range), red-headed and red-bellied woodpeckers, wood thrush, black-and-white warbler, American redstart, eastern towhee, rose-breasted grosbeak, and eastern wood pewee. Other notable breeders or probable breeders include wood duck, American bittern, gray partridge (rare), least tern, sora and Virginia rail, long-eared owl, Bell's, red-eyed, and warbling vireos, and Savannah sparrow (a possible or very local breeder). A total of 259 bird species have been reported for the park, including many vagrant gulls. There are modern cabins and camping facilities. State park entry permit required. For information, see URL: http://www.ngpc.state.ne.us/parks/guides/parksearch/showpark.asp?Area_No=126. Map location K-2.

Antelope County (Northern Portion)

Antelope County is an Elkhorn Valley county with less than 900 acres of surface water and over 21,000 acres of wooded habitats, and historically it had nearly 200,000 acres of grasslands. There are tourist accommodations at Elgin, Neligh, and Orchard.

Ashfall Fossil Beds State Historical Park

Area 360 acres. Managed by Nebraska Game and Parks Commission. Located two miles west and six miles north of Royal. This extremely important paleontological site preserves the Miocene fossils of horses, rhinos, camels, and other animals (including a crane closely resembling the African crowned cranes) interred under a thick layer of volcanic dust that settled here 10-12 million years ago. The center is open from Memorial Day through Labor Day. The area is mostly rugged range country, with mixed-grass bird species such as upland sandpipers common. Rock wrens often can be seen near the excavation site, and Bewick's wrens have sometimes been present in summer. Admission fee, and a state park permit is also required. For information write Box 66, Royal NE 68773, or see URL: http://www.ngpc.state.ne.us/parks/guides/parksearch/showpark.asp?Area_No=279. Map location A-1.

Grove Lake WMA

Area 1,746 acres, with a 35-acre reservoir. Managed by Nebraska Game and Parks Commission. Located three miles north of Royal. Mainly mixed hardwoods and grasslands along Verdigre Creek. This is an area of rolling grassland, with scattered trees along East Verdigre Creek. There is also a small reservoir and a trout-rearing facility. Most of the birds are grassland and woodland-edge species, but ospreys and belted kingfishers are sometimes present. Map location A-2.

Pierce County (Western Portion)

Pierce County is an Elkhorn Valley county with less than 400 acres of surface water and about 5,000 acres of wooded habitats, and historically it had nearly 125,000 acres of grasslands. There are tourist accommodations at Osmond and Plainview. There are no sites of special biological interest in western Pierce County.

Glossary

Accidental An individual occurring well beyond its species' normal geographic range; sometimes called a "vagrant."

Adaptation An evolved structural, behavioral, or physiological trait that increases an organism's ability to survive and reproduce.

Allospecies Two or more geographically separated populations that appear to have the necessary criteria to be considered separate species but are geographically isolated (allopatric) and thus cannot be tested for possible reproductive isolating mechanisms.

Alluvial Moved or deposited by water. *See also* eolian.

Amphicyonidae An extinct doglike predator family.

Aplodontidae A primitive family of mostly extinct rodents having a single surviving species, the North American mountain beaver.

Aquifer A subterranean zone of saturated sands, gravels, and so on constituting the "water table."

Arikaree Group A geologic unit of sediments from the upper Oligocene to the lower Miocene, which in the greater Niobrara region includes (in older to more recent sequence) the Ash Creek, Monroe Creek, and Harrison–Upper Harrison formations. The Rosebud formation is sometimes also included.

Artiodactyls Those hoofed mammals (ungulates) with symmetrically paired ("cloven") hooves, such as deer and goats. *See also* ungulates.

Association A specific type of biotic community having a high degree of floristic uniformity and occurring regularly in similar environments. Associations are usually named for one or more plant species or genera that consistently occur as stable dominants within that community. *See also* community *and* dominant.

Avian Relating to birds. "Avifauna" describes the collective bird life of a particular locality or region.

Badlands Vernacular term for highly eroded sedimentary landforms, best developed in arid and unglaciated regions of the Great Plains, such as along the White and Cheyenne rivers.

Biodiversity The measure of the relative species richness of a region's plants and animals.

Biogeography The study of the geographic distributions of organisms, including the historical events and ecological factors determining them.

Biomass The total organism weight (of a specified species or all organisms collectively) present within a stated area.

Biota A general term including both flora and fauna.

Blowout A local area of bare, eroding sand in an otherwise vegetated dune.

Bog A groundwater wetland that accumulates peat and is highly acidic (pH 0–4.4) in association with very low plant nutrient availability. *See also* fen.

Boreal Having northern affinities, such as the coniferous forests of Canada.

Brontothere A now-extinct group of large rhinolike herbivores that survived into the Oligocene and included the very large *Brontotherium*, common in the early Oligocene of western Nebraska.

Browse To forage on the twigs and leaves of woody plants. "Browse" is also sometimes used to refer to the vegetation itself. *See also* graze.

Bryophyte A member of the moss and liverwort plant group.

Calcareous Containing calcium carbonate.

Cambrian period The first major interval of the Paleozoic era, lasting from about 570–590 to 505 million years ago. *See also* Paleozoic era *and* Precambrian period.

Camelidae The mammalian camel and llama family.

Candidate A term used by the Office of Endangered Species in classifying a taxon for which there is substantial information to support a proposal to list it as threatened or endangered.

Canidae The mammalian dog family; its members are sometimes called canids.

Castoridae The mammalian beaver family.

Cenozoic (or Cainozoic) era The geologic era encompassing the past 65 million years, often called the "Age of Mammals." It has traditionally been divided into the (older) Tertiary and (newer) Quaternary periods. Recently two more equally chronologically defined terms, Paleogene and Neogene periods, have instead been proposed. *See also* Neogene period, Paleogene period, Quaternary system, *and* Tertiary system.

Centimeter A metric measurement equal to 0.39 inch and representing 10 millimeters.

cfs Flow rates of cubic feet per second. Sometimes also measured as gallons per minute (gpm).

Chalicotheriidae A family of extinct (Eocene to Pleistocene) large mammals related to the tapir family. Chalcotheres include the horselike *Moropus*, with long, clawed legs and teeth adapted for browsing.

Clay Fine-grained earth materials with particles that form colloidal suspensions or pastes in water and highly adherent solids when dry and heated. *See also* silt.

Coleopteran A member of the beetle order of insects (Coleoptera).

Colluvium (adj., colluvial) Materials accumulated by gravity at the base of a slope or cliff; colluvial soils are an example. *See also* alluvial, loess, *and* palustrine.

Community In ecology, an interacting group of plants, animals, and microorganisms in a specific location, tending to recur in different areas but similar habitats and usually responding similarly to their biotic and physical environments. *See also* ecosystem *and* habitat.

Coniferous Cone-bearing. Conifers are cone bearing, usually nondeciduous, trees. *See also* deciduous.

Courtship Communication between individuals of opposite sexes of a species that promotes pair bonding, pair maintenance, or fertilization. *See also* display.

Cretaceous period The geologic interval that extended from about 146 to 65 million years ago, ending the Mesozoic era. *See also* Mesozoic era, Niobrara Chalk, *and* Pierre Shale.

Deciduous Descriptive of shedding, especially of those trees (mostly broad-leaved species) that drop their leaves after each growing season. *See also* coniferous.

Display An evolved ("ritualized") behavior that communicates information within or between species. *See also* courtship, signals, *and* territory.

Diurnal Active during the daytime.

Dominant In ecology, descriptive of taxa that exert the strongest ecological effects within a community. *See also* community.

Drift In geology, glacially transported and deposited materials, either not sorted by size (till) or size-sorted (stratified drift). *See also* glacial erratics, moraine, *and* till.

Ecological segregation The process by which competition between potentially competing individuals or populations is reduced through the development of niche or habitat differences. *See also* niche.

Ecosystem An interacting group of plants, animals, microorganisms, and their physical environment.

Ecotone A transitional zone between two community types.

Edge species A species that is more common in or most characteristic of ecotone communities, such as forest-edge species.

Endangered A conservation category, usually defined as being those taxa that are in clear danger of extinction and whose survival is unlikely if the factors causing their decline continue operating. *See also* threatened *and* rare.

Endemics Taxa that are both native to and limited to a specific area, habitat, or region. *See also* indigenous.

Entelodontidae An extinct (Eocene to Miocene) family of giant pigs ("entelodonts") with elongated skulls and bony knobs on the lower jaws.

Environment The natural surroundings of an organism or community of organisms. *See also* habitat.

Eocene epoch A major early subdivision of the Cenozoic period, following the Paleocene epoch and extending from about 54 to 35 million years ago. *See also* Cenozoic era.

Eolian (or aeolian) Shaped, carried, or influenced by wind, such as loessal soils. *See also* loess.

Equidae The mammalian horse and zebra family.

Era (or erathem) A major geological unit of time, as in Cenozoic era, Mesozoic era, and Paleozoic era.

Escarpment A steep, eroded slope; popularly called a "scarp."

Evolution Any gradual change. Biological ("organic") evolution results from changing gene frequencies in successive generations associated with biological adaptations, typically through natural selection. *See also* natural selection.

Extinct A taxon that no longer exists anywhere. *See also* extirpated.

Extirpated A taxon that has been eliminated from some part of a previously occupied range.

Family A taxonomic category representing a group of one or more related genera; usually spelled for animals with an "idae" suffix and for plants with a "ceae" suffix.

Felidae The mammalian cat and lion family.

Fen A wetland characterized by having a boglike substrate of organic matter (peat or marl) but, unlike typical bogs, having favorable plant nutrition levels (especially calcium availability) and much greater organic productivity. *See also* bog *and* marsh.

Fire-influenced species Any of several groups of organisms affected by fire. *Fire-*

dependent species are those whose continued existence in a community depends on the periodic occurrence of fire. *Fire-tolerant* species may survive fires but not depend on them for their continued presence. *Fire-sensitive* species may decline or even disappear with the periodic occurrence of fires.

Floodplain The part of a river valley that is subjected to occasional flooding.

Forb A herbaceous plant that is not a grass or sedge, thus including many broad-leaved and nonwoody plants. *See also* grass, herb, *and* sedge.

Forest A general term for a community dominated by trees with heights (typically more than about twenty feet) much greater than the average distance between them, and an overhead plant canopy that is more or less continuous. *See also* savanna *and* woodland.

Form A nontechnical term usually referring to a species or well-differentiated subspecies, especially one whose exact taxonomic status is still in doubt. *See also* species.

Formation In ecology, a major type of plant community that extends over broad regions sharing similar climates, soils, and biological succession patterns and having similar life forms of dominant plants, at least at their final vegetational stages. Plant formations usually include several subcategories, or "associations." In stratigraphy, a specific lithographic unit of sediments of definable age and geographic distribution. Several formations may compose a stratigraphic "group," and each geological formation may in turn have several "members." *See also* association, dominant, group, *and* succession.

Gallery forest Narrow forests that follow rivers or other waterways out into non-forested habitats. *See also* riparian, savanna, *and* woodland.

Geomyidae The mammalian pocket gopher family.

Glacial erratics Large rocks and boulders that have been glacially transported and randomly deposited over the landscape, having a composition different from that of the bedrock below. *See also* drift *and* moraine.

Gomphotheres A extinct (Miocene to mid-Pleistocene) family of long-jawed mastodonts (Gomphotheridae), once widespread in the Great Plains. Among the Nebraskan genera were *Gomphotherium, Ambelodon,* and *Stegomastodon.*

Gram A metric unit of weight; 28.3 grams equal an ounce, and 454 grams equal a pound.

Grass Herbaceous plants (family Poaceae), typically having hollow stems and narrow leaves that are parallel-veined. *See also* forb *and* sedge.

Gravel Sedimentary particles larger than two millimeters in diameter. *See also* sand *and* silt.

Graze To feed on the leaves of herbaceous plants. *See also* browse.

Great Plains The nonmountainous region of interior North America lying east of the Rocky Mountains and west of the Central Lowlands of the Mississippi and lower Missouri drainages.

Groundwater Subsurface water carried by aquifers, such as the Ogallala aquifer. *See also* water table.

Group A geological term for associated sediments (typically subdivided into formations) laid down over a substantial period of geologic time. Major Nebraska groups represented in the Niobrara region include (oldest to youngest) the White River, Arikaree, and Ogallala, which cover a period extending from late Eocene to early Miocene, or from about 40 to 5 million years ago. *See also* formation.

Habitat The ecological situation or natural community in which a species survives; its natural "address." *See also* community, ecosystem, *and* niche.

Hectare (ha) A metrically defined area (10,000 square meters), equal to 2.47 acres. A square mile contains 259 hectares or 2.59 square kilometers.

Herb Any plant having no aboveground woody parts, including grasses, sedges, and forbs. *See also* forb, grass, *and* sedge.

Herpetile (or "herp") A member of the amphibian and reptile assemblage. Herpetology refers to the study of such animals.

Holocene epoch The roughly 11,000-year interval extending from the end of the last (Wisconsin) glaciation to the present time. *See also* Recent epoch.

Hybrid An individual produced by the crossing of taxonomically different populations, usually between subspecies, less often between species, and rarely between genera.

Hypertragulidae An extinct Oligocene and Miocene family of antelope-like mammals.

Hypsodont "High-toothed," in reference to the elongated and flattened teeth of horses, modern elephants, and other grazers that continue to grow and replace abraded enamel, thus being able to grind grasses rich in silica.

Indigenous Descriptive of taxa that are native to, but not necessarily limited to, a particular area or region. *See also* endemics.

Interspecific Pertaining to relationships or interactions between species.

Intraspecific Pertaining to relationships or interactions within species.

Introgression The movement and exchange of genes between two genetically distinct populations through hybridization.

Isohyet A line connecting points of equal amounts of precipitation on a map.

Jurassic period The second major period of the Mesozoic era, following the Triassic period. It lasted from about 210 to 145 million years ago (the beginning of the Cretaceous period) and marked the peak of dinosaur abundance and diversity. *See also* Cretaceous period *and* Triassic period.

Kilogram (kg) A metric measure equal of 1,000 grams, or about 2.2 pounds.

Kilometer (km) A metric distance of 1,000 meters, or 0.62 mile. A square kilometer equals 0.386 square mile.

Lacustrian Referring to lakes and their biota or substrates, such as lacustrian vegetation or soils. *See also* palustrine.

Lake A freshwater or saline wetland that is typically large enough to have barren, wave-washed shorelines and deep enough to develop seasonal temperature stratification. *See also* marsh.

Larimide revolution The period of mountain building in the central Rocky Mountains (named for Wyoming's Laramie Range), beginning during the late Mesozoic and extending into early Cenozoic times. *See also* Cenozoic era, Mesozoic era, *and* orogeny.

Latilong A geographic area measuring one degree of latitude by one degree of longitude.

Legumes A family of plants (Leguminaceae or Fabiaceae), many of which harbor in their roots bacteria that can convert gaseous nitrogen into a molecular form usable by other plants.

Lek A display ground in which males of a species congregate and competitively interact to establish individual territories and determine their relative dominance, providing females a means of assessing the males' desirability as mating partners.

Leporidae The mammalian rabbit and hare family

Life form A term broadly descriptive of plant categories, such as coniferous or deciduous trees (or forests), broad-leaved shrubs, perennial grasses, annual forbs, and so on.

Litter Dead, nonwoody plant matter lying on the ground surface.

Loam (or loamy) Refers to soils containing a mixture of particle sizes, including sand, silt, and clay. *See also* clay, loess, sand, *and* till

Loess (or loessal) Silt-sized materials (larger than clays, but smaller than sand) that have been transported and deposited by wind. Loess soils show little or no vertical stratification and are easily eroded. The word is of German origin, meaning "loose," and is pronounced "luss." *See also* alluvial *and* till.

Macroinvertebrates Invertebrates visible to the unaided human eye. Microinvertebrates are visible only with a microscope.

Marsh A wetland type ("palustrine") in which the soil is saturated for long periods but peat does not accumulate. Marshes, excepting the most alkaline ones, typically have extensive shoreline vegetation and are shallow enough that emergent aquatic plants cover most or all their surface. Marshes often grade into the edges of lakes. *See also* bog, fen, *and* lake.

Mastodonts Extinct (Oligocene to Pleistocene) elephants (families Gomphotheridae and Mammutidae) that differed from the now extinct mammoths and modern elephants (family Elephantidae) in having distinctly cusped and ridged teeth adapted for browsing in forests rather than rasplike teeth adapted for grazing in grasslands. *See also* Gomphotheres.

Mating system Patterns of mating within a population, including length and strength of a pair bond, if any, the number of mates, degree of inbreeding, and the like.

Member In geology, a temporal subdivision of a stratigraphic formation. *See also* formation.

Merycoidodontidae An extinct family of Oligocene and Miocene even-toed ungulates somewhat intermediate anatomically between the pigs and camels. *See also* Tylopoda *and* ungulates.

Mesic A habitat with an intermediate level of soil moisture (or other moderated environmental conditions). *See also* xeric.

Mesozoic era The "Age of Dinosaurs," extending from about 225 to 65 million years ago, or to the start of the Cenozoic era. *See also* Cenozoic era *and* Paleozoic era.

Meter A metric measurement equal to 100 centimeters, 1.094 yards, or 39.37 inches.

Microtine (synonym, arvicoline) Referring to a subfamily of rodents that includes voles, lemmings, and muskrats. The word is derived from the vole genus *Microtus See also* vole.

Migration The regular, usually seasonal, movements of animals ("migrants") between two locations, usually breeding and nonbreeding areas. Irregular or one-way movements may include dispersals, emigrations, immigrations, and periodic irruptions.

Miocene epoch The interval within the Tertiary system (and the associated geologic strata deposited during that interval), from the end of the preceding Oligocene epoch (24 million years ago) to the start of the Pliocene epoch (5 million years ago). *See also* Oligocene epoch *and* Pliocene epoch.

Mixed-grass (or midgrass) prairie Perennial grasslands that are dominated by grasses of intermediate heights (often from 1.5 to 3 feet tall at maturity) between those typically found in tallgrass and shortgrass prairies. Mixed-grass prairies usually occur in areas of low precipitation and are situated geographically between tallgrass and shortgrass prairies. *See also* shortgrass prairie *and* tallgrass prairie.

Moraine Gently rolling landscapes of glacial deposits, marking a glacier's lateral or terminal margins. *See also* drift *and* till.

Mosasaurs Now extinct marine lizards of the Mesozoic era, with very large heads and large, muscular tails used for propulsion.

Mustelidae The mammalian family of weasels, ferrets, minks, otters, badgers, and so on; its members are often called "mustelids."

mya Abbreviation for millions of years ago.

Natural selection The differential survival and reproduction of the fittest individuals within interbreeding populations, producing changes in gene frequencies and associated traits in those populations. *See also* sexual selection.

Neogene period A subdivision of the Cenozoic era. It followed the Paleogene period and lasted from 24 million years ago to the present, from the Miocene to Holocene epoch. *See also* Paleogene period.

Niche The behavioral, morphological, and physiological adaptations of a species to its habitat. Sometimes defined as the range of ecological conditions in which a species potentially or actually exists. *See also* habitat.

Nimravids Members of an extinct (Oligocene to Miocene) family of primitive catlike predators (Nimravidae); sometimes called "false sabertooths."

Niobrara Chalk Sedimentary chalk deposits dating from the late Cretaceous period (ca. 70–80 million years ago), and representing the bottom of the Cretaceous sea (Western Interior Seaway) that once covered much of interior North America. *See also* Cretaceous period.

Niobrara National Scenic River A seventy-six-mile stretch of the Niobrara River, so named by the Niobrara Scenic River Designation Act. *See also* Wild and Scenic Rivers Act.

Odonata The insect order of dragonflies and damselflies, collectively often called odonates.

Ogallala (High Plains) aquifer An enormous subsurface layer of water-saturated sand, gravel, silt, clay, siltstone, and sandstone, extending from South Dakota to Texas.

Ogallala group A geologic unit of sediments from the upper half of the Oligocene, which in the greater Niobrara region includes (in approximate older to more recent sequence) the Runningwater, Box Butte, Valentine, and Ash Hollow formations.

Oglala Name that refers to a tribe of Lakota-speaking members of the Dakota (Sioux) tribe and for which the Oglala National Grassland is named.

Oligocene epoch A major subdivision of the Cenozoic era, extending from about 37 to 18 million years ago. *See also* Cenozoic era.

Oreodont An extinct (late Eocene to early Pleistocene) group (family Merycoidodontidae) of four-toed ungulates linking the swine and the deer–giraffe assemblage. *See also* ungulates.

Orogeny The geological process of mountain building.

Orographic Mountain related, such as orographic precipitation.

Orthopteran A member of the insect order Orthoptera, including mantids, stick insects, grasshoppers, locusts, crickets, and others.

Pair-forming and pair-bonding behaviors Sexual behaviors that respectively relate to (1) mate choice and associated pair formation and (2) pair-bond maintenance.

Paleocene epoch The first epoch of the Cenozoic era, extending from about 65 to 54 million years ago. *See also* Cenozoic era.

Paleogene period A subdivision of the Cenozoic era. lasting from 65 to 24 million years ago and encompassing the Paleocene, Eocene, and Oligocene epochs. *See also* Neogene period.

Paleosol The buried remnants of an ancient soil layer.

Paleozoic era The geologic era of "ancient life," beginning about 570 million years ago, at the start of the Cambrian period, and lasting until the beginning of the Mesozoic era, about 225 million years ago. *See also* Precambrian period *and* Mesozoic era.

Palustrine Descriptive of marshes, such as palustrine vegetation or palustrine soils. *See also* lacustrian, marsh, *and* riparian.

Passerine (or passeriform) Descriptive of members of the avian order Passeriformes; popularly called "perching birds" or "songbirds."

Peat Incompletely decomposed organic matter that accumulates at the bottom of some wetlands, especially bogs and fens. *See also* bog *and* fen.

Perissodactyls Those hoofed mammals (ungulates) having their third digit medially located and largest, such as horses. *See also* ungulates.

Phenotype (adj., phenotypic) The external appearance of an individual, reflecting both its genetic makeup (genotype) and nongenetically mediated influences.

Pierre Shale Sedimentary deposits dating from the late Cretaceous period and representing the bottom of the Cretaceous-age sea (Western Interior Seaway) that once covered much of interior North America.

Pleistocene epoch The interval extending from about 1.8 million years ago (the end of the Pliocene epoch) to 11,000 years ago (the start of the current Holocene or Recent epoch). This epoch includes part or all of several glacial periods (and their associated interglacial intervals), of which in North America the traditionally named Nebraskan glaciation was the earliest and the Wisconsin glaciation the most recent. The Kansan and Illinoisan glaciations were of intermediate age, and like the others were named after their southernmost extensions. *See also* Pliocene epoch.

Plesiosaurs Carnivorous and now extinct marine reptiles of the Mesozoic era, having flipperlike legs and necks of greatly variable length.

Pliocene epoch The interval (and associated geologic strata deposited during that interval) extending from the end of the preceding Miocene epoch (5 million years ago) to the start of the Pleistocene epoch (about 1.8 million years ago). *See also* Miocene epoch *and* Pleistocene epoch.

Prairie A native plant community dominated by perennial grasses. Prairies may be broadly classified by the relative stature of their particular dominant grass taxa (tallgrass, mixed-grass, or shortgrass) or by the characteristic form of these grasses (e.g., bunchgrasses or sod-forming grasses. *See also* shortgrass prairie, mixed-grass prairie, sandsage prairie, *and* tallgrass prairie.

Precambrian period Refers to that time in the earth's history before the Cambrian period, or at least 550 million years ago. *See also* Cambrian period *and* Paleozoic era.

Prongbucks Members of an extinct North American family (Procerotidae) of even-toed ungulates (those related to deer and cattle) having up to three pairs of bony head outgrowths in males, the frontal pair often forming Y-shaped prongs. *See also* ungulates.

Quaternary system The last 1.8 million years of the earth's history, including the Pleistocene and Holocene epochs. *See also* Holocene epoch, Pleistocene epoch, *and* Tertiary system.

Race An informal term for the subspecies category.

Rare A conservation category often defined as including those forms having populations that are small but not currently considered either endangered or vulnerable.

Recent epoch Refers to the current geological epoch, from the end of the Pleistocene (ca. 11,000 years ago) to the present time; also called the Holocene epoch.

Refugium (pl., refugia) An area where populations can locally survive during prolonged, generally unfavorable environmental conditions.

Relict A population geographically isolated from a species' main range, suggesting that the species' range was once more extensive and has since become fragmented.

Resident (adj., residential) A sedentary (nonmigratory or nonnomadic) population.

Rhinocerotidae The mammalian rhinoceros family.

Riparian Associated with shorelines, especially river or stream shorelines. Riverine is a synonym. *See also* gallery forest.

Sand Fine-grained natural materials larger than silt but smaller than gravel. Sandstone is a sedimentary rock composed mostly of hardened sand. *See also* gravel *and* silt.

Sandsage prairie Mixed grass and shrubs (mostly sand sagebrush) developed over sandy substrates and with an abundance of sand-adapted species. *See also* prairie.

Sandstone A sedimentary rock composed of cemented sand grains. Siltstone is similar but is composed of smaller (silt-sized) particles. *See also* shale.

Savanna Any grassland-dominated community within which scattered trees occur. *See also* woodland.

Scientific name The Latin or Latinized combination of a general (generic) and a specific (species-level) name that collectively uniquely identifies an organism. Some scientific names include a third and final component, a race or subspecies (in animals) or a variety (in plants). *See also* species *and* subspecies.

Sedentary Descriptive of nonmobile individuals or populations. *See also* migration.

Sedge Herbaceous, grasslike plants (of the family Cyperaceae) having solid stems and narrow, parallel-veined leaves that are often arranged in three ranks (as seen from above). *See also* grass.

Seep A groundwater wetland with less horizontal water flow than a spring.

Sensitive A term (comparable to "vulnerable") that is often used by conservation agencies to identify rare or declining species of possible future threatened conservation status. *See also* endangered, rare, *and* threatened.

Sexual selection A type of natural selection in which the evolution and maintenance of traits of one sex result from the social interactions (such as competitive interactions within the members of one sex or differential rates of attraction among members of the two sexes) that produce differential individual reproductive success. *See also* natural selection.

Shale A sedimentary rock composed of highly compressed mud.

Shortgrass prairie A grassland (sometimes called "steppe grassland") dominated by short-stature perennial grasses. *See also* mixed-grass prairie, steppe, *and* tallgrass prairie.

Shrub A woody plant that typically is less than twelve feet tall at maturity and usually has many aboveground stems. Shrublands are communities dominated by shrubs with varied degrees of canopy cover; shrubsteppes are mixed communities of shrubs and grasses. *See also* forest, tree, *and* woodland.

Signals Behaviors that have become evolutionarily modified to transmit information among members of a social group. Such signals ("displays") include postures, movements, vocalizations, and species- or sex-specific odors.

Silt Sedimentary materials of a size intermediate between sand and clay.

Speciation The process of species proliferation through the gradual development of reproductive isolation between geographically separated populations.

Species A "kind" of organism. More technically, one or more populations whose members share the same isolating mechanisms and thus are reproductively isolated from all other populations. "Species" is spelled the same in both singular and plural, but the singular abbreviation is sp., the plural spp. *See also* scientific name *and* subspecies.

Springbranch canyon A local name for canyons associated with spring-fed tributaries of the Niobrara River.

Steppe Temperate-zone shortgrass communities, the term originally applied to arid central Asian grasslands. *See also* shortgrass prairie.

Stratum (pl., strata) In geology, a body or layer of sedimentary rock, sometimes composed of a number of definable "beds."

Subspecies (abbreviated ssp., plural sspp.) A geographically defined and morphologically recognizable subdivision of a species. Subspecies epithets are the last segment of a three-part name ("trinomial"). *See also* species.

Succession The series of gradual plant and animal changes that occur in biotic communities over time, as temporary (successional) taxa are sequentially replaced by others that are able to persist and reproduce for a more prolonged or even indefinite period. *See also* community.

Swamp As used here, a freshwater wetland with standing or variably submerged woody vegetation. *See also* marsh *and* lake.

Sympatric Populations that overlap at least in part, especially during the breeding season. By definition, sympatrically distributed but noninterbreeding populations are never considered the same species. *See also* species.

System A term for the two major subdivisions of the Cenozoic era (the Quaternary and Tertiary systems).

Tallgrass prairie Perennial grasslands that are dominated by tall-stature grasses. These grasslands typically occur in areas that are more mesic than those supporting shorter grasses (midgrass or mixed-grass prairies) but are still too arid or too frequently burned to support forests. *See also* shortgrass prairie *and* mixed-grass prairie.

Terrace A flat area above an active floodplain, representing the deposited remains of an earlier floodplain.

Territory A definable area having resources that an animal permanently or seasonally defends against others of its species (intraspecific territories); sometimes territorial behavior is also directed toward individuals of other species (interspecific territories).

Tertiary system The first of the two major subdivisions of the Cenozoic era, beginning about 65 million years ago (at the end of the Cretaceous period) and lasting until about 1.8 million years ago (the start of the Quaternary system). *See also* Quaternary system.

Threatened A legal category used by state and federal wildlife agencies to designate taxa that are not yet believed to be endangered but whose known numbers place them at risk of falling into that category. *See also* endangered and rare.

Till Unsorted glacial drift deposits. *See also* drift.

Titanotheres Very large horned mammals ("titanic beasts") of the early Cenozoic era that were vegetarians and ancestors of such odd-toed modern ungulates as rhinos.

Trait A measurable phenotypic attribute (behavioral, structural, physiological), especially one that is at least in part genetically controlled.

Tree A woody plant that is usually well above twelve feet tall at maturity and typically has a single main stem. *See also* shrub.

Triassic period The first major geologic period of the Mesozoic era, lasting from about 245 to 210 million years ago, or the start of the Jurassic period. *See also* Jurassic period *and* Mesozoic era.

Tylopoda A group of even-toed ungulates that includes the camel-like mammals and many now extinct families.

Ungulates Hoofed mammals, either even-toed (e.g., deer, antelope, pigs, and other artiodactyls) or odd-toed (e.g., horses, rhinos, and other perissodactyls). *See also* artiodactyls *and* perissodactyls.

Vagrant An individual occurring well outside its population's normal migratory or nomadic limits. *See also* accidental.

Volcanic ash Fine-grained materials produced during volcanic eruptions and often carried great distances before final deposition.

Vole Any of a group of short-legged field mice, especially those of the meadow mouse genus *Microtus*.

Water table The upper edge of a saturated underground layer of water, or aquifer. *See also* aquifer.

White River group A geologic unit of sediments from the upper Eocene to the mid-Oligocene, which in the greater Niobrara region includes (in older to more recent sequence) the Chamberlain Pass, Chadron, and Brule formations.

Wild and Scenic Rivers Act A congressional act of 1968 that designated selected rivers as wild or scenic and prohibited their impoundment. These rivers must be free flowing and possess remarkable scenic recreational, geological, biological, historical, cultural, or other significant values. *See also* Niobrara National Scenic River.

Woodland A partially wooded community in which the height of the trees is usually less than the distances between them, so that the overhead canopy is discontinuous. More widely scattered trees in grasslands may form savannas. *See also* forest.

Xeric Characterized by dry conditions. *See also* mesic.

References

Note: This reference list includes works that were used in preparing the text but are not specifically cited.

Chapter 1. The Ancient Niobrara Valley

Axelrod, D. I. 1985. Rise of the grassland biome, central North America. *Botanical Review* 51:163–201.

Bleed, A. 1998. Groundwater. In *An atlas of the Sand Hills*, 3rd ed., ed. A. Bleed and C. Flowerday, 67–92. Resource Atlas no. 5. Lincoln: Conservation and Survey Division, Univ. of Nebraska–Lincoln.

Bleed, A., and C. Flowerday, eds. 1989. *An atlas of the Sand Hills*, 1st ed. Resource Atlas no. 5. Lincoln: Conservation and Survey Division, Univ. of Nebraska–Lincoln.

———. 1998. *An atlas of the Sand Hills*, 3rd ed. Resource Atlas no. 5. Lincoln: Conservation and Survey Division, Univ. of Nebraska–Lincoln.

Bradley, B. E. Miocene stratigraphy of the Niobrara River Valley, western Cherry County, Nebraska. MS thesis, Univ. of Nebraska–Lincoln.

Buchanan, J. P., and Schumm, S. A. 1990. Niobrara River. In *Surface water hydrology: The geology of North America*, 314–21. Boulder CO: Geological Society of America.

Burchett, R. R. 1986. Geologic bedrock map of Nebraska. Nebraska Geological Survey, Univ. of Nebraska–Lincoln. Updated in 1991 by R. R. Burchett and R. K. Pabian.

Carlson, M. P. 1993. *Geology, geologic time and Nebraska*. Lincoln: Conservation and Survey Division, Univ. of Nebraska–Lincoln.

Condra, G. E., E. C. Reed, and E. D. Gordon. 1950. *Correlation of the Pleistocene deposits of Nebraska*. Bull. 15A. Lincoln: Conservation and Survey Division, Univ. of Nebraska–Lincoln.

Cook, H. C., and M. C. Cook. 1933. Faunal lists of the Tertiary of Nebraska and adjacent areas. *Nebraska Geological Survey Paper* 5:1–58.

Diffendal, R. F., Jr., and M. R. Voorhies. 1993. Geological framework of the Niobrara River drainage basin and adjacent areas in South Dakota generally east of the 100th meridian west longitude and west of the Missouri River. In *Research symposium: Environmental and natural resources of the Nebraska River basin*, ed. R. Kuzelka. Ainsworth NE, October 14–15, 1993. Lincoln: Water Center/Environmental Programs, Univ. of Nebraska–Lincoln.

———. 1994. *Geological framework of the Niobrara River drainage basin and adjacent areas in South Dakota generally east of the 100th meridian west longitude and west of the Missouri River.* Report of Investigations 9. Lincoln: Conservation and Survey Division, Univ. of Nebraska–Lincoln.

Ducey, J. 1992. Fossil birds of the Nebraska region. *Transactions of the Nebraska Academy of Sciences* 19:83–96.

Eiseley, L. 1969. *The unexpected universe*. New York: Harcourt, Brace and World.

Falk, C. R., R. E. Pepperl, and M. R. Voorhies. 1985. *Cultural and paleontological investigations within the proposed Norden Unit, Nebraska: Final report.* Technical Report 83-02. Lincoln: Dept. of Anthropology, Univ. of Nebraska–Lincoln.

Flowerday, C. A., and R. F. Diffendal Jr., eds. 1997. *Geology of Niobrara State Park, Knox County, Nebraska, and adjacent areas: With a brief History of the park, Gavin's Point Dam, and Lewis and Clark Lake.* Educational Circular 13. Lincoln: Conservation and Survey Division, Univ. of Nebraska–Lincoln.

Frick, C. 1937. Horned ruminants of North America. *Bulletin of the American Museum of Natural History* 69:1–669.

Graham, A. 1999. *Late Cretaceous and Cenozoic history of North American vegetation north of Mexico.* New York: Oxford Univ. Press.

Hearty, P. J. 1978. The biogeography and geomorphology of the Niobrara River Valley near Valentine, Nebraska. MS thesis, Univ. of Nebraska–Omaha.

Hunt, R. M., Jr. 1978. Depositional setting of a Miocene mammal assemblage, Sioux County, Nebraska (U.S.A). *Palaeogeography, Palaeoclimatology, Palaeoecology* 24:1–52.

Kitchen, D. W., and P. T. Bromley. 1971. Agonistic behavior of territorial pronghorns. In *The behaviour of ungulates in relation to management*, ed. V. Geist and F. Walter, 365–81. Publication 24. Morges, Switzerland: IUCN.

Kurtén, B., and D. C. Anderson. 1983. *Pleistocene mammals of North America.* New York: Columbia Univ. Press.

Love, J. D., and J. C. Reed, Jr. 1971. *Creation of the Teton landscape*. Moose WY: Grand Teton Natural History Association.

Lugn, A. L. 1934. *Outline of Pleistocene geology of Nebraska*. State Museum Bulletin B-1-41. Lincoln: Univ. of Nebraska.

———. 1935. *The Pleistocene of Nebraska*. Nebraska Geological Survey Bulletin 10, 2nd ser. Lincoln: Univ. of Nebraska.

———. 1939. Classification of the Tertiary system in Nebraska. *Bulletin of the Geological Society of America* 50:1245–76.

Maher, H. D., G. F. Engelmann, and R. D. Shuster. 2003. *Roadside geology of Nebraska*. Missoula MT: Mountain Press.

Martin, J. E. 1985. Fossiliferous Cenozoic deposits of western South Dakota and northwestern Nebraska. *Dakoterra* 2 (2): 7 (Museum of Geology, South Dakota School of Mines, Rapid City).

Mosel, S. 2004. From water hole to rhino barn. *Natural History* 113 (7): 56–57.

Osborn, H. F. 1910. *The age of mammals in Europe, Asia and North America*. New York: Macmillan.

Palmer, D., ed. 1999. *The Simon and Schuster encyclopedia of dinosaurs and prehistoric creatures: A visual Who's Who of prehistoric life*. New York: Simon and Schuster.

Peterson, O. A. 1906a. The Agate Spring fossil quarry. *Annals of the Carnegie Museum* 3 (4): 487–94.

———. 1906b. The Miocene beds of western Nebraska and eastern Wyoming and their vertebrate fauna. *Annals of the Carnegie Museum* 4 (1): 21–72.

Savage, D. E., and D. E. Russell. 1983. *Mammalian paleofaunas of the world*. Reading MA: Addison-Wesley.

Schultz, C. B. 1934. The Pleistocene mammals of Nebraska. *Nebraska State Museum Bulletin* 1 (41): 19–37.

———. 1961. *Field conference on the Tertiary and Pleistocene of western Nebraska*. Special Publication. Lincoln: Univ. of Nebraska State Museum.

Schultz, C. B., and C. H. Falkenbach. 1968. The phylogeny of the oreodonts. *American Museum of Natural History Bulletin* 139:1–498.

Scott, W. B. 1937. *A history of land mammals in the Western Hemisphere*. New York: Macmillan.

Sears, P. 1935. Glacial and postglacial vegetation. *Botanical Review* 1:37–51.

Skinner, M. F., and C. W. Hibbard. 1972. Early Pleistocene pre-glacial rocks and faunas of north-central Nebraska. *Bulletin of the American Museum of Natural History* 148:1–148.

Skinner, M. F., and F. W. Johnson. 1984. Tertiary stratigraphy and the Frick Collection of fossil vertebrates from north central Nebraska. *Bulletin of the Museum of Natural History* 178:215–368.

Skinner, M. F., and O. C. Kaisen. 1947. The fossil *Bison* of Alaska and a preliminary revision of the genus. *Bulletin of the American Museum of Natural History* 89:123–256.

Skinner, M. F., S. M. Skinner, and R. J. Gooris. 1977. Stratigraphy and biostratigraphy of late Cenozoic deposits in central Sioux County, western Nebraska. *Bulletin of the American Musem of Natural History* 158:263–70.

Swinehart, J. B. 2004. Little dunes on big dunes: More tall tales from the Sand Hills. Oral presentation, Sandhills Discovery Experience, Ainsworth NE, July 13, 2004.

Swinehart, J. B., and R. F. Diffendal Jr. 1998. Geology of the pre-dune strata. In *An atlas of the Sand Hills*, 3rd ed., ed. A. Bleed and C. Flowerday, 29–42. Resource Atlas no. 5. Lincoln: Conservation and Survey Division, Univ. of Nebraska–Lincoln.

Swinehart, J. B., V. L. Souders, H. M. DeGraw, and R. F. Diffendal Jr. 1985. Cenozoic paleogeography of western Nebraska. In *Cenozoic paleogeography of west-central United States*, ed. R. F. Flores et al., 209–29. Symposium 3. Denver: Rocky Mountain Section, Society of Economic Paleontologists and Mineralogists.

Trimble, D. E. 1980. *The geologic story of the Great Plains*. Geological Survey Bulletin 1493. Washington DC: U.S. Department of Interior, U.S. Geological Survey.

U.S. Department of Interior, National Park Service. 1980. *Agate Fossil Beds National Monument*. Handbook 107. Washington DC: National Park Service.

Voorhies, M. R. 1987. Late Cenozoic stratigraphy and geomorphology, Fort Niobrara, Nebraska. In *Centennial field guide—North Central Section*, 1–6. Boulder CO: Geological Society of America.

———. 1990. Nebraska wildlife: Ten million years ago. *NEBRASKAland* 68 (5): 8–17.

———. 1994. The ancient seas, Jungles and savannas, and The Ice Age. In The cellars of time: Paleontology and archeology in Nebraska, 8–81. *NEBRASKAland* 72 (1): 1–162.

Voorhies, M. R., and R. G. Corner. 1993. An inventory and evaluation of vertebrate paleontological sites along the Niobrara/Missouri Scenic River corridors. Typescript report prepared for U.S. Department of Interior, National Park Service.

Wayne, W. J., J. S. Alber, S. S. Agard, R. N. Bergantino, J. P. Bluemle, D. A. Coates, M. E. Cooley, R. F. Madole, J. E. Martin, B. Mears Jr., R. B. Morrison, and W. M. Sutherland. 1991. Quaternary geology of the northern Great Plains. In *Quaternary nonglacial geology: Conterminous US. The Geology of North America*, vol. K-2, ed. R. B. Morrison, 441–76. Boulder CO: Geological Society of America.

Woodburne, M., ed. 1987. *Cenozoic mammals of North America: Biochronology and biostratigraphy*. Berkeley: Univ. of California Press.

Yatkola, D. A. 1978. Tertiary stratigraphy of the Niobrara River Valley, Marsland Quadrangle, western Nebraska. *Nebraska Geological Survey Paper* 19:1–66.

Chapter 2. Human Footprints in the Niobrara Valley

Agenbroad, L. D. 1978. *The Hudson-Meng site: An Alberta bison kill site in the Nebraska High Plains*. Caldwell ID: Caxton.

Baltensberger, B. M. 1985. *Nebraska: A geography*. Boulder CO: Westview Press.

Barry, R. 1983. Climatic environment of the Great Plains, past and present. *Transactions of the Nebraska Academy of Sciences* 11:45–55.

Beel, M. B., ed. 1986. *A Sandhills century. Book 1. The land: A history of Cherry County. Book 2. The people: A history of the People in Cherry County*. Valentine NE: Cherry County Centennial Committee.

Bleed, A. 1998. Groundwater. In *An atlas of the Sand Hills*, 3rd ed., ed. A. Bleed and C. Flowerday, 67–92. Resource Atlas no. 5. Lincoln: Conservation and Survey Division, Univ. of Nebraska–Lincoln.

Bozell, J. R. 1994. The Ice Age and the first immigrants. In The cellars of time: Paleontology and archeology in Nebraska. *NEBRASKAland* 72 (1): 1–162.

Carlson, M. P. 1993. *Geology, geologic time and Nebraska*. Lincoln: Conservation and Survey Division, Univ. of Nebraska–Lincoln.

Clark, K. H. 1997. An environmental history of the Niobrara River basin. MA thesis, Univ. of Nebraska–Lincoln.

Condra, G. E., E. C. Reed, and E. D. Gordon. 1950. *Correlation of the Pleistocene deposits of Nebraska*. Bull. 15A. Lincoln: Conservation and Survey Division, Univ. of Nebraska–Lincoln.

Cook, J. H. 1923. *Fifty years on the Old Frontier*. New Haven CT: Yale Univ. Press. Repr. Norman: Univ. of Oklahoma Press, 1980.

Dick, E. N. 1975. *Conquering the great American desert*. Nebraska State Historical Society Publications, vol. 27. Lincoln NE: State Historical Society.

Ducey, J. E. 2000. *Birds of the untamed west: The history of bird life in Nebraska, 1750 to 1875*. Omaha NE: Making History Press.

Falk, C. R., R. E. Pepperl, and M. R. Voorhies. 1985. *Cultural and paleontological investigations within the proposed Norden Unit, Nebraska: Final report*. Technical Report 83-02. Lincoln: Dept. of Anthropology, Univ. of Nebraska–Lincoln.

Fitzpatrick, L. L. 1960. *Nebraska place-names.* Lincoln: Univ. of Nebraska Press.

Franklin, R., M. Grant, and M. Hunt. 1994. *Historical overview and inventory of the Niobrara/Missouri National Scenic Riverways, Nebraska/South Dakota.* Omaha NE: National Park Service.

Grier, R. 1983a. The Elkhorn. NEBRASKA*land* 61 (2): 66–71.

———. 1983b. The Pine Ridge streams. NEBRASKA*land* 61 (2): 120–27.

Hanson, J. A. 1983. *Northwest Nebraska's Indian people.* Chadron NE: Chadron Centennial Committee.

Hoffman, R. S., and J. K. Jones Jr. 1970. Influence of late-glacial and postglacial events on the distribution of Recent mammals on the northern Great Plains. In *Pleistocene and Recent environments of the central Great Plains,* ed. W. Dort and J. K. Jones, 355–96. Lawrence: Univ. Press of Kansas.

Howard, J. H. 1965. The Ponca tribe. *Bureau of American Ethnology Bulletin* 195: 1–191. Repr. Lincoln: Univ. of Nebraska Press, 1995.

Hutton, H. 1999. *The river that runs.* Freeman SD: Pine Hill Press.

Johnsgard, P. A. l995. *This fragile land: A natural history of the Nebraska Sandhills.* Lincoln: Univ. of Nebraska Press.

Lawson, M. P., K. F. Dewey, and R. E. Neild. 1977. *Climatic atlas of Nebraska.* Lincoln: Univ. of Nebraska Press.

Lowie, R. H. 1954. *Indians of the Plains.* New York: McGraw-Hill. Repr. Lincoln: Univ. of Nebraska Press, 1982.

Ludwickson, J., and J. R. Bozell. 1994. The early potters. In The cellars of time: Paleontology and archeology in Nebraska, 111–19. NEBRASKA*land* 72 (1): 1–162.

Lugn, A. L. 1935. *The Pleistocene of Nebraska.* Nebraska Geological Survey Bulletin 10, 2nd ser. Lincoln: Univ. of Nebraska.

Maher, H. D., G. F. Engelmann, and R. D. Shuster. 2003. *Roadside geology of Nebraska.* Missoula MT: Mountain Press.

McCarraher, D. B. 1977. *Nebraska's Sandhills lakes.* Lincoln: Nebraska Game and Parks Commission.

McMurtry, M. S., R. Craig, and G. Schildmann. 1972. *Nebraska wetland survey.* Lincoln: Nebraska Game and Parks Commission.

Mengel, R. M. 1970. The North American central plains as an isolating agent in bird speciation. In *Pleistocene and Recent environments of the central Great Plains,* ed. W. Dort and J. K. Jones, 280–340. Lawrence: Univ. Press of Kansas.

Moulton, G., ed. 1983. *The journals of the Lewis and Clark expedition: August 25, 1804–April 6, 1805.* Lincoln: Univ. of Nebraska Press.

Nebraska Game and Parks Commission. 1984. The first voices. *NEBRASKAland* 62
　　(1): 1–130.

——— 1986. Fort Robinson illustrated. *NEBRASKAland* 64 (1): 1–114.

———. 1994. The cellars of time: Paleontology and archeology in Nebraska.
　　NEBRASKAland 72 (1): 1–162.

Olson, J. C. 1966. *History of Nebraska*. 2nd ed. Lincoln: Univ. of Nebraska Press.

Reece, C. S. 1945. *An early history of Cherry County, Nebraska*. Simeon NE:
　　Published by the author. Repr. Valentine NE: Plains Trading Company,
　　1992.

Steinauer, J. 1998. The Loup: Lifeblood of central Nebraska. *NEBRASKAland* 76
　　(5): 24–33.

Van Metre, O. 1977. *The Old Town, 1880–1889*. Norfolk NE: Norfolk Printing
　　Company.

Voorhies, M. 1994. The ancient seas, Jungles and savannas, and The Ice Age. In
　　The cellars of time: Paleontology and archeology in Nebraska, 8–81.
　　NEBRASKAland 72 (1): 1–162.

Warren, G. T. 1875. *Preliminary report of explorations in Nebraska and Dakota,
　　in the years 1855–56–57*. Washington DC: U.S. Army Corps of
　　Topographical Engineers.

Wells, P. V. 1970a. Postglacial vegetational history of the Great Plains. *Science*
　　167:1574–82.

———. 1970b. Historical factors controlling vegetation patterns and floristic
　　distributions in the central plains region of North America. In
　　Pleistocene and Recent environments of the central Great Plains, ed. W.
　　Dort Jr. and J. K. Jones Jr., 211–21. Lawrence: Univ. Press of Kansas.

———. 1983. Late Quaternary vegetation of the Great Plains. *Transactions of the
　　Nebraska Academy of Sciences* 11:83–89.

Wright, H. E., Jr. 1970. Vegetational history of the Great Plains. In *Pleistocene
　　and Recent environments of the central Great Plains*, ed. W. Dort Jr. and
　　J. K. Jones Jr., 157–72. Lawrence: Univ. Press of Kansas.

Chapter 3. The Distributions and Habitats of Niobrara Plants

Baltensberger, B. M. 1985. *Nebraska: A geography*. Boulder CO: Westview Press.

Barkley, T. M., ed. 1986. *Flora of the Great Plains*. Lawrence: Great Plains Flora
　　Association and Univ. Press of Kansas.

Briggs, J. M., G. A. Hoch, and L. C. Johnson. 2002. Assessing the rate,
　　mechanisms and consequences of the conversion of tallgrass prairie to
　　Juniperus virginianus forest. *Ecosystems* 5:578–86.

Churchill, S. P. 1982. Mosses of the Great Plains. VI. The Niobrara basin of
　　Nebraska. *Transactions of the Kansas Academy of Sciences* 85:1–12.

Churchill, S. P., C. C. Freeman, and G. E. Kantak. 1988. The vascular flora of the Niobrara Valley Preserve and adjacent areas in Nebraska. *Transactions of the Nebraska Academy of Sciences* 16:1–15.

Crosby, C. S. 1988. Vegetation of the coniferous-deciduous forest overlap region along the Niobrara River Valley of north-central Nebraska. MS thesis, Univ. of Nebraska–Omaha.

Farrar, J. 1997. Red cedar: The good, the bad and the ugly. NEBRASKA*land* 75 (2): 22–31.

———. 2000. Burning for wildlife. NEBRASKA*land* 78 (2): 20–25.

Gehring, J. L., and T. B. Bragg. 1992. Changes in prairie vegetation under eastern redcedar (*Juniperus virginianus* L.) in an eastern Nebraska bluestem prairie. *American Midland Naturalist* 128:209–17.

Harrison, A. T. 1980. The Niobrara Valley Preserve: Its biogeographic importance and description of its plant communities. Working report, typescript. Minneapolis MN: Nature Conservancy.

Ingwersen, M. B. 1998. A study of the floristic composition, zonation and abiotic parameters of three fens in the Sand Hills of Nebraska. PhD diss., Univ. of South Dakota.

Johnson, J. R., and G. E. Larson. 1999. *Grassland plants of South Dakota and the northern Great Plains*. South Dakota Agricultural Experiment Station Publication B566, rev. Brookings: South Dakota State Univ.

Kantak, G. 1995. Terrestrial plant communities of the middle Niobrara Valley, Nebraska. *Southwestern Naturalist* 49:129–38.

Kaul, R. B. 1986. Physical and floristic characteristics of the Great Plains. In *Flora of the Great Plains*, ed. T. M. Barkley, 7–10. Lawrence: Univ. Press of Kansas.

———. 1998. Plants. In *An atlas of the Sandhills*, 3rd ed., ed. A. Bleed and C. Flowerday, 127–42. Resource Atlas no. 5. Lincoln: Conservation and Survey Division, Univ. of Nebraska–Lincoln.

Kaul, R. B., G. E. Kantak, and S. P. Churchill. 1988. The Niobrara River Valley, a postglacial migration corridor and refugium of forest plants and animals in the grasslands of central North America. *Botanical Review* 54:44–81.

Kaul, R. B., and S. B. Rolfsmeier. 1993. *Native vegetation of Nebraska*. Lincoln: Conservation and Survey Division, Institute of Agriculture and Natural Resources, Univ. of Nebraska–Lincoln. (Map plus text supplement. A 1975 version of this map by Kaul was titled Vegetation of Nebraska [circa 1850].)

———. 1994. Diversity of vascular plants and intensity of plant collecting in Nebraska. *Transactions of the Nebraska Academy of Sciences* 21:13–20.

Kaul, R. B., D. H. Sutherland, and S. B. Rolfsmeier. 2006. *Flora of Nebraska.* Lincoln: Conservation and Survey Division, Univ. of Nebraska–Lincoln.

Larson, G. E., and J. R. Johnson. 1999. *Plants of the Black Hills and Bear Lodge Mountains.* South Dakota Agricultural Experiment Station Publication B732. Brookings: South Dakota State Univ.

McCarraher, D. B. 1977. *Nebraska's Sandhills lakes.* Lincoln: Nebraska Game and Parks Commission.

Nixon, E. S. 1967. A vegetational study of the Pine Ridge of northwestern Nebraska. *Southwestern Naturalist* 12:134–45.

Pound, R., and F. C. Clements. 1900. *The phytogeography of Nebraska.* 2nd ed. Univ. of Nebraska Botanical Survey I: General Survey. Lincoln: Univ. of Nebraska Botanical Seminar.

Rolfsmeier, S., and G. Steinauer. 2003. Vascular plants of Nebraska. Version 1. Lincoln: Nebraska Game and Parks Commission.

Steinauer, G. 1992. Sandhills fens. NEBRASKA*land* 70 (6): 16–32.

———. 1993a. The Niobrara Valley forests. In Walk in the woods. NEBRASKA*land* 71 (1): 1–98.

———. 1993b. Sandhills fens in Cherry County, Nebraska: Description, inventory and general assessment. In *Research symposium: Environmental and natural resources of the Niobrara River basin*, ed. R. Kuzelka. Ainsworth NE, October 14–15, 1993. Water Center/Environmental Programs. Lincoln: Univ. of Nebraska–Lincoln.

Steinauer, G., and S. B. Rolfsmeier. 1995. Rare plant survey of selected areas of the McKelvie National Forest. Unpublished report to the U.S. Forest Service, Chadron NE.

———. 2003. *Terrestrial natural communities of Nebraska.* Version 3. Lincoln: Nebraska Game and Parks Commission.

Steinauer, G., S. B. Rolfsmeier, and J. P. Hardy. 1996. Inventory and floristics of Sandhills fens in Cherry County, Nebraska. *Transactions of the Nebraska Academy of Sciences* 23:9–21.

Tolstead, W. L. 1942. Vegetation of the northern part of Cherry County, Nebraska. *Ecological Monographs* 12:255–92.

Tunnell, S. J., J. Stubbendieck, J. Huddle, and J. Brollier. 2004. Seed dynamics of eastern redcedar in the mixed-grass prairie. *Great Plains Research* 14:129–42.

Warren, G. T. 1875. *Preliminary report of explorations in Nebraska and Dakota, in the years 1855–56–57.* Washington DC: U.S. Army Corps of Topographical Engineers.

Weaver, J. E. 1965. *Native vegetation of Nebraska.* Lincoln: Univ. of Nebraska Press.

Chapter 4. The Distributions and Habitats of Niobrara Animals

Austin, J. E., and A. L. Richert. 2001. A comprehensive review of observational and site evaluation data of migrant whooping cranes in the United States, 1943–99. Report, U.S. Geological Survey. Jamestown ND: Northern Prairie Wildlife Research Center.

Baker, G. T., and J. R. Simon. 1970. *Wyoming fishes*. Bulletin 4. Cheyenne: Wyoming Game and Fish Department.

Beed, W. E. 1936. *A preliminary study of the animal ecology of the Niobrara Game Preserve*. Bulletin 10. Lincoln: Conservation and Survey Division, Univ. of Nebraska–Lincoln.

Benedict, R. A. 2004. Reproductive activity and distribution of bats in Nebraska. *Western North American Naturalist* 64:231–48.

Benedict, R. A., H. H. Genoways, and P. W. Freeman. 2000. Shifting distribution patterns of mammals in Nebraska. *Transactions of the Nebraska Academy of Sciences* 26:55–84.

Bliss, Q. P., and S. Schainost. 1973. Niobrara River stream inventory report. Unpublished report, Nebraska Game and Parks Commission, Lincoln.

Bogan, M. A. 1995. *A biological survey of the Fort Niobrara and Valentine National Wildlife Refuges*. Fort Collins CO: Midcontinent Ecological Service Center, National Biological Service, U.S. Department of Interior.

———. 1997. Historical changes in the landscape and vertebrate diversity of north central Nebraska. In *Ecology and conservation of Great Plains vertebrates*, ed. F. L. Knopf and F. B. Samson, 105–30. New York: Springer-Verlag.

Brock, J. P., and K. Kaufman. 2003. *Butterflies of North America*. Boston: Houghton Mifflin.

Brogie, M. A., and M. J. Mossman. 1983. Spring and summer birds of the Niobrara Valley Preserve area, Nebraska. *Nebraska Bird Review* 51:44–51.

Ducey, J. E. 1988. *Nebraska birds: Breeding status and distribution*. Omaha NE: Simmons-Boardman.

———. 1989. Birds of the Niobrara River Valley, Nebraska. *Transactions of the Nebraska Academy of Sciences* 17:37–60.

Dunkle, S. W. 2000. *Dragonflies through binoculars*. New York: Oxford Univ. Press.

Farrar, J. 1998. Amphibians and reptiles. In *An atlas of the Sand Hills*, 3rd ed., ed. A. Bleed and C. Flowerday, 168–72. Resource Atlas no. 5, Lincoln: Conservation and Survey Division, Univ. of Nebraska–Lincoln.

———. 2004. Birding Nebraska. *NEBRASKAland* 82 (1): 1–179.

Griebel, R. L., S. L. Winter, and A. A. Steuter. 1998. Grassland birds and habitat structure in Sandhills prairie managed for cattle or bison plus fire. *Great Plains Research* 8:255–68.

Gutzmer, M. P., J. W. King, D. P. Overhue, and E. Y. Crisp. 2002. Fish species-richness trends in the Niobrara River, Nebraska, below the Spencer Dam. *Transactions of the Nebraska Academy of Sciences* 28:57–63.

Hesse, L. W., G. Zuerlein, R. Vancil, B. Newcomb, and L. A. Retelsdorf. 1979. *Niobrara-Missouri fisheries investigations.* Lincoln: Nebraska Game and Parks Commission.

Johnsgard, P. A. 1987. The ornithogeography of the Great Plains states. *Prairie Naturalist* 10:97–112.

———. 1998. Endemicity and regional biodiversity in Nebraska's breeding birds. *Nebraska Bird Review* 66:115–21.

———. 2005. *The birds of Nebraska.* Rev. ed. Lincoln NE: Printed by the author.

Johnson, J. R., and G. E. Larson. 1999. *Grassland plants of South Dakota and the northern Great Plains.* South Dakota Agricultural Experiment Station Publication B566, rev. Brookings: South Dakota State Univ.

Johnson, K. 1973. The butterflies of Nebraska. *Journal of Research on the Lepidoptera* 11:1–64.

Jones, J. K., Jr. 1964. Distribution and taxonomy of mammals of Nebraska. *University of Kansas Publications, Museum of Natural History* 16:1–356.

Kingery, H. E., ed. 1998. *Colorado breeding bird atlas.* Denver: Colorado Bird Atlas Partnership and Colorado Division of Wildlife.

Kitchen, D. W., and P. T. Bromley. 1971. Agonistic behavior of territorial pronghorns. In *The behaviour of ungulates in relation to management,* ed. V. Geist and F. Walter, 365–81. Publication 24. Morges, Switzerland: IUCN.

Kondratieff, B. C., coordinator. 2000. Dragonflies and damselflies of the United States. Jamestown ND: Northern Prairie Wildlife Research Center home page: http://npwrc.usgs.gov/resource/distr/insects/dflyusa.htm (Version 26JUN2002).

Labedz, T. E. 1998. Birds. In *An atlas of the Sand Hills,* 3rd ed., ed. A. Bleed and C. Flowerday, 173–92. Resource Atlas no. 5. Lincoln: Conservation and Survey Division, Univ. of Nebraska–Lincoln.

Lanyon, W. E. 1994. Western meadowlark (*Sturnella neglecta*). In *The birds of North America,* ed. A. Poole and F. Gill, no. 104. Philadelphia: Birds of North America.

———. 1995. Eastern meadowlark (*Sturnella magna*). In *The birds of North America,* ed., A. Poole and F. Gill, no. 160. Philadelphia: Birds of North America.

Larson, G. E., and J. R. Johnson. 1999. *Plants of the Black Hills and Bear Lodge*

Mountains. South Dakota Agricultural Experiment Station Publication B732. Brookings: South Dakota State Univ.

Longfellow, S. 1977. Birds of the Norden Dam site area: A supplemental study. Report to U.S. Department of Interior, Bureau of Reclamation. June 1977 report plus December 1977 supplement. In *Supplement, final environmental statement, O'Neill Unit, Lower Niobrara Division, Pick-Sloan Missouri Basin Program, Nebraska.* Appendix C, Vegetative and Wildlife Assessment. Grand Island: Nebraska Reclamation Office.

Lott, D. F. 1971. Sexual and aggressive behavior of adult male American bison (*Bison bison*). In *The behaviour of ungulates in relation to management,* ed. V. Geist and F. Walter, 382–94. Publication 24. Morges, Switzerland: IUCN.

Luce, R., R. Oakleaf, A. Cervoski, L. Hunter, and J. Priday. 1997. *Atlas of birds, mammals, reptiles and amphibians of Wyoming.* Lander: Wyoming Game and Fish Department.

Madsen, T. I. 1985. The status and distribution of the uncommon fishes of Nebraska. MA thesis, Univ. of Nebraska–Omaha.

Maier, C. R. 1993. The Niobrara River Valley—a crossroads of nature. In *Research symposium: Environmental and natural resources of the Nebraska River basin,* ed. R. Kuzelka. Ainsworth NE, October 14–15. 1993. Lincoln: Water Center/Environmental Programs, Univ. of Nebraska–Lincoln.

Maret, T. R. 1988. A water-quality assessment using aquatic macroinvertebrates from streams of the Long Pine Creek watershed in Brown County, Nebraska. *Transactions of the Nebraska Academy of Sciences* 16:69–84.

———. 1989. The use of Sand Hills fish communities to assess water quality and designate aquatic-life uses. In *An atlas of the Sand Hills,* 1st ed., ed. A. Bleed and C. Flowerday, 155–56. Resource Atlas no. 5. Lincoln: Conservation and Survey Division, Univ. of Nebraska–Lincoln.

Mestl, G. E. 1993. Fifteen years later: Fish sampling in the Niobrara River. In *Research symposium: Environmental and natural resources of the Niobrara River basin,* ed. R. Kuzelka. Ainsworth NE, October 14–15, 1993. Lincoln: Water Center/Environmental Programs, Univ. of Nebraska–Lincoln.

Mollhoff, W. L. 2001. *The Nebraska breeding bird atlas: 1984–1989.* Lincoln: Nebraska Game and Parks Commission.

Moulton, M. P. 1972. The small playa lakes of Nebraska: Their ecology, fisheries and biological potential. In *Playa lakes symposium transactions,* 15–23. International Center for Arid and Semi-arid Land Studies. Lubbock: Texas Tech Univ.

Mussetter, R. A., and C. G. Wolf. 1993. Modeling the dynamics of the Niobrara/

Missouri River confluence. In *Research symposium: Environmental and natural resources of the Niobrara River basin*, ed. R. Kuzelka. Ainsworth, NE, October 14–15, 1993. (Lincoln: Water Center/Environmental Programs, Univ. of Nebraska–Lincoln.

Page, L. M., and B. M. Burr. 1991. *Freshwater fishes*. Boston: Houghton Mifflin.

Rich, T. C., et al., eds. 2004. *North American landbird conservation plan*. Ithaca NY: Partners in Flight and Cornell University Laboratory of Ornithology.

Roehrs, Z. P. 2004. Biogeography and population dynamics of the prairie dog *Cynomys ludovicianus* Ord in Nebraska from 1965 to 2003. MS thesis, Univ. of Nebraska–Lincoln.

Rosche, R. 1982. *The birds of northwestern Nebraska and southwestern South Dakota: An annotated checklist*. Crawford NE: Cottonwood Press.

Rundquist, D. C. 1983. *Wetland inventories of Nebraska's Sandhills*. Resource Report 9. Lincoln: Conservation and Survey Division, Univ. of Nebraska, Institute of Agriculture and Natural Resources.

Schainost, S. 1975. Threatened fishes survey. Unpublished mimeo report. Nebraska Game and Parks Commission, Lincoln. Sharpe, R. S., W. R. Silcock, and J. G. Jorgensen. 2001. *Birds of Nebraska: Their distribution and temporal occurrence*. Lincoln: Univ. of Nebraska Press.

Steinauer, G., and S. B. Rolfsmeier. 2003. *Terrestrial natural communities of Nebraska*. Version 3. Lincoln: Nebraska Game and Parks Commission.

Tallman, D. A., D. L. Swanson, and J. S. Palmer. 2002. *Birds of South Dakota*. Aberdeen: South Dakota Ornithologists' Union.

U.S. Bureau of Reclamation. 1978. *Supplement, final environmental statement, O'Neill Unit, Lower Niobrara Division, Pick-Sloan Missouri Basin Program, Nebraska*. Denver: Bureau of Reclamation.

Chapter 5. Biogeography and Biodiversity in the Niobrara Valley

Bates, J. N. 1983. *The relationship between densitometry and dominant species composition of natural plant communities of the Niobrara Valley Preserve*. Lincoln: Conservation and Survey Division, Univ. of Nebraska, Institute of Agriculture and Natural Resources.

Bessey, C. E. 1887. A meeting-place of two floras. *Bulletin of the Torrey Botanical Club* 14:189–91.

Crosby, C. S. 1988. Vegetation of the coniferous-deciduous forest overlap region along the Niobrara Valley of north-central Nebraska. MS thesis, Univ. of Nebraska–Omaha.

Ducey, J. E. 1989. Birds of the Niobrara River Valley, Nebraska. *Transactions of the Nebraska Academy of Sciences* 17:37–60.

Dunkle, S. W. 2000. *Dragonflies through binoculars*. New York: Oxford Univ. Press.

Harrison, A. T. 1980. The Niobrara Valley Preserve: Its biogeographic importance and description of its plant communities. Working report, typescript. Minneapolis MN: Nature Conservancy.

Hearty, P. J. 1978. The biogeography and geomorphology of the Niobrara River Valley near Valentine, Nebraska. MS thesis, Univ. of Nebraska–Omaha.

Johnsgard, P. A. 1998. Endemicity and regional biodiversity in Nebraska's breeding birds. *Nebraska Bird Review* 66:115–21.

———. 2005. *Prairie dog empire: A saga of the shortgrass prairie*. Lincoln: Univ. of Nebraska Press.

Jones, J. K., Jr. 1964. Distribution and taxonomy of mammals of Nebraska. *University of Kansas Publications, Museum of Natural History* 16:1–356.

Kantak, G. E. 1994. An ordination of the Niobrara plant communities. *Transactions of the Nebraska Academy of Sciences* 21:9–12.

———. 1995. Terrestrial plant communities of the middle Niobrara Valley, Nebraska. *Southwestern Naturalist* 40:129–38.

Kantak, G. E., and S. P. Churchill. 1993. The Niobrara Valley Preserve: Inventory of a biogeographical crossroads. *Transactions of the Nebraska Academy of Sciences* 20:1–12.

Kaul, R. B., G. E. Kantak, and S. P. Churchill. 1988. The Niobrara River Valley, a postglacial migration corridor and refugium of forest plants and animals in the grasslands of central North America. *Botanical Review* 54:44–81.

Kondratieff, B. C., coordinator. 2000. Dragonflies and damselflies of the United States. Jamestown ND: Northern Prairie Wildlife Research Center home page: http://npwrc.usgs.gov/resource/distr/insects/dflyusa.htm (Version 26JUN2002).

Lott, D. F. 1971. Sexual and aggressive behavior of adult male American bison (*Bison bison*). In *The behaviour of ungulates in relation to management*, ed. V. Geist and F. Walter, 382–94. Publication 24. Morges, Switzerland: IUCN.

Maier, C. R. 1992. Communities of the biological crossroads: An extraordinary outdoor classroom. *BioScience* 18:11–19.

———. 1993. The Niobrara River Valley—a crossroads of nature. In *Research symposium: Environmental and natural resources of the Nebraska River basin*, ed. R. Kuzelka. Ainsworth NE, October 14–15. 1993. Lincoln: Water Center/Environmental Programs, Univ. of Nebraska–Lincoln.

Mollhoff, W. L. 2001. *The Nebraska breeding bird atlas: 1984–1989*. Lincoln: Nebraska Game and Parks Commission., Lincoln NE.

Morgan, G. R. 1962. The geographical distribution and environment of white birches along the Niobrara River in north-central Nebraska. MA thesis, Univ. of Nebraska–Lincoln.

Nixon, E. S. 1967. A vegetational study of the Pine Ridge of northwestern Nebraska. *Southwestern Naturalist* 12:134–45.

Pound, R., and F. C. Clements. 1900. *The phytogeography of Nebraska.* 2nd ed. Univ. of Nebraska Botanical Survey I: General survey. Lincoln: Univ. of Nebraska Botanical Seminar.

Roehrs, Z. 2004. Biogeography and population dynamics of the prairie dog *Cynomys ludovicianus* Ord in Nebraska from 1965 to 2003. MS thesis, Univ. of Nebraska–Lincoln.

Steinauer, G. 1993. Sandhills fens in Cherry County, Nebraska: Description, inventory and general assessment. In *Research symposium: Environmental and natural resources of the Niobrara River basin*, ed. R. Kuzelka. AinsworthNE, October 14–15, 1993. Water Center/ Environmental Programs. Lincoln: Univ. of Nebraska–Lincoln.

Steinauer, G., S. B. Rolfsmeier, and J. P. Hardy. 1996. Inventory and floristics of Sandhills fens in Cherry County, Nebraska. *Transactions of the Nebraska Academy of Sciences* 23:9–21.

Chapter 6. Bird Populations and Interactions in the Niobrara Valley

Anderson, C. D, C. D. Becker, and P. S. Gibson. 2004. Impacts of river recreation on birds at Fort Niobrara National Wildlife Refuge, 2000–2002. Research summary. Manhattan: Kansas Cooperative Fish and Wildlife Unit, Kansas State Univ.

Anderson, B. W., and R. J. Daugherty. 1974. Characteristics and reproductive biology of grosbeaks (*Pheucticus*) in the hybrid zone of South Dakota, *Wilson Bulletin* 86:1–11.

Austin, J. E., and A. L. Richert. 2001. A comprehensive review of observational and site evaluation data of migrant whooping cranes in the United States, 1943–99. Report, U.S. Geological Survey. Jamestown ND: Northern Prairie Wildlife Research Center.

Brogie, M. A., and M. J. Mossman. 1983. Spring and summer birds of the Nio-brara Valley Preserve area, Nebraska. *Nebraska Bird Review* 51:44–51.

Brown, C. R, P. A. Johnsgard, J. Kren, and W. C. Scharf. 1996. Birds of the Cedar Point Biological Station area, Keith and Garden counties, Nebraska. *Transactions of the Nebraska Academy of Sciences* 29:91–108.

Corbin, K. W., and C. G. Sibley. 1977. Rapid evolution of the genus *Icterus*. *Condor* 79:335–42.

Corbin, K. W., C. G. Sibley, and A. Ferguson. 1979. Genic changes associated with the establishment of sympatry in orioles of the genus *Icterus*. *Evolution* 33:624–33.

Ducey, J. E. 1988. *Nebraska birds: Breeding status and distribution*. Omaha NE: Simmons-Boardman.

———. 1989. Birds of the Niobrara River Valley, Nebraska. *Transactions of the Nebraska Academy of Sciences* 17:37–60.

Emlen, S. T., J. D. Rising, and W. L. Thompson. 1975. A behavioral and morphological study of sympatry in the indigo and lazuli buntings of the Great Plains. *Wilson Bulletin* 87:145–79.

Griebel, R. L., S. L. Winter, and A. A. Steuter. 1998. Grassland birds and habitat structure in Sandhills prairie managed for cattle or bison plus fire. *Great Plains Research* 8:255–68.

Johnsgard, P. A., and R. W. Wood. 1968. Distributional changes and interactions between prairie chickens and sharp-tailed grouse in the Midwest. *Wilson Bulletin* 80:173–88.

Kingery, H. E., ed. 1998. *Colorado breeding bird atlas*. Denver: Colorado Bird Atlas Partnership and Colorado Division of Wildlife.

LaGrange, T. 2005. *Guide to Nebraska's wetlands and their conservation needs*. 2nd ed. Lincoln: Nebraska Game and Parks Commission.

Lanyon, W. E. 1994. Western meadowlark (*Sturnella neglecta*). In *The birds of North America*, ed. A. Poole and F. Gill, no. 104. Philadelphia: Birds of North America.

———. 1995. Eastern meadowlark (*Sturnella magna*). In *The birds of North America*, ed., A. Poole and F. Gill, no. 160. Philadelphia: Birds of North America.

Longfellow, S. 1977. Birds of the Norden Dam site area: A supplemental study. Report to U.S. Department of Interior, Bureau of Reclamation. June 1977 report plus December 1977 supplement. In *Supplement, final environmental statement, O'Neill Unit, Lower Niobrara Division, Pick-Sloan Missouri Basin Program, Nebraska*. Appendix C, Vegetative and wildlife assessment. Grand Island: Nebraska Reclamation Office.

Luce, R., R. Oakleaf, A. Cervoski, L. Hunter, and J. Priday. 1997. *Atlas of birds, mammals, reptiles and amphibians of Wyoming*. Lander: Wyoming Game and Fish Department.

Mengel, R. M. 1970. The North American central plains as an isolating agent in bird speciation. In *Pleistocene and Recent environments of the central Great Plains*, ed. W. Dort and J. K. Jones, 280–340. Lawrence: Univ. Press of Kansas.

Mollhoff, W. L. 2001. *The Nebraska breeding bird atlas: 1984–1989*. Lincoln: Nebraska Game and Parks Commission.

Moore, W. S., and W. D. Koenig. 1986. Comparative reproductive success of yellow-shafted, red-shafted and hybrid flickers across a hybrid zone. *Auk* 103:42–51.

Peterson, R. A. 1995. *The South Dakota breeding bird atlas*. Aberdeen: South Dakota Ornithologists' Union.

Rising, J. D. 1970. Morphological variation and evolution in some North American orioles. *Systematic Zoology* 19:315–51.

———. 1983. The Great Plains hybrid zones. *Current Ornithology* 1:131–57.

Rising, J. D., and F. W. Schueler. 1980. Identification and status of wood peewees (*Contopus*) from the Great Plains: What are sibling species? *Condor* 80:301–6.

Rosche, R. 1982. *Birds of northwestern Nebraska and southwestern South Dakota: An annotated checklist*. Crawford NE: Cottonwood Press.

Rounds, R. C., and H. L. Munro. 1982. A review of hybridization between *Sialia sialis* and *S. currucoides*. *Wilson Bulletin* 94:219–23.

Sharpe, R. S., W. R. Silcock, and J. G. Jorgensen. 2001. *Birds of Nebraska: Their distribution and temporal occurrence*. Lincoln: Univ. of Nebraska Press.

Short, L. L., Jr. 1961. Notes on bird distribution in the central plains. *Nebraska Bird Review* 29:2–22.

———. 1965a. Bird records from northern Nebraska during the breeding season. *Nebraska Bird Review* 33:2–5.

———. 1965b. Hybridization in the flickers (*Colaptes*) of North America. *Bulletin of the American Museum of Natural History* 129:311–428.

———. 1969. Taxonomic aspects of avian hybridization. *Auk* 86:84–105.

Sibley, C. G., and L. L. Short Jr. 1959. Hybridization in the buntings (*Passerina*) of the Great Plains. *Auk* 76:443–63.

———. 1964. Hybridization in the orioles of the Great Plains, *Condor* 66:130–50.

Sibley, C. G., and D. A. West. 1959. Hybridization in the rufous-sided towhees of the Great Plains. *Auk* 76:326–38.

Tallman, D. A., D. L. Swanson, and J. S. Palmer. 2002. *Birds of South Dakota*. Aberdeen: South Dakota Ornithologists' Union.

U.S. Fish and Wildlife Service. 1981. *The Platte River ecology study*, ed. G. Krapu. Special Scientific Report. Jamestown ND: Northern Prairie Research Station.

West, D. A. 1962. Hybridization in grosbeaks (*Pheucticus*) of the Great Plains. *Auk* 79:399–424.

Chapter 7. Conservation Prospects and Portraits in the Niobrara Valley

Bischof, R., M. I. Fritz, and M. A. Hack. 2004. Preliminary report: Aerial survey of black-tailed prairie dogs (*Cynomys ludovicianus*) in Nebraska. Internal report. Nebraska Game and Parks Commission, Lincoln.

Ducey, J. E. 1989. Birds of the Niobrara River Valley, Nebraska. *Transactions of the Nebraska Academy of Sciences* 17:37–60.

Farrar, J. 1998. The Nebraska Environmental Trust. NEBRASKA*land* 76 (6): 30–40.

———, 2003. Last stand for Blanding's turtles? NEBRASKA*land* 81 (6): 28–35.

Forsberg, M. 1997. Jewel on the Niobrara. NEBRASKA*land* 75 (6): 8–15.

Johnsgard, P. A. l995. *This fragile land: A natural history of the Nebraska Sandhills*. Lincoln: Univ. of Nebraska Press.

———. 2001. *The nature of Nebraska: Ecology and biodiversity*. Lincoln: Univ. of Nebraska Press.

———. 2002. *Grassland grouse and their conservation*. Washington DC: Smithsonian Institution Press.

———. 2003. *Great wildlife of the Great Plains*. Lawrence: Univ. Press of Kansas.

———. 2005. *Prairie dog empire: A saga of the shortgrass prairie*. Lincoln: Univ. of Nebraska Press.

Johnsgard, P. A., and R. W. Wood. 1968. Distributional changes and interactions between prairie chickens and sharp-tailed grouse in the Midwest. *Wilson Bulletin* 80:173–88.

Roehrs, Z. 2004. Biogeography and population dynamics of the prairie dog *Cynomys ludovicianus* Ord in Nebraska from 1965 to 2003. MS thesis, Univ. of Nebraska–Lincoln.

Chapter 8. The Niobrara as a Scenic River

Bachelor, R. 1993. An environmental impact study of a Sandhills ranch. In *Research symposium: Environmental and natural resources of the Niobrara River basin*, ed. R. Kuzelka. October 14–15, Ainsworth NE. Lincoln: Water Center/Environmental Programs, Univ. of Nebraska–Lincoln.

Bouc, K. 1992. The scenic Niobrara. NEBRASKA*land* 70 (2): 30–39.

Clark, K. H. 1997. An environmental history of the Niobrara River basin. MA thesis, Univ. of Nebraska–Lincoln.

Farrar, J. 1983a. The Niobrara. NEBRASKA*land* 61 (2): 103–13.

———, ed. 1983b. Nebraska rivers. NEBRASKA*land* 61 (1): 1–145.

———. 2003a. A long and tortuous course. NEBRASKA*land* 81 (4): 10–19.

———. 2003b. Looking back, looking ahead. NEBRASKA*land* 81 (5): 20–27.

Klataske, R. 1987. The Niobrara Valley: Unique and enduring. NEBRASKA*land* 65 (7): 20–29.

Kuzelka, R., ed. 1993. *Research symposium: Environmental and natural resources of the Niobrara River basin*. Ainsworth NE, October 14–15, 1993.

Lincoln: Water Center/Environmental Programs, Univ. of Nebraska–Lincoln.

Roeder, J. 2004. The One Hundred and Second Congress and the Niobrara Scenic River: Old arguments and new compromises. *Nebraska History* 85:116–27.

Smith, R. J. 1993. Property rights, the environment, and the Niobrara River. In *Research symposium: Environmental and natural resources of the Niobrara River basin*, ed. R. Kuzelka. Ainsworth NE, October 14–15, 1993. Lincoln: Water Center/Environmental Programs, Univ. Of Nebraska–Lincoln.

U.S. Bureau of Reclamation. 1978. *Supplement, final environmental statement, O'Neill Unit, Lower Niobrara Division, Pick-Sloan Missouri Basin Program, Nebraska*. Denver: Bureau of Reclamation.

U.S. Department of Interior, National Park Service. 1996. *Draft general management plan, environmental impact statement, Niobrara National Scenic River, Niobrara/Missouri National Scenic Riverways*. Denver: National Park Service.

Vawser Wolley, A. M., and A. J. Osborne. 1995. Archeological overview and assessment, Niobrara/Missouri National Scenic Riverways, Nebraska and South Dakota. Draft typescript report, Midwest Archeological Center, Lincoln NE.

Voorhies, M. R. 1983. *Vertebrate paleontology of the proposed Norden Dam Reservoir area, Brown, Cherry and Keya Paha counties, Nebraska*. Technical Report 82–109, appendix A. Denver: U.S. Bureau of Reclamation.

Voorhies, M. R., and R. G. Corner. 1993. An inventory and evaluation of vertebrate paleontological sites along the Niobrara/Missouri Scenic River corridors. Typescript report prepared for National Park Service, U.S. Department of Interior.

Chapter 9. The Niobrara as a Recreational River

Anderson, C. D., C. D. Becker, and P. S. Gibson. 2004. Impacts of river recreation on birds at Fort Niobrara National Wildlife Refuge, 2000–2002. Research summary. Manhattan: Kansas Cooperative Fish and Wildlife Unit, Kansas State Univ.

Farrar, J. 2003. Study describes Niobrara floaters. *NEBRASKAland* 81 (10): 46.

Gudgel, D. 1992. *Niobrara River canoeing guide*. Valentine NE: Plains Trading Company.

McPeak, K. 2004. River recreation use levels and patterns on Fort Niobrara National Wildlife Refuge. Unpublished report, Fort Niobrara National Wildlife Refuge.

Chapter 10. The Now and Future Niobrara Valley

Bauer, D. 2004. A history of agricultural practices in Brown, Rock and Keya Paha counties. Oral presentation. Sandhills Discovery Experience, Ainsworth, Nebraska, July 13, 2004.

Benedict, R. A., H. H. Genoways, and P. W. Freeman. 2000. Shifting distribution patterns of mammals in Nebraska. *Transactions of the Nebraska Academy of Sciences* 26:55–84.

Clark, K. H. 1997. An environmental history of the Niobrara River basin. MA thesis, Univ. of Nebraska–Lincoln.

Mussetter, R. A., and C. G. Wolf. 1993. Modeling the dynamics of the Niobrara/Missouri River confluence. In *Research symposium: Environmental and natural resources of the Niobrara River basin*, ed. R. Kuzelka. Ainsworth, NE, October 14–15, 1993. Lincoln: Water Center/Environmental Programs, Univ. of Nebraska–Lincoln.

U.S. Department of Interior, National Park Service. 1996. *Draft general management plan, environmental impact statement, Niobrara National Scenic River, Niobrara/Missouri National Scenic Riverways.* Denver: National Park Service.

———. 2005. *Niobrara National Scenic River: Brown, Cherry, Keya Paha and Rock counties, Nebraska; Draft general management plan and environmental impact statement.* O'Neill NE: National Park Service.

Voorhies, M. R., and R. G. Corner. 1993. An inventory and evaluation of vertebrate paleontological sites along the Niobrara/Missouri Scenic River corridors. Typescript report prepared for U.S. Department of Interior, National Park Service.

Appendixes

Baker, G. T., and J. R. Simon. 1970. *Wyoming fishes.* Bulletin 4. Cheyenne: Wyoming Game and Fish Department.

Ballinger, R. E., J. W. Meeker, and M. Thies. 2000. A checklist and distribution maps of the amphibians and reptiles of South Dakota. *Transactions of the Nebraska Academy of Sciences* 26:29–46.

Barkley, T. M., ed. 1977. *Atlas of the flora of the Great Plains.* Ames: Iowa State Univ. Press.

Behler, J. L., and F. W. King. 1979. *The Audubon Society field guide to North American reptiles and amphibians.* New York: Knopf.

Benedict, R. A., H. H. Genoways, and P. W. Freeman. 2000. Shifting distribution patterns of mammals in Nebraska. *Transactions of the Nebraska Academy of Sciences* 26:55–84.

Berry, C. R., and B. Young. 2004. Fishes of the Missouri Recreational River, South Dakota and Nebraska. *Great Plains Research* 14:89–114.

Bischof, R., M. I. Fritz, and M. A. Hack. 2004. Preliminary report: Aerial survey of black-tailed prairie dogs (*Cynomys ludovicianus*) in Nebraska. Internal report. Nebraska Game and Parks Commission, Lincoln.

Brogie, M. A., and M. J. Mossman. 1983. Spring and summer birds of the Niobrara Valley Preserve area, Nebraska. *Nebraska Bird Review* 51:44–51.

Churchill, S. P, C. C. Freeman, and G. E. Kantak. 1988. The vascular flora of the Niobrara Valley Preserve and adjacent areas in Nebraska. *Transactions of the Nebraska Academy of Sciences* 16:1–15.

Dankert, N., and H. G. Nagel. 1988. Butterflies of the Niobrara Valley Preserve. *Transactions of the Nebraska Academy of Sciences* 16:17–30.

Dankert, N., H. G. Nagel, and T. Nightengale. 1993. Butterfly distribution maps—Nebraska. Univ. of Nebraska–Kearney.

Ducey, J. E. 1989. Birds of the Niobrara River Valley, Nebraska. *Transactions of the Nebraska Academy of Sciences* 17:37–60.

Dunkle, S. W. 2000. *Dragonflies through binoculars.* New York: Oxford Univ. Press.

Freeman, P. 1998. Mammals. In *An atlas of the Sand Hills*, 3rd ed., ed. A. Bleed and C. Flowerday, 193–200. Resource Atlas no. 5. Lincoln: Conservation and Survey Division, Univ. of Nebraska–Lincoln.

Gutzmer, M. P., J. W. King, D. P. Overhue, and E. Y. Crisp. 2002. Fish species-richness trends in the Niobrara River, Nebraska, below the Spencer Dam. *Transactions of the Nebraska Academy of Sciences* 28:57–63.

Hesse, L. W., G. Zuerlein, R. Vancil, B. Newcomb, and L. A. Retelsdorf. 1979. *Niobrara-Missouri fisheries investigations.* Lincoln: Nebraska Game and Parks Commission.

Higgins, K. F., E. D. Stukel, J. M. Goulet, and D. C. Backlund. 2000. *Wild mammals of South Dakota.* Pierre: South Dakota Department of Game, Fish, and Parks

Hrabik, R. A. 1998. Fishes. In *An atlas of the Sand Hills*, 3rd ed., ed. A. Bleed and C. Flowerday, 155–68. Resource Atlas no. 5. Lincoln: Conservation and Survey Division, Univ. of Nebraska–Lincoln.

Johnsgard, P. A. 2005. *The birds of Nebraska.* Rev. ed. Lincoln NE: Printed by the author.

Johnson, J. R., and G. E. Larson. 1999. *Grassland plants of South Dakota and the northern Great Plains.* South Dakota Agricultural Experiment Station Publication B566, rev. Brookings: South Dakota State Univ.

Johnson, R. E. 1942. The distribution of Nebraska fishes. PhD diss., University of Michigan, Ann Arbor.

Jones, D. 1963. *A History of Nebraska's Fishery Resources.* Lincoln: Nebraska Game and Parks Commission.

Jones, J. K., Jr., and J. R. Choate. 1980. Annotated checklist of the mammals of
    Nebraska. *Prairie Naturalist* 12:43–53.
Kantak, G. E., and S. P. Churchill. 1993. The Niobrara Valley Preserve: An
    inventory of a biological crossroads. *Transactions of the Nebraska
    Academy of Sciences* 20:1–12.
Kaul, R. B., D. H. Sutherland, and S. B. Rolfsmeier. 2006. *Flora of Nebraska*.
    Lincoln: Conservation and Survey Division, Univ. of Nebraska–Lincoln.
Kondratieff, B. C., coordinator. 2000. Dragonflies and damselflies of the United
    States. Jamestown ND: Northern Prairie Wildlife Research Center home
    page: http://npwrc.usgs.gov/resource/distr/insects/dflyusa.htm
    (Version 26JUN2002).
Larson, G. E., and J. R. Johnson. 1999. *Plants of the Black Hills and Bear Lodge
    Mountains*. South Dakota Agricultural Experiment Station Publication
    B732. Brookings: South Dakota State Univ.
Luce, R., R. Oakleaf, A. Cervoski, L. Hunter, and J. Priday. 1997. *Atlas of birds,
    mammals, reptiles and amphibians of Wyoming*. Lander: Wyoming
    Game and Fish Department.
Lynch, J. D. 1985. Annotated checklist of the reptiles and amphibians of
    Nebraska. *Transactions of the Nebraska Academy of Sciences* 13:33–57.
Marrone, G. M. 2002. *Field guide to butterflies of South Dakota*. Pierre: South
    Dakota Department of Game, Fish and Parks.
Mestl, G. E. 1993. Fifteen years later: Fish sampling in the Niobrara River.
    In *Research symposium; Environmental and natural resources of the
    Niobrara River basin*, 3rd ed., ed. R. Kuzelka. Ainsworth NE, October
    14–15, 1993. Lincoln: Water Center/Environmental Programs, Univ. of
    Nebraska–Lincoln.
Mollhoff, W. L. 2001. *The Nebraska breeding bird atlas: 1984–1989*. Lincoln:
    Nebraska Game and Parks Commission.
Morris, J., L. Morris, and L. Witt. 1974. *The fishes of Nebraska*. Lincoln: Nebraska
    Game and Parks Commission.
Mossman, M. J., and M. A. Brogie. 1983. Breeding status of selected bird species
    on the Niobrara Valley Preserve area, Nebraska. *Nebraska Bird Review*:
    51:52–62.
Opler, P. A., R. E. Stanford, and H. Pavulaan. 2002. Butterflies of North
    America. Northern Prairie Wildlife Research Center home page:
    http://npwrc.usgs.gov/resource/distr/lepid/bflyusa/bflyusa.htm.
Page, L. M., and B. M. Burr. 1991. *Freshwater fishes*. Boston: Houghton Mifflin.
Partners in Flight. 2004. *North American landbird conservation plan*. Ithaca NY:
    Cornell Laboratory of Ornithology.

Peterson, R. A. 1995. *The South Dakota breeding bird atlas*. Aberdeen: South Dakota Ornithologists' Union.

Rolfsmeier, S., and G. Steinauer. 2003. Vascular plants of Nebraska. Version 1. Lincoln: Nebraska Game and Parks Commission.

Rosche, R. 1982. *The birds of northwestern Nebraska and southwestern South Dakota: An annotated checklist*. Crawford NE: Cottonwood Press.

Steinauer, G. 1993. Sandhills fens in Cherry County, Nebraska: Description, inventory and general assessment. In *Research symposium: Environmental and natural resources of the Niobrara River basin*, ed. R. Kuzelka. AinsworthNE, October 14–15, 1993. Water Center/ Environmental Programs. Lincoln: Univ. of Nebraska–Lincoln.

Steinauer, G., S. B. Rolfsmeier, and J. P. Hardy. 1996. Inventory and floristics of Sandhills fens in Cherry County, Nebraska. *Transactions of the Nebraska Academy of Sciences* 23:9–21.

Tallman, D. A., D. L. Swanson, and J. S. Palmer. 2002. *Birds of South Dakota*. Aberdeen: South Dakota Ornithologists' Union.

U.S. Bureau of Reclamation. 1978. *Supplement, final environmental statement, O'Neill Unit, Lower Niobrara Division, Pick-Sloan Missouri Basin Program, Nebraska*. Denver: Bureau of Reclamation.

U.S. Department of Interior, National Park Service. 2005. *Niobrara National Scenic River: Brown, Cherry, Keya Paha and Rock counties, Nebraska; Draft general management plan and environmental impact statement*. O'Neill NE: National Park Service.

Index